YORK HANDBOOKS

GENERAL EDITOR:
Professor A. N. Jeffares
(*University of Stirling*)

A DICTIONARY OF LITERARY TERMS

Martin Gray

MA (OXFORD) M PHIL (LONDON)
Senior Lecturer in English Studies, University of Stirling

LONGMAN
YORK PRESS

YORK PRESS
Immeuble Esseily, Place Riad Solh, Beirut

PEARSON EDUCATION LIMITED
Edinburgh Gate, Harlow,
Essex CM20 2JE, England
Associated companies, branches and representatives
throughout the world

First published 1984
Second revised edition 1992
Ninth impression 1999

ISBN 0 582 08037 1

Produced by Pearson Education Asia Pte Ltd
Printed in Singapore (PH)

Contents

Introductory note

In this dictionary anyone who wants to discover or clarify the meaning of a literary term will find a relatively simple and straightforward account of how the term is used, along with some relevant historical information and examples. Cross-references, printed in SMALL CAPITALS, are made in two ways. Some are listed at the end of entries, directing the reader to other entries relating to the same subject. Other cross-references will be found in the text of the entries; these advise the reader that the term in question is explained under its own entry in the dictionary. To help the reader find terms discussed in the middle of another entry, such terms are printed in **bold** type. Foreign words and titles of books, long poems and plays are in *italic* type.

The grammatical status of a word which forms the subject of an entry is given only if the word has more than one grammatical status, or if confusion might arise about its meaning.

For the reader's convenience, an appendix at the end of this book lists in alphabetical order all the writers mentioned in the text, with their dates of birth and death. There is also a chronological list of the English sovereigns, followed by a list of the main periods of English literature. In the text the dates of works refer to first publication, except in the case of plays, which are dated by their first performance.

For all the attempts of scholars and interpreters of literature to be scientific and rigorously exact in their terminology, much critical vocabulary is metaphoric: where a style is described as 'dense', 'pungent' or 'anodyne' an ordinary dictionary will provide a clear enough definition of these adjectives to assist the reader, and I have eschewed such 'terms', though they permeate literary discourse.

I have attempted to explain how terms are actually used rather than how they should be used. With a few exceptions ('involute' and 'phonaestheme'), I have avoided including unusual terms which might be used more often. In general, the terms here defined are culled from the traditional stock of critical vocabulary. However, I have tried to bring the second edition of this dictionary up to date with entries on the terminology of critical and theoretical movements and debates which have flourished since the first edition of this dictionary in 1984. Clear definitions are offered, I hope, for thorny concepts and critical terms. Some such terms I do not use myself (though I may find myself doing so in the future); some may even soon be forgotten. Nonetheless it would have been wrong to ignore the way in which literary criticism has persevered in elaborating a specialist jargon, still predominantly metaphorical, which is difficult for the outsider to penetrate. In doing this, criticism is only continuing the trend begun by Modernist critics like Pound and Eliot, who used terms borrowed from the sciences and psychology, like 'catalyst' and 'complex'. And, of course, literary studies is doing no more than following the example of other academic subjects, which renew and redefine themselves through invented and modified vocabularies. It has been difficult to define words like 'empiricism' and 'common sense', which look familiar, but which can have a special tendentious resonance when used in present-day literary discussion; some of these expressions are like icebergs, seeming superficially innocent, but trailing beneath them a great weight of assumptions and attitudes for those who recognise and believe in their implications.

I have been perplexed about whether or not to include entries on topics like the 'Crisis in English Studies', or words which are currently fashionable in critical debate like 'interrogate'. Though it is difficult to imagine in what circumstances someone might *start* by looking up these words, they still seemed worthy of inclusion, if only to allow cross-referencing from other terms.

I expect critics on all sides of the various present-day critical controversies will find some of these new definitions annoying, either because they appear to be giving currency and approving ideas with which they disagree, or for what may seem their reductive shortness, the result perhaps of simple ignorance or impatience.

In the first case, pretending or hoping that such words and concepts will go away seems now an impossible course of action, irrespective of where one stands in the current debates, and simple definitions at least provide a starting point for further discussion, refinement, or rejection of unpalatable terms and untenable ideas. Sometimes I have offered suggestions as to how certain approaches and terms may seem to me flawed or partial, but in general I have left such ideas to stand or fall on their own merits. Dictionaries must by their nature be pluralistic and 'dialogic' in their relationship with their subject matter. Readers should not presume that because I here define a term I necessarily believe in its usefulness, accuracy, 'truth' or value.

Whole books have been written about concepts like 'ideology' and 'postmodernism'; but such words must appear here too, if only in a form that scratches at their surface. My aim has been to help someone understand a puzzling word or expression encountered in a book or lecture, by offering a swift sketch of possible meanings; exhaustive and definitive accounts and discussions must be sought elsewhere.

Some information about the origins of most words is provided, because it seems useful to remind readers of the way in which words adapt or are adapted, and may conceal in their history some straightforward meaning which sharpens our understanding of their modern use. Readers who wish for more complete information concerning the history of a word will find it in the many-volumed *Oxford English Dictionary*, or in *The Oxford Dictionary of English Etymology* (1966) by C.T. Onions. It would be foolish for any writer of dictionaries not to examine and pay due respect to the dictionaries that already exist. This present dictionary will, I hope, satisfy a need for definitions of most basic literary terms. For a reader wanting to discover the meaning of arcane or rare terms such as 'magody' or 'narodne pesme' I recommend J.A. Cuddon's *A Dictionary of Literary Terms* (third edition 1991), which also contains long and interesting historical entries on certain minor genres such as the spy story or the detective story. Another work which goes beyond the scope of this present dictionary is M.H. Abrams's *A Glossary of Literary Terms* (fifth edition 1985), which has excellent, impartial and lengthy explanations of many critical-theoretical areas or controversies, such as 'speech-act theory', 'narratology' and 'reader-response criticism', of which only a short account is provided here. No one dictionary will satisfy the needs of every possible reader: as with cookery books, it is likely that enthusiasts will need to possess more than one such work of reference.

ABBREVIATIONS

AD	*Anno Domini* (Lat. 'in the year of the Lord') after Christ	**It.**	Italian
		Jap.	Japanese
		Lat.	Latin
adj.	adjective	**Med. Lat.**	medieval Latin
Ar.	Arabic	**Mid. E.**	Middle English
b.	born	*n.*	noun
BC	before Christ	**N.B.**	*nota bene* (Lat. 'note well')
c.	*circa* (Lat. 'about')		
compl.	completed	**Norw.**	Norwegian
d.	died	**O.E.**	Old English
e.g.	*exempli gratia* (Lat. 'for example')	**O.E.D.**	*Oxford English Dictionary*
etc.	*et cetera* (Lat. 'and the rest')	**O. Fr.**	Old French
		O.H. Ger.	Old High German
fl.	*floruit* (Lat. 'flourished')	**O.N.**	Old Norse
		Pr.	Provençal
Fr.	French	**R.P.**	Received Pronunciation
Gael.	Gaelic		
Ger.	German	**Russ.**	Russian
Gk.	Greek	**San.**	Sanskrit
Heb.	Hebrew	**Sp.**	Spanish
i.e.	*id est* (Lat. 'that is')	*v.*	verb

A

Abridgement. (O. Fr. 'shorten') A shortened and sometimes simplified or BOWDLERISED version of a work. Abridged editions of famous literary works are often made for children's reading. *The Reader's Digest* often publishes abridged novels.

Abrogation. *See* POST-COLONIAL LITERATURE.

Abstract. (Lat. 'drawn away') (*n.*) A summary of the argument of a piece of writing. (*adj.*) Concerned with ideas rather than things (in this sense abstract is often opposed to CONCRETE). In criticism the terms 'abstract' and 'concrete' may be applied somewhat loosely to characterise the subject matter or language of literature. Thus the opening of Nashe's 'Song' (1600) is abstract in its treatment of death:

> Adieu, farewell earth's bliss!
> This world uncertain is:
> Fond are life's lustful joys,
> Death proves them all but toys.

The terms are sometimes used to distinguish different kinds of words within a metaphorical expression. In Keats's opening line of *Hyperion* (1820), 'Deep in the shady sadness of a vale', an abstraction, sadness, is linked with the shade of a valley, which is, relatively, a concrete thing. This way of particularising abstractions is common in poetry: it is an inherent effect of PERSONIFICATION.

Avoiding excessive abstraction became almost a programme for some twentieth-century poets. Pound writes in his essay 'A Retrospect' (1918):

> Don't use such an expression as 'dim lands *of peace*'. It dulls the image. It mixes an abstraction with the concrete. It comes from the writer's not realizing that the natural object is always the *adequate* symbol.

As a pejorative, 'abstract' might be applied to an argument that is too theoretical, too divorced from close contact with the observable evidence with which it should be dealing.

Absurd, Theatre of the Absurd. The philosophy of EXISTENTIALISM tends to depict human beings as isolated in an indifferent and incomprehensible universe of space and time. Lacking any essential motive or guiding principles, or any inherent sense of truth or meaning, human existence is characterised by anguished anxiety (ANGST) and absurdity, the condition in which all action and endeavour is perceived as ineffectual, ridiculous, even comical, taking place as it does in a world void of purpose. One notable description of absurdity is contained in the collection of essays by the French philosopher and novelist Albert Camus called *The Myth of Sisyphus* (1942).

During the twentieth century many writers have depicted the absurd status of humanity. The European literary movements of EXPRESSIONISM and SURREALISM provided techniques well adapted for elaborating this vision. In prose, works by the Austrian novelist Franz Kafka, such as *The Trial* (1925) and *Metamorphosis* (1915), focus on protagonists who have to endure bizarre and incomprehensible situations. In the theatre, surrealism and FARCE came together to form a new kind of drama. The label 'Theatre of the Absurd' has been common since Martin Esslin's book of that title, published in 1961.

'Absurd' drama flourished in the 1950s: Ionesco, Beckett and Pinter are notable playwrights whose works have been thus labelled. Ionesco's *Rhinoceros* (1960), for example, is a fable in which people are continually turning into rhinoceroses, emphasising the alienation of human beings from each other and their meaningless, sterile existence. *See also* ANTI-HERO, AVANT-GARDE, BLACK COMEDY, TRAGEDY.

Accent. (Lat. 'like song') Another word for STRESS. The emphasis placed on a syllable. 'Accent' is frequently used to denote stress in descriptions of verse.

Accentual verse. Strongly rhythmical verse organised by a simple pattern of major stresses or 'accents'. Songs, ballads and nursery rhymes, and other forms of verse that are popular and oral in origin, often use this kind of patterning. This example has four stresses per line:

Humpty Dumpty sat on a wall.
Humpty Dumpty had a great fall.
All the king's horses and all the king's men
Couldn't put Humpty together again.

See also ALLITERATIVE VERSE, METRE, SPRUNG RHYTHM.

Acrostic. (Gk. 'end of verse-lines') Verse in which the first letters of each line (or, more rarely, the middle or final letters), when read together, make up a word, or a verbal pattern, for instance, ABC etc.

Act. (Lat. 'thing done') (*n.*) A division in the ACTION of a play, often further divided into SCENES. Frequently these divisions correspond with time changes in the development of the play. On the stage the divisions of the action may be punctuated by exits and entrances of actors, changes of scenery, lighting effects, or, in the case of a theatre with a PROSCENIUM arch, by closing the stage with a curtain.

Elizabethan dramatists copied the five-act structure from Seneca and other Roman playwrights, and this became the standard form for all plays till Ibsen and Chekhov experimented with four-act plays in the late nineteenth century. Modern playwrights show great freedom in their methods of structuring drama. Plays of three acts are perhaps most common.

Actant. The narratologist Greimas defines six 'actants' in oppositional pairs as basic constituents of all NARRATIVES: subject/object, sender/ receiver and helper/opponent. Characters, or even significant objects, embody aspects of one or more of these actants. The analysis of stories in terms of elemental forms is typical of STRUCTURALIST CRITICISM and NARRATOLOGY.

Action. (Lat. 'doing') The main sequence of developing events in any story; most often used in relation to drama. Action is often synonymous with PLOT; but it can be used to discriminate between the unfolding of the story, and its overall pattern as understood retrospectively.

Active and passive. A grammatical distinction which is easy to understand by example. 'A man bought the book' is active. 'The book was bought by a man' is passive. In a sentence with an active verb the grammatical subject is the 'actor'. In a passive sentence the grammatical subject is 'acted upon', in other words is the recipient or 'goal' of the action.

Adage. (Lat. 'saying') A MAXIM, PROVERB or saying.

Addisonian. In the style of the essayist Joseph Addison (1672–1719) who contributed frequently to *The Tatler* and *The Spectator*: clear, relaxed, elegant, urbane, BALANCED, perhaps a bit bland. *See also* AUGUSTAN AGE, NEOCLASSICISM, PERIODICAL.

Aesthetic distance. *See* DISTANCE.

Aestheticism or The Aesthetic Movement. A European movement in the arts, including literature, flourishing in the second half of the nineteenth century, which stressed the paramount value and self-sufficiency of art. There are many early examples of aesthetic points of view, such as De Quincey's essay 'On Murder Considered as One of the Fine Arts' (1827) or Keats's enigmatic ending to the 'Ode on a Grecian Urn' (1820):

Beauty is truth, truth beauty – that is all
Ye know on earth, and all ye need to know.

The main exponents of Aestheticism as a self-conscious movement were the French (Gautier, Baudelaire, Flaubert, Mallarmé, Huysmans). In America, Poe propounded a theory of 'the poem for the poem's sake' ('The Poetic Principle', 1850), and in Britain, Pater, Wilde, Dowson, Lionel Johnson and Symons adopted many elements of the aesthetic approach; Tennyson, Morris and Swinburne were also influenced. '**Art for art's sake**' was the catch-phrase of Aestheticism. Art is viewed as the supreme human achievement, and it should be subservient to no moral, political, didactic or practical purpose: its purpose is to exist solely for the sake of its own beauty. It can be judged only by aesthetic criteria.

Aestheticism can be partially explained as a reaction against the UTILITARIANISM and PHILISTINE materialism of the nineteenth century. During the later phase of Aestheticism some of its more extreme tenets, in particular the notion that life was opposed to art, were exaggerated, giving rise to the movement called DECADENCE.

Aesthetics. (Gk. 'things perceptible to the senses') The name given to the philosophical study of the nature of beauty: it concerns the appreciation, definition and criticism of the beautiful, and the theory of taste. Some philosophers, notably the German philosopher Immanuel Kant, used 'aesthetic' in a broader sense to mean 'pertaining to the philosophy of perception through the senses'. Its current use dates from *Aesthetica* (1750–8), by the German philosopher A.G. Baumgarten, which examines the theory of taste.

Aesthetic (*adj.*) is sometimes used colloquially in a weak sense to mean beautiful or tasteful. It may refer to the study of aesthetics, or apply to the ideas of the cultural phenomenon called AESTHETICISM.

Affectation. (Lat. 'aspiration') The use of a false or pretentious literary style, inappropriate for the subject being discussed.

Affective criticism. 'Affect' is a psychological term denoting feeling or emotion attached to an idea. Affective criticism examines literature in terms of the feelings it evokes in the reader, a procedure denounced by the NEW CRITICS as liable to be distorted by personal subjectivity (*see* AFFECTIVE FALLACY).

READER-RESPONSE CRITICISM has renewed interest in the affective quality of literature. Close examination of the process of reading as a changing and dynamic experience has shown how the constant modification and manipulation of feeling plays a significant part in the experience of the text.

Affective fallacy. The title of an essay by the American critics W.K. Wimsatt and M.C. Beardsley, printed in Wimsatt's *The Verbal Icon* (1954). They argue that judging a poem by its effect or emotional impact on the reader is a fallacious method of criticism, resulting only in IMPRESSIONISTIC CRITICISM. *See also* CRITICISM, INTENTIONAL FALLACY, NEW CRITICISM.

Age of Reason. A loose term for the RESTORATION and AUGUSTAN AGE (jointly covering the period 1660–1745), and for the eighteenth century in general, when the ideal of reason dominated intellectual activity in the arts. Its literature is characterised by balanced judgment, lack of excess, DECORUM and restraint. *See also* NEOCLASSICISM.

Age of Sensibility. *See* SENSIBILITY.

Agitprop. An abbreviation of the Russian word for 'Department of Agitation and Propaganda' which was established by the Communist Party in Russia in 1920 to ensure that the arts which flourished after the 1917 Revolution were in line with communist ideology. The term is used now to describe politically motivated writing with a left-wing bias. During the 1970s and 80s the 7:84 Theatre Company in Scotland, for example, performed drama that might be described as agitprop; its name referred to the fact that 7 per cent of the population of the United Kingdom own 84 per cent of its wealth and property.

Alazon. A self-deceiving braggart. One of the stock characters from Greek comedy, often a foil to the EIRON. Shakespeare's Falstaff is a modern version of the type.

Alba. A Provençal name for the AUBADE, or dawn song.

Aleatory, aleatoric. (Lat. 'depending on a throw of the dice') Poetry and music composed out of elements chosen at random by the performer or writer, or sometimes assembled by the reader out of material provided by the writer. Mallarmé's experimental poem 'Un coup de dés jamais n'abolira le hazard' ('A dice throw will never abolish luck', 1897) discusses and demonstrates the nature of aleatory writing. Exponents of SURREALISM and DADA often employed random methods of composition or organisation, including COLLAGE. Indeed the remarkably apt name 'Dada' is supposed to have been chosen by Tzara at random by stabbing at the Larousse dictionary with a paperknife. The poet-artist Kurt Schwitters constructed what he called *Merzpoems*, like *Anna Blume* (1919), out of collections of litter, newspaper cuttings, jingles, phrases from popular songs, and so on.

The contemporary American John Ashbery writes poems that appear to follow the uncontrolled drift of consciousness, in a manner that sometimes gives the impression of aleatory composition. This is the opening of 'Houseboat Days' (1977):

'The skin is broken. The hotel breakfast china
Poking ahead to the last weekend in August, not really
Very much at all, found the land where you began . . .'
The hills smouldered up blue that day, again
You walk five feet along the shore, and you duck
As a common heresy sweeps over.

See also ANTI-NOVEL.

Alexandrine. *Vers héroïque* (Fr. 'heroic verse'), the most common METRE in French poetry since the sixteenth century: a line of twelve syllables. The name is derived from a late twelfth-century Old French romance about Alexander the Great, the *Roman d'Alexandre*, in which the metre is used. The nearest English equivalent is the IAMBIC HEXAMETER. Spenser uses this for the last line of his SPENSERIAN STANZA in *The Faerie Queene* (1590, 1596), but in general it is not a popular metre. Pope illustrates the unwieldy effect of the six feet in *An Essay on Criticism* (1711):

A needless Alexandrine ends the song,
That like/a woun/ded snake/drags its/slow length/along.

Alienation effect. (In German, *Verfremdungseffekt*) Brecht, the German playwright and dramatic theorist, noted that in dramatic performances where the actors identified with their parts the spectators were liable to be swept away by the illusion of reality created, allowing their sympathies for the characters to be manipulated in a way that led only to vague emotional satisfaction, excitement or confusion, rather than critical judgment of the play's subject matter. He argued that the actors should distance themselves from their parts so as to remind the audience that they were watching a play, only a representation of reality. In order to help to achieve this detachment and awareness in his audience, Brecht's plays are interspersed with songs and summaries of the action, and even his heroic characters tend to be marred by unsympathetic faults, which makes it difficult for the audience to identify with them. *See also* CATHARSIS.

Allegory. (Gk. 'speaking otherwise') Allegory is difficult to define neatly because the word refers as much to the method by which a piece of literature is interpreted as to any inherent aspects of the work itself. The simplest form of allegory consists of a story or situation written in such a way as to have two coherent meanings. Thus in Dryden's *Absalom and Achitophel* (1681) biblical figures represent contemporary historical personalities: King David is Charles II, Absalom is Charles's bastard son the Duke of Monmouth, Achitophel is the Earl of Shaftesbury, and so on. The Bible story is used to make a concealed satirical comment on politics. The poem exists as an autonomous narrative, but for those who understand its hidden system of meanings it has a clear and specific political significance. This coherent system of a hidden second meaning is characteristic of allegory.

An allegory may, however, suggest more than one system of meanings and interpretations. In Spenser's *The Faerie Queene* (1590, 1596) the Fairy Queen herself is both Elizabeth I of England, and Glory, an ideal. *The Faerie Queene* is too varied a narrative to lend itself to one single thread of interpretation.

Another famous allegory, but of a different kind, is Bunyan's *The Pilgrim's Progress* (1678), in which the hero Christian's journey from the City of Destruction illustrates Christian salvation. A short passage demonstrates Bunyan's allegorical methods:

Now a little before it was day, good Christian, as one half amazed, brake out in this passionate speech, 'What a fool,' quoth he, 'am I, thus to lie in a stinking Dungeon, when I may as well walk at liberty? I have a Key in my bosom, called Promise, that will, (I am persuaded) open any Lock in Doubting-Castle.' Then said Hopeful, 'That's good news; good Brother pluck it out of thy bosom, and try.' Then Christian pulled it out of his bosom, and began to try at the Dungeon door, whose bolt (as he turned the Key) gave back, and the door flew open with ease, and Christian and Hopeful both came out.

Clearly the spiritual meaning of Bunyan's narrative is kept completely explicit by the use of PERSONIFICATIONS such as 'Hopeful' and 'Christian', and the moral labelling of the journey to places like the 'Slough of Despond' and 'Vanity Fair'.

The term allegory is now most often used in relation to works of some length, like *The Faerie Queene* or *The Pilgrim's Progress*. Shorter allegorical forms might be called FABLES or PARABLES. Allegorical figures are common in painting and sculpture.

Allegorical interpretation as a way of understanding literature is a more influential and pervasive mode of thought than might be imagined from the narrow definition of allegory as a critical term. All interpretation of literature, any way of understanding a work as containing meanings other than those explicit on the level of its literal surface, can be called allegorical.

Special kinds of allegorical interpretation dominated the reading of literature from the end of the Classical period right up to the end of the Renaissance. Christian thinkers explored Classical literature for allegorical meanings. Roman and Greek literature and the myths of the pagan gods became acceptable if they could be shown to contain Christian truths in allegorical forms. The story of Orpheus and Eurydice, for example, can be understood as an allegorical treatment of Christian redemption and salvation. Classical allegorical works, such as Prudentius's *Psychomachia* (*c.*AD405), in which vices and virtues fight for the possession of a soul, were highly influential.

'**Typological allegory**' is the explanation of the Old Testament in terms of prophecies of New Testament events. The New Testament already contains examples of this method of interpretation: the story of Jonah and the whale is seen as an allegory of Christ's descent into Hell and resurrection (Matthew 12:40–2). The concluding book of the New Testament, the Revelation of St John, is regarded as an allegorical vision of events leading up to the Day of Judgment.

Allegorical interpretation permeated the medieval way of looking at the world to the extent that all human knowledge came to be treated allegorically and explored for concealed Christian truths. History, for example, was read as a revelation of the providential purpose of God. Contemporary events were used to prove that the Seventh Age of man was drawing to its end as described in the Revelation. The whole world came to be seen mystically as a visible allegory of the invisible God, and nothing in it was unavailable to Christian interpretation. Numbers and letters of the alphabet were used so as to have mystical significance ('numerical' and 'alphabetical' allegory).

Given this climate of opinion it is not surprising that many of the greatest works of the medieval period, such as Dante's *Divine Comedy* or Langland's *Piers Plowman*, both written in the fourteenth century, are explicitly allegorical. Dante, in his *Convivio* (*c.*1304–7), following St Thomas Aquinas in the *Summa Theologica* (thirteenth century), described four methods of interpreting literature, which may be summarised as literal, allegorical or poetical, moral and ANAGOGICAL.

Allegorical literature became much less common after the Renaissance. Swift's *Gulliver's Travels* (1726) is a famous example from the eighteenth century. Orwell's *Animal Farm* (1945) is a modern political allegory.

Allegory may be distinguished from the SYMBOL, though the two terms are often used in such a way that their meanings overlap. Symbols usually have a wider and more suggestive range of meaning, and a more obvious, less tenuous relationship with what they represent. In allegory the TENOR AND VEHICLE are kept further apart, so that understanding the relationship involves a more clearly defined act of 'translation', like peeling off a label.

Alliteration. (Lat. 'more letters') A sequence of repeated consonantal sounds in a stretch of language. The matching consonants are usually at the beginning of words or stressed syllables. Alliteration is common in poetry and prose, and is one of the most easily identifiable figures of speech. In some poems alliteration is insistent and obvious for special effect, as in Hopkins's 'The Windhover' (written 1877):

> I caught this morning morning's minion, king-
> dom of daylight's dauphin, dapple-dawn-drawn Falcon, in his
> riding
> Of the rolling level underneath him steady air, and striding
> High there, how he rung upon the rein of a wimpling wing
> In his ecstasy!

More often it is less assertive, but still a powerful means of introducing pattern into language. Keats plays on 's', 'm', 'f', 'v' and 'r' sounds in the opening of 'To Autumn' (1820):

> Season of mists and mellow fruitfulness,
> Close bosom-friend of the maturing sun;
> Conspiring with him how to load and bless
> With fruit the vines that round the thatch-eaves run.

In prose alliteration is also very frequent, though its effect may be less immediately obvious than in verse. Dickens plays with 'l', 'm' and 'w' sounds in the opening of *Bleak House* (1852–3):

> London. Michaelmas term lately over, and the Lord Chancellor sitting in Lincoln's Inn Hall. Implacable November weather. As much mud in the streets, as if the waters had but newly retired from the face of the earth, and it would not be wonderful to meet a Megalosaurus, forty feet long or so, waddling like an elephantine lizard up Holborn Hill.

Alliteration is often used in prose and verse for jocular or comic effect. De Quincey, in his *Confessions of an English Opium Eater* (1821), here jokingly comments on the pleasures of opium, playing on hard 'c' and 'p' sounds:

> Happiness might now be bought for a penny, and carried in the waistcoat pocket: portable ecstasies might be had corked up in a pint bottle...

See also ASSONANCE, CONSONANCE, ONOMATOPOEIA.

Alliterative revival. The ALLITERATIVE VERSE of the fourteenth century (*Pearl*, *Gawain*, Langland's *Piers Plowman*, several Scots poems) perceived both as a revival and as a continuation of alliterative forms dating back to the Anglo-Saxon period.

Alliterative verse. Anglo-Saxon poetry was written in a metre based on ALLITERATION. The verse was organised into stretches of language dominated by four heavily stressed syllables, of which the first three usually shared an initial consonant. Words beginning with vowels were considered to alliterate.

Here is some of 'The Seafarer' (ninth or tenth century?) rendered into a modern English version of the Old English metre (by M. Alexander):

> for men's laughter
> there was curlew-call, there were the cries of gannets,
> for mead-drinking the music of the gull.
> To the storm striking the stone cliffs
> gull would answer, eagle scream
> from throats frost-feathered.

Many of the greatest poems of the Middle Ages, such as Langland's *Piers Plowman* (*c*.1372–89), the anonymous *Sir Gawain and the Green Knight* and *Pearl* (both late fourteenth century), also use alliterative metres. In Middle English alliterative verse the organisation is looser, and the poet has more licence to play on the repeated sounds. Various modern poets, such as Hopkins and Auden, have experimented with alliterative verse forms.

Allusion. (Lat. 'to play with, to touch lightly upon') A passing reference in a work of literature to something outside itself. A writer may allude to legends, historical facts or personages, to other works of literature, or even to autobiographical details.

Literary allusion requires special explanation. Some writers include in their own works passages from other writers, or IMITATIONS or PARODIES of the style of other writers, in order to introduce implicit contrasts or comparisons. T.S. Eliot's *The Waste Land* (1922) is almost a COLLAGE of allusions of this kind, many of which are explained in his own notes to the poem:

But at my back from time to time I hear
The sound of horns and motors, which shall bring
Sweeney to Mrs Porter in the spring.

(from 'The Fire Sermon')

In his notes Eliot refers the reader to Marvell's famous 'To His Coy Mistress' (1681):

But at my back I always hear
Time's wingèd chariot hurrying near;
And yonder all before us lie
Deserts of vast Eternity.

He also quotes another, less well-known, poem, John Day's *The Parliament of Bees* (written c.1607):

When of the sudden, listening, you shall hear,
A noise of horns and hunting, which shall bring
Actaeon to Diana in the spring,
Where all shall see her naked skin . . .

Presumably Eliot hopes that his own lines will be enriched by the reader's memory of the witty but sadly urgent tone of Marvell's poem, and by the ironic contrasts and parallels between the Classical deities and his own modern, vulgar characters. Clearly literary allusions of this kind are useful for achieving compression in a work of literature, and for widening its frame of reference. But as such allusions rely on prior knowledge or patience with a reference book, their effect may go unnoticed by the general reader. *See also* INTERTEXTUALITY.

Alternate rhyme. The rhyming of alternate lines in verse, as in the STANZA form *abab*. *See also* RHYME.

Ambience. (Lat. 'going around') In its literary use, another word for the ATMOSPHERE or MOOD of a literary work.

Ambiguity. (Lat. 'doubtful, shifting') The capacity of words and sentences to have double, multiple or uncertain meanings. A PUN is the simplest example of ambiguity, where a word is used so as to have two sharply different possible meanings, usually with comic or wry effect. The English critic William Empson in his influential *Seven Types of Ambiguity* (1930) extended the meaning of ambiguity to 'any verbal nuance, however slight, that gives room to alternative reactions to the same piece of language'. Here is an example:

No worst, there is none, Pitched past pitch of grief,
More pangs will, schooled at forepangs, wilder wring.

(written c.1885)

Hopkins's lines play with the different possible meanings of 'pitch': it is difficult to determine whether the primary meaning of 'pitched' is musical, or if it suggests 'highly wrought', or simply 'thrown'. The final word of the second line seems to confirm a musical meaning, in the sense that a high-pitched note 'rings', but the spelling 'wrings' makes its primary meaning 'to squeeze and twist strongly'. 'Pitch', in the sense of an oily substance produced by boiling tar, is proverbial for its blackness ('pitch-black'), and therefore the word may add by implication the idea of darkness to the despair which is the poem's subject. Other meanings of 'pitch', which can be discovered in a large dictionary (such as O.E.D.) in relation to architecture and falconry, may also have played a part in aiding Hopkins's choice of the word.

Ambiguity may be syntactical:

> many a time,
> At evening, when the earliest stars began
> To move along the edges of the hills,
> Rising or setting, would he stand alone,
> Beneath the trees, or by the glimmering lake.

(Wordsworth, 'There was a Boy', 1800)

'Rising or setting' refers to the movement of the stars, but it is so placed in the line that it could also refer to the hills, and though the hills cannot 'rise' or 'set' literally, Wordsworth gives them a sense of movement or creates an impression of their shape by the fluidity of his syntax, a nuance of meaning which is borne out by the fragment's subject matter, the reciprocity between the boy as observer and the landscape which surrounds him.

A piece of literature may also be ambiguous in feeling. The first stanza of Yeats's 'Sailing to Byzantium' (1928) appears to oscillate between celebration and condemnation, resulting in an uneasy but fascinating complexity of tone:

> That is no country for old men. The young
> In one another's arms, birds in the trees
> – Those dying generations – at their song,
> The salmon-falls, the mackerel-crowded seas,
> Fish, flesh, or fowl, commend all summer long
> Whatever is begotten, born, and dies.
> Caught in that sensual music all neglect
> Monuments of unageing intellect.

Ambivalence. (Lat. 'strong on both sides') AMBIGUITY of feeling; the co-existence of two different attitudes to the same object. The reader may feel ambivalent towards the character of Heathcliff in *Wuthering Heights* (1847), for example, simultaneously sympathising with him in his passionate love for Catherine and his rejection by her, while being repelled by his violence.

'Ambivalence' is a more general quality of a text, and is less precisely located in individual words than 'ambiguity'. It is most often created by building up several different ways of looking at a character or event. Used to describe a piece of writing, 'ambivalent' suggests the expression of opposing points of view, or an openness to diverse and even possibly mutually exclusive interpretations.

American Renaissance or **American Romantic period.** A label for the flowering of American literature that took place between about 1830 and the end of the Civil War in 1865. The novelists Hawthorne (*The Scarlet Letter*, 1850) and Melville (*Moby-Dick*, 1851), the essayists Emerson and Thoreau (*Walden*, 1854), and the poets Poe and Whitman (*Leaves of Grass*, 1855), all contributed to the development of new kinds of literature with a distinctly American national character. *See also* TRANSCENDENTALISM.

Amphibrach. (Gk. 'short at both ends') A trisyllabic metrical FOOT in Classical prosody, consisting of 'short–long–short'. In English stress-based prosody: x / x, ti-tum-ti. Rare except as a substitute foot. *See also* METRE.

Amphimacer. (Gk. 'long at both ends') A trisyllabic FOOT in Classical prosody, consisting of long–short–long. Its stress-based equivalent (/ x /, tum-ti-tum) is rare in English verse. *See also* METRE.

Amplification. (Lat. 'enlargement, copiousness') A rhetorical term used to describe passages in prose or verse in which a statement is extended so as to add to its effect: for example, continual emphasis by REPETITION, as in the opening to Dickens's *Bleak House* (1852-3):

> Fog everywhere. Fog up the river, where it flows among green aits and meadows; fog down the river, where it rolls defiled among the tiers of shipping, and the waterside pollutions of a great (and dirty) city.

Anachronism. (Gk. 'refer to a wrong time') The inclusion of some action or object in a work of art which is out of time with the historical period being depicted. A famous example is Shakespeare's reference to a clock (II.1) in *Julius Caesar* (1599). Anachronisms may be simple mistakes, or they may be deliberate, in order to suggest the timelessness of human behaviour. Modern-dress productions of plays by Shakespeare, or any other non-modern playwright, are deliberate anachronisms, to emphasise the enduring qualities of the language and ideas of the drama.

Anachrony. The deliberate shuffling of time-sequences in a narrative. A common feature of novels, for example, is that the order in which the PLOT develops is quite different from the chronological sequence of events of the original STORY. In many instances these differences may be highly complex, as, for example, in Emily Brontë's *Wuthering Heights* (1847), in which the narrative moves forward through a developing story while simultaneously explaining a large span of events that took place before the beginning of the novel.

'Prolepsis' is a glimpse forward, anticipating things that will be described fully later. A glimpse backward, or, in the cinematic term, a 'flashback', supplying necessary background information, is 'analepsis'. See also IN MEDIAS RES, NARRATOLOGY.

Anacoluthon. (Gk. 'lacking sequence') Breaking the grammatical sequence of a sentence. A sudden change of grammatical construction within a sentence or passage, either in error, or for deliberate effect, as, for example, 'If you fail to do your duty – let's not think of that!'

Anacreontics. Anacreon was a Greek lyric poet of the sixth century BC of whose works only a few fragments remain, all of them short, clear poems in praise of the muses, love, wine and song, some with a satirical edge. About sixty poems by other poets imitating this style are gathered together in the collection called the *Anacreontea.* Various English poets have also written anacreontic verse, notably Abraham Cowley, and Thomas Moore, who translated the *Odes of Anacreon* (1800). Here is a fragment of a translation by Byron, called 'From Anacreon', in *Hours of Idleness* (1807):

My harp shall all its powers reveal,
To tell the tale my heart must feel;
Love, love alone, my lyre shall claim,
In songs of bliss and sighs of flame.

Anacrusis. (Gk. 'prelude') One or more extra syllables at the beginning of a line of verse, not counted as part of the METRE. W.H. Auden's 'Lullaby' (1940) is written in trochaic TETRAMETER, but occasional lines have an extra slack syllable at the beginning, as in the second line quoted below:

Grave the vision Venus sends
Of supernatural sympathy,
Universal love and hope . . .

Anadiplosis. (Gk. 'doubling') A rhetorical device in which a word or words that appear at the end of one clause or sentence are repeated at the start of the next. Keats's 'Ode to a Nightingale' (1820) provides an example in which the repeated word links stanzas:

. . . in faery lands forlorn.

Forlorn! the very word is like a bell
To toll me back from thee to my sole self!

See also REPETITION.

Anagnorisis. (Gk. 'recognition') Aristotle, in his *Poetics* (fourth century BC), uses this term to refer to the moment when truth is discovered by the characters in a play. A famous example, which Aristotle knew, occurs in Sophocles's *Oedipus Rex* (*c*.430BC) when Oedipus gradually realises that it is he himself who has killed Laius, and that therefore he has married his mother, caused the plague in Thebes, fulfilled his predicted destiny, and so on. There are many such moments in TRAGEDIES. Similar moments of discovery exist in COMEDIES. When Viola sheds her disguise at the end of Shakespeare's *Twelfth Night* (*c*.1600), Orsino's sudden and uncomfortable new perspective on events is comparable with the tragic anagnorisis. *See also* PERIPETEIA, PLOT.

Anagogical. (Gk. 'elevating') The mystical, spiritual or hidden ALLEGORI-CAL meaning of a text, especially of the Bible.

Anagram. (Gk. 'writing anew') A word puzzle: the letters of a word or words are muddled up to make another word. Thus the words 'Ah speak, seer!' are an anagram of 'Shakespeare'.

Analepsis. (Gk. 'take back') A FLASHBACK in narratives. *See also* ANACHRONY.

Analogue. (Gk. 'proportion') A parallel word or thing; used in literary scholarship to refer to stories with similar or comparable plots occurring in the literatures of different ages or countries. *See also* PARALLEL, SOURCE.

Analogy. (Gk. 'equality, proportion') Another word for a literary PARALLEL. An analogy is a word, thing, idea or story, chosen for the purpose of comparison, which can help to explain whatever it is similar to: for example, Gloucester's relationship with his two sons in the SUBPLOT of Shakespeare's *King Lear* (*c*.1605) is analogous to Lear's relationship with his daughters.

Analysis. (Gk. 'unloose, undo') The detailed study and attempted explana-tion of an individual literary work and its effect. Analysis usually adopts the method of dividing up the work under examination in order to distinguish its component parts and to speculate how and why it is put together in the way that it is. 'Critical analysis' implies evaluation as well as explanation.

Anapaest. (Gk. 'reversed') A trisyllabic metrical FOOT consisting of two unstressed syllables followed by a stressed syllable: ti-ti-tum. Anapaes-tic metres are not uncommon in English verse, though the strong stresses tend to over-assert themselves: in a poor reading the verse structure will then dominate the sense of the poem. Because of this headlong, galloping quality, it is popular (like DACTYLIC metre) in poems about headlong motion, such as Browning's 'How They Brought the Good News from Ghent to Aix' (1845).

The following example, the first stanza of Swinburne's 'A Forsaken Garden' (1878), illustrates a predominantly anapaestic rhythm; seven lines of anapaests (mixed with IAMBS, and even a TROCHEE in line three) are concluded by a short line of three heavily stressed syllables:

> In a coign of the cliff between lowland and highland,
> At the sea-down's edge between windward and lee,
> Walled round with rocks as an inland island,
> The ghost of a garden fronts the sea.
> A girdle of brushwood and thorn encloses
> The steep square slope of the blossomless bed
> Where the weeds that grew green from the graves of its roses
> Now lie dead.

See METRE for further discussion of these terms.

Anaphora. (Gk. 'carrying back, repetition') The name for a rhetorical device, common in prose, verse and speech, in which a word or phrase is repeated in several successive clauses. Often this kind of syntactical REPETITION is associated with the depiction of strong feelings. York's complaint to Richard II is a straightforward example:

> How long shall I be patient? Ah how long
> Shall tender duty make me suffer wrong?
> Not Gloucester's death, nor Hereford's banishment,
> Nor Gaunt's rebukes, nor England's private wrongs,
> Nor the prevention of poor Bolingbroke
> About his marriage, nor my own disgrace,
> Have ever made me sour my patient cheek,
> Or bend one wrinkle on my Sovereign's face.
>
> (Shakespeare, *Richard II* (*c*.1595), II.1)

Dickens was particularly fond of this repetitive effect, as, for example, in his opening account of Mr Bounderby in *Hard Times* (1854):

> He was a rich man: banker, merchant, manufacturer, and what not. A big, loud man, with a stare and a metallic laugh. A man made out of a coarse material, which seemed to have been stretched to make so much of him. A man with a great puffed head . . . A man who could never sufficiently vaunt himself a self-made man. A man who was always proclaiming, through that brassy speaking-trumpet of a voice of his, his old ignorance and his old poverty. A man who was the Bully of humility.

Anaphora may be the basis for a simple poetic metre, as in the contemporary American poet Allen Ginsberg's *Howl* (1956), or in Psalm 29:

> The voice of the Lord is powerful: the voice of the Lord is
> full of majesty . . . the voice of the Lord shaketh the wilderness.

See also INCREMENTAL REPETITION.

Anatomy. (Gk. 'cut up') The detailed examination of a subject. The most
famous example is Burton's *The Anatomy of Melancholy* (1621),
subtitled 'what it is, with all the kinds, causes, symptomes, prognos-
tickes, and severall cures of it in three partitions, with their severall
sections, members and subsections, Philosophically, Medicinally, Historically opened and cut up'. Exhaustive erudition is a major characteristic of the anatomy. The Canadian critic Northrop Frye's *Anatomy of
Criticism* (1957) discusses the form at some length, as might be expected
from its title. Frye suggests that the anatomy, the NOVEL, CONFESSION
and ROMANCE, are the four chief forms of FICTION. He explains how a
work such as Melville's *Moby-Dick* (1851) combines strands of romance
and anatomy: the theme of the hunt develops into an encyclopaedic
examination of whales and whaling.

Androcentric. (Gk. 'man-centred') Like PHALLOCENTRIC, a term used in
FEMINIST CRITICISM . It refers to the way in which Western culture is
inherently organised according to masculine values.

Androgyny. (Gk. 'man-woman-y') Containing elements of both sexes.
Virginia Woolf contemplates the meaning of the term (which she
ascribes to a remark by Coleridge, that great minds are androgynous) in
the last chapter of *A Room of One's Own* (1929). Her novel *Orlando*
(1928) has a central character who is first male, then female. The
concept, or fact, of androgyny is of interest to FEMINIST CRITICS (though
repudiated by some, because 'andro-' still refers to man), as it presents
an escape from the gender polarity of masculine versus feminine. *See
also* BINARY OPPOSITION.

Anecdote. (Gk. 'things unpublished') The *Anecdota* (c.AD550) of the Greek
historian Procopius consists of short stories and incidents of court life
told as an attack on the Emperor Justinian and his wife Theodora.
Anecdotes are narratives of small incidents or events, told for the
purpose of entertainment, mirth, malice, or to reveal character. The
anecdote is not in itself a literary form, and it is often despised as
evidence of a gossiping interest, but none the less many literary works of
lasting interest, notably biographies, such as Boswell's *The Life of
Samuel Johnson* (1791) or De Quincey's *Recollections of the Lake Poets*
(1834–9), are crammed with anecdotes.

Anglo-Norman period. The period from 1100 to 1350 when Anglo-
Norman (a dialect of French) was the chief vehicle for literature in
England (after Latin). *See also* MIDDLE ENGLISH PERIOD.

Anglo-Saxon period. *See* OLD ENGLISH PERIOD.

Angry Young Men. A catch-phrase used of certain British writers and
public figures of the 1950s. Several novels of the period featured ANTI-
HEROES, comic or unpleasant, as their protagonists, for example,
Kingsley Amis's *Lucky Jim* (1954), John Braine's *Room at the Top*
(1957) and John Wain's *Hurry on Down* (1953): the vaguely anti-

Establishment and anti-middle-class feeling of these works seemed the stamp of a new literary stance or movement. In fact the writers and their novels had little, if anything, in common with each other.

John Osborne's play *Look Back in Anger* (1956) is perhaps the most famous and enduring work of this vaguely defined literary movement or trend. The play's hero, Jimmy Porter, who indulges his anguished consciousness in long tirades against the middle-class gentility of his wife and her family, is the quintessential 'Angry'. Another writer labelled an Angry Young Man was Colin Wilson; when his book of literary criticism, *The Outsider* (1956), was published, he was living in a tent in a London park, ' and newspapers made much of this bohemianism.

Angst. (Ger. 'anxiety, anguish') In EXISTENTIALIST philosophy *Angst* is the state of dread which results from a person's realisation that the future must be determined solely by freely chosen actions and decisions. The burden of being continually responsible for one's own fate causes a constant state of anxiety.

Annals. (Lat. 'yearly') Historical records, or CHRONICLES written year by year, like the *Anglo-Saxon Chronicle* (ninth–twelfth centuries).

Anonymous. (Gk. 'without name') Literary works of which the author is not known, either through deliberate choice, or because details of authorship have been lost, are so designated. Much of the lyric poetry of the Middle Ages, for example, is of unknown authorship.

Antagonist. (Gk. 'struggle against') The chief opponent of the hero or PROTAGONIST in a story; especially used of drama. Thus Iago is the antagonist in Shakespeare's *Othello* (c.1604). Satan is the 'Antagonist of Heaven's Almightie King' in Milton's *Paradise Lost* (1667). In spite of its specific sense the word is usually used to refer to anyone in opposition to anything.

Anthem. (O.E. contraction of 'antiphon') A song asserting the beliefs of a group, whether bound together by religion, nationality, politics, or some more particular social organisation, such as a school.

Anthology. (Gk. 'flower collection') A collection of poems by different poets, without any particular linking theme or principle of organisation, though the poems may be arranged according to poet, according to subject matter, or chronologically. The word originates from the *Greek Anthology*, a compilation of lyric poems and epigrams, some dating back as far as 700BC, made by Constantine Cephalas in the late ninth century.

Many well-known pre-Elizabethan and Elizabethan poems first appeared in anthologies of lyric poetry like *Tottel's Miscellany* (1557), *The Phoenix Nest* (1593) and *England's Helicon* (1600).

The most famous anthology in English literature is probably *The Golden Treasury of the Best Songs and Lyrical Poems in the English*

Language (1861), compiled, with the advice of Tennyson, by F.T. Palgrave, which influenced British taste for several generations. Anthologies may create or influence the public response to poetry, but they are also often modified to cater for changing interests and attitudes.

Anthropomorphism. (Gk. 'human-form-ism') The attribution of a human form to God, to abstractions or even to animals and inanimate objects. Ted Hughes's 'Hawk Roosting' (1960), for example, is one among many of his early poems that endow birds and beasts with human qualities: it is an exercise in EMPATHY, beginning 'I sit in the top of the wood, my eyes closed'. *See also* PATHETIC FALLACY, PERSONIFICATION.

Anticlimax. (Gk. 'down-ladder') A rhetorical term, but in colloquial use. A sudden effect of banality, either intentional or unintentional, in prose or verse. According to Dr Johnson, 'A sentence in which the last part expresses something lower than the first.'

By extension anticlimax refers to a similar effect in the action of a play, or plot of a novel, when some high point of excitement is not achieved, or the seriousness of a literary work is dissipated by a comical, digressive, meaningless or boring development. A writer may manipulate this kind of apparent anticlimax to add rather than destroy suspense: a famous example of this is provided by the digressive speeches of the porter just after the murder of Duncan in Act II, Scene 3 of Shakespeare's *Macbeth* (*c*.1606). *See also* BATHOS.

Anti-hero. An unheroic PROTAGONIST of a play or novel. A character whose attractiveness or interest consists of the inability to perform deeds of bravery, courage or generosity. Anti-heroic elements have existed in comedy from the earliest times. The term is usually reserved for a special kind of character in modern literature, though the antecedents can clearly be seen in Cervantes's *Don Quixote* (1605, 1615), Sterne's *Tristram Shandy* (1760–7) and in Defoe's rogues, for example in *Moll Flanders* (1722). T.S. Eliot's 'J. Alfred Prufrock' with his 'Love Song' (1917) and Joyce's Leopold Bloom in *Ulysses* (1922) were early examples of the ordinary, unheroic protagonist, which has been fully explored in twentieth-century literature, to the extent of becoming a STEREOTYPE in the fiction of the 1950s and 1960s.

In drama the middle- or working-class protagonists of modern tragedies, such as Willy Loman in Arthur Miller's *Death of a Salesman* (1949), might be called anti-heroes to distinguish them from the kings, princes and noblemen who figured in the great tragedies of the past.

Antimasque. An addition to the conventions of the MASQUE made by Ben Jonson in 1609; the antimasque is a contrasting episode of clowning before or during the masque proper, of which it was often a grotesque and farcical BURLESQUE.

Antinomy. (Gk. 'opposite law') Contradiction between opposite principles: antinomies are mutually exclusive truths, which remain true in spite of the fact that they contradict each other. The poet Blake was fascinated by such PARADOXES, and incorporated them into his personal mythology. What seem, for example, to be contrary definitions of love are given in the short poem 'The Clod and the Pebble' (1794), though in fact they are mutually dependent:

'Love seeketh not Itself to please,
Nor for itself hath any care,
But for another gives its ease,
And builds a Heaven in Hell's despair.'

So sung a little Clod of Clay,
Trodden with the cattle's feet,
But a Pebble of the brook
Warbled out these metres meet:

'Love seeketh only Self to please,
To bind another to Its delight,
Joys in another's loss of ease,
And builds a Hell in Heaven's despite.'

Anti-novel. Modern experimental fiction which deliberately refuses to make use of elements considered essential in the traditional NOVEL, such as plot, characterisation or ordered narrative sequence.

French exponents of the NOUVEAU ROMAN (new novel) have written many works of fiction which might be classed as anti-novels. In Britain, B.S. Johnson attempted structural and narrative experiments which abandon traditional ideas of the novel form. *The Unfortunates* (1969) consists of twenty-seven short sections in a case, which can be shuffled about and read in any order. In *Albert Angelo* (1964) Johnson breaks into his story with 'an almighty aposiopesis', which suddenly reveals the author sitting in his study commenting on the dishonesty of the fiction which he has been creating for the reader.

A large number of the techniques and preoccupations of modern experimental fiction are foreshadowed in Sterne's remarkable novel *Tristram Shandy* (1760-7) which, like *Albert Angelo*, plays with the reader's sense of illusion and which contains several typographical novelties and jokes, such as a completely black page (representing mourning). See also STREAM OF CONSCIOUSNESS.

Antiphonal. (Gk. 'responsive') A hymn, prayer or poem which is split up into two parts, one a response, or echoing reply to the other.

Antiphrasis. (Gk. 'anti-tell') An ironical figure of speech, by which a word is used to mean its exact opposite, such as calling a bald man 'Curly'.

Antistrophe. *See* STROPHE.

Antithesis. (Gk. 'opposite placing') (1) A rhetorical term. Opposing or contrasting ideas in next-door sentences or clauses, using opposite or strongly contrasting forms of words, for example: 'I am going north by bicycle, but she is coming south by car.' This kind of verbal mirroring is common in speech and literature. *See also* OXYMORON, PARADOX. (2) The second of two opposed ideas. An argument in opposition to some original proposition, and thus those ideas or forces tending to change or correct an original THESIS. *See also* DIALECTIC.

Antitype. That which is represented by the TYPE or SYMBOL. In typological interpretation of the Bible (*see* ALLEGORY), the Old Testament figures are the 'types' which prefigure the 'antitypes'; Adam (the type) is read as a figure or image of Christ (the antitype).

Antonomasia. (Gk. 'anti-name') The use of an EPITHET instead of a proper name: for example, 'Her Majesty' for Queen Elizabeth; 'the Bard' for Shakespeare. The appropriation of a famous proper name to indicate a person's qualities, as in 'she's a real Jezebel', or 'he's a bit of a Scrooge', is also antonomastic.

Antonym. (Gk. 'opposite name') A word of opposite meaning: the antonym of 'good' is 'bad'.

Anxiety of influence. The title of a book, published in 1973, by the American critic Harold Bloom, in which he describes the different ways in which writers (especially poets) react to the crushing weight of the literary tradition that precedes them. This anxiety may take the form of a general fear that nothing significant remains to be written; or writers may reshape and rewrite influential works; or anxiety may be visible in distortions or gaps caused when seeking to avoid apparent or even invisible influences. Criticism is also a result of re-writing and mis-reading poems. Bloom describes his central principle thus:

> Poetic Influence – when it involves two strong, authentic poets, – always proceeds by a misreading of the prior poet, an act of creative correction, that is actually and necessarily a misinterpretation. The history of fruitful poetic influence, which is to say the main tradition of Western poetry since the Renaissance, is a history of anxiety and self-saving caricature, of distortion, of perverse, wilful revisionism, without which modern poetry as such could not exist.

Mixing quotations from Freud and Nietzsche with his own poetic critical prose, Bloom creates a special vocabulary with which to discriminate between different varieties of influence. An aspiring writer is an 'ephebe' who has to overcome anxiety at the work of 'strong' poets by 'mis-readings' or 'misprisions'. Most of his terms ('clinamen', 'tessera', 'kenosis', 'daemonization', 'askesis' and 'apophrades') have not become part of the ordinary currency of literary debate, unlike the catchphrase 'anxiety of influence' and his general emphasis on the significance of influence in the development of poetry, which has been widely accepted.

Aperçu. (Fr. 'glimpse') A moment of understanding, experienced by anyone, be they real or fictional, but especially by a reader in suddenly appreciating some aspect of a work.

Aphorism. (Gk. 'definition') A MAXIM. A generally accepted principle or truth expressed in a short, pithy manner. PROVERBS are traditional aphorisms. The *Aphorisms* of Hippocrates (*c*.415BC) were statements of the medical knowledge and principles of his age. The opening sentence reads: 'Life is short, the art long, opportunity fleeting, experiment treacherous, judgment difficult.' Other collections of medical aphorisms were made up till the eighteenth century, but 'aphorism' has come to be applied to any kind of pithily expressed precept, not just statements of scientific truth.

In English literature the poetry of the eighteenth century is particularly rich in aphorisms. The HEROIC COUPLET provided a specially suitable vehicle for this kind of witty, conclusive statement. Pope's *An Essay on Criticism* (1711), for example, is a discussion composed of aphoristic statements about the judgment of poetry. The following definition is well known:

True Wit is Nature to Advantage dress'd,
What oft was Thought, but ne'er so well Express'd,
Something, whose Truth convinc'd at Sight we find,
That gives us back the Image of our mind.

Some writers, such as Oscar Wilde, are remembered as much for their witty conversation and their ability to coin aphorisms as for their literary output. Similarly Boswell's *The Life of Samuel Johnson* (1791) is a record of that gentleman's remarkable capacity for aphoristic statement. Other writers are famed for private collections of aphorisms: Samuel Butler's *Notebooks* (1912) were published a decade after his death, though he himself preserved and organised them with great care. *See also* APOPHTHEGM, GNOMIC VERSE, PENSÉE, SENTENTIOUSNESS.

Apocalypse. (Gk. 'disclosure') Another name for the Book of Revelation of St John, the last book of the New Testament, which describes in visionary detail the future destruction of the world prior to the second coming of the Messiah, including the opening of the seven seals, the great conflict with the Dragon and other Beasts, the downfall of Babylon, the Day of Judgment, and the construction of the New Jerusalem. Other literary or artistic visions of violent and cataclysmic happenings can be described as 'apocalyptic'.

Apocalypse, New. *See* NEW APOCALYPSE.

Apocrypha. (Gk. 'hidden, of unknown authorship') A plural word. Apocrypha are works of unknown or disputed authorship which are considered spurious and not authentic. The word is applied specifically to those books, which, though not written in Hebrew and not considered genuine by the Jews, were included in the Septuagint and VULGATE versions of the Old Testament. They were excluded from the sacred CANON by the Protestants during the Reformation.

An 'apocryphal story' is therefore one that is almost certainly untrue, fictitious or fabulous, because its origins are unknown and its authenticity in doubt. Works falsely or dubiously ascribed to famous authors are also called 'apocryphal'.

Apollonian/Dionysian. The German philosopher Nietzsche coined these terms in *The Birth of Tragedy* (1872) to distinguish two opposite sides of the human psyche. The Apollonian stands for civilisation and the serene daylight of reason; the Dionysian represents the stormy, primitive, instinctive and passionate aspects of human nature. *See also* ROMANTICISM.

Apology. (Gk. 'defence') AUTOBIOGRAPHICAL, CONFESSIONAL, critical or philosophical literature in which the author argues a case for his or her beliefs, opinions or actions. A justification or vindication, not necessarily apologetic in tone. The most famous example in English literature is John Henry Newman's *Apologia Pro Vita Sua* ('Apology for His Life') which he wrote in 1864 to justify his changing from the Anglican to the Roman Catholic faith, and to refute fiercely the accusations of dishonesty made against him by Charles Kingsley.

Other famous examples are Plato's *Apology* (fourth century BC) in which Socrates defends himself against the government of Athens, and Sir Philip Sidney's *An Apology for Poetry* (1595) in which the nature of poetry is explored.

Apophthegm or **apothegm.** (Gk. 'speak one's opinions clearly') A terse, pithy, witty or weighty saying, embodying a truth. Synonymous with APHORISM and MAXIM. Bacon, who called the short sections of his *Novum Organum* (1620) 'Aphorisms', and whose 'Maxims of the Law', in *The Elements of the Common Laws of England* (1630), is a discussion of twenty-five brief legal statements, defined the apophthegm as 'pointed speeches' in his collection *Apophthegms New and Old* (1624).

Aporia. (Gk. 'unpassable path') A rhetorical term for the pondering of a difficult question; a famous instance is Hamlet's soliloquy, 'To be or not to be'.

'Aporia' is used by the French linguistic philosopher Derrida to refer to that point in all DISCOURSES (or so he asserts) at which some internal contradiction or irresolvable paradox proves the instability of meaning. According to Derrida, this instability is the condition of all language. The critical process of DECONSTRUCTIVE CRITICISM consists of discovering such knots of contradiction in texts.

Aposiopesis. (Gk. 'to keep silent') A rhetorical term. A sudden break in speech or writing, suggesting unwillingness or inability to proceed. In his *Of the Art of Sinking in Poetry* (1727) Pope defines it thus:

An excellent figure for the Ignorant, as, 'What shall I say?' when one
has nothing to say: or 'I can no more' when one really can no more.
Expressions which the gentle reader is so good as never to take in
earnest.

Such halts are likely to occur at points of extreme crisis in drama.

Apostrophe. (Gk. 'turning away') A rhetorical term for a speech addressed
to a person, idea or thing, often placed at the start of a poem or essay,
but also acting as a digression or pause in an ongoing argument. 'Oh
just, subtle and mighty opium', De Quincey apostrophises in the
Confessions of an English Opium Eater (1821), modifying Sir Walter
Raleigh's 'O eloquent, just and mighty Death' from *The History of the
World* (1614). The convention is mocked by Chekhov, whose character
Gayev in *The Cherry Orchard* (1904) is addicted to addressing domestic
objects with high-flown sentiments, to the amused embarrassment of his
family.

The apostrophe is a common element in the LYRIC, especially perhaps in ODES and ELEGIES. Shelley's 'Ode to the West Wind' (1820)
consists of five fourteen-line sections, each one addressed throughout to
the wind:

O Wild West Wind, thou breath of Autumn's being,
Thou, from whose unseen presence the leaves dead
Are driven . . .

This device has proved a robust convention in poetry of all kinds;
indeed it almost amounts to a minor genre, as a means of initiating a
poem in a manner that is self-consciously artificial, but conventionally
acceptable. Nowadays it is often used in a semi-serious, semi-mocking
manner, such as in Douglas Dunn's 'Ode to a Paper-clip' (1981):

When I speak to you, paperclip, urging you
To get a move on and metamorphose,
You sit there mating with the light that shines
Out of your minerals, a brighter glint
Where, rounding at a loop, you meet the sun.
Paperclip, I like you, I need you.
Please, turn into something wonderful.

See also INVOCATION.

Apparatus. (Lat. 'make ready') Scholarly editions of texts often include
prefaces, notes of various kinds, a glossary, collections of historical and
critical material and appendices, all deemed helpful in reading the work
in question: this extra material is called the apparatus, from the Latin
apparatus criticus, which denoted information specifically about textual
variations and changes.

Appropriation. *See* POST-COLONIAL LITERATURE.

Aptronym. (Coined by an American journalist) In literature a character's name that explains or gives a clue to his or her personality, morality or purpose in the story: for example, Squire Allworthy in Fielding's *Tom Jones* (1749) or Mr Knightley in Jane Austen's *Emma* (1816). Such names are common in novels, and in allegorical works, like Bunyan's *The Pilgrim's Progress* (1678, 1684). The term also applies to surnames that denote a job, like 'Smith', 'Thatcher', 'Butler' or 'Baker'.

Arcadia. Originally a mountainous district of Greece. Virgil followed Greek precedents in locating his idealised PASTORAL life in his *Eclogues* (42–37BC) in Arcadia. During the Renaissance 'Arcadia' became the typical name for an idealised rural society where the harmonious Golden Age still flourished. Sir Philip Sidney's prose ROMANCE is entitled *Arcadia* (1590). *See also* PRIMITIVISM.

Archaism. (Gk. 'ancient, old-fashioned') In literature archaism is the deliberate retention or imitation of obsolete words or syntax, which may have been the characteristic usage of an earlier period. A simple instance is the preservation in nineteenth-century poetry of the pronouns 'thee' and 'thou', along with their appropriate verbal forms, long after they had passed out of ordinary speech. Archaism has been an acceptable licence in verse till recent times.

Except for specific purposes of parody or historical reconstruction, archaism is not common in prose, though the Authorised Version of the Bible (1611) is a notable exception. Archaic forms were used by the translators to lend authority and dignity to their style.

What amounts almost to a tradition of deliberate, ostentatious archaism was introduced into the language of English poetry by Elizabethan poets, especially Spenser. In *The Faerie Queene* (1590, 1596) Spenser used many obsolete forms of English, with Chaucer as his model, to help to create the atmosphere of the medieval chivalric past, for which the Elizabethans had a nostalgic longing. The opening lines of Canto I suggest something of this subject matter and language:

A Gentle Knight was pricking on the plaine,
Ycladd in mightie armes and silver shielde,
Wherein old dints of deepe wounds did remaine.

'Pricking' and the prefix 'y' in 'ycladd' are both archaisms, redolent of Middle English poetry, especially Chaucer.

Some of this kind of archaism became fossilised into POETIC DICTION. The nineteenth century saw another revival of MEDIEVALISM, and this helped to maintain archaic forms in poetry, though Keats, for example, favours words like 'darkling' and 'brede' (for 'braid') even in poems that have no need of a historical atmosphere.

Archaisms may be used on false assumptions about old-fashioned linguistic forms. The 'Ye' as in 'Ye Olde Tea Shoppe' etc. is based on a misinterpretation of the Icelandic and Old English runic letter pronounced 'th', which dropped out of the alphabet towards the end of the Middle English period (late fifteenth century).

Doubts about whether individual words are archaistic or not can often be resolved by referring to the twenty-volume *Oxford English Dictionary* which is 'compiled on historical principles' and therefore gives details of the development and usage of words.

Archetype. (Gk. 'original pattern, first model') A surprisingly old word (first usage recorded in O.E.D.: 1599) which, having been taken up as a technical or jargon term in anthropology, psychology and literary criticism, has passed into everyday usage; used in its weakest form, 'archetypal' means not much more than 'typical'.

The recurrent themes, images, patterns and characters which occur in all literatures, as well as in MYTHS and perhaps even dreams, may be called archetypes. According to the theories of Jung archetypes are inherent in our COLLECTIVE UNCONSCIOUS: they are a kind of ready-formed mythology or mental furniture which exists in the human brain as a consequence of past human experiences. Before Jung developed his psychological theories, anthropologists, especially J.G. Frazer in *The Golden Bough* (1890–1915), had been collating myths and rituals from different cultures so as to reveal the many comparable or common patterns.

Literature's manifest subject matter contains a vast number of recurrent interests, situations, plots and personalities which may be classed as archetypal without recourse to myth or to the unconscious mind. Northrop Frye has attempted a comparative study of literature in this light in his *Anatomy of Criticism* (1957).

The essential facts and conditions of human experience give rise to archetypal situations: the cycle of the seasons, sowing and harvesting, childhood and old age, love, family conflict, birth and death, all these may be dealt with in literature in a way which brings to mind their archetypal quality as events. Archetypal themes and plots include the difficult journey or quest, the search for lost parents, the descent into the underworld, the heavenly ascent, redemption by death, and so on. Some of the characters which may be deemed archetypal are the scapegoat, the Promethean rebel, the blind seer, the avenger, the earth goddess, the siren and the witch. Certain animals, such as the lion, or plants, such as the rose, or places, such as the paradisal garden, may have meanings as SYMBOLS which give them archetypal significance. *See also* IMAGERY.

Architectonics. (Gk. 'pertaining to buildings') Properly the science of architecture, or the classification of knowledge; but used of literature as a jargon word for the structural principles underlying a work or works.

Argument. (Lat. 'making clear, proving') The word has many applications with regard to literature. A short summary of the PLOT or subject matter of a long piece of poetry or prose is called 'the argument'. A statement of the purpose or 'argument' at the start of an EPIC is part of the conventions of that form.

Basically the 'argument' of a literary work is the ideas or views which it sets out to assert or prove. Some literary works, therefore, have a strong sense of argument; others have little or no argument, existing for no other purpose than to be the object of aesthetic pleasure. *See also* DIDACTICISM.

Aristotelian. Pertaining to the ideas of Aristotle (384–322 BC) whose wide-ranging philosophical ideas had enormous prestige in the Middle Ages.

In relation to literature, his *Poetics* (observations about Greek TRAGEDY collected by his followers) is an early and influential example of empirical criticism (*see* EMPIRICISM). By the examination of examples Aristotle attempts to analyse those features that make some tragedies more successful than others. He focuses on the nature of the PLOT and its connections with a moral pattern, the typifying features of the tragic hero, and the play's intensity of focus in time and place (later called the UNITIES). The characteristic shape of the tragic plot is defined, with labels like PERIPETEIA (reversal), ANAGNORISIS (recognition) and CATHARSIS (purgation).

The CHICAGO CRITICS, or 'Chicago Aristotelians', associated themselves with Aristotle's empirical method, and his emphasis on the significance of the plot.

Art for art's sake. *See* AESTHETICISM.

Arthurian legend. *See* ROMANCE.

Artifice. (Lat. 'make art') In a literary sense, 'artifice' refers either to the skill of the writer in contriving a work of art, or to the work of art itself. The word draws attention to the fact that the world of art and literature is a man-made, created fiction, not the same as the real world. The fact that literature is an 'artifice' or is artificial, may be lamented or may be enjoyed as the licence for exuberant ingenuity. The mythical maze-maker, Daedalus, the 'old artificer', is James Joyce's symbol for the artist in *A Portrait of the Artist as a Young Man* (1916).

Aside. (*n.*) An aside is a common dramatic CONVENTION in which a character speaks in such a way that some of the characters on stage do not hear what is said, while others do. It may also be a direct address to the audience, revealing the character's views, thoughts, motives and intentions so as to create DRAMATIC IRONY. *See also* SOLILOQUY.

Association. (Lat. 'sharing, allied') First used in its special philosophical sense by Locke (in 1690; O.E.D.), association refers to the mental connection between an object and ideas that have some relation to it. Hume extended the meaning of the word to include the sometimes arbitrary relationships between ideas in the mind. Twentieth-century psychoanalysts use free association of ideas as a means of exploring the subconscious mind.

In Britain several early nineteenth-century poets were interested in the theory of association, and its relevance to poetry. Many of Wordsworth's and Coleridge's CONVERSATION POEMS are studies in this function of the human mind: the poet typically associates his mood and ideas with his surroundings, and contemplates the connections which he feels between ideas and things both in the present and in his memory. Coleridge's 'Frost at Midnight' (1798) not only is about association and the way in which the mind forges links between things and ideas, but it progresses by association: the poem's structure follows the movement of the poet's contemplation, drifting from subject to subject freely, naturally and explicably, but not in a severely rational or ordered manner.

In the twentieth century the theory of association, given further credibility by the development of psychology, gave rise to the STREAM OF CONSCIOUSNESS novel, which is also associative in its form and narrative structure. Virginia Woolf's *To the Lighthouse* (1927) is a famous example.

Assonance. (Lat. 'to answer to') The correspondence, or near-correspondence, in two words of the stressed vowel, and sometimes those which follow, but not of the consonants (unlike RHYME). Thus, can and fat, food and droop, child and silence, nation and traitor, and reticent and penitence are all assonantal. It is thus the vocalic, or vowel, equivalent of ALLITERATION. This method of making patterns in sound is used in the versification of Old French, Spanish, Celtic and other languages. It is a common feature of English verse, and is often the explanation of some particularly EUPHONIOUS effect in verse, as in this passage from Tennyson's *In Memoriam* (1850), XCV:

> Till now the doubtful dusk reveal'd
> The knolls once more where, couch'd at ease,
> The white kine glimmer'd, and the trees
> Laid their dark arms about the field.

Now, doubtful, couch'd and about are all assonantal. Note also the paired examples of assonance, white kine and dark arms, and a sequence of four nearly corresponding vowel sounds in one line, 'The knolls once more where, couch'd at ease'. These effects, coupled with the rhymes and alliterations, subtly but pervasively bind the chosen words together into a coherent pattern of sound, which is one aim of poetic language. See also CONSONANCE, HALF-RHYME.

Asyndeton. (Gk. 'unconnected') The omission of small words (definite and indefinite articles, prepositions, conjunctions) for the sake of speed and conciseness. A rhetorical device common in modern poetry. In Louis MacNeice's 'Snow' (1935) 'the' is omitted in such a way to suggest and provoke surprise:

World is crazier and more of it than we think,
Incorrigibly plural.

See also POLYSYNDETON.

Asyntactic. (Gk. 'not arranged') Describing language which is lacking full grammatical arrangement: ungrammatical word order.

Atmosphere. (Gk. 'ball of vapour') A common though vague term for the mood – moral, sensational, emotional or intellectual – which dominates a piece of writing, a play, a film, or even a painting. Atmosphere is built up in literature by a series of clues, subtle or obvious. Shakespeare is a master of the swift creation of a particular atmosphere. The opening of *Macbeth* (c.1606), for example, is a tiny scene of a dozen lines, yet the three witches introduce the element of suspense ('When shall we three meet again?') with which they link Macbeth himself; and they fix the violent and evil atmosphere of the play in their discussion of the 'hurlyburly' of the battle, and in their inversion of values:

Fair is foul, and foul is fair:
Hover through the fog and filthy air.

Attic style. Direct, simple, and unadorned by excessive rhetorical flourishes and complexity. A style of speech-making modelled on the Athenian orators of the fourth century BC, of whom the most famous was Demosthenes.

Aubade. (Lat. 'white, dawn') A song or salute at dawn, usually by a lover lamenting parting at daybreak. Such poems are common in LYRIC poetry in many different literatures. A famous if perhaps unusually complicated example is Donne's 'The Sun Rising' (1633). Aubades may also occur at appropriate moments in longer works, such as Chaucer's *Troilus and Criseyde* (c.1380–5) or Shakespeare's *Romeo and Juliet* (c.1595).

Augustan age. Before and during the reign of the Emperor Augustus (27BC –AD14), Roman writers enjoyed a period of peace and prosperity which resulted in an astonishingly fertile literary output, including Virgil's *Georgics* and *Aeneid*, Horace's *Odes* and *Epistles*, the *Elegies* of Sextus Propertius, and Ovid's *Metamorphoses*. In imitation of this brilliant literary period English poets and writers of the first half of the eighteenth century, particularly the reign of Queen Anne (1702–14), have also been called Augustan. Addison, Steele, Pope and Swift admired the Roman writers of the Augustan age and attempted to imitate them in style and subject matter. DECORUM, BALANCE, elegant wit, patriotism, and a concern for society and for good taste are characteristics of both Augustan ages. The implication of the term is that it is applied to the period of highest purity and refinement in a national literature.

Aureate language. (Lat. 'decorated with gold') Brilliantly decorative poetic language, rejoicing in learned words borrowed from Latin, internal rhymes and ALLITERATION: language as if embellished and refined with gold. The term is usually restricted to certain poems, mostly religious, by English and Scottish poets of the fifteenth and early sixteenth centuries. The monk-poet Lydgate probably invented this eloquent, ornate and precious diction in imitation of the Latin liturgical style. The SCOTTISH CHAUCERIANS occasionally used aureate language.

Author. (Lat. 'originator') A person who writes any kind of literary or non-literary work. From most points of view the concept of authorship requires no explanation: publishers, lawyers, accountants, reviewers, readers and authors themselves know exactly what is meant by the 'author' of a book.

In the NEW CRITICISM it was considered wrong to examine a work in the light of the author's intentions or biography, because the text was supposed to be AUTONOMOUS. This concentration on text still allowed writing to be perceived as the creation of an author. However, the concept and significance of authorship has been put under attack by French critics like Roland Barthes, in his essay 'The Death of the Author' (1968), and Michel Foucault in 'What is an Author?' (1969). The first argues that the critic's obsession with authorship is a way of falsely pinning down the meaning of a text and refusing to contemplate it as an infinite 'tissue of signs'. The second places authorship in a historical context to show that the concept is culturally determined, and that different societies at different times have not perceived books necessarily as the original creations of gifted individuals. For example, in the Middle Ages some kinds of text would have been expected to be wholly indebted to traditional sources, to the extent of excluding all personal originality.

Those critics who object to a HIERARCHY OF DISCOURSES in a text point out that the concept of 'author' relates to the idea of *author*ity. In the view of DECONSTRUCTIVE CRITICISM, to think of the author as a kind of absolute and specially privileged creator of meaning is a falsification of the nature of language: as meaning is constructed by the readers (not the writer), no final meaning is available for any text. To view literary works as the mysterious creations of god-like beings, in the view of MARXIST critics, tends to be a way of ignoring the social and political contexts in which writing is produced. *See also* PRODUCTION.

Autobiography. (Gk. 'self-life-writing') The story of a person's life written by that person. A surprisingly modern word (coined at the end of the eighteenth century), though this is an old literary form: examples have been found even in ancient Egyptian literature. St Augustine's *Confessions* (*c.*AD397–9) is an influential early model. In England the seventeenth century is particularly rich in autobiography: there are many religious life-accounts by Puritans such as Richard Baxter and Bunyan. Rousseau's *Confessions* (published posthumously between 1781 and 1788) introduced a new candour and intimacy into autobiographical writing.

An unusual example of the genre, but one of the greatest autobiographies in literature, is Wordsworth's *The Prelude* (written from *c.*1798, published 1850). In this poem, which is a kind of internal epic, Wordsworth established the seriousness of autobiography as a genre by his rigorous investigation of his own experience, memory, psychology, creativity and sense of values. It is perhaps not an exaggeration to say that it is characteristic of modern literature to follow Wordsworth in assuming that values and meaning must be derived from the self rather than from any general rules, laws and principles outside the self.

Autobiography is now a common and popular form. The famous and the infamous alike are expected to write their life-story. *See also* APOLOGY, BILDUNGSROMAN, BIOGRAPHY, CONFESSION, EPIPHANY, INVOLUTE, MEMOIRS.

Automatic writing. Writing performed without any kind of conscious control or intention, of interest for different reasons to spiritualists and psychologists, but also occasionally used by experimental writers such as the SURREALISTS, for whom automatism was a basic creative method. In his first *Manifesto of Surrealism* (1924) André Breton describes the technique of emptying the mind and swiftly writing down whatever surfaces. Aesthetic and psychological explanations are suggested for the resulting dream images. *See also* ALEATORY.

Autonomy, autonomous. (Gk. 'self-law') The right of self-government: the word is used especially in twentieth-century criticism to suggest the way in which an individual work of art can be viewed free from its sociological or biographical context, and must be judged solely by artistic criteria. *See also* NEW CRITICISM.

Autotelic. (Gk. 'self-ended') A work of art is 'autotelic' in so far as it contains its own end-purpose and justification. The word was used by the NEW CRITICS to emphasise the AUTONOMY of an artistic work, and the way in which it can (or should) be perceived as referring only to itself, and having no aims or purposes other than its own existence as a work of art.

Avant-garde. (Fr. 'before the guard') A military expression: the vanguard or foremost part of an army. *Avant-garde* is now commonly used to describe modern artists and writers whose works are (or were) deliberately and self-consciously experimental, who set out to discover new forms, techniques and subject matter in the arts.

B

Balance. (Lat. 'twin scales') The quality in literature of seeming rational and fair-minded; a balanced statement creates the impression of being the consequence of serious thought on the matter in question, and allows the existence of several possible points of view, without emotive or confusing language.

Certain syntactic forms help create a sense of balance, such as 'On the one hand . . . on the other hand'. ANTITHESIS, CHIASMUS and PARALLEL-ISM, ABSTRACT vocabulary and GENERALISATIONS are common in the style of a writer such as Dr Johnson who valued balance as a criterion. The following is from *The Rambler* No.129 (1751):

> According to the inclinations of nature, or the impressions of precept, the daring and the cautious may move in different directions without touching upon rashness or cowardice.

See also NEOCLASSICISM.

Ballad. (Fr. 'dancing song') A poem or song which tells a story in simple, colloquial language. There are traditional or ORAL ballads, BROADSIDE ballads and literary ballads: some scholars feel that the term 'ballad' should be used only to refer to the traditional oral folk ballads.

Oral ballads, though probably composed originally by a brilliant individual, have been transmitted from singer to singer for centuries, and in the process are remade by the singer or reciter at every performance. There are, therefore, many variant texts, and no single text of any ballad. Some have several tunes. Nevertheless folk ballads share many themes and techniques, though no single ballad will exhibit every typifying feature.

The subject matter of ballads is usually tragic and often violent. The story is told through dialogue and action, with sudden transitions from point to point in the narrative (called **'leaping and lingering'**). Abrupt beginnings, starting with a climactic episode, are common. Imagery is sparse and immediate. Stock EPITHETS, such as 'blood-red wine', 'yellow hair' or 'merry men', are used. REFRAINS and INCREMEN-TAL REPETITION (repetition with modification which advances the story) are common features. Oral ballads are usually starkly impersonal, with little or no comment on the action described. The following four verses of 'The Douglas Tragedy' are typical also in that they are in so-called BALLAD METRE, QUATRAINS of alternate four- and three-stress lines rhymed *abcb*:

> 'Rise up, rise up, now, Lord Douglas,' she says,
>   'And put on your armour so bright;
> Let it never be said that a daughter of thine
>   Was married to a lord under night.'

'Rise up, rise up, my seven bold sons,
  And put on your armour so bright,
And take better care of your youngest sister,
  For your eldest's awa the last night.'

He's mounted her on a milk-white steed,
  And himself on a dapple grey,
With a bugelet horn hung down by his side,
  And lightly they rode away.

Lord William lookit o'er his left shoulder
  To see what he could see
And there he spy'd her seven brethren bold
  Come riding over the lee.

The outcome of this ballad is tragic and bloody, involving the death of the seven brothers, the father, Lord William and his beloved. Many of the Scottish or 'Border' ballads, of which this is an example, probably date back to the fifteenth century.

Ballads with a more self-conscious narrative style are called **minstrel ballads** to differentiate them from the anonymous and impersonal folk ballad. Many of the Robin Hood ballads of the fifteenth and sixteenth centuries are of this type. The opening of 'Robin Hood and Allen a Dale' is typical:

Come listen to me, you gallants so free,
  All you that love mirth for to hear,
And I will tell of a bold outlaw
  That lived in Nottinghamshire.

Broadside ballads lack the timeless quality of the folk ballads because they often deal with topical events; they were also printed, rather than orally transmitted. But many of the traditional ballads were also published as broadsides, though sometimes in a sensational form.

With the exception of a famous commendation by Sidney in his *An Apology for Poetry* (1595), ballads were largely ignored till the eighteenth century. In 1711 two essays by Addison in *The Spectator* (Nos. 70 and 74) aroused interest. Thomas Percy's *Reliques of Ancient English Poetry* (1765) established the ballad's literary respectability. Poets started to be influenced by the form. Scott collected his *Minstrelsy of the Scottish Border* (1802–3). Many nineteenth-century poets wrote literary or artificial ballads, imitating traditional ballad features: Coleridge's 'The Rime of the Ancient Mariner' from his and Wordsworth's paradoxically entitled *Lyrical Ballads* (1798) and Keats's 'La Belle Dame Sans Merci' (1820) are notable examples. The literary ballad is also common in twentieth-century verse.

The standard collection of traditional ballads is F.J. Child's *English and Scottish Popular Ballads* (1882–98). This scholarly life's work did much to establish the historical authenticity and the text of the oral folk ballads. Popular ballads are still being collected in America and Australia as well as in Britain. *See also* FOLKLORE.

Ballad metre. A QUATRAIN (four-lined STANZA) of alternate four-stress and three-stress lines, usually roughly IAMBIC (*see* METRE for further discussion of these terms). A common form for the traditional and literary BALLAD. This example is from Coleridge's 'The Rime of the Ancient Mariner' (1798):

> I fear thee, ancient Mariner!
> I fear thy skinny hand!
> And thou art long, and lank, and brown,
> As is the ribb'd sea-sand.

Ballade. (Fr. 'dancing song') An Old French verse form, often used by Villon and popular in the fourteenth and fifteenth centuries. Examples exist in medieval English poetry; late nineteenth-century poets such as Swinburne and Belloc revived this complicated form. A typical *ballade* has three eight-line stanzas, rhyming *ababbcbc*, with a four-line *envoi* (Fr. 'message'), a kind of summing up of the poem, rhyming *bcbc*.

Bard. (Welsh 'poet') In the Gaelic cultures of Ireland, Scotland and Wales, the bard was an official poet whose role was to celebrate events, especially deeds of heroism. In Wales the tradition still exists, and bards compete with their poems at a yearly gathering called the Eisteddfod, which dates back to the twelfth century, and which was revived, after a long break, in the nineteenth century.

The word 'bard' is associated with a particular view of the poet as perhaps the unwilling medium for passionate, prophetic poetry expressing the consciousness of a community. 'The Bard' is also a common nickname for Shakespeare.

Bardolatry. A portmanteau word, combining 'Bard' and 'idolatry', and implying an exaggerated reverence for Shakespeare and his works.

Baroque. (Sp. 'imperfect pearl') Chiefly an architectural term, meaning irregular, odd and whimsical, with specific application to the florid, ornamental style of late Renaissance architecture. Highly ornate writing of the seventeenth century is called 'baroque' by analogy. The prose of Sir Thomas Browne, like his *Urn Burial* (1658), might be called baroque; so might the verse of some of the METAPHYSICAL POETS, especially the more extravagant CONCEITS of Cleveland or Crashaw, like the latter's description of Mary Magdalene's eyes in 'The Weeper' (1646):

> Two walking Baths; two weeping motions;
> Portable and compendious oceans.

See also CULTERANISMO, EUPHUISM, GONGORISM, MARINISM.

Bathos. (Gk. 'deep') A ludicrous descent from the elevated treatment of a subject to the ordinary and dull. Pope's *Of the Art of Sinking in Poetry* (1727), a parody of Longinus's *On the Sublime* (first century AD), established the critical use of this term. Whereas ANTICLIMAX is a controlled bathetic effect for comic purposes, bathos is used to indicate a writer's failure to achieve a serious effect apparently aimed at: to some extent, therefore, recognition of bathos is a matter of taste. Few would dispute one of Pope's own illustrations:

> Ye Gods! annihilate but Space and Time
> And make two lovers happy.

The verse of the nineteenth-century Scottish poet William McGonagall is perversely enjoyed for its banality and bathos. *The Stuffed Owl* (1930), edited by D.B. Wyndham Lewis and Charles Lee, is a famous anthology of over-pompous verse.

Beat generation. A group of American writers of the 1950s. The best-known were Jack Kerouac, Allen Ginsberg, Gregory Corso and Lawrence Ferlinghetti. Ferlinghetti's City Lights Press, based in San Francisco, published many of their works, including Ginsberg's *Howl* (1956), a long THRENODY, which was in part a manifesto of the Beats' point of view. The novelist Jack Kerouac also depicted the Beats' way of life in *On the Road* (1957) and in *The Dharma Bums* (1958), a fictionalised account of his friendship with the poet Gary Snyder. William Burroughs's *The Naked Lunch* (1959) was another influential 'beat' novel, much more experimental in technique and AVANT-GARDE than Kerouac's prose.

'Beat' living signifies the rejection of American middle-class society, embracing poverty and searching for truth through drugs, sexuality, Zen Buddhism and mysticism. Beat poetry is loose in structure, sensational, autobiographical, full of HYPERBOLE and SURREALISM and aiming for the effect of spontaneity. Kerouac's novels are written in what he called 'spontaneous prose'; some imitate the unrevised and improvisatory quality of jazz.

Belles-lettres. (Fr. 'fine letters') A literary parallel to *beaux arts* (Fr. 'beautiful arts'). Originally the term distinguished artistic from scientific writings, but in practice it refers to the writings of nineteenth-century essayists and 'men of letters', who wrote in an elegant, amusing and sometimes learned manner about literary topics. Modern 'literary critics' tend to regard '*belles-lettrists*' as trifling and unscholarly in their attitude to literature, and use the word as a pejorative. The caricaturist, wit and parodist Max Beerbohm might be cited as typical of the lightweight *belles-lettrist*.

Bestiary. (Lat. 'connected with beasts') A collection of descriptions of real and mythical animals, usually hinting at allegorical interpretations of their supposed habits and appearances. Bestiaries were a popular form of literature in the Middle Ages.

Bibliography. (Gk. 'writing about books') A list of the complete writings of a given author, or a list of books, essays and articles on a given subject. Bibliography is also the study of the production of books, changing printing techniques, the history of publication, and so on.

Bildungsroman. (Ger. 'formation-novel') A NOVEL which describes the protagonist's development from childhood to maturity. Joyce's *A Portrait of the Artist as a Young Man* (1916) is a famous *Bildungsroman*; Goethe's *Wilhelm Meister's Apprenticeship* (1795-6) is an early and influential example. This common genre developed in popularity at the same time as AUTOBIOGRAPHY, which also tends to focus on the relationship between experience, education, character and identity. *See also* KÜNSTLERROMAN.

Binary opposition. The fundamental contrasts (such as in/out, off/on, good/bad, cops/robbers) used in STRUCTURALIST methods of linguistic analysis, and in criticism, anthropology and feminism. Lévi-Strauss's examinations of societies in terms of the raw/the cooked, nature/culture, and so on, are notable examples.

Literature can be interpreted through frameworks of oppositions of this kind, and indeed it has been argued that binarism is fundamental to all learning and interpretation of experience, and that all processes of understanding involve discrimination and choice between opposed possibilities. If we ask ourselves whether an action is good, then this is only comprehensible in terms of its opposite, bad. 'Up' and 'down' are relative terms, not absolutes: they only have meaning in relation to each other.

Feminists point out that lists of binary oppositions (such as active/passive, head/heart, reason/feeling, strength/weakness, sun/moon) often coincide with the gender opposition of male/female; and in a male-dominated society, the masculine side of the opposition tends to be perceived as having more intrinsic value than its feminine counterpart. Thus anti-woman attitudes are constantly but often unnoticeably recycled and re-affirmed in day-to-day language. The evaluation of experience through binarism, they argue, is characteristic of Western PATRIARCHAL society.

According to Robert Pirsig in *Zen and the Art of Motorcycle Maintenance* (1974), the Japanese word *mu* 'points outside the process of dualistic discrimination'. It describes a neutral state between binary oppositions (neither 'off' nor 'on').

Biography. (Gk. 'life-writing') An account of a person's life; literature which consists of the histories of individuals.

In Ancient Greece and Rome biography was considered a branch of historical writing. Historians such as Tacitus (first century AD) and

Suetonius (second century AD) included much biographical material. Shakespeare borrowed many plots from Plutarch's *Parallel Lives* (*c*.AD110).

HAGIOGRAPHY (the lives of saints) was the chief medieval form of biography. From the sixteenth century onwards the art of biography developed steadily until, at the end of the eighteenth century, Dr Johnson's *Lives of the Poets* (1781) and Boswell's *The Life of Samuel Johnson* (1791) fully established the genre as a significant literary activity. Johnson's exquisite but critical 'Life' of his friend Savage illustrates his decision not to overpraise his subjects.

During the last two centuries both scholarly and popular biographies have become commonplace. The belief in the value of biography is enshrined in the *Dictionary of National Biography* (commonly abbreviated to D.N.B.) begun in 1885. The tendency for nineteenth-century biographers to be scholarly but reticent about their subjects' weaknesses was overturned by Lytton Strachey's debunking and irreverent *Eminent Victorians* (1918).

The biographical approach to literature, which interprets an author's work in terms of the events of a person's life and development of ideas, has tended to be out of fashion since the NEW CRITICISM. A 'critical biography' is an account of a writer's life for the purpose of explaining and evaluating his or her writings.

Black comedy. Drama (or other kinds of literature) in which potentially tragic or unpleasant situations are treated with a cynical amusement. Many modern plays exhibit this disillusioned comic despair. Some of the plays by those twentieth-century playwrights whose work is characterised as ABSURD, like Ionesco, Beckett, Genet, Albee or Pinter, are black comedies. In plays such as Beckett's *Waiting for Godot* (1953), human beings are depicted as the helpless puppets of brutal, nightmarish forces which they do not understand; this makes their despair, anger or attempts to occupy themselves absurd and comical to the audience, and even to themselves. Black comedy has its antecedents in TRAGICOMEDIES like Shakespeare's *The Merchant of Venice* (*c*.1596), but the mood of twentieth-century EXISTENTIALISM and atheism accounts for its prevalence in modern literature.

Black comedy is also common in twentieth-century novels, such as Joseph Heller's *Catch-22* (1961).

Black letter. Heavy, angular gothic printing types used by the early printers, as opposed to the white letter roman typefaces. German printers used this type until recent times: Hitler considered it more Germanic.

Black Mountain school. A group of poets associated with the Black Mountain College near Asheville in North Carolina, from which was published the *Black Mountain Review* between 1954 and 1957. Characteristic of the 'school' is a short verse line, and a concern with perception and the creative process. Black Mountain poets include Robert Creeley, Robert Duncan and Charles Olson, who was the theorist of their kind of writing in his essay on **'projective verse'**, which defines poems as 'open fields' conducting energy from poet to reader, with poetic form being created in the gap between the poet's breath and the visual spacing generated by the typewriter. The opening of Robert Creeley's 'The Rocks' (1966) illustrates the thoughtful, dislocated feel of the short line that is typical of this kind of verse:

Trying to think of
some way out, the
rocks of thought

which displace,
dropped in
the water . . .

Blank verse. Unrhymed IAMBIC PENTAMETER: a line of five IAMBS. One of the commonest English METRES; indeed, the form for much of the finest verse in English. Blank verse was introduced into England by Henry Howard, Earl of Surrey, who used it in his translation of Virgil's *Aeneid* (1557). Thereafter it became the normal medium for Elizabethan and Jacobean drama, being used expertly by Shakespeare. In narrative and meditative verse it has been widely used: it is the metre of Milton's *Paradise Lost* (1667), Wordsworth's *The Prelude* (1850) and Tennyson's *Idylls of the King* (1842–85).

The popularity of blank verse is due to its flexibility and relative closeness to spoken English. It allows a pleasant variation of full strong stresses per line, generally four or five, while conforming to the basic metrical pattern of five iambs. Long sentences can be built up into VERSE PARAGRAPHS; ENJAMBMENT is natural because of the lack of rhyme, and endless variations in the play between the syntax and the metrical line are allowable. This short example is the final ten lines of Coleridge's meditation 'Frost at Midnight' (1798):

Therefore all seasons shall be sweet to thee,
Whether the summer clothe the general earth
With greenness, or the redbreast sit and sing
Betwixt the tufts of snow on the bare branch
Of mossy apple-tree, while the nigh thatch
Smokes in the sun-thaw; whether the eave-drops fall
Heard only in the trances of the blast,
Or if the secret ministry of frost
Shall hang them up in silent icicles,
Quietly shining to the quiet Moon.

Blazon. (Fr. 'coat-of-arms') A description of a woman's beauty in the form of a list of her excellent physical features. It is a common device for Elizabethan lyricists, for whom the immediate model was the fourteenth-century Italian poet Petrarch. *See also* CONCEIT, LYRIC.

Blockbuster. A best-seller in the book trade. Originally a kind of bomb designed to wreak havoc over a large area, then applied metaphorically to people with explosive personalities, this word is now used almost exclusively to designate the kind of popular novel that, through a shrewd combination of publicity and marketing, has achieved sales of hundreds of thousands of copies.

Bloomsbury group. The name given to those writers who were associated with the Bloomsbury area of London from about 1907 until 1939. The home of Virginia and Vanessa Stephen was one gathering place for writers such as Leonard Woolf, Clive Bell, Lytton Strachey and E.M. Forster. Virginia Stephen became a well-known novelist after her marriage to Leonard Woolf. All were much influenced by the philosopher G.E. Moore.

'Bloomsbury' never had a group aim, being merely a loose coterie of like-minded people who valued honesty of thought and feeling, art, literature and mutual friendship. It was often derided as effete by writers such as D.H. Lawrence.

Blue book. One of the official reports of Parliament and the Privy Council, issued in a blue paper cover. Disraeli drew information for his mid-nineteenth-century political novels from such documents.

Blurb. (Coined by an American humorist) The short summary of a book's contents printed on its jacket, often advertising in a sensational form special features of the work.

Bob and wheel. Some Middle English ALLITERATIVE VERSE, like *Sir Gawain and the Green Knight* (late fourteenth century), is divided into short sections by this metrical device of a single stress line (the 'bob') followed by a stanza of four three-stress lines (the 'wheel').

Bodice-ripper. A disparaging and salacious term for modern popular 'romantic' novels, which depict steamy passions in historical settings.

Bohemian. A word for a socially unconventional person or way of life: artists and writers of loose and irregular habits, vagabonds and adventurers are often so called. The word was originally applied in France to gipsies, who were thought to have arrived in Western Europe from Bohemia, a central European state.

Bombast. (O. Fr. 'silk, cotton wool') Formerly the name for cotton-wool, or the material used for stuffing and padding clothing. Now 'bombast' refers to turgid and inflated language. Polonius in Shakespeare's *Hamlet* (*c*.1601) is a character given to bombastic speeches, full of unnecessary padding; Gertrude begs him for 'more matter with less art' (II.2).

'Bourgeois' realism. *See* 'CLASSIC BOURGEOIS' REALISM.

Bowdlerise. To EXPURGATE; to remove material considered undesirable from a literary work. In 1818 Dr Bowdler published an edition of Shakespeare's plays 'in which those words or expressions are omitted which cannot with propriety be read aloud in a family'. Greater frankness about sexual matters in the first decades of the twentieth century has rendered Dr Bowdler's efforts absurd, though adaptation of Shakespeare's plays to fit in with changing attitudes was (and to some extent still is) the norm.

Braggadocio. (Mid. E. 'brag', with It. pejorative suffix) A boastful, idle, vain, coarse, violent and cowardly liar, often a soldier; a STOCK CHARACTER in drama. Braggadocchio, a character in Spenser's *The Faerie Queene* (1590, 1596), established the type. Also called MILES GLORIOSUS and ALAZON.

Brechtian. The dramatic theories and stage techniques of the German playwright and poet Bertolt Brecht (1898–1956). 'Brechtian' refers most frequently to his break with the conventions of dramatic realism in EPIC THEATRE, and the attempt to shatter an audience's easy sympathetic identification with 'good' characters by means of the ALIENATION EFFECT. *See also* SOCIALIST REALISM.

Bricolage. (Fr. 'odd-jobbery') A vogue word amongst STRUCTURALISTS after the anthropologist Lévi-Strauss in *La Pensée sauvage* ('The Savage Mind', 1962) defined mythical thought as 'a kind of intellectual *bricolage*'. Structuralist critics use the term to suggest the way in which intellectual systems (such as myths or literary theory) freely swap concepts and methods in order to develop and expand.

Broadside. A large sheet of paper printed on one side only. Therefore the name given to a TRACT, popular song or BALLAD sold in the streets from the sixteenth century onwards. The earliest extant broadside is probably Skelton's elegy on the death of Henry VII (*c*.1509). In the mid-sixteenth century broadside printers were legally obliged to register their ballads, and between 1557 and 1709 more than 3000 were listed. The diarist Pepys had a large collection (over 1500).

Most broadsides are sensational in subject matter: murders, executions, tales of adventure or terrible bad luck, and scandals formed the staple fare. They were purchased by poor town-dwellers. They were collected into 'garlands' and sold by chapmen (pedlars), or they were sung by 'patterers' or posted on walls. Often they were illustrated with crude wood-cuts.

Public events were often publicised in broadside verses. Falstaff in Shakespeare's *Henry IV, Part 2* (*c*.1598) demands that his prowess in battle be properly recorded, 'or by the Lord, I will have it in a particular ballad else, with mine own picture on the top on it' (IV.3). Even as late as the early nineteenth century broadsides on public events made fortunes for their printers, but the growth of cheap newspapers replaced this popular form of literature and communication.

Broken rhyme. The fracturing of a word at the end of a line of verse with the purpose of rhyming a syllable other than its final one. Very rare, except in the verse of Gerard Manley Hopkins, who uses a forced ENJAMBMENT to ENACT his meaning in the following example, from 'No Worst, There is None' (written *c*.1885):

> . . . on an age-old anvil wince and sing –
> Then lull, then leave off. Fury had shrieked 'No ling-
> ering! Let me be fell . . . '

Broken rhymes are often used in LIGHT VERSE for comic effect.

Bucolic. (Gk. 'to do with herdsmen') Rustic verse. *See also* PASTORAL.

Burden. (O. Fr. 'drone') Originally a bass 'undersong' accompanying a song. Now more commonly a song's REFRAIN or CHORUS. Also, having assimilated the meaning of O.E. *burden* ('load'), 'burden' can refer to the main theme or message of a literary work, especially a poem.

Burlesque. (It. 'ridicule') A special kind of comic writing: the mockery of serious matter or style, achieved by dealing with a subject in a deliberately incongruous manner. There are many different kinds of burlesque. The following different types may be distinguished. (1) PARODY: the comic imitation of a particular work or author, often achieved by mimicking an author's style and applying it to a ridiculous subject. Thus Fielding's *Shamela* (1741) mocks Richardson's *Pamela* (1740-1). (2) The mock poem: the burlesque of a whole class of literature achieved by parody, for example Pope's mock EPIC *The Rape of the Lock* (1712, 1714) in which epic conventions are applied to the theft of a lock of hair. (3) TRAVESTY: the mockery of a subject by treating it in an absurdly low style. Byron's *The Vision of Judgment* (1822) is an absurd version of Southey's poem about the death of George III, *A Vision of Judgment* (1821). Tom Stoppard's play *Travesties* (1974) involves James Joyce, Freud and Trotsky in a ridiculous series of incidents concerning a pair of trousers.

Burlesque writing has flourished in all kinds of literature from the seventeenth century onwards. Butler's *Hudibras* (1662-78) is a notable example of a 'low' burlesque aimed generally at Puritan religion and politics. Mock-poems achieved perfection during the eighteenth-century NEOCLASSICAL period because the theory of fixed genres and conventions (epic, pastoral, tragedy, and so on) led to a clear sense of the appropriate, and also, therefore, the inappropriate.

Burlesque writing has also thrived in drama. The play put on by the 'Rude Mechanicals' within Shakespeare's *A Midsummer Night's Dream* (*c*.1595-6) is a well-known example: it burlesques the theatrical INTER-LUDE. Whole plays may be burlesques, such as Fielding's *The Tragedy of*

Tragedies, or the Life and Death of Tom Thumb the Great (1731), or some of the libretti of W.S. Gilbert in the late nineteenth century. In prose, parodies are not uncommon. Stella Gibbons's *Cold Comfort Farm* (1932) is a genial mock version of novels of rural PRIMITIVISM. Max Beerbohm's *A Christmas Garland* (1912) is a witty collection of prose parodies.

In America a 'burlesque' may be a variety show featuring music, comedians and strip-tease.

Burns metre. A six-line verse form frequently used by Robert Burns, as in 'To a Mouse' (1786):

Wee, sleekit, cow'ring, tim'rous beastie,
O, what a panic's in thy breastie!
Thou need na start awa sae hasty
    Wi' bickering brattle!
I wad be laith to rin an' chase thee,
    Wi' murdering pattle!

Lines one, two, three and five have four stresses; four and six have two stresses each. The STANZA rhymes *aaabab*.

Buskin. (Derivation unknown) A thick-soled boot (or **cothurnus**) worn by actors in Greek and Roman tragedy, as opposed to the *soccus* or 'sock' or low shoe used in comedy. Hence 'buskin' came to stand for tragedy, and 'buskined' means concerned with tragedy, elevated, or written in an elevated style.

Byronic hero. A character type portrayed by Byron in many of his early narrative poems, especially *Childe Harold's Pilgrimage* (1812, 1816, 1818), *The Giaour* (1813), *Manfred* (1817) and *Cain* (1821). The type is prefigured in eighteenth-century GOTHIC NOVELS, and in the 'romantic' misinterpretation of Satan in Milton's *Paradise Lost* (1667).

The Byronic hero is a brooding solitary, who seeks exotic travel and wild nature to reflect his superhuman passions. He is capable of great suffering and is guilty of some terrible, unspecified crime, but bears this guilt with pride, as it sets him apart from society, revealing the meaninglessness of ordinary moral values. He is misanthropic, defiant, rebellious, nihilistic and hypnotically fascinating to others.

Byron's own tempestuous character and life fostered the allure of this gloomy, heroic type: he was 'mad, bad and dangerous to know', as Lady Caroline Lamb wrote in her diary. The poetry containing this melo-dramatic self-portrait continued to be popular long after Byron's ostracism by English society. The Byronic hero re-emerges in many forms in nineteenth-century literature, grinding his teeth and flashing his eyes. Heathcliff in Emily Brontë's *Wuthering Heights* (1847) and Pushkin's *Eugene Onegin* (1833) are two notable examples. *See also* POÈTE MAUDIT, ROMANTICISM, WERTHERISM.

C

Cacophony. (Gk. 'unpleasant sound') Discordant, rugged or harsh-sounding effects in prose or verse, usually produced by clusters of consonants arranged so as to make pronunciation difficult. Cacophony is frequent in comical verse and tongue-twisters; it is often allied to ONOMATOPOEIA. *See also* DISSONANCE, EUPHONY.

Cadence. (Lat. 'falling') A vague term: in its more precise use it denotes the individual rhythmical pattern of a fragment of verse or prose, especially a RHYTHM which coincides with a conclusion or finishing effect – the end of a sentence or line, for example.

In a general way 'cadence' is often used simply to mean the rhythm of prose or verse, caused by the varied stresses placed on syllables and words. *See also* METRE.

Caesura. (Lat. 'cutting') A pause within a line of verse, caused by the natural organisation of the language into phrases, clauses and sentences, which do not conform to the metrical pattern. In English verse such a pause may be strong or weak; a single line may have no caesura, a single caesura, or two or more such breaks. The caesura (with ENJAMBMENT) is a vital method of introducing variety into metrical forms suitable for long poems, such as BLANK VERSE. A passage from Book 1 of Wordsworth's *The Prelude* (1850) demonstrates this variety; only the strong caesurae have been marked:

One summer evening//(led by her)//I found
A little boat tied to a willow tree
Within a rocky cave,//its usual home.
Straight I unloosed her chain,//and stepping in
Pushed from the shore.//It was an act of stealth
And troubled pleasure,//nor without the voice
Of mountain echoes did my boat move on.

In Greek and Latin prosody, rules were elaborated explaining where the caesura might occur and what variation in choice of FOOT might be allowed in consequence. Imitating this, Neoclassical writers, in the eighteenth century, attempted to regulate the caesura in English verse, so that in the HEROIC COUPLET the caesura is usually medial (in the middle of the line) rather than initial (towards the beginning) or terminal (towards the end). But in general the use of the caesura in English verse has been very free; it may occur between feet in the metrical pattern, or divide feet.

In some verse we may choose to explain certain rhetorical effects in terms of the caesura. For example, in Wordsworth's emotive sonnet about the death of his daughter, 'Surprised by Joy' (1815), the rhetorical syntax results in two caesurae, one after the first word of the poem, underlining the significance of the opening word, which is also accentuated by repetition. This break also has the effect of turning the first foot into something approaching a SPONDEE:

Love,//faithful love,//recalled thee to my mind.

See also METRE, RHYME.

Calligramme. (Gk. 'beautiful letters') A kind of word-picture invented by the French poet Apollinaire. His book *Calligrammes* was published in 1918. *See also* CONCRETE POETRY.

Cambridge school of critics. I.A. Richards's *Practical Criticism* (1929), William Empson's *Seven Types of Ambiguity* (1930) and a series of works by F.R. Leavis, including *The Great Tradition* (1948) and *The Common Pursuit* (1952), were all expressions of new attitudes to criticism and the teaching of literature which were associated with Cambridge University from the late 1920s till the 1950s. The Cambridge-based journal *Scrutiny* (1932–53) was an influential medium for what later became known as the LEAVISITE view of literature.

Richards was influenced by Coleridge and contemporary psychological theory. Empson was a poet, as well as a critic of exceptional complexity and intelligence. They shared with F.R. and Q.D. Leavis a belief in the educative value of literature and 'close reading' or PRACTICAL CRITICISM, but the notion of a 'school' encompassing all these figures is something of a simplification. *See also* NEW CRITICISM.

Camp. A word of disputed origin which has now come to be associated mainly with deliberately affected and ostentatious behaviour by people pretending to be homosexuals. For a time in the late 1960s the word was used to indicate a way of looking with enjoyment or pleasure at works of art and artefacts, to which the spectator felt superior, but towards which critical attitudes had been suspended. *See also* KITSCH.

Campus novel. A NOVEL about university life. Nineteenth-century examples (perhaps not strictly speaking 'campus' novels) include *The Adventures of Mr Verdant Green, an Oxford Freshman* (1853–7) by 'Cuthbert Bede' (Edward Bradley) and Thomas Hughes's *Tom Brown at Oxford* (1861). In the twentieth century Kingsley Amis's *Lucky Jim* (1954) is an early example of what has now come to be a minor genre. Usually indulgently satiric, such works explore the foibles of academics and their activities, in Britain, the USA and further afield, and offer the pleasures of examining closed communities, populated by eccentrics, who in a variety of ways are at odds with society and each other. Professors David Lodge and Malcolm Bradbury are British exponents of the form; their work has been successfully televised.

Canon. (Gk. 'rule') A law or decree of the Church, hence any list of such rules, and particularly the list of books of the Bible accepted as genuine and inspired (not APOCRYPHAL). Thus a reverential term for the works of any writer: the Shakespearean canon, for example.

In this sense the word has come to be used for the collection of 'great works' of literature which for a long time was presumed to form the bulk of worthwhile reading matter for students of literature. LEAVISITES argued about the merits of individual writers and works, partly in order to establish a 'great tradition' of the best texts for the purposes of a proper moral and cultural education. But the whole concept of such a core has been attacked from a variety of points of view since the advent of STRUCTURALISM and DECONSTRUCTION. MARXIST critics maintain that 'canonical' literature merely represents those kinds of works that foster the intellectual climate for the perseverance of the bourgeois *status quo*. They seek to replace the traditional texts with their own canon of SUBVERSIVE texts. FEMINIST critics attack the canon for acting as a means of disseminating and enforcing PATRIARCHAL values and interests, composed as it is mostly of writing by and about men, and therefore they too have established their own counter-canons of feminist texts. POST-STRUCTURALISTS argue that there is no theoretical justification for valuing some kinds of writing at the expense of others, and therefore the canon should be abandoned to allow the study of a culture conceived as more wide-ranging and all-inclusive than just the 'high culture' of the past. POST-COLONIALIST critics and writers from English-speaking countries outside England resent the canon for what they see as its 'metropolitan' grip on literary taste, leading to the exclusion of writing from different kinds of culture and society. *See also* ANTHOLOGY, CRISIS IN ENGLISH STUDIES, ENG. LIT.

Cant. (Lat. 'sing') (*n.*) The whining manner of speech used by beggars. Thus any kind of language or JARGON particular to a class or profession: thieves' cant. Also used pejoratively, often with a suggestion of hypocrisy, of the typical content of such language, such as CLICHÉS, or boringly commonplace ideas accepted by certain classes or kinds of people without thought or justification.

Canto. (It. 'song') A division of a long poem, especially an EPIC or mock epic. Dante's *Divine Comedy* (*c.*1304–21), Byron's *Don Juan* (1819–24) and, obviously, Pound's *Cantos* (1930–69) are all divided into these chapter-length sections.

Canzone. (It. 'song') A French or Italian LYRIC poem, with repeated stanzas of various forms, but usually concluding with a shortened stanza, called an *envoi*. *Canzoni* were imitated in the nineteenth and early twentieth century by poets interested in Provençal and medieval Italian poetry, such as Hilaire Belloc and Ezra Pound. *See also* BALLADE.

Caricature. (It. 'to load, exaggerate') A grotesque or ludicrous rendering of character, achieved by the exaggeration of personality traits. In the visual arts it is easy to distinguish a caricature from a realistic portrait, in so far as it departs from an exact and credible reproduction of the human form. In literature it is more difficult to know to what extent an author wants a character to be understood as a caricature. Few would argue against defining Sir Andrew Aguecheck, Sir Toby Belch and Malvolio in Shakespeare's *Twelfth Night* (*c*.1600) as caricatures: the first two are dissipated drunks, the third a self-righteous puritan. It might be a matter for disagreement whether their exaggerated and at times improbable or incredible behaviour is regarded as delightfully comic or as a serious, even distasteful description of human vice or folly. Names which suggest a particular behaviour or personality (like Sir Toby Belch), called APTRONYMS, often suggest caricature.

Obviously caricature is most frequent in comic works. In comic dramas or novels it is very common. But it is not infrequent even in tragedy; see, for example, Osric, the ridiculous courtier in Shakespeare's *Hamlet* (*c*.1601).

Carnivalisation. A literary phenomenon described by the Russian critic Mikhail Bakhtin, especially in his work *Rabelais and His World* (1965). According to him some writers use their works as an outlet for the spirit of carnival, of popular festivity and misrule. They 'subvert' the literary culture of the ruling classes, undermining its claim to moral monopoly. Such forms and genres are open and DIALOGIC. They allow multiple points of view to co-exist (rather than working through a single dominating, 'monologic' voice), and are valued for their availability to 'plural' interpretations.

Carol. (Probably connected with Gk. CHORUS) Originally a ring-dance accompanied with song. Now used of joyous Christmas songs (usually religious); but in medieval verse any love song or religious poem could be called a carol.

Caroline period. (*Carolus*, Lat. 'Charles') The period of Charles I's reign (1625–49). Several of the later METAPHYSICAL POETS, including Herbert, Crashaw, Vaughan and Carew, were writing during this time, as were Herrick, Milton, and the CAVALIER POETS, Suckling and Lovelace. As this diverse list shows, there is no single 'Caroline' style of writing, and 'Caroline' is therefore chiefly a chronological term, though the flamboyant cynicism of Cavalier poetry is distinctive enough to be considered a special and typical product of the age. The period was dominated by the Civil War between the 'Cavalier' Royalists and the Puritan 'Roundheads' which eventually resulted in Charles's execution. *See also* TRIBE OF BEN.

Carpe diem. (Lat. 'seize the day') A quotation from one of the *Odes* of the Roman poet Horace. The tag denotes a theme or subject common in all literature, especially lyric verse: the invitation or plea to enjoy youth and life quickly, before the onset of dull maturity or death. This is often combined with an offer of love: Marvell's 'To His Coy Mistress' (1681) and Herrick's 'To the Virgins, to Make Much of Time' (1648) are two famous versions of the *carpe diem* MOTIF. Here are the first and last verses of the latter poem:

> Gather ye Rose-buds while ye may,
>   Old Time is still a-flying:
> And this same flower that smiles today,
>   Tomorrow will be dying.

> Then be not coy, but use your time,
>   And while ye may, go marry:
> For having lost but once your prime,
>   You may forever tarry.

Catachresis. (Gk. 'use wrongly') Misuse of a word: the application of a term to a thing which the term does not denote. Also used of mixed metaphors (*see* METAPHOR), like 'the tongues of flame bit into the wood'.

Catalexis, catalectic. (Gk. 'leave off') The omission of a syllable in the last FOOT of a line of verse. The most common example of catalexis is the omission of the final syllable in a line of TROCHAIC metre, creating a MASCULINE ENDING:

> Tiger/tiger/burning/bright.

See METRE for further discussion of these terms. *See also* DEFECTIVE FOOT.

Catalogue verse. Verse which lists names of people or places or things. In ancient literature its function may have been to help to memorise genealogies and facts. It is common in EPICS: Milton includes several geographical and mythological catalogues in *Paradise Lost* (1667). A more modern instance is the American poet Walt Whitman's *Song of Myself* (1855), which, like much of his other verse, includes catalogues of many diverse subjects, such as scenery, animals, jobs and other activities, giving an impression of the variety of the huge continent of America.

Catastrophe. (Gk. 'overturning') The climactic final moments of a TRAGEDY when the PLOT is resolved: the tragic DÉNOUEMENT. *See also* FREYTAG'S PYRAMID.

Catharsis. (Gk. 'purgation, purification') A term devised by Aristotle in his *Poetics* (fourth century BC) to explain the effect of tragic drama on an audience. The exact interpretation of the idea is much disputed. Aristotle discusses the way in which the tragic downfall of the PROTAGONIST arouses the pity and fear of the audience; these emotions are 'purged' by the cathartic final outcome. Possibly he wished to find a way of justifying literature against Plato's argument that it appealed only to the feelings and did nothing to engage the audience's or reader's powers of reasoning. If so, the cathartic 'purgation' rids the audience of its feeling, and allows them to contemplate the tragic fate in thoughtful calm. Certainly the concept is often used to explain the fact that the audience's feeling at the end of a TRAGEDY is often one of exultation and relief rather than suffering and distress, though this is to interpret Aristotle's concept psychologically. It may be also that the 'catharsis' should be applied as much to the protagonist's feelings of guilt and anguish as to the audience's response. *See also* ALIENATION EFFECT.

Cavalier poets. English lyric poets of the reign of Charles I (1625–49). Lovelace, Suckling, Carew, Waller and Herrick are often so named; they are sometimes also termed the 'sons' or TRIBE OF BEN, because they greatly admired Ben Jonson's work. Cavalier poetry is concerned with love, and employs a variety of lyric forms; it is highly polished and frequently elegantly cynical, in the manner of this verse from Suckling's 'Song' (1646), which concludes with 'The devil take her!':

> Why so pale and wan, fond lover?
> Prithee, why so pale?
> Will, when looking well can't move her,
> Looking ill prevail?
> Prithee, why so pale?

Celtic Renaissance. Yeats's poetry and the plays of Synge and O'Casey are the major elements in the Irish Literary Revival, a particularly creative period in Irish letters from about 1885 to 1940. Other poets of the time include AE (George Russell) and Oliver St John Gogarty.

Chanson. (Fr. 'song') A varied Provençal form of love-song, usually in the COURTLY LOVE tradition.

Chanson de geste. (Fr. 'song of deeds') A medieval French EPIC poem composed between the late eleventh and the early fourteenth centuries. There are more than eighty of these popular poems extant: they were chanted by JONGLEURS with musical accompaniment. The subject matter of the *chansons* was in part legendary and in part historical, dealing with famous battles, often between Christians and Moors, the Crusades, or the struggle for power between barons and their king. The *Geste du Roi* cycle, to which belongs the most famous, *Chanson de Roland* (c.1100), deals with the struggles of the twelve peers of Charlemagne against the Saracens. Another celebrated group of poems concentrates on the exploits of Guillaume d'Orange and his family. The *Chansons* were influential all over Europe in the development of epic poetry and the ROMANCE.

Chapbook. An inexpensive, crudely printed and illustrated book, such as those sold by chapmen (pedlars), from the sixteenth to the eighteenth century; BALLADS, FAIRY TALES, LEGENDS, puzzles, TALL STORIES, practical advice, rhymes and other popular,literary materials were the typical contents.

Character. (Gk. 'instrument for marking, distinctive nature') Characters are the invented, imaginary persons in a dramatic or narrative work, which are given human qualities and behaviour. We learn about them through dialogue, action and description.

The 'character' is also a minor literary genre, dating back to the *Characters* (c.320BC) of the Greek writer Theophrastus, which consisted of short prose sketches of different types of human behaviour. There was a vogue for such collections in the seventeenth century. Translations of Theophrastus led to Joseph Hall's *Characters of Virtues and Vices* (1608) and Sir Thomas Overbury's *Characters* (1614). John Earle's *Microcosmographie* (1628) and the French writer Jean La Bruyère's *Les Caractères* (1688) are celebrated examples of the form. The 'character' is closely connected with the ESSAY: it points towards the novel in its examination and typification of human personality.

Characterisation. The way in which a writer creates characters in a narrative so as to attract or repel our sympathy. The varieties of characterisation presented in literature are as numerous as those of the real people who surround us in the world; but different kinds of literature have certain conventions of characterisation. Often in dealing with a literary character we learn more of his or her motives than we would ever expect to be certain of in real life: consistency of motivation seems a necessary fact in literary characterisation.

There are as many different methods of characterisation as there are ways of telling a story. Many of the entries on subjects like IRONY, NARRATIVE or POINT OF VIEW also touch on characterisation. *See also* ROUND CHARACTER, SHOWING AND TELLING, STOCK CHARACTER.

Chaucerian stanza. *See* RHYME ROYAL.

Cheville. (Fr. 'plug') An insignificant word or phrase filling out a metrical line to achieve the proper number of syllables.

Chiaroscuro. (It. 'light-dark') A word describing painting or drawing which accentuates effects of light and shade; sometimes applied to literary works which move rapidly from mood to mood, such as Milton's two poems on melancholy and happiness, 'L'Allegro' and 'Il Penseroso' (1645).

Chiasmus. (Gk. 'crossing over') A common figure of speech in which the word order of similar phrases in a sentence is inverted. In the following example the order of adverb–verb–subject is followed by subject–adverb–verb:

Smooth flow the waves, the zephyrs gently play.

Chiasmus is common in eighteenth-century verse. The fragment above is from Pope's *The Rape of the Lock* (1712, 1714). In a longer example, from Coleridge's 'Frost at Midnight' (1798), the chiasmus consists of words repeated at the beginning and end of the sentence:

By lakes and sandy shores, beneath the crags
Of ancient mountain, and beneath the clouds,
Which image in their bulk both lakes and shores
And mountain crags.

Chicago critics. A group of critics associated with the University of Chicago, whose ideas are represented in the collection of essays *Critics and Criticism: Ancient and Modern* (1952), edited by their leader, R.S. Crane. Developing concepts about form based on Aristotle's *Poetics* (fourth century BC), they emphasised the significance of examining the overall structure and plot of literary works.

Chivalric romance. *See* ROMANCE.

Choral character. A character, specially in plays, but also in other narrative forms, who, like the CHORUS in Greek drama, comments as an observer on the action. Usually the choral character is not a major participant in the events witnessed, and his or her comments are full of ironic insight: the Fool, for example, acts as a choral commentator on Lear's predicament in Shakespeare's *King Lear* (*c.*1605).

Chorus. (Gk. 'band of dancers') In the TRAGEDIES of the ancient Greek playwrights Aeschylus and Sophocles the 'chorus' is a group of characters who represent ordinary people in their attitudes to the action which they witness as bystanders, and on which they comment. For example, in Aeschylus's *Agamemnon* (458BC) the chorus consists of twelve Elders of Argos who describe the situation of the play as it occurs and react with increased agitation to Clytemnestra's terrible doings, but are powerless to affect events.

Before its special use in the theatre, the chorus had been participants in Greek religious festivals, dancing and chanting; hence the connection of certain poetic terms and forms, such as the STROPHE and the ODE, with choric conventions.

In modern drama the chorus is fairly rare, though CHORAL CHARACTERS are common enough. Two plays which do imitate the Greek convention quite closely are Milton's CLOSET DRAMA *Samson Agonistes* (1671) and T.S. Eliot's *Murder in the Cathedral* (1935).

The word chorus may also mean a repeated REFRAIN in a song, which the audience may join in singing.

Chronicle. (Gk. 'to do with time') An early form of historical writing: lists of events often mixing fact and legendary fiction covering an extensive period of time. King Alfred started the *Anglo-Saxon Chronicle* during the ninth century: it continued to be written for 300 years. Chronicles both of national history and of more local interest, for example, the twelfth-century *Chronicle* of his monastery by Jocelin de Brakelond, were written throughout the Middle Ages, but the most famous example is Holinshed's *Chronicles of England, Scotland and Ireland*

(1577, 1587), which became a source book for Elizabethan HISTORY PLAYS.

Chronicle play. Patriotic feeling after the defeat of the Spanish Armada in 1588 led to a vogue for plays recounting the history of England. Playwrights drew their material from Holinshed's *Chronicles* (1577, 1587). Marlowe's *Edward II* (*c*.1592) explores the consequences of weak kingship; and Shakespeare's two cycles of HISTORY PLAYS, covering English history from Richard II to Henry VIII, and culminating in the intense patriotism of *Henry V* (*c*.1598), support the slender Tudor claim to the throne. Shakespeare's history plays are fully dramatised examinations of historical and political events. The early chronicle plays relied on pageantry and stage-battles.

Some critics use 'chronicle play' to mean the same as 'history play': any play which deals with recorded historical facts rather than legends or myths.

Chronology. (Gk. 'time study') Determination of the proper sequence of historical events; and those events carefully dated and arranged in some kind of table, usually simply a list.

Ciceronian. Prose style modelled on that of the Roman orator Cicero (106–43BC): BALANCED, clear, ordered and dignified. Eighteenth-century writers of FORMAL prose, such as Dr Johnson and Gibbon, aspired to achieve these effects. *See also* NEOCLASSICISM, PERIODIC SENTENCE.

Circumlocution. (Lat. 'speaking around') Words which move roundabout their subject rather than announcing it directly, either by mistake, or for EUPHEMISTIC or IRONIC purposes. Henry James in *What Maisie Knew* (1897), in creating an impression of the thought processes of a young girl, uses circumlocutions to skirt around ideas which Maisie dislikes or does not understand (in the following example, the word 'fat'):

> [Maisie felt] she was deficient in something that would meet the general desire. She found out what it was: it was a congenital tendency to the production of a substance to which Moddle, her nurse, gave a short ugly name, a name painfully associated at dinner with the part of the joint that she didn't like.

Claque. (Fr. 'clap') Professional clappers hired in French theatres in the nineteenth century to spur on the audience's applause. The word is now used to suggest a group of sycophantic admirers.

Classic, classical. The second-century Roman essayist Aulus Gellius divided literature into *classicus*, 'for the upper classes', and *proletarius*, 'for the lower classes'. Thence the word *classicus* came to mean 'writing of the highest quality', and because from the RENAISSANCE until the eighteenth century works of Greek and Latin literature were considered models of excellence, 'classic' came to mean 'ancient Greek and Roman', and 'the classics' consisted of Greek and Latin literature.

In modern use 'classic' or 'classical' can therefore mean 'excellent' or 'of the best and most typical'; or 'to do with ancient Greek or Roman culture'; or 'dignified, balanced and clearly ordered in the manner of certain Greek and Roman models'. *See also* NEOCLASSICISM.

'Classic bourgeois' realism. The French critic Roland Barthes, whose early work was STRUCTURALIST, throughout his career attacked REALISM, which he regarded as the literary form which expressed and underpinned bourgeois values and IDEOLOGY. Other POST-STRUCTURALIST critics, some Marxist, have continued this attack. The features deemed to characterise classic realism are ILLUSIONISM, which is supposed to hoodwink the unthinking reader into forgetting that the text is a fictional production; a HIERARCHY OF DISCOURSES, by which the AUTHOR dominates the narrative and disallows a plural reading; and, combined with this, a movement throughout the narrative towards CLOSURE, the apparent (and false) completion of meaning.

In *S/Z* (1970) Barthes analyses the opening paragraphs of a classic bourgeois realist text, Balzac's story 'Sarrasine' (1830), and discovers, paradoxically, many explicit instances of the author/narrator reminding the reader that the work is a constructed fiction.

Classicism. A vague word used of a variety of literary or cultural attitudes, all of which in some way look back to the conventions of Greek and Latin literature, or to the qualities supposed to be redolent of Greek and Roman society, such as dignity, proportion, balance, restraint, precision of analytic reasoning, and so on. Many attempts have been made to display a fundamental distinction in human attitudes and ways of thinking by special definitions of the opposed concepts of 'classicism' and 'ROMANTICISM': an interesting modern example of this is to be found in Robert Pirsig's autobiographical novel *Zen and the Art of Motorcycle Maintenance* (1974). *See also* NEOCLASSICISM.

Clerihew. A short comic verse form consisting of rhymed pairs of lines of any length, invented by E. Clerihew Bentley (1875–1956). They are most often mild jokes about famous people, ranging from the EPIGRAMMATIC to the nonsensical:

Elizabeth Barrett Browning
Was always frowning;
Good humour left her by degrees
While writing *Sonnets from the Portuguese.*

Cliché. (Fr. 'stereotype') A boring phrase, made tedious by frequent repetition. Clichés usually seek to be clever or sound fine, but are enfeebled by constant use: examples in ordinary speech are 'in the fullness of time', 'bright-eyed and bushy-tailed' and 'with all due respect'. In literature writers seek to 'make it new' in Ezra Pound's phrase, and try to avoid the clichéd use of words, or clichéd situations, unless they are using such clichés ironically. In his *An Essay on Criticism* (1711) Pope mocks the untalented poets, whose ideas and rhymes are predictable:

> Where'er you find 'the cooling western breeze,'
> In the next line it 'whispers through the trees'.

Climax. (Gk. 'ladder') In FREYTAG'S PYRAMID the point at which the PROTAGONIST's fortunes reach their highest point before the 'turning point' which initiates the 'falling action'. In general, any point of great intensity in a literary work; in a narrative the culminating moment of the action. *See also* PLOT.

Close reading. The scrupulous and balanced critical examination of a text so as to extract its meaning and identify its effects: after the NEW CRITICISM, for a long time the standard initial approach to literary works.

Closed couplet. *See* HEROIC COUPLET.

Closet drama. A literary work in the form of a play, but not intended to be staged in a theatre. Milton's *Samson Agonistes* (1671), Byron's *Manfred* (1817), Shelley's *Prometheus Unbound* (1820) and Hardy's *The Dynasts* (1904–8) are notable examples.

Closure. The impression of completeness and finality achieved by the ending of some literary works, or parts of literary works: 'and they all lived happily ever after.' During the latter half of the twentieth century critics have tended to prefer 'open' texts, which defy closure and refuse to leave the reader comfortably satisfied; and, by an extension of this predilection, it is argued that criticism itself should avoid closure, leaving the text available to multiple interpretations, and refuse to offer conclusive judgments. *See also* READABLE.

In the discussion of poetry, 'closure' can have the narrow sense of referring to the way in which the syntax of a piece of verse can coincide with the metrical unit, either in the case of a line (when it is 'end-stopped') or a stanza. Some poems achieve a strong sense of closure simply because the final line is the only line in the poem not to be run-on, and therefore the expectation of ENJAMBMENT which has been created is denied by the poem's ending.

Cockney school of poetry. A derisive term for certain London-based writers, including Leigh Hunt, Shelley, Hazlitt and Keats; the term was invented by the Scottish journalist John Gibson Lockhart in an anonymous series of articles on 'The Cockney School of Poetry', published in *Blackwood's Magazine* (during October 1817, and 1818), in which he mocked the supposed stylistic vulgarity of these writers.

Coda. (Lat. 'tail') A term borrowed from music, meaning a concluding passage, sometimes with the slightly derogatory sense that it is not an essential part of the work as a whole, but has been tacked on, either as a summary, or to offer a different point of view from that demonstrated by the work as a whole.

Code. STRUCTURALISM and SEMIOTICS have demonstrated that meaning is inherent in systems of SIGNS shared by a group. These systems operate according to rules and conventions; however familiar the signs, the underlying rules that govern the system may be invisible to their users. In this respect languages are like codes that require deciphering.

Literature also functions according to rules, some obvious, some invisible, that operate between writer and reader, and the critic's task may be to explain or catalogue these rules, and decipher literature as if it was a code. *See also* COMPETENCE, HERMENEUTICS, LEXIE.

Codex. (Lat. 'block of words') A word originally describing ancient writing materials which came to be used to denote collections of early paper and parchment manuscripts. The *Vercelli Book* (tenth century), a collection of various Anglo-Saxon writings, is a famous codex.

Cognitive language. (Lat. 'investigating') Another term for REFERENTIAL LANGUAGE. *See also* DENOTATION.

Cohesion. (Lat. 'stuck together') Amongst a number of meanings in linguistic analysis, cohesion describes the linking together of sentences or larger units of meaning, for example, by means of pronouns, articles and some adverbs. In the following pair of sentences, the full meaning of some words depends upon knowledge not gleaned from within each sentence considered on its own: 'The man went for a walk. However, he did not take long.' (Why 'The' and not 'A'? Why 'However'? Who is 'he'?) The study of cohesion explores the nature of these links, gaps and explanations. *See also* DEICTIC.

Collage. (Fr. 'glueing') A technique popular in the early twentieth century with painters such as the Cubists Braque and Picasso: pieces of material, newspaper or other fragments of 'real' objects are incorporated within the painting. Later artists have produced whole works by pasting together pictures, printed items and fragments of materials of all kinds. The term is used by analogy to describe one of the effects common in modernist poetry: the swift jumping from topic to topic by means of fragmentary images, ALLUSIONS and quotations. Pound's *Cantos* (1930–69) are full of this kind of writing, as are parts of Eliot's *The Waste Land* (1922) from which the following is taken:

> I sat upon the shore
> Fishing, with the arid plain behind me
> Shall I at least set my lands in order?
> London Bridge is falling down falling down falling down
> *Poi s'ascose nel foco che gli affina*
> *Quando fiam uti chelidon* – O swallow swallow . . .

Collate. (Lat. 'bring together') To compare different editions of a text in order to note all differences for the purposes of correction or emendation, or to establish which text is genuine and original.

Collective unconscious. The psychologist Jung believed that we all inherit racial memories which include the ARCHETYPES, figures and situations that appear to us in dreams and MYTHS, and are expressed in artistic creations. In his autobiographical notes, *Memories, Dreams and Reflections* (1963), he describes his own developing relationship with this collective unconscious, including encounters with legendary figures such as Salome and Elijah. Poets as diverse as W.B. Yeats and Ted Hughes share similar beliefs in the role of poetry as a means of drawing upon a world of truths and forces that lie partially hidden in the human mind. *See also* SHAMANISM.

Colloquialism. (Lat. 'like speech') The use of the kinds of expression and grammar associated with ordinary, everyday speech rather than FORMAL language. Colloquialisms may simply be part of a relaxed style of speaking or writing; or they may be employed, perhaps with SLANG, to provide additional colour and word-play, as in the opening lines of 'Good Sport' (1968) by Bruce Dawe:

Good sport, she laughed about her weight
And jogged about the court in shorts,
Her butt the butt of many a joke
– She turned the other cheek in sports . . .

Colloquy. (Lat. 'conversation') A discussion, usually of a learned topic. A colloquium is a meeting of learned persons for the purpose of such discussion.

Colophon. (Gk. 'summit, finishing touch') In old books a note stating authorship, title, printing and publishing facts, placed (unlike in modern books) at the end. In modern use 'colophon' refers to the publisher's emblem, initials or trademark.

Comedy. (Gk. 'merry-making, comic poet') A broad genre which encompasses a large variety of different kinds of literature; however, 'comedy' is used most often with reference to a kind of drama which is intended primarily to entertain the audience, and which ends happily for the characters.

In this meaning of the word, 'comedy', like TRAGEDY, is an ancient form dating at least as far back as the fifth century BC. It probably originated in the seasonal festivities, often obscene, which were part of the Dionysiac fertility cult. By the end of the fifth century BC great individual playwrights had already emerged: Aristophanes is the most notable. His plays, such as *The Frogs* and *Lysistrata*, combine lyrical poetry, buffoonery, satire and fantastical plots and characters. Another highly prized writer of comedies was Menander, who flourished at the end of the fourth century BC: his plays are only known because of his strong influence on the Roman playwrights Plautus and Terence. Their comedies are more social in their focus, contain songs, and have elaborate plots, involving STOCK CHARACTERS, such as the bragging soldier, spendthrift young men, wily servants, and so on, many of whom were copied by Renaissance playwrights; Shakespeare's *The Comedy of Errors* (*c*.1592–3), for example, is modelled on the *Menaechmi* of Plautus.

During the Middle Ages the word 'comedy' referred to narrative poetry in which the plot ends happily. Dante's *Divine Comedy* (*c*.1304–21) is perhaps not typical of this usage, though Dante's progress through the 'Inferno' and 'Purgatory' to 'Paradise' shows the basic 'comic' pattern of movement from trouble and misery towards happiness. There were farcical INTERLUDES in the medieval MYSTERY PLAYS, but it was during the Renaissance that comic drama flourished once more and developed a wide variety of styles and interests.

Perhaps because Aristotle concentrated on tragedy in the *Poetics* (fourth century BC), comedy was never subject to the same attempt to impose rules concerning its conventions. But none the less most comedies from the Renaissance until the present day share certain features: they do not concentrate on the fortunes of an individual, but the interest is spread over a group of people; they tend to deal with low life and humble people, rather than with kings and nobles; their plots are usually elaborate, involve misunderstandings and deceptions, and move from the possibility of disaster towards a happy ending, often symbolised by a wedding. All these elements distinguish comedy strongly from tragedy (though, of course, the forms are mixed in TRAGICOMEDY from the Renaissance onwards).

Different forms of comedy are also clearly discernible. **Romantic comedy**, like Shakespeare's *As You Like It* (*c*.1599), involves idealised lovers sorting out their tangled relationship and achieving happiness: it is light-hearted and unrealistic. **Satiric comedy** in the manner of Ben Jonson's *Volpone* (1605–6) may be painfully unflinching in its depiction of human folly, vice and greed: it concentrates on the clever unscrupulousness of tricksters and the stupid gullibility of their dupes. The **comedy of manners**, which reaches its point of perfection during the Restoration and the eighteenth century, focuses on the love intrigues of cynical and sophisticated young aristocrats in high society: it relies heavily on verbal wit, while the other comic styles often contain farcical elements or even SLAPSTICK. FARCE, which concentrates wholly on provoking laughter, is quite a late development in drama.

Since the Renaissance, dramatic comedy has remained a constant form of popular entertainment, at times in decline because of the occasional general decline of drama, but reflecting all the changing styles and interests of literature in general. Though its prestige as a literary form, because of its very nature and purpose, to amuse and delight, has tended to be eclipsed by 'serious' tragedy, critics have analysed and examined its conventions and techniques. The nineteenth-century writer Meredith in 'The Idea of Comedy' (1877) invented the labels HIGH COMEDY and LOW COMEDY, distinguishing, at the furthest extremes, intellectual comedy of wit and merriment, from buffoonery. Perhaps the twentieth century is more sympathetic to comedy than any other age. Many modern critics have tended to regard the comic and ironic vision of works such as Shakespeare's *Twelfth Night* (*c*.1600) or the Russian Chekhov's *The Cherry Orchard* (1904) as as much a triumph of technique and artistic perception as any tragic masterpiece, though a counter-argument is that the pattern of human life is essentially tragic, ending as it inevitably does in death, and so the comic vision is limited and partial. Since the 1950s, in the Theatre of the ABSURD, comedy has even been used to express the ironic techniques and philosophical outlooks typical of MODERNISM and EXISTENTIALISM. In the Theatre of the Absurd works like Beckett's *Waiting for Godot* (1953) employ comic conventions and even farce to convey a profoundly serious view of human existence.

The term 'Comedy' is often applied to novels or other narratives in so far as they are similar in plot or point of view to dramatic comedies.

Comedy of manners. *See* COMEDY.

Comic. (*adj.*) Provoking laughter, either sympathetic or derisive.

Comic relief. Comic incidents, characters or speeches placed in a serious work, even a tragedy, for the purpose of contrast. Two famous instances in Shakespeare's plays are the drunken porter's speech in *Macbeth* (*c*.1606), II.3, which brings back the world of normality after the murder of Duncan, and Hamlet's conversation with the gravediggers in *Hamlet* (*c*.1601), V.1, providing a lull in the action that prepares for the funeral of Ophelia. The swift manipulation of the audience's feelings can be a vital ingredient in building up suspense in a play. Shakespeare is a master of such effects. Comic relief, however, can overbalance a play: the tragic effect of Marlowe's *Dr Faustus* (*c*.1588) is diluted by the heavy-handed buffoonery in the middle acts (which may not all have been written by Marlowe).

Commedia dell'arte. (It. 'comedy of the professional actors') A form of drama evolved in sixteenth-century Italy in which travelling companies of actors improvised comic plays around standard plots, using STOCK CHARACTERS. A typical play might involve a young lover, the 'Inamorato', tricking Pantaleone ('Pantaloon'), a rich old father, into giving up his daughter. Arlecchino ('Harlequin'), the cunning servant, and Pulcinella ('Punch'), the hunchback clown, were other stock types. The play was enlivened by dancing, singing and SLAPSTICK buffoonery. Many elements of the form are visible in comic plays by Shakespeare and

Molière in the sixteenth and seventeenth centuries, and the influence is still seen in plots of operas well into the nineteenth century.

Commitment. A writer or artist who sees literature as necessarily serving a political or social programme or set of beliefs, and not merely aimed at achieving literary ends, is said to be 'committed'. In practice the word is used most often of socialist and communist writers.

Common measure. A QUATRAIN of alternating four-stress and three-stress lines, rhymed either *abcb* or *abab*; also called BALLAD METRE. *See also* METRE, RHYME.

Common sense. A concept that, from a common-sense point of view, requires no explanation, but which has special connotations in some contemporary literary criticism. Some POST-STRUCTURALIST critics argue that 'common sense', while seeming to be a simple and generally agreed collection of normally acceptable truths, is actually a construction of a specific political IDEOLOGY. According to this point of view, 'common sense' always reflects and authenticates the prevailing power structures within society. Thus, far from being an innocent collection of straightforward and uncomplicated attitudes, it is a powerful instrument for maintaining an existing social hierarchy. *See also* DECONSTRUCTION, DISCOURSE, INTERPELLATION, PHENOMENOLOGY.

Common sense was also a disputed concept in eighteenth-century philosophical debate. Thomas Reid (1710–96) was the originator of the Scottish 'Common Sense' school of philosophy. In his *Enquiry into the Human Mind on the Principles of Common Sense* (1764) he attacked the scepticism of EMPIRICISTS like Hume and Locke, and defended the view that our senses allow a contact with a reality which is independent of the mind.

Commonplace. A 'commonplace' is a well-known saying, or possibly a recurrent MOTIF or subject in literature. The word usually has a pejorative meaning: 'commonplace' as an adjective means ordinary, common, platitudinous and dull.

Commonplace book. A book chiefly composed of interesting quotations, but also including ideas and notes, compiled privately by any individual. Occasionally the commonplace book of a writer is published: W.H. Auden compiled such a collection, called *A Certain World* (1971), in place of writing an autobiography.

Commonwealth literature. The various English-language literatures of countries that belong to the Commonwealth of Nations, which includes many African countries, Australia, Canada, India and the West Indies. The literatures of South Africa and Ireland are sometimes included, though neither country is currently a member of the Commonwealth. *See also* POST-COLONIAL LITERATURE.

Commonwealth period. From the execution of Charles I, at the end of the Civil War in 1649, until the Restoration of the Stuart monarchy with the return of Charles II in 1660, England was ruled by Parliament led by Oliver Cromwell. The Puritans banned theatrical performances in 1642, so dramatic writing ceased. Prose, however, flourished: Sir Thomas Browne, Jeremy Taylor and Izaak Walton were three highly individual writers of non-fictional prose. Some of the METAPHYSICALS, including Vaughan and Marvell, were poets of this period, as also were Cowley and Waller. Milton was involved in writing political pamphlets in support of the Puritans. Thomas Hobbes published his political and philosophical study *Leviathan* in Paris in 1651, and so scandalised the exiled Royalist court with his 'atheistic' notions that he had to return to England.

Comparative literature. The study and analysis of parallels in the literatures of different nations and cultures. The comparative literary approach regards all literature as a manifestation of interests and activities common to all peoples of the world, and seeks to illuminate particular works through cross-cultural comparison and contrast.

Competence. Knowledge of language is 'competence'; **performance** is its use. These terms were invented by the linguistic philosopher Noam Chomsky. They echo and extend the fundamental distinction between LANGUE and *parole* enunciated by Saussure, the Swiss linguistician. Linguistic competence is the possession, mostly unconscious, of a huge fund of information, rules, counter-rules and patterns, that allow us with an extraordinary degree of sophistication to recognise errors in highly complex grammatical systems. Very few of us can explain these systems, or label the grammatical rules by which we communicate. But we can still use the language, and thus provide examples of performance, which the linguistician examines in order to understand competence, and reveal grammar.

Critical theorists have borrowed Chomsky's terms to suggest that readers must possess **literary competence** in order to understand the conventions of a narrative or poem. For example, when Wordsworth begins a poem 'Behold her, single in the field, yon solitary Highland lass!' ('The Solitary Reaper', 1807), even unsophisticated readers know that he is not addressing a particular person, but adopting a rapt mode of communing with himself and his future unknown readers, which is appropriate in poetry. Making explicit the implicit rules by which literature functions is one task of criticism.

Cultural competence is the knowledge of the vast array of cultural references and assumptions that differentiate national, religious or social groups. Many Australians, for example, are privileged by having potential access to two areas of cultural competence, their Australian heritage, and the heritage of whatever country their family may have originally come from, be it Ireland, England, Greece, Thailand, or wherever.

Complaint. (Lat. 'bewailing') A common MOTIF or minor genre in LYRIC poetry: the poet complains of ill-luck, poverty, of the cruelty or faithlessness of a loved one, or of the rotten state of the world. Chaucer wrote several such works, including 'A Complaint unto Pity' and the 'Complaint of Chaucer to His Purse' (fourteenth century). Wyatt's 'They Flee from Me' (1557) is another notable example. The stance of the poet lamenting or grumbling, and the use of 'Complaint' as a title, is common in lyric verse until the seventeenth century. *See also* ELEGY, LAMENT.

Complexity. (Lat. 'encompassing, woven') Often used as an evaluative critical word, suggesting the subtle combination of the parts in a literary work (especially IRONIES and AMBIGUITIES), and also usually drawing attention to the cleverness of the critic who appreciates and unravels this literary quality.

Conceit. (Lat. 'concept') Originally 'conceit' meant simply a thought or an opinion. The term came to be used in a derogatory way to describe a particular kind of far-fetched metaphorical association. It has now lost this pejorative overtone and simply denotes a special sort of figurative device, usually a SIMILE.

The distinguishing quality of a conceit is that it should forge an unexpected comparison between two apparently dissimilar things or ideas. The classic and familiar example is Donne's parallel between the nature of his love and a pair of geometric compasses in 'A Valediction: Forbidding Mourning' (1633):

> If they be two, they are two so
>   As stiff twin compasses are two,
> Thy soul the fixed foot, makes no show
> To move, but doth, if th'other do.

The comparison is ingeniously continued for two more verses. Conceits of this kind are a common and distinctive feature of METAPHYSICAL POETRY. Whole poems might grow out of an idea, like Donne's conceit in 'The Flea' (1633), arguing that being bitten by a flea is equal to sexual intercourse and marriage. In the later Metaphysicals, like Carew, Crashaw and Cleveland, the conceit became even more extravagant and fantastical, as in the following series of bizarre, jocular metaphors from Cleveland's 'The Antiplatonick' (1651):

> The soldier, that man of iron,
> Whom ribs of *Horror* all environ;
> That's strung with wire, instead of Veins,
> In whose embraces you're in chains,
> Let a Magnetic girl appear,
> Straight he turns *Cupid's* Cuirasseer,

Love storms his lips, and takes the Fortress in,
For all the Bristled Turn-pikes of his chin.

This kind of forced fantasy led to Dr Johnson's judgment on the DISCORDIA CONCORS of Metaphysical poetry in which 'the most heterogeneous ideas are yoked by violence together' (*Life of Cowley*, 1779). Conceits are also found outside the poetry of the so-called Metaphysical school. **Petrarchan conceits** are common in Elizabethan poetry and before: they are the kind of metaphor used by the Italian poet Petrarch in his love poetry. Extravagant claims for the beauty of the poet's loved one, with fanciful comparisons, are typical. Shakespeare often uses such conceits, but in Sonnet 130 (1609) he mocks the conventional similes:

My mistress' eyes are nothing like the sun;
Coral is far more red than her lips' red;
If snow be white, why then her breasts are dun,
If hairs be wires, black wires grow on her head.
I have seen roses damask'd, red and white,
But no such roses see I in her cheeks.

The poem ends by twisting round into a compliment.

Conceits can also be found in other kinds of verse. T.S. Eliot's enthusiasm for Donne's poetry has led critics to discern conceited figures in his own writing, such as the famous description of the evening 'spread out against the sky/Like a patient etherised upon a table' in 'The Love Song of J. Alfred Prufrock' (1917).

Conceptismo. (Sp. 'conceit') The seventeenth-century Spanish poetic movement which espoused the use of elaborate and difficult METAPHORS, CONCEITS and PUNS in the attempt to grapple with occult philosophical ideas. Its master was Francisco Quevedo. *See also* CULTERANISMO, GONGORISM, MARINISM, METAPHYSICAL POETS.

Concordance. (Lat. 'harmonising') A reference book listing all the uses of an individual word in a text or in the complete works of an author, thus making it possible to look up every usage of any particular word in, for example, the Bible or Shakespeare's works.

Concrete. (Lat. 'grown together') (*adj.*) A passage in a literary work is said to be 'concrete' if it refers to things (people or objects), rather than to ideas. Language is almost always a mixture of ABSTRACT and concrete in this sense; but it is still possible to contrast language which is mostly abstract with that which is mostly concrete: compare 'the green frog hopped into the muddy pond' with 'ideals of beauty have motivated humanity throughout history'.

Concrete poetry. An AVANT-GARDE form of poetry or art in which TYPOGRAPHY is used to make pictures or visual jokes. Such poems often imitate the appearance of the object described, like Apollinaire's 'Il pleut' (1918), one of his *Calligrammes*, in which the words run verticall down the page like rain falling. Concrete verse is usually immediate and total in its effect, and because of this its exponents have claimed it transcends ordinary, sequential language, allowing words (if words are used) their full potentiality of meaning.

Condensation. *See* PSYCHOANALYTIC CRITICISM.

Confession. (Lat. 'to admit') A variety of AUTOBIOGRAPHY which tends to dwell on the author's honesty in admitting and describing former sinfulness or wrong-doing. One classic model for the form is St Augustine's *Confessions* (*c.*AD397-9), which is chiefly religious in its focus; another example is Rousseau's *Confessions* (1781, 1788), which gives a remarkable insight into human psychology. De Quincey's mildly sensational *Confessions of an English Opium Eater* (1821) is a typical example of the form.

Confessional poetry. A kind of poetry originating in the late 1950s and 1960s in the work of several American poets who rejected the idea that poetry should be impersonal (*see* IMPERSONALITY), a view that had dominated the poetic world since T.S. Eliot's strictures on the subject, reinforced by the attitudes of the NEW CRITICISM. The poetry of Theodore Roethke, often describing events from his own childhood, was an important influence in establishing the confessional trend, as was also the immense popularity of the BEAT poets, showing the academics that there was a market for poetry that was less self-consciously clever and controlled. Robert Lowell's *Life Studies* (1959) is a landmark in the development of the confessional manner. John Berryman, Sylvia Plath and Anne Sexton are the other notable confessional poets.

Confidant(e). (Lat. 'trustworthy') A STOCK CHARACTER in novels and, especially, in drama: the trusted friend of the PROTAGONIST, with whom the latter discusses plans and aspirations, thus providing a convenient method of allowing the audience to learn of motives and probable developments. Horatio acts as Hamlet's confidant in Shakespeare's *Hamlet* (*c.*1601).

Connotation. (Lat. 'mark in addition') The connotations of a word are its various secondary meanings and overtones: that which it suggests and implies rather than means. The connotations of words make METAPHOR possible. The word 'tiger' denotes a large carnivorous quadruped, *Panthera tigris*: its connotations are ferocity and stripiness. A tiger-lily is orange-striped; a 'tiger smile' would be menacingly ferocious. Each combination uses only those connotations of 'tiger' that make sense in the given context. When Blake writes, 'Tiger! tiger! burning bright' (1794), he is drawing out the connotations inherent in the word, by the metaphorical association with fire ('burning bright'), another colourful and ferocious phenomenon. *See also* DENOTATION, REFERENTIAL LANGUAGE.

Consonance. (Lat. 'sounding together') Repeated arrangements of consonants, with a change in the vowel that separates them: flip–flap, limp–lump–lamp, reader–rider–ruder–raider. Common as a kind of HALF-RHYME in poetry. *See also* RHYME.

Constructivism. A Soviet literary movement of the 1920s: its aim was to adopt a technological approach to writing, but in literature (rather than in the plastic arts) constructivism was neither very coherent nor significant.

Conte. (Fr. 'tale') From the nineteenth century the word has been used simply to denote a SHORT STORY, but during the seventeenth and eighteenth centuries a *conte* was a special kind of short narrative, usually amusing and involving fantasy and sometimes allegory, like Charles Perrault's *Contes de ma Mère l'Oye* (1697).

Content. What is 'contained' in a literary work. Usually the word implies a simple and unified notion of a work's central idea and THEME, its main argument, in effect some message that is expressible in non-literary language, a boiled down moral, rather than a summary of its action.

Content is an abstract and vague word, and its common antithetical pairing with FORM scarcely helps clarify the meaning of either. It is a cliché, though nonetheless true, that in literature form and content are indivisible. The two concepts are indeed mutually dependent: form is what contains; content is what is contained.

This inseparability of form and content has led to the argument that poetry, to take an example of a kind of writing in which form is highly significant, can be neither translated nor paraphrased (because both processes would lead to radical changes of form). Yet the practice of paraphrasing and translating poetry continues unabated, suggesting that the content even of poetry is to some extent transferable and resistant to changes of form.

Some writers concentrate on the formal patterning of what they write, aspiring towards musical effects, or abstraction. Others adopt the opposite view, that the content or message of their work is of vital significance, and the form needed to communicate this should be as transparent and disposable as possible, and is of no interest in itself.

Context. (Lat. 'woven together') The parts immediately before or after a chosen passage in a literary work: the words and ideas which surround a statement, and give it its particular meaning. To quote 'out of context' therefore is to distort a piece of language by ignoring its place in the larger whole of which it is a part. Obviously words change their meaning according to their context: the tree's <u>bark</u> is brown/the dog's <u>bark</u> is loud. More subtle interpretations of the metaphorical associations or CONNOTATIONS of words can be justified by reference to their context. In plays, the dramatic context is also highly significant: for example, in Shakespeare's *King Lear* (*c*.1605), Gloucester's despairing

speech 'As flies to wanton boys are we to the gods' (IV.1), is undercut by the fact that at that very moment his son is about to take care of him.
Contextualisation. To reveal the context of a statement or idea. Usually to 'contextualise' is to explain the nature of the DISCOURSE in which a comment occurs, in terms of its historical, social and political background.
Conventions. (Lat. 'coming together, agreement') All forms of literature can be best understood or enjoyed when the reader or audience is aware of certain common features of the particular kind of literature in question: these common features are the 'conventions' of that form.

Often the conventions of a particular form are a consequence of its nature. Drama, for example, cannot exist without certain radical conventions: we watch a play in near silence, and pretend that the stage in front of us is a room, a battlefield, a forest, kitchen, or whatever. Other aspects of drama are also conventions, though less basic than the method of staging a play common in Western society: we accept jumps in time-span, and multiple scene-changes (although the theory of the UNITIES of time and space was an attempt to create a different convention); we also understand SOLILOQUIES, and other absolutely non-naturalistic events that help the audience follow the action, such as characters reading letters out loud, or a narrator commenting on the action. Of course different kinds of drama make use of different conventions. Nineteenth-century realistic playwrights such as Ibsen and Chekhov try to avoid non-naturalistic devices like those mentioned above.

Metre is a convention of all poetry until the twentieth century. GENRES, like the epic, the tragedy, the pastoral elegy, and so on, are defined by those conventional features which they share. STOCK CHARACTERS in drama and the novel, such as the boastful soldier, the bohemian student or the fair young heroine, are also conventions, though they may not be definitive. Recurring elements, whether of technique or subject matter, in all kinds of literature turn into the conventions of that form which new authors may copy, alter or reject. Writers who seek originality may invent entirely new forms, totally dismissing the conventions which preceded them: yet these new conventional examples become, in their turn, new conventions. Even the most AVANT-GARDE of literature and art is in the process of forging new conventions by which it can be understood.

Misunderstanding or misinterpreting conventional features of a literary kind is a basic error in literary criticism, like complaining that the actors are singing during an opera. To complain, for example, that Shelley's treatment of Keats's death in *Adonais* (1821) is artificial and does not seem based on real friendship, would be to misunderstand the conventions of pastoral elegy.

Conversation poem. A kind of BLANK VERSE poem: several poems written by Coleridge and Wordsworth around 1798 (including 'Frost at Midnight', 'This Lime-tree Bower My Prison' and 'Lines Composed a Few Miles above Tintern Abbey') are often grouped together as 'conversation poems'. They are not conversational in the sense of being colloquial, nor are they dialogues (though they are addressed or dedicated to other persons), but are informal meditations on the relationship between self and surroundings.

Copernican theory. The model of the solar system which recognises that the Earth and other planets revolve around the sun. The theory was explained in *De Revolutionibus Orbium Caelestium* (1543) by the Pole Nicolas Copernicus (1473–1543). After much opposition and controversy, the new hypothesis prevailed against the PTOLEMAIC astronomy, in which the Earth was perceived to be at the centre of the universe. Copernicus's system was defective in that he thought the planetary orbits were circular: Kepler later proved them to be elliptical. But it swept away the medieval cosmology, and provided a modern perception of our place in the universe. *See also* RENAISSANCE.

Copyright. The legal ownership by the author, publisher or some other assigned person, of a piece of writing. Laws prevent the copying, printing or publishing without permission of works protected by copyright for a fixed number of years (in Britain for fifty years after the author's death). Before the early eighteenth century no such laws existed, and writers often had their works printed without their consent and without payment; this kind of literary theft is called a **pirate edition**.

Coronach. (Gael. 'roaring together') A Scottish and Irish word for a funeral DIRGE.

Correctness. In relation to literature, the notion that texts (especially poetry) should subscribe to established and clear 'rules', for example, about kinds of subject matter and appropriate approaches to it, genre, choice of language or departures from metrical regularity. Such ideas have only prevailed in relation to English literature in the seventeenth and eighteenth centuries. The *Académie Française* (started 1634) regulated the correctness of French literature right up till the nineteenth century, insisting, for example, on the maintenance of the Aristotelian UNITIES in drama; it still makes pronouncements about language and new words in French. Ideas for such an academy in Britain foundered, not least because Shakespeare had broken every 'rule' thought to exist for the proper construction of plays. However, 'correctness' was much prized by eighteenth-century writers who subscribed to the conventions and ideals of NEOCLASSICISM. *See also* DECORUM, POETIC DICTION.

Correlative. *See* OBJECTIVE CORRELATIVE.

Correspondances. The title of a poem by the French poet Baudelaire, published in *Les fleurs du mal* (1857), which uses SYNAESTHESIA to express relationships between nature, sounds, perfumes, colours, sensations. The doctrine of 'correspondences', this way of perceiving the world through poetic intuitions of the hidden links between all kinds of experience, became a significant aspect of the SYMBOLIST MOVEMENT.

Cosmic irony. *See* IRONY.

Coterie. (Fr. 'tenants holding land together') A group of like-minded people who enjoy each other's company: members of a literary coterie, like the BLOOMSBURY GROUP, share values and styles, but lack the self-conscious coherence and aim of a deliberate movement.

Co-text. A word sometimes used to refer to the specifically linguistic environment of a stretch of language, the other language which surrounds it, rather than its general context, or situation.

Cothurnus. *See* BUSKIN.

Coup de théâtre. (Fr. 'theatrical blow') A sudden and spectacular turn to events in the PLOT of a play, such as a surprise revelation or unmasking, that changes the audience's perception of the action.

Couplet. (O. Fr. 'little pair') A pair of rhymed lines, of any METRE. Herrick's 'Delight in Disorder' (1648) is composed of seven couplets of IAMBIC TETRAMETER:

A sweet disorder in the dress
Kindles in clothes a wantonness.
A lawn about the shoulders thrown
Into a fine distraction;
An erring lace, which here and there
Enthrals the crimson stomacher;
A cuff neglectful, and thereby
Ribbons to flow confusedly;
A winning wave, deserving note,
In the tempestuous petticoat;
A careless shoestring, in whose tie
I see a wild civility:
Do more bewitch me than when art
Is too precise in every part.

See also RHYME.

Courtesy book. A book of etiquette: the most famous is Castiglione's *Il Libro del Cortegiano* ('The Book of the Courtier'), published in 1528, which describes the model behaviour of the gentleman at court, who should endeavour to be an ideal combination of statesman, soldier, artist, scholar, philosopher and friend. The work was translated into English by Sir Thomas Hoby in 1561. Many other works outlining gentlemanly standards of behaviour and educational aims were published during the sixteenth and seventeenth centuries. Lord Chesterfield's *Letters to His Son* (1774) may be considered a late example of the form.

Courtly love. The term *amour courtois* was invented in the nineteenth century to refer to the phenomenon of courtly love which is generally thought to have originated in the poetry of the Provençal TROUBADOURS of southern France in the late eleventh century. It is a matter for dispute to what extent the conventions of courtly love are realistic accounts of social behaviour in the Middle Ages, or a stylised literary artifice. Courtly love is based on the idea that human love is an ennobling, even spiritual experience, a novel view for that age. Since medieval marriages were arranged according to political or financial motives, this noble love is seen as being essentially adulterous. The lover adores his lady in spite of the fact that she is the wife of another man. She becomes the idealised object of his veneration. The vassal-lover suffers constantly in his unswerving devotion to all his lady's orders and desires. Indeed, he proves his honour by this total devotion; he fights his battles and pursues the high ideals of chivalric behaviour for her sake. Such is the love that Lancelot suffers for Guinevere, who is King Arthur's wife; it is described in countless ROMANCES and LYRIC poems from the twelfth to the sixteenth century.

The development of these conventions has been explained in terms of the social patterns of the day: the need to serve a feudal lord is easily displaced into serving his lady. The cult of the Virgin Mary is clearly another factor which confirms this particular convention: Christian patterns of worship, rule, sin, guilt, repentance and grace are easily transferred into the courtly love framework. Another factor, it is claimed, was the misreading, as if it was a serious work, of the Roman poet Ovid's mildly satirical and exaggerated *Ars Amatoria* ('The Art of Loving'), written at the start of the Christian era.

The conventions of courtly love spread throughout Europe into the twelfth-century Arthurian romances of Chrétien de Troyes, into the thirteenth-century lyric poetry of the Italian DOLCE STIL NUOVO, and into the *Vita Nuova* (*c.*1292) of Dante. In England its influence is clear in fourteenth-century works such as *Sir Gawain and the Green Knight* and Chaucer's *Troilus and Criseyde*, which is a criticism of courtly love. The concept continued to provide the basic material for lyric poetry for Petrarch, whose ideas and images recur in Tudor and Elizabethan verse. In the seventeenth century the METAPHYSICALS and the CAVALIER POETS still toyed with some of the conventions.

C.S. Lewis's *The Allegory of Love* (1936) is a famous but controversial study of the origins and development of courtly love.

Courtly makers. A name applied by Puttenham, the Elizabethan critic, to the poets at the court of Henry VIII (1509–47), of which the 'two chieftains' were Sir Thomas Wyatt and Henry Howard, Earl of Surrey. These poets introduced many new metrical forms into English verse, including the SONNET and BLANK VERSE; most of their poetry first appeared publicly (in revised form) in the influential Elizabethan anthology *Tottel's Miscellany* (1557), some ten years after both were dead.

Cowleyan ode. *See* ODE.

Creolisation. *See* PIDGIN.

Crisis. (Gk. 'decision') A medical word for the turning point of a disease, which is used of any vitally decisive moment in the PLOT of a drama, or other kind of narrative.

Crisis in English Studies. The title of the introduction to *Re-Reading English* (1982), edited by P. Widdowson, a collection of essays which discusses the role of POST-STRUCTURALIST and MARXIST approaches to literature in secondary and tertiary education, and the future of the discipline of 'English'. He argues that new critical methodologies and theories have revealed the bourgeois IDEOLOGY inherent in the conventional educational methods and procedures, which, he concedes, were (and probably still are) entrenched in most English departments throughout Britain – practices that can be summed up as the exercise of teaching students to interpret and enjoy a collection of special and valued texts.

Rather than predicting or causing a crisis, Widdowson's book was part of a campaign by exponents of post-structuralism in universities and polytechnics to modify the teaching of English as a subject. Their programme includes eradicating the concept of a special kind of writing called 'Literature', demystifying the 'myth' of 'literary value', exposing 'criticism' as an 'ideological practice', and examining literature (perceived as all kinds of writing, not just the 'Literary') in relation to the 'material' facts of political and social history.

Critics of the 'new paradigm', as they sometimes call themselves, have developed a special language in which to express their ideas. This 'discursive practice' makes their work sometimes not immediately comprehensible to 'unreconstituted' readers, who are apt to be puzzled by the pleasureless dislike for literary texts which often seems to characterise such critical writing. A decade of 'crisis' has not altered the mixed methods of teaching English that prevail in most institutions, though LITERARY THEORY and CULTURAL STUDIES have become subjects for study in their own right.

Criterion. (Gk. 'means of judging, test') A standard of judgment. In considering an evaluation of a literary work, it is essential to be aware of what critical criteria have been used. Even sophisticated critics sometimes complain that a work falls short in some manner that is irrelevant to the writer's achievement. F.R. Leavis, for example, in his essay 'Shelley' in *Revaluation* (1936), subtly misconstrues Shelley's 'Ode to the West Wind' (1820): 'what again, are those "tangled boughs of Heaven and Ocean"? They stand for nothing that Shelley could have pointed to in the scene before him.' Yet the whole drift of the poem shows that Shelley is not attempting to describe 'the scene before him', but writing a poem which is symbolist rather than realistic in its logic.

Criticism. (Gk. 'judgment') The INTERPRETATION, analysis, classification, and ultimately judgment of works of literature, which has become a kind of literary genre itself. A broad division can be made between PRACTICAL CRITICISM, which focuses on the examination of individual texts, and theoretical criticism, which discusses the nature of literature, and the relationship between literature, the critic and society. A similar distinction also exists between DESCRIPTIVE CRITICISM, which attempts to describe literature as it is, and PRESCRIPTIVE CRITICISM, which (sometimes unconsciously) argues how literature ought to be.

The aims and conventions of literary criticism, like literature itself, have changed constantly through the ages, and there are many different types of critical approach. In an essay on the 'Orientation of Critical Theories', the opening chapter of *The Mirror and the Lamp* (1953), the contemporary American critic M.H. Abrams explores the diversity of critical approach via a simple diagram of the elements involved:

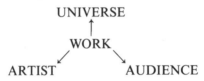

Abrams explains that theories of art can be defined according to the way in which they tend to concentrate on any of the three variables at the corners of the triangle, the universe, the artist or the audience. Thus a MIMETIC theory of art sees the work of art as reflecting the universe like a mirror: Aristotle, who defined art as imitation in his *Poetics* (fourth century BC), is the prime example. A PRAGMATIC theory of art sees the work as a means to an end, to teach or instruct: the focus is changed to the work's effect on an audience. The assumption of most NEOCLASSICAL criticism from Sir Philip Sidney's *An Apology for Poetry* (1595) to Dr Johnson's many critical studies at the end of the eighteenth century is that literature serves a pragmatic purpose to teach by delighting. Expressive theories centre on the artist: Wordsworth's definition of poetry as 'the spontaneous overflow of powerful feelings' in his 'Preface' to the *Lyrical Ballads* (1800) is typical, and nearly all Romantic and nineteenth-century criticism generally regards art as primarily concerned with expressing the poet's feelings or psyche.

The NEW CRITICISM of the twentieth century, and many of the other critical theories which followed it, dominated the study of literature in universities and schools until the 1980s. This may be termed OBJECTIVE CRITICISM, which focuses chiefly on the text, the work of art itself, and attempts to regard it as standing free from the poet, the audience and the world. From about 1950 till 1980 'criticism' tended to mean practical criticism. Sometimes in this sense 'criticism' is distinguished from scholarship: 'criticism' concerns itself exclusively with the appreciation and interpretation of individual texts, while scholarship encompasses literary history and the establishment of correct versions of texts (TEXTUAL CRITICISM).

The analysis of individual texts, combined with some literary history and critical theory, is still the basic menu of undergraduate study provided in modern universities. Students, when given an essay title 'Write a critical study of X', need to avoid confusing the literary meaning of 'criticism' with its day-to-day meaning of 'adverse judgment': this error is easily made, because many twentieth-century critics (notably the influential English critic, F.R. Leavis) often justify their high evaluation of a particular text or author by savagely dismissing other similar texts or authors, turning the evaluation of literature into a kind of boxing match, in which 'minor writers' are eliminated by 'great works'.

Since the 1970s traditional understanding of the relationships between universe, writer, audience and text has been put into turmoil by the approaches to language known as STRUCTURALISM and DECONSTRUCTION, which place in doubt any simple mimetic notion of language itself, and therefore literature; the security that words have meaning because they directly symbolise the things contained in the world outside (the universe) has been attacked. Language has come to be seen as a framework creating 'truth' and 'reality', rather than simply describing things. The consequences of these ideas for literature and criticism have been wide-ranging. One result has been the proliferation of LITERARY THEORY as a subject for study in its own right, usually concentrating on the theory of criticism rather than literature itself. Another has been the shift away from the internal mechanisms of texts themselves in order to show them in the context of society and politics, possibly by adopting MARXIST or FEMINIST critical perspectives. Both these approaches have attacked the concept of the CANON, the idea that literature should be composed of a collection of special and highly valued texts. The specific disciplines of NARRATOLOGY and READER-RESPONSE CRITICISM have also grown out of the ferment caused by structuralism.

Critics of consciousness. *See* GENEVA SCHOOL OF CRITICISM.

Critique. (Fr., from Gk. 'fault-finding, judgment') A reasoned critical account of an artistic work, or of any intellectual endeavour, usually expressing a carefully argued adverse judgment, or contrary point of view.

Crown of sonnets. A sequence of seven SONNETS, with the last line of the first the same as the first line of the second, and so on until the last line of the seventh is the same as the opening line of the whole sequence. Donne's 'La Corona' is an example, standing as the Introduction to his 'Holy Sonnets' (1633).

Crusoe myth. *See* ROBINSON CRUSOE MYTH.

Crux. (Lat. 'cross') Short for *crux interpretum*, 'torment of interpreters'. A crux is a difficult point in a text, about which critics disagree; different solutions to the problem may result in widely divergent interpretations of the whole work.

Culteranismo. (Sp. *culto*, 'learned'; a pejorative term due to association with *luteranismo*, 'Lutheranism') A literary movement of seventeenth-century Spain, characterised by its extreme artificiality of style and its elaborate Latinate language. It was opposed by the poet and dramatist Lope de Vega who argued that poetry should be more comprehensible and popular. Also called GONGORISM, after its most famous exponent, Góngora. It was considered antithetical to CONCEPTISMO, in so far as it aimed at artificiality and obscurity of style and allusion, rather than difficulty of subject matter; but in fact the two movements share many features.

Cultural competence. *See* COMPETENCE.

Cultural studies. A name for the educational approach which considers society and its various cultural manifestations – institutions and political systems, the media, plastic arts such as painting and sculpture, music, writing of all kinds. Traditional literature (in the form of an established CANON of highly valued texts) may (or may not) be considered alongside other kinds of writing and other modes of artistic expression.

Culture. (Lat. 'cultivation, tilled ground') This concept can be used in at least three different ways, which interconnect, and are, to some extent, liable to be in competition with each other. In its broadest sense 'culture' refers to all activities and value systems within a society. Less inclusively, it encompasses the intellectual and artistic activities and products of a society. Or it can be used evaluatively and selectively, to describe the 'best' artistic activities and products in a society.

In general the wider, neutral definition has tended to gain currency in the late part of the twentieth century, and the evaluative use of the term (as in Arnold's *Culture and Anarchy*, 1869) has been replaced by the notion of 'high' culture, with the concomitant concept of 'popular' or 'mass' culture.

Cultures, The Two. A controversy chiefly between F.R. Leavis and C.P. Snow about the relative merits of education in the sciences or the humanities; it started after a lecture delivered by Snow in 1959 (published as *The Two Cultures and the Scientific Revolution* in the same year). Snow, who was both a scientist and a novelist, stressed the need to bridge the gap between the traditional 'literary' culture and the world of science and technology.

Curtal sonnet. A short (ten-line) version of the SONNET invented by G.M. Hopkins. His well-known poem 'Pied Beauty' (written 1877) is an example.

Cycle. (Gk. 'circle') A group of poems, plays, stories or novels which are grouped together, either by the author or by tradition, and which all deal, more or less, with some central theme or themes. Shakespeare's *Sonnets* (published 1609) are one of many sonnet-cycles in the sixteenth and seventeenth centuries, while his history plays are commonly organised into two cycles, *Henry VI* to *Richard III*, written between 1590 and 1593, and *Richard II* to *Henry V*, written between 1595 and 1599.

Cynghanedd. Poetic conventions, involving INTERNAL RHYMES and ALLITE-RATION, in Welsh poetry. In the nineteenth century G.M. Hopkins and in the twentieth century Robert Graves were interested in this technique.

D

Dactyl. (Gk. 'finger joints') A metrical FOOT. In English versification a strongly stressed syllable, followed by two weak ones: tum-ti-ti, as in the word 'strawberry'. Dactylic metres are not very common in English verse. Thomas Hardy's 'The Voice' (1914) is an example:

> Woman much missed, how you call to me, call to me,
> Saying that now you are not as you were
> When you had changed from the one who was all to me,
> But as at first, when our day was fair.

See also METRE.

Dada. (Fr. 'hobby-horse') A deliberately meaningless title for an anarchical literary and artistic movement begun in 1916 at the Cabaret Voltaire in Zurich by the Romanian Tristan Tzara with the French sculptor Hans Arp and the German pacifist H. Ball. The purpose of Dada was a NIHILISTIC revolt against all bourgeois ideas of rationality, meaning, form and order. Its artists and poets used COLLAGE to arrange objects and words into meaningless and illogical patterns. By the early 1920s it was overtaken by SURREALISM which allied many dadaist techniques to psychological theory. *See also* ALEATORY, AVANT-GARDE, MODERNISM.

Dance of Death, *Danse macabre.* A MOTIF popular in medieval and Renaissance art and literature: a procession in which the living are led to the grave by the dead. Allegorical pictures and verses in the cloisters of the church of the Holy Innocents in Paris are a famous example. So too is a series of woodcuts (*c.*1538), said to be by Hans Holbein, representing Death dancing with all kinds of different persons, starting with Adam and Eve, and moving through the various professions and social classes from the king to the beggar. The Dance of Death is more common in artistic representation than in literature, but Chaucer's *The Pardoner's Tale* (late fourteenth century) alludes to the idea: three revellers set out in a search for Death, who has killed one of their friends, and they find him.

The Dance of Death is a specific example of the general fascination with death in medieval and Renaissance art, showing itself in the occurrence of MEMENTO MORI (reminders of death) such as skulls and skeletons. REVENGE TRAGEDIES, as, for instance, Webster's *The Duchess of Malfi* (*c*.1613), show a similar preoccupation with the macabre.

Danse macabre. *See* DANCE OF DEATH.

Dead metaphor. *See* METAPHOR.

Débat. (Fr. 'contest') A poetic debate on some moral or political subject. In the thirteenth-century Middle English poem ascribed to Nicholas of Guildford, *The Owl and the Nightingale*, the two birds represent two contrasting points of view, or different kinds of poet: the solemnly religious owl versus the worldly, amorous nightingale. Chaucer has his birds in *The Parliament of Fowls* (late fourteenth century) discuss the various merits of three eagles who wish to marry a female. The *débat* was popular also in French poetry of the twelfth and thirteenth centuries.

Decadence. (Lat. 'falling away') Applied usually to certain aspects of French FIN DE SIÈCLE literature (*c*.1870–1900). Many writers at this time cultivated the most artificial kinds of literature and manners, searching for bizarre, even perverse subjects. Gautier summed up many Decadent ideas in the 'Notice' to an edition of Baudelaire's poems *Les fleurs du mal* in 1868. Art was opposed to 'nature', including 'natural' morality and behaviour. The cultivated dandy, elaborately unnatural and self-consciously artificial in every aspect of appearance and behaviour, was esteemed. The young poet Rimbaud's programme of 'the systematic derangement of the senses' led to further excesses of behaviour, both in sexual experiments and in drug-taking. Huysmans's *A rebours* ('Against Nature'), published in 1884, describes many of the precepts of Decadence in the form of a novel.

A few English writers copied the style and subjects of the French Decadents. Oscar Wilde and Ernest Dowson both wrote poetry about prostitutes, and other such subjects which would have been unheard of in the mid-nineteenth century. Wilde's *The Picture of Dorian Gray* (1891) is about a decadent way of life.

The term 'decadent' can also apply to any culture in decline, like the late Roman Empire after *c*.AD50 or the Byzantine era of Greek culture; any work of art or literature which takes pleasure in perversity, cruelty, violence, death or immorality may also be justly labelled decadent. *See also* AESTHETICISM.

Decasyllable. (Gk. 'ten syllables') A line of verse of ten syllables: extremely common in French and English verse, but in English stress-based scansion it is usually resolved into a line of PENTAMETER. *See also* METRE.

Decentre, decentring. The process of removing power from some perceived centre of authority, whether it be Man or the TRANSCENDENTAL SIGNIFIED, as in the case of ANDROCENTRIC and LOGOCENTRIC world-views respectively. In much POST-STRUCTURALIST criticism, literature itself, previously regarded as a collection of highly valued texts with special authority, has been 'decentred'. *See also* CANON, PRIVILEGING.

Deconstruction, deconstructive criticism. A blanket title for certain radical critical theories which revise and develop the tenets of STRUCTURALIST criticism. Many of the ideas of deconstruction originate in three books by the French philosopher Jacques Derrida, all of which were published in France in 1967 and have been translated into English with the following titles: *Speech and Phenomena* (1973), *Of Grammatology* (1976) and *Writing and Difference* (1978). Derrida's books are difficult to read and he freely coins new terms for his concepts, not all of which have become common in the discussion of literature.

Derrida believes that all notions of the existence of an absolute meaning in language (a 'TRANSCENDENTAL SIGNIFIED') are wrong. He argues that even in speech, the idea that the speaker might fully possess the significance of the spoken words, if only for a moment, is unproven and a false assumption. Yet this assumption about speech and writing (where there is not even the consciousness of the speaker present to validate meaning) has dominated Western thought, and it should be the aim of the philosopher and critic to 'deconstruct' the philosophy and literature of the past to show this false assumption and reveal the essential paradox at the heart of language. As in structuralist analysis, Derrida sees any individual statement as depending for its meaning on its relationship with its surrounding system of language: it can only derive its meaning by its DIFFERENCE (which Derrida spells *différance*) from all the other possible meanings, unlimited in number. No more than the illusory effect of meaning is possible in contact with these unlimited different possible readings: meaning does not reside in the SIGNIFIER. Interpretation of meaning is then an endless movement that can never arrive at an absolute, ultimate signified. Thus the 'play of signification' is endless ('playful' was a favourite approving word for criticism in the 1980s). To 'deconstruct' a text is merely to show how texts deconstruct themselves because of this fundamental indeterminateness at the core of language. One reason for the difficulty of Derrida's own writing is that he is aware of his own texts deconstructing themselves.

'Deconstruction' attacks the very basis of Western scholarship and thought. Derrida's ideas have been taken up, developed and fiercely attacked, especially in America. British criticism, with its strong educational, pragmatic emphasis, has tended to lag behind in the area of highly abstract theoretical dispute. Most British studies of critical theory consist of re-working and explaining ideas which have originated in France and the USA. The word 'deconstruction' is now often used merely to refer to the revelation of partially hidden meanings in a text, especially those that illuminate aspects of its relationship with its social and political context, as is common in MARXIST CRITICISM. Indeed in its weakest use, to 'deconstruct' may mean no more than to reveal the way meaning in any kind of text is a 'construction' by the writer or the reader, open to dissection by the critic, who also has to construct meaning; in other words, it has become a jargon word for 'analyse' or 'interpret'. *See also* APORIA, LOGOCENTRICISM, MISE-EN-ABYME, PLURAL-ISM, POST-STRUCTURALISM, SUPPLEMENT.

Decorum. (Lat. 'what is decent') To use the proper and fitting style for every literary kind is to obey the principle of 'decorum'. Horace's *Ars Poetica* (*c*.20BC) and Aristotle's *Poetics* (fourth century BC) were major Classical precedents for the doctrine of literary decorum, which reached a peak of significance during the seventeenth and eighteenth centuries. The hierarchy of genres, with epic and tragedy at the top, was part of the concept. It was thought that epic and tragedy should deal only with gods, heroes, kings and the highest social classes, and that this elevated subject matter should be dealt with only in a suitably high style. In Britain the models of the Bible and Shakespeare meant that writers always had before their eyes great literature which mixed low incidents with matters of the utmost seriousness. Nevertheless the theory of decorum led writers to cultivate a specialist POETIC DICTION; Wordsworth's and Coleridge's *Lyrical Ballads* (1798) was a deliberate rejection of decorum in style, genre and subject matter. *See also* NEOCLASSICISM.

Deep structure. The basic 'deep' structures of meaning in a language can be described in abstract terms (not unlike mathematical formulae); hypothetical elemental forms are transformed into the actual **surface structure** of language by means of the grammar known to native speakers. This distinction, invented by Chomsky, is used in linguistic and semantic analysis. A commonly cited example is the difference between active and passive sentence forms. 'The boy kicked the ball' shares the same deep structure as 'the ball was kicked by the boy', but has a different surface structure.

Similar concepts have been applied to the analysis of narratives: the elemental content of a work can be inferred, so as to be able to clarify aspects of its final 'surface' form. Exploring the 'deep structure' of narratives is more abstract than deducing the basic STORY of an individual work; its aim is to arrive at a kind of overall grammar applicable to narrative structures. *See also* ACTANT, DISCOURS, HISTOIRE, NARRATOLOGY.

Defamiliarisation. 'Making strange'; the capacity of some kinds of writing to strip away familiarity from the world about us, so that we see things anew. With some writers this method or purpose has become almost a programme. Wordsworth in the 'Preface' to *Lyrical Ballads* (1800) describes his intention to choose 'incidents and situations from common life' and 'to throw over them a certain colouring of imagination, whereby ordinary things should be presented to the mind in an unusual aspect'. Shelley is even more direct in *The Defence of Poetry* (1840, written 1821): 'Poetry lifts the veil from the hidden beauty of the world, and makes familiar objects be as if they were not familiar.' In the 1970s MARTIAN poets invented riddle-like metaphors with which to amuse and refresh their readers' perceptions.

The concept of defamiliarisation (or **estrangement**) was formulated by the Russian FORMALISTS who argued that literary language was different from ordinary language not least because of its capacity to 'make strange'. Departures from linguistic norms lead to the FOREGROUNDING of unusual features, which is common in literary language. *See also* LITERARINESS.

Defective foot. In verse an incomplete FOOT, common especially in TROCHAIC verse, where the final foot of each line often loses a syllable to create a MASCULINE ENDING, an effect called CATALEXIS. *See* METRE for further discussion of these terms.

Deictic, deixis. (Gk. 'showing directly') A term from linguistics: deictics are words (referring to person, place and time), which are dependent for their meaning on the surrounding context in which a statement is made. Pronouns like 'I', 'you', 'that' and 'them', and adverbs like 'there' or 'then', may rely for meaning on information outside the sentences in which they occur. Poets often use deixis to imply situations and attitudes that are not fully articulated in the poem's surface meaning. Yeats, for example, often uses 'that' and 'those' to suggest a rhetorical urgency in his poetry, as in the opening line of 'Sailing to Byzantium' (1928), '*That* is no country for old men', or 'Byzantium' (1933):

> *Those* images that yet
> Fresh images beget,
> *That* dolphin-torn, *that* gong-tormented sea.

Deism. (Lat. *deus*, 'God') The doctrine, typical of the eighteenth-century ENLIGHTENMENT, that belief in God is a natural consequence of reasonableness, and does not need the dogma of religious institutions or divine revelations to support it. Deists tend to blur all religions together as manifestations of the same God. They see the perfection of the world as rational evidence for God's existence, and feel that God, having completed the Creation, leaves the Universe to pursue its proper existence. Humanity has its allotted role in the world, dignified by the maturity of intellect; religion should be above the superstitions and rituals of particular cultures. Some Deists, such as Rousseau, also allowed an appeal to feeling to be natural proof of the existence of God.

Demotic. (Gk. 'of the people') A word applied to the popular, simplified form of the ancient Egyptian script (as distinguished from the HIERATIC). A demotic style in English is one based on the language of ordinary speech, and intended to be readily comprehensible to ordinary people.

Demotion. This term, in conjunction with PROMOTION, can be used to describe different forms of metrical SUBSTITUTION in lines of English stress-based verse. Demotion is the use of a stressed syllable in a position normally occupied by an unstressed one. Promotion is the opposite effect, that occurs when an insignificant and weakly stressed syllable bears the metrical beat. A stanza (LXVII) from Tennyson's *In Memoriam* (1850) illustrates both:

> When on my bed the moonlight falls,
> I know that in thy place of rest
> By that broad water of the west,
> There comes a glory on the walls.

'Broad' in line three is demoted; 'of' in the same line is promoted, as are several other small words in the example (like 'in' and 'on'). The frustration or fulfilment of an established metrical norm is an essential aspect of verse, and, in a reading, variations like these lead to the careful enunciation of the lines and avoid monotony: demoted syllables do not lose all their natural stress, nor are promoted syllables fully stressed. *See also* METRE.

Denotation, denote. (Lat. 'mark out') To denote is to signify; to mean exactly; the meaning 'denoted' by a word or group of words is that to which the words refer most simply and precisely. Denotation is commonly opposed to CONNOTATION, which is all the possible ASSOCIATIONS, nuances, hints and suggestions contained in words, that may also be a part of their meaning. To take an individual example: the word 'Autumn' denotes the time of year between summer and winter, in Britain September to November; but the word is full of connotations (which may be different for different people): Keats's 'To Autumn' (1820) gives one person's response to the word's connotations.

Poets continually use words in such a way as to suggest their connotative meanings; when Shelley in 'Ode to the West Wind' (1820) refers to 'The Blue Mediterranean, where he lay,/Lulled by the coil of his crystalline streams', the single word 'coil', because of its conno-

tations, is enough to turn the Mediterranean into a serpent. *See also*
REFERENTIAL LANGUAGE.

Dénouement. (Fr. 'unknotting') The final unfolding of a PLOT: the point at
which the reader's expectations, be they hopes or fears, about what will
happen to the characters are finally satisfied or denied.

Description. (Lat. 'writing down') One of the basic skills and pleasures of
literature: the creation or representation in words of objects, people,
behaviour or scenes. Along with DIALOGUE and the unfolding of the·
events of a NARRATIVE, description is a vital element in the novel, but
vital also in poetry and all kinds of literary activity.

Description involves the selection of details, and no two writers will
select identical details even in describing similar objects. Description is
therefore a key to the writer's or narrator's POINT OF VIEW, and quickly
acquires significance and meaning beyond the barely representational.

Descriptive criticism. The critical approach to literature which attempts, in
the phrase used by Matthew Arnold in 'The Function of Criticism at the
Present Time' (1864), 'to see the object in itself as it really is', and
describe the individuating features of texts so as to allow discrimination
between different kinds of writing, without reference to any over-riding
linguistic, literary or social theory.

Sometimes weak critical writing may be labelled 'merely descriptive',
suggesting that it does no more than retell what is already clear, explicit
and obvious in the text, and thereby fails to analyse those aspects of the
text that are most significant and special. *See also* CRITICISM.

Detachment. *See* DISTANCE.

Deus ex machina. (Lat. 'god out of a machine') In Greek drama a god was
sometimes lowered on to the stage by a piece of machinery, if such an
intervention was needed to assist or complete the unfolding of the plot.
The phrase is often used pejoratively to indicate an unexpected,
improbable and unwarranted twist in a plot, merely there apparently
because the writer can think of no other way of resolving the situation
which has been created. Improbable coincidences are common in novels
with elaborate plots such as Fielding's *Tom Jones* (1749) or Dickens's
Bleak House (1852–3).

Device. (Lat. 'control, divide') Any literary method or technique can be
called a device; the word usually implies, in a non-derogatory way, an
understanding of the text as a carefully wrought stretch of language
carefully designed to manipulate the reader's responses. *See also*
FUNCTION, LITERARINESS.

Diachronic (Gk. 'through time') A term invented by Saussure in his
influential *Course in General Linguistics* (1915) to designate the study of
language through its developing history. This had been the characteristic approach to language by nineteenth-century philologists.

The historical approach is distinguished from the other way of investigating language, the 'synchronic', which involves the very different task of examining language as a system in use at a particular moment in time.

Dialect. (Gk. 'way of speaking, language of a district') In most European languages the particular style and manner of speaking of one particular area has come to be considered the chief language in which to compose literary works, either for cultural or political reasons. During the MIDDLE ENGLISH PERIOD, a variety of different dialects, the versions of English spoken in different areas, were considered equally good as media for literary expression. After about 1400 the dialect of London and the south Midlands gradually came to dominate literature, partly because Chaucer seemed foremost in the poetic world, but also because of the rising importance of London as the commercial and political centre of England, and eventually Britain. Meanwhile the spoken varieties of English have continued in use until the present day, and have been used also for literary purposes, for example, in the Dorset dialect poems of William Barnes. In Scotland a coherent tradition of Scottish literature can be traced back to the Middle Ages: Scots do not like to think of their language as a dialect of English and prefer to consider themselves as speaking a separate language.

The standard variety of English is called **R.P.** (Received Pronunciation). Up till about 1950 it was thought desirable to speak in this manner, but the growth of regional feeling in Britain, combined with a shift in attitudes to class and culture, has made the dominance of R.P. less significant in contemporary Britain.

Dialectic. (Gk. 'art of discourse') Logical disputation; the investigation of truth by discussion, especially as exercised by Socrates in Plato's dialogues (fourth century BC), a process of question and answer which gradually eliminates error and moves towards the truth.

The German philosopher Hegel saw the progression of thought and, therefore, human history as a THESIS which gives rise to an ANTITHESIS, and out of this opposition emerges a SYNTHESIS, which in turn becomes a new thesis. MARXISTS have borrowed this pattern of reality discerned by Hegel; they too see history as an inevitable dialectic.

Dialogic. Texts which allow the expression of a variety of points of view, in the manner of dialogue in drama, leaving the reader with open questions, are 'dialogic'. The opposite kind of text is **monologic**, dominated by a single way of perceiving things, usually presumed to be the author's. A vogue word in the 1980s, borrowed from the writings of the Russian critic Bakhtin. In *Problems of Dostoevsky's Art* (1929) Bakhtin contrasts the monologic novels of Tolstoy, in which all the characters reflect Tolstoy's purposes, with the dialogic or POLYPHONIC forms created by Dostoevsky, in which a variety of independent and equal voices are allowed to speak through the characters. In a long essay, 'Discourse on the Novel' (1934–5), Bakhtin argues that the novel form is essentially dialogic. *See also* PLURALISM.

Dialogue. (Gk. 'conversation') (1) The speech and conversation of characters in any kind of literary work. (2) A genre consisting of a discussion between characters. Plato's dialogues of Socrates (fourth century BC) are amongst the earliest and most famous examples of the dialogue genre. The form has been revived from time to time; a notably successful version was Landor's *Imaginary Conversations* (1824–9) in which he invented discussions on all kinds of topics between famous men, living and dead.

Diary. (Lat. 'daily') A day-by-day record of a person's life, written for his or her own use and not necessarily with any intention to publish it. The *Diaries* (1660–9) of Samuel Pepys, written in his own secret shorthand, are justly renowned; they combine his interest in public events with candid examination of his own sexuality, resulting in a document fascinating both as history and psychology. The *Journals* (1762–95) of James Boswell are equally varied in their interests: they were written with some view to publication, or at least circulation among his friends. Since the development of AUTOBIOGRAPHY as a common literary form, from the early nineteenth century onwards many writers have kept diaries with the intention eventually of publishing their recollections of their life. Politicians also commonly write diaries of their time in office, for the benefit of future historians.

Fictional diaries are not infrequent as the basis for novels: Defoe's *Robinson Crusoe* (1719), Goethe's *The Sorrows of Young Werther* (1774) and Sartre's *Nausea* (1938) are three very different examples.

Diatribe. (Gk. 'waste, while away, discourse') A severely critical discourse; an angry, violent and uncontrolled verbal attack on something or someone. *See also* FLYTING, INVECTIVE, LAMPOON.

Diction. (Lat. 'saying, mode of expression') The choice of words in a work of literature; the kind of vocabulary used. The diction of a work may be ABSTRACT or CONCRETE, simple or elaborate, colloquial or formal, racy or dignified, LATINATE or Anglo-Saxon in derivation, LITERAL or full of FIGURATIVE LANGUAGE, exact or vague, densely packed with nouns, floridly adjectival or full of active verbs, etc. *See also* POETIC DICTION, STYLE.

Didacticism. (Gk. 'teaching') Didactic literature is designed to instruct or to persuade. Its purpose is not purely or primarily imaginative, though many didactic works are prodigious works of the imagination, in which the imaginative material is ordered to illustrate a particular doctrine.

Nowadays, of course, there is an enormous quantity of didactic writing published, but educational textbooks or works of reference are not usually considered to be 'literature'. However, in former ages, this distinction did not exist. Greek and Roman literature, for example, is rich in didactic works. Hesiod's *Works and Days* (eighth century BC) gives a realistic picture in poetry of rustic life, filled with advice, as does Virgil's *Georgics* (37–30BC), which was based on the Greek model. In English literature didactic poetry has also been written as a guide to practical matters, such as John Philips's *Cyder* (1708), on the technology of cider-making, an example of the eighteenth-century vogue for GEORGICS. Or it may simply aim to inform the reader in a more general way, like Erasmus Darwin's scientific poem *The Botanic Garden* (1789, 1791). The aim of the poem may be philosophical exposition, or theological, like Milton's *Paradise Lost* (1667). Clearly allegories, such as Bunyan's *Pilgrim's Progress* (1678, 1684), and satires, which aim to persuade the reader to a point of view (typical of eighteenth-century poets like Pope), in quite different ways are both didactic. Didactic poetry of the practical kind has been unfashionable from the mid-eighteenth century onwards; and nowadays the word 'didactic' is often used as a pejorative, suggesting that the work of art has somehow been betrayed into serving a purpose other than its own artistic ends. In the twentieth century the NEW CRITICS stressed the autonomy of the literary text, endorsing the 'art for art's sake' doctrine of the late nineteenth century. *See also* AESTHETICISM, PROPAGANDA.

Diegesis. (Gk. 'guide through') An old word for NARRATIVE, originally employed by Plato to denote reported speech in drama as opposed to imitations of direct speech, which he called MIMESIS.

'Diegesis' is used in NARRATOLOGY to specify the elemental STORY 'level' of a narrative, to be distinguished from the 'higher' level of its actual narration. Thus the diegetic level of *Wuthering Heights* (1847), a tale that begins with Heathcliff's arrival at the house long before the actual moment at which the book opens, has to be unravelled from the levels of its two main narrators and complicated time schemes. Lockwood and Nelly Dean are both **intradiegetic** narrators, as they are characters in the story on the diegetic level, and they do not know more than other characters. Strictly speaking Nelly is a third-degree narrator (**hypodiegetic**), since she tells the story to Lockwood.

A narrator who is 'above' the narrated story, such as the omniscient narrator of *Tom Jones* (1749), is called **extradiegetic**. Both intradiegetic and extradiegetic narrators may participate in the stories they tell. Nelly Dean and Lockwood are participants, and are therefore **homodiegetic**, while the narrator of *Tom Jones* is **heterodiegetic**.

It is easy to confuse these various terms, and indeed they are more elastic than they may seem, and require careful application in individual cases. For example, in *Wuthering Heights*, Nelly knows much more than Lockwood about the events that occur in the novel, and therefore it might be argued that she is an extradiegetic narrator, or at some subtle level between intra- and extradiegetic.

Difference, *différance,* *différence.* A major feature of STRUCTURALISM is the network of insights that originate in the Swiss linguistician Saussure's account of language as a system working through differentiation: the meaning of 'cat' is not that of 'vat' or 'bat' or 'sat', by means of a structured pattern of differences in sound (PHONEMES). The French linguistic philosopher Derrida agrees with Saussure's emphasis on *différence,* but replaces it with the invented term *différance.* He argues that meaning is never 'present' in words. 'Cat' has no meaning on its own, but only because it is not, 'vat' and 'sat': therefore meaning is always dependent on everything that is not the word itself, and is constantly in a state of being 'deferred'. Derrida's word *différance* is unstable in itself, hovering in French between 'differ' and 'defer', a kind of pun which can never mean one thing, since single, absolute meaning is impossible.

However, *différance* results in more than just AMBIGUITY, which still deals with fixed, if various meanings. The dispersal of meaning, called **dissemination** (another suggestive word implying 'de-' or 'un-meaning', as well as 'spreading widely'), leads to the 'free play' of INTERPRETA-TIONS, without a single fixed signification. Derrida's theories about the instability of meaning in language have obviously offered a striking challenge to many of the practices of traditional literary study and criticism, as well as COMMON-SENSE views of language. *See also* DECON-STRUCTION, LOGOCENTRICISM.

Digression. (Lat. 'step apart') A straying away from the main subject in any kind of writing. The nineteenth-century essayist De Quincey was so digressive that often his digressions far exceed in length his discussion of the supposed subject of the essay: an explanation for this habit might be found in his belief in the value of the mind's intuitive powers of ASSOCIATION.

Dimeter. (Gk. 'two measures') In English versification a line consisting of two feet (*see* METRE). 'Mushrooms' (1960), by Sylvia Plath, is a modern example, each line containing two strong stresses:

> Overnight, very
> Whitely, discreetly,
> Very quietly
>
> Our toes, our noses
> ·Take hold on the loam,
> Acquire the air.

Dionysian. *See* APOLLONIAN/DIONYSIAN.

Diphthong. (Gk. 'two sounds') A syllable in which the tongue and mouth move through different vowel sounds, slurring them together. The following words offer examples: 'foul', 'fear', 'fate'. Diphthongs are usually counted as single syllables in metrical analysis.

Dirge. Originally the religious service in honour of the dead, which commenced with a Psalm beginning *Dirige, Domine . . .* ('Direct me, Lord . . .'). *Dirige* was contracted to 'dirge'. A dirge is now any song of mourning, shorter and less formal that an ELEGY, and intended for singing. Ariel's song for Ferdinand's father, 'Full Fathom Five Thy Father Lies', at I.2 of Shakespeare's *The Tempest* (*c*.1611), is probably the best-known example. *See also* MONODY, PASTORAL ELEGY, THRENODY.

Disbelief, Willing suspension of. *See* ILLUSION.

Discordia concors. (Lat. 'discord in harmony') Dr Johnson's unflattering phrase for the WIT of the METAPHYSICAL POETS in his *Life of Cowley* (1779) which he explains thus: 'a combination of dissimilar images or discovery of occult resemblances in things apparently unlike.'

Discours. A French term with a number of different meanings in relation to the description of texts. It is sometimes translated into English as 'DISCOURSE', a confusingly varied term in itself, and sometimes left in its French form to suggest either of the two following semi-technical uses. *Discours* is opposed to *histoire* in discussing two broadly different types of narration. *Histoire* ('story, history') is a narrative that is impersonal and makes claims to being objective, as, for example, most historical writing or dictionary definitions. *Discours*, on the other hand, is a kind of writing that characteristically assumes a relationship between the 'I' of the writer and the 'you' of the reader, with all the sense of intimacy and colouring that such a method allows.

In NARRATOLOGY *discours*, confusingly, is one of the several terms for the actual final NARRATIVE of the text, as opposed to the raw material of the STORY.

Discourse. (Lat. 'run to and fro, speak at length') Traditionally, conversation, or a serious discussion or examination of a learned topic. In general, 'discourse' refers to the 'how' of a narrative, as opposed to its 'what'. In contemporary literary criticism 'discourse' has come to have many different meanings and emphases. Sometimes it is used to mean not much more than 'a piece of writing'.

The term is used in linguistics to refer to utterances longer than a sentence: **discourse analysis** studies the links between sentences and defines the rules that govern these links. By extension of this idea, 'discourse' can be used to refer to any self-contained body of ideas, opinions, approaches, methods, and the language which contains them. It is the framework of references which are commonly used in relation to a particular topic: for example, a football commentary, a thesis on chemistry, and a story for small children will all have quite separate ways of using language, with different expectations of what their audiences will know and expect, different kinds of grammar and argument, different JARGONS. Considering examples of the 'discursive practices' of a group, such as chemists or football fans, ties language to its social context rather than considering it in abstraction.

Literature contains many different 'discourses' of this kind, and in its entirety is itself a 'discourse', using particular kinds of language in particular ways. A student essay, a work of literary criticism, and a play by Shakespeare are all 'discourses'. When applied to literature 'discourse' is a non-evaluative term in a way that the label 'literature' is not. Its use thus undermines LITERARI-NESS. *See also* DISCOURS.

Discourse analysis. *See* DISCOURSE.

Discovery. The word often used to translate 'anagnorisis', Aristotle's term in his *Poetics* (fourth century BC) for the moment when the PROTAGON-IST in a play learns facts which were formerly unknown, and which will probably lead to the PERIPETEIA or reversal of fortune. Oedipus's realisation that he has married his mother and murdered his father is clearly the classic model, but such moments of discovery are common in comedy and TRAGEDY, and in the DÉNOUEMENT of many novels. *See also* PLOT.

Displacement. *See* PSYCHOANALYTIC CRITICISM.

Dissemination. *See* DIFFERENCE.

Dissertation. (Lat. 'discussion, debate') A written discussion of some learned topic; now most frequently used of scholarship and research work done in academic institutions as part of a degree programme.

Dissociation of sensibility. The phrase invented by T.S. Eliot in his essay 'The Metaphysical Poets' (1921):

> Tennyson and Browning are poets, and they think; but they do not feel their thought as immediately as the odour of a rose. A thought to Donne was an experience: it modified his sensibility. When a poet's mind is perfectly equipped for its work, it is constantly amalgamating disparate experience . . .
> The poets of the seventeenth century . . . possessed a mechanism of sensibility which could devour any kind of experience . . . In the seventeenth century a dissociation of sensibility set in, from which we have never recovered.

Eliot goes on to explain that the influence of Milton and Dryden aggravated this dissociation: 'While the language became more refined, the feeling became more crude.'

This view of English literature had considerable vogue until the 1950s. The shift in poetic sensibility was thought to be connected with the growth of scientific thought. It is now generally felt that Eliot's fascinating theory has no historical validity, though it is a valuable indication of Eliot's own tastes and interests in poetry.

Dissonance. (Lat. 'disagreement in sound') The arrangement of words so as to create a harsh jangling or disharmony of sounds or rhythm. Poets such as Donne and Browning were criticised for their use of dissonant effects in verse. It is a common effect in modern poetry. Fragments of Ted Hughes's 'Wind' (1957) demonstrate various degrees of dissonance:

> Through the brunt wind that dented the balls of my eyes
> The tent of the hills drummed and strained its guyrope . . .
>
> The wind flung a magpie away and a black-
> Back gull bent like an iron bar slowly.

See also CACOPHONY.

Distance. A word and concept, much the same in meaning as **detachment**, which underlies many comments on literature and criticism. It is almost a premise of critical procedure that a reader should not be too involved with a work of literature: it should exercise the range of his or her sympathies, but in order to appreciate it properly he or she needs to be detached, at a distance from it, and 'disinterested', that capacity to be aloof from practical, immediate and local concerns which was defined and praised by Matthew Arnold in his essay 'The Function of Criticism at the Present Time' (1864). If a reader identifies too strongly with a work of art, whether for sentimental, personal or political reasons, it is felt this will distort a proper judgment of it.

This concept of **aesthetic distance** can be applied also to the relationship between an author and his or her material. Some writers are apparently more involved with their material than others. George Eliot has been criticised (probably wrongly) for being too sympathetic towards the character of Maggie in *The Mill on the Floss* (1860): the book is clearly based on autobiographical experience. It is true that she is close to her characters in this novel, and treats them throughout with seriousness and sympathy: though no less sympathetic or serious in *Middlemarch* (1871–2), she does appear to stand further away from her characters there and guides the reader's reactions towards them, as if she had made clearer and more complete moral judgments about their behaviour. A satirical novelist like Thackeray is even more detached from his characters: in *Vanity Fair* (1847–8) they sometimes seem like dolls or puppets being manipulated for the enjoyment of the reader, and we may find that our easy judgment of their silly goodness or nastiness precludes our full sympathetic engagement with them as imaginary people. These different levels of involvement create different pleasures for the reader: it is not a question of good or bad writing.

For writers of certain political persuasions the notion of aesthetic detachment may seem a false view of the correct relation between writer, material and reader. A COMMITTED writer sees it as his or her duty to write on particular themes in a particular way, and, as a critic will judge according to the same criteria. A MARXIST critic might perceive aesthetic distance as merely another aspect of the IDEOLOGY by which the bourgeoisie subtly reinforces its political and cultural control, a kind of willed neutrality in dealing with texts, which ignores their origins and purposes in society. *See also* ALIENATION EFFECT, INVOLVEMENT.

Distich. (Gk. 'two rows') Another word for a COUPLET: a two-line verse STANZA.

Dithyramb. A Greek choric hymn in honour of Dionysus. Dryden attempts an imitation of the form in *Alexander's Feast* (1697), in which the length of the line is varied from two to seven feet. In general 'dithyrambic' is applied to a wildly enthusiastic song or chant. *See also* FOOT, RHAPSODY.

Divergence. (Lat. 'bending apart') In linguistics, divergence is the tendency of DIALECTS to grow less and less like each other, in the absence of strong links with a standard dialect. The word also indicates a departure from supposed linguistic norms, which can lead to FOREGROUNDING and DEFAMILIARISATION, common enough in many areas of language use, and readily observable in poetry, for example.

Document. (Lat. 'official paper, proof') Written evidence or information of an official or exactly 'truthful' sort, such as certificates of identity, state papers, letters, diaries, newspapers.

Documentary. (*adj.*) The adjective can be applied to any play or novel based on documents of various kinds, which attempts therefore a reconstruction of an event in an exact historical rather than imaginative manner. The author will, of course, provide his or her own interpretation of events, and may be forced by gaps in the documentary evidence into invention. In film and television a documentary (*n.*) is a non-fictional account of a political or social issue or event. *See also* BLUE BOOK, FACTION.

Doggerel. (Presumably from the contemptuous associations of 'dog': 'Dog-Latin' is bad Latin) Bad verse. Ill-constructed, rough, clumsy, crude versification. It may be deliberately written to amuse; or 'doggerel' may be a pejorative term. *See also* HUDIBRASTIC VERSE, LIGHT VERSE, MACARONIC VERSE, NONSENSE, SKELTONICS.

Dolce stil nuovo. (It. 'sweet new style') A term used by Dante in his *Purgatory* (*c*.1310) to describe his own style, but referring more widely to the lyric style of thirteenth-century writers like Guinizelli and Cavalcanti who were much influenced by the COURTLY LOVE poetry of the TROUBADOUR tradition.

Domain. (O. Fr. 'private property') A word with a variety of meanings in linguistics, two of which are sometimes drawn upon in discussing literature. It may designate the area of experience referred to by a particular set of related terms, such as colour words or sociological terms. More often, however, it refers to the 'area' of a social group or institution (such as the school, the seminar room, the family home, the law court), each of which has its own linguistic norms and expectations. Thus the 'domain' of literary criticism is the school and academic institution. *See also* DISCOURSE.

Don Juan myth. Don Juan is the proverbial seducer of women, heartless and wicked, but charming. Traditionally the wife he betrays is called Elvira. The Spanish story was first dramatised by Tirso de Molina in *El Burlador de Sevilla* (*c*.1630). Molière's *Dom Juan ou Le Festin de Pierre* (1665) is a version of the story. In Mozart's operatic treatment of the story, *Don Giovanni* (1787), the seducer, watched by his servant Leporello, is finally dragged off to hell by the animated statue of the Commendatore who has been murdered earlier in the opera while attempting to stop the Don ravishing his daughter.

In English literature, Shadwell's play *The Libertine* (1675) deals with the theme, as does Shaw's *Man and Superman* (1905), and Browning's poem *Fifine at the Fair* (1872). Byron's enormous epic satire *Don Juan*, published in sixteen cantos between 1819 and 1824, gives a new perspective to the myth by turning the Don into a would-be virtuous young man pursued and seduced by women.

Donnée. (Fr. 'given') A *donnée* is the experience, idea, word or phrase which was the original impulse for a complete work of art.

Double entendre. (Fr. 'hearing twice') From the French term for an AMBIGUITY, *à double entente*; used in English almost exclusively to imply a PUN with a sexual or bawdy meaning.

Double plot. Many Elizabethan plays generate interest via their PLOT plus a strong SUBPLOT, the latter either containing a parallel series of events, such as the relationship between Gloucester and his sons mirroring that of Lear and his daughters in Shakespeare's *King Lear* (*c*.1605); or the subplot may be a contrast to the main story, in the manner of Falstaff's comic episodes in *Henry IV*, Parts 1 and 2 (*c*.1597, *c*.1598). Triple or multiple plots, as in *A Midsummer Night's Dream* (*c*.1595-6), are also common.

Double rhyme. Another name for FEMININE RHYME, or a RHYME involving two syllables.

Drama. (Gk. 'deed, action, play') The form of literature intended to be performed usually in some kind of theatre: drama comes to life when it is interpreted in the performance of actors, who adopt the roles of the characters and speak the dialogue, along with appropriate actions, all of which have usually been invented for them by a playwright. Reading plays, without trying to imagine them on the stage or in performance, is apt to distort them. *See also* ACT, CHORUS, CHRONICLE PLAY, COMEDY, DRAMATIC IRONY, DUMB SHOW, FOLK DRAMA (*under* FOLKLORE), MASQUE, MELODRAMA, MIRACLE PLAY, MORALITY PLAY, PANTOMIME, PLOT, SCENERY, SOLILOQUY, TRAGEDY, TRAGICOMEDY.

Dramatic irony. A feature of many plays: it occurs when the development of the PLOT allows the audience to possess more information about what is happening than some of the characters themselves have. The most famous example is from Sophocles's *Oedipus Rex* (*c*. 430BC), when the audience has understood that Oedipus has killed his father and married his mother, while he himself remains ignorant of this truth, insistently and angrily questioning the other characters, a process which eventually leads to his painful recognition of his fate. *See also* IRONY.

Dramatic monologue. *See* MONOLOGUE.

Dramatis personae. (Lat. 'characters of the play') A list of the characters in a play, usually printed at the beginning of the text.

Dramatisation. A play constructed from some pre-existing narrative. The MYSTERY PLAYS were dramatisations of Bible stories. From the eighteenth century on, novels have been frequently and successfully dramatised. The practice is still common in television.

Dramaturgy. The practice and theory of drama. The word comes from an old word for a playwright: dramaturge (Gk. 'play-worker').

Dream vision. A term usually restricted to certain medieval narrative poems, in which the narrator falls asleep, and dreams the events which he relates. Often he may be guided by a person or animal to some other world. Dante being guided by Virgil through Hell in *The Divine Comedy* (*c*.1304–21) is a typical example. Many others of the greatest medieval poems are also dream visions, including the *Roman de la Rose* (thirteenth century) by Guillaume de Lorris and Jean de Meun, Langland's *Piers Plowman*, the anonymous *Pearl*, and Chaucer's early *The Book of the Duchess* and *The House of Fame* (all fourteenth century). The form is a natural vehicle for ALLEGORY: Bunyan's *The Pilgrim's Progress* (1678, 1684) is set in the frame of a dream.

Examples of the dream vision can be found in the poetry of nineteenth-century ROMANTICS, such as Keats and Shelley, and twentieth-century SYMBOLISTS, such as Yeats. A prose version of the form is Lewis Carroll's *Alice's Adventures in Wonderland* (1865).

Dub poetry. A special kind of PERFORMANCE POETRY originating in Jamaica in the 1970s, and popular in England during the 1980s. Its name is said to have come from the practice of disc-jockeys who 'dubbed' their own words on to records. It is characterised by the energetic speech idioms and strongly marked rhythms of West Indian English, and it usually deals with the urban experience of black Britons, politics, music and relationships. By 1990, its practitioners, who include Linton Kwesi Johnson, Jean Binta Breeze and Benjamin Zephaniah, had emerged as separate voices, rendering shortlived the stereotyping of their poetry under a single name.

Dumb show. A not uncommon feature of Elizabethan plays was a MIMED version of the PLOT, as is demonstrated by the example which precedes the play-within-the-play in Shakespeare's *Hamlet* (*c*.1601). In *A Mid-summer Night's Dream* (*c*.1595–6) the comic players give a SYNOPSIS of the plot before the real play, and presumably this introductory dumb show was similarly intended to help the audience follow what was about to happen. 'Dumb show' also refers to mimed scenes within a play, also frequent enough, as, for example, the banishment of the heroine in Webster's *The Duchess of Malfi* (*c*.1613).

Duodecimo. (Lat. 'twelfth') A printer's term for the size of book produced when each sheet of paper is folded so as to produce twelve small pages. See also FOLIO, OCTAVO, QUARTO.

Duple metre. A metre based on two-syllable feet, using either the IAMB or TROCHEE. Triple metres are based on three-syllable feet, such as the ANAPAEST and DACTYL. See METRE for further discussion of these terms.

Dysphemism. (Gk. 'unfavourable expression') A harsh or disagreeable manner of description; the opposite of EUPHEMISM. Obscene slang expressions for bodily functions and sex organs are often dysphemisms.

Dystopia. (Gk. 'bad place') An unpleasant imaginary world, the opposite of a UTOPIA.

E

Eclectic. (Gk. 'chosen') Used of philosophers not attached to any school. Now the word usually means 'wide-ranging in taste' or 'drawing upon a large number of sources and influences'.

Eclogue. (Lat. 'short poem', from Gk. 'selection') Virgil's *Bucolics* or *Eclogues* (42–37BC) were modelled on the Greek pastoral poetry of Theocritus. An eclogue is therefore another word for PASTORAL.

Écriture. (Fr. 'writing') A word often kept in French in literary theoretical discussion because of the special meanings that French writers have at times attached to it. Sartre described the neutral and colourless language of Camus as *l'écriture blanche*. Barthes countered this argument, asserting that no language is style-free (and therefore no language can avoid offering a particular perspective on reality), and he uses the word to mean something like 'personal utterances', or the effect produced by all the features of a literary work that give it individuality. In DECONSTRUCTION the word is often employed in contrast with speech, which, Derrida argues, in Western thought tends to be considered more 'authentic' than writing.

Like DISCOURSE, *écriture* offers a word for writing that avoids separating 'literature' from other kinds of human written expression, and thereby makes the activity of critical writing, for example, on a par with composing a poem. Both are specific examples of *écriture* as a social institution. 'AUTHOR' and 'reader' should be discerned from within the text itself, and are constructed out of the expectations established in different kinds of writing.

Écriture féminine. (Fr. 'feminine writing') A distinctively feminine kind of writing defined by the French feminist Hélène Cixous, in which the sexual, psychic and physical identity of the female gender is given a voice. It is not simply 'what women write', nor indeed does it have to be written by a woman (gender, unlike sexual identity, is considered to be a socially constructed category), but is observable in certain qualities in the text, especially in its escape from the BINARY OPPOSITIONS that characterise the PATRIARCHAL version of reality.

Edda. (O.N. 'poetry' or 'grandmother') The so-called Prose Edda is a list of metres with extensive prose commentary, in effect a handbook of the art of the SKALD and a store of information about Icelandic literature, written by Snorri Sturluson in the thirteenth century.

Eddaic poetry is anonymous Icelandic poetry written down c.1270 but belonging to an older ORAL tradition, though probably none of the poems dates back before the ninth century. They are divided into mythological poems on the Norse gods and heroic lays recounting incidents from the lives of legendary characters such as Sigurd the dragon-slayer.

Edit, edition. (Lat. 'production') The various forms in which a literary work is produced or published are called 'editions'. A 'new edition' is a version of a book in which changes have been made. Details of the printing and publication history of a book should appear on the back of the title-page. To edit a book is to prepare it for the press and publication: this may involve annotating difficult passages, writing an introduction, and even making an ABRIDGEMENT.

Edwardian period. After Queen Victoria's death (1901), Edward VII reigned until 1910. The First World War (1914-18) led to vast changes in the fabric of British society: consequently the fifteen or so years before 1914 are remembered as the last years of a way of life soon to be changed for ever. This Edwardian period was rich in novelists: Conrad, F.M. Ford, Kipling, Wells and Henry James were all publishing prolifically. In the theatre Synge, Shaw and Barrie, and in poetry Hardy, Alfred Noyes and Yeats were the chief writers.

Ego. *See* PSYCHOANALYTIC CRITICISM.

Egotistical sublime. Keats's description of Wordsworth's poetical character in a letter. *See* NEGATIVE CAPABILITY.

Einfühlung. (Ger. 'feeling into') A German word for EMPATHY.

Eiron. A STOCK CHARACTER from Greek comedy. The eiron is a self-deprecatory, modest, understating individual who contrasts with the ALAZON, the self-deceiving and boastful impostor. Socrates often adopts the role of the eiron in his dialogues with philosophical adversaries in Plato's dialogues (fourth century BC). The word is the root of IRONY.

Elegy. (Gk. 'lament') A poem of lamentation, concentrating on the death of a single person, like Tennyson's *In Memoriam* (1850), which describes his grief at the death of his friend Arthur Hallam, or Yeats's 'In Memory of Major Robert Gregory' (1919). The death celebrated may be that of a public figure rather than a personal friend.

In Greek and Roman literature the elegiac metre (alternate HEXA-METERS and PENTAMETERS) was used in solemn poems, and the word 'elegy' may thus also be used of any gravely meditative poem, such as Gray's 'Elegy Written in a Country Churchyard' (1751).

The PASTORAL ELEGY is a significant species of elegiac writing. *See also* PASTORAL.

Elision. (Lat. 'crush out') The slurring of a syllable or a word to achieve the correct number of syllables in a metrical line ('th'arts' instead of 'the arts'). The verb is 'to elide'.

Elizabethan age. Elizabeth I's reign (1558-1603) was a period of relative internal stability, commercial expansion and the growth of patriotic feeling, combined with the changes in outlook referred to as the RENAISSANCE, which had been infiltrating into Britain since the late fifteenth century. One of the great ages of English literature, especially in drama: its chief writers include Shakespeare, Jonson, Marlowe, Sidney, Spenser and Bacon.

Ellipsis. (Gk. 'leaving out') In grammar, the omission of words thought to be essential in the complete form of the sentence. Ellipsis is not uncommon as a figure of speech in poetry, where it allows the maximum meaning to be condensed into the shortest form of words. The first stanza of Edwin Muir's 'The Animals' (1956) misses out 'they' twice, and these ellipses create intriguing contortions in the syntax:

> They do not live in the world,
> Are not in time and space.
> From birth to death hurled
> No word do they have, not one
> To plant a foot upon,
> Were never in any place.

See also ASYNDETON, PARATAXIS.

Emblem. (Gk. 'insertion') A SYMBOLIC or ALLEGORICAL picture: its meaning is hidden ('inserted') rather than obvious. A fish is an emblem for Christ; a pair of scales is an emblem of justice; three ostrich feathers are the emblem for the Prince of Wales. Heraldic crests and coats-of-arms are emblematic.

Sometimes an object, scene or animal in a poem is given a special significance or meaning, which is not spelt out in systematic detail, as in the manner of allegory; nor is it full of nuance and suggestiveness like a symbol: such a device can be called an emblem. Wordsworth calls his description of a moonlit panorama of mountains 'the emblem of a mind/That feeds upon infinity' (*The Prelude*, 1850 text, Book 14, 70–1).

Emblem-book. Popular books of the sixteenth and seventeenth centuries, filled with emblematic pictures and explanations of their meanings. The best-known were Quarles's *Emblems* (1635) and *Hieroglyphics* (1638) and George Wither's *A Collection of Emblems* (1635), all with verse expositions. The METAPHYSICAL POETS sometimes drew on the tradition of emblematic meanings for their CONCEITS. Emblematic poems were also written in the seventeenth century, in the shape, for example, of a cross or a bottle; Herbert's 'The Altar' (1633) is a PATTERN POEM of this kind:

A broken Altar, Lord, thy servant rears,
Made of a heart, and cemented with tears:
Whose parts are as thy hand did frame;
No workman's tool hath touch'd the same.
A   Heart   alone
Is   such a   stone,
As   nothing but
Thy pow'r doth cut.
Wherefore each part
Of my hard heart
Meets in this frame,
To praise thy Name:
That, if I chance to hold my peace,
These stones to praise thee may not cease.
O let thy blessed Sacrifice be mine,
And sanctify this Altar to be thine.

Emotive language. *See* REFERENTIAL LANGUAGE.

Empathy. (Gk. 'affection, feeling into') A kind of sympathy, but stronger: empathy suggests total involvement with the object of sympathy, so that we seem to be inside it for a moment. Keats's observation of a sparrow outside his window, which made him 'take part in its existence and pick about the gravel' (letter to Bailey, 22 November 1817) is a famous example of strong sympathetic imagination. Poems in which the writer pretends to be an animal or bird are exhibitions of empathy. Certain highly descriptive passages in poetry or prose, which almost evoke a physical response, may also be termed empathic. Keats is expert at this effect, as in the opening of his 'The Eve of St Agnes' (1820):

St Agnes' Eve – Ah, bitter chill it was!
The owl, for all his feathers, was a-cold;
The hare limp'd trembling through the frozen grass . . .

The object of empathy may be human, animal or inanimate.

Empirical criticism. *See* EMPIRICISM.

Empiricism. (Gk. 'concerned with experience') A philosophical tradition which regards observation of sense experience as the basis of knowledge. It is often contrasted with various forms of IDEALISM, which considers that the mind encounters the world already equipped with ideas; another contrast is with the rationalist argument that knowledge can be arrived at by the power of reasoning alone.

Francis Bacon and Thomas Hobbes are forerunners of the British empirical school of philosophers, which includes Locke and Hume. Locke argued that at birth the mind was 'white paper, devoid of all characters', and that therefore ideas could only develop from experience. The flourishing of experimental science during the eighteenth century is connected with the ascendancy of empirical philosophy; and the emphasis placed on the imagination by poets like Wordsworth and Coleridge at the turn of the century is a movement both within and against empiricism.

Empirical criticism starts and ends with the scrupulous examination of texts, devoting itself to describing their meanings and forms, the facts surrounding them, and the processes by which they are understood. As this procedure can be undertaken without the intermediary abstraction of a methodology, or theoretical approach, 'empiricist' has come to be used as a word of contempt by some contemporary literary critics, who argue that no interpretation or description of a text can be free of a theoretical and ideological standpoint, and that to pretend otherwise is a dishonest refusal to contemplate the social and political function of literature and literary studies. On the other hand empiricists argue that no valid literary theory can be devised without experience of texts. *See also* HERMENEUTIC CIRCLE.

Enact, enactment. (Med. Lat. 'decree, performance') If the form of a sentence or line of verse seems to echo what it is describing, it is said to 'enact' its meaning. In the following example from Hopkins's poem 'No Worst, There is None' (written *c.*1885) a word is split across a line-ending so as to emphasise its meaning:

> Then lull, then leave off. Fury had shrieked 'No ling-
> ering! Let me be fell: force I must be brief!

Encomium. (Gk. 'concerned with triumph or praise') A literary work written in praise of a person or noble event is so called. The Odes (*c.*464–456BC) of the Greek poet Pindar were encomiums written to celebrate the winners of the Olympic games and other sporting contests.

Encyclopaedia. (Gk. 'general education') A book containing information on all branches of knowledge, usually set out alphabetically.

Encyclopédie. In France the *Encyclopédie ou Dictionnaire raisonné des sciences, des arts et des métiers* appeared in thirty-five volumes between

1751 and 1772. The editors Diderot and d'Alembert transformed a modest project into an ambitious demonstration of the powers of reason, and an attack on the religious and political forces which sought to fetter the minds of men through tradition. It did much to spread the scientific, rationalist and HUMANIST views typical of the ENLIGHTENMENT, despite the opposition of the Church and Louis XV.

End-rhyme. The most common form of RHYME in English versification: syllables rhymed at the end of lines of verse.

End-stopped line. A line of verse in which the end of the line coincides with an essential grammatical pause usually signalled by punctuation. *See also* ENJAMBMENT.

Engagé. A French word used of writers who have committed themselves to some political viewpoint or programme. *See also* COMMITMENT.

English sonnet. *See* SONNET.

Eng. Lit. A usually belittling nickname for the study of English literature in academic institutions. From the point of view of those who use it as a pejorative, it suggests an array of critical methods based on the following: a refusal to consider the nature and purpose of literary studies; an unexamined acceptance of a traditional CANON of great works; a reliance on interpretation as an exercise supposed to be value-free, but actually élitist in its methods and assumptions; and a refusal to acknowledge the insights of POST-STRUCTURALIST critical theories such as DECONSTRUCTION.

A traditional practitioner might offer the following counter-assertions: that literary studies should be organised so as to allow the understanding and enjoyment of texts; that the traditional canon of great works, though subject to continual modification, is a historical fact, and to prevent students from studying what have been considered 'great works' is to deny them the chance of judging the justice of such a classification; that interpretation may not be value-free, but nor is the post-structuralist attack on literature; and that to discuss the theory of literature and criticism divorced from the analysis of individual texts is a meaningless activity. *See also* CRISIS IN ENGLISH STUDIES.

Enjamb(e)ment. (Fr. 'striding') The term used to describe a line of poetry which is not END-STOPPED, that is to say, in which the sentence continues into the next line without any pause being necessary to clarify the grammar, and therefore without any punctuation mark.

A skilful poet, however, will use the line-ending to reinforce meaning: consider the way Wordsworth makes use of a pause at the line-endings to emphasise and ENACT his meaning (which concerns pauses, silence, suspense and surprise) in the following lines from 'There was a Boy' (1800):

> And, when there came a pause
> Of silence such as baffled his best skill:

Then sometimes, in that silence, while he hung
Listening, a gentle shock of mild surprise
Has carried far into his heart the voice
Of mountain-torrents . . .

The available contrast between end-stopped and enjambed lines in BLANK VERSE, in which the grammar flows freely into the metre, allowing a combination of sameness with variation, must be one of the explanations for the popularity and durability of that metrical form.

Enlightenment. A term for aspects of the intellectual atmosphere of Europe, especially in France, during the eighteenth century. The overriding feature of this phase of thought was the conviction that reason would solve the problems of humanity and rid the world of all undesirable elements, superstition, barbarity and ignorance. Reason was thought to lead naturally to scientific discovery. Pope's epitaph for the scientist Sir Isaac Newton, who died in 1727, sums up some of the optimism of Enlightenment thinking:

Nature and Nature's Laws lay hid in Night.
God said, *Let Newton be!* and All was *Light.*

William Godwin, whose *Enquiry Concerning Political Justice* (1793) was admired for a short while by many English intellectuals who supported the French Revolution, is generally considered the last in a line of Rationalist philosophers starting with Bacon and including Locke. In France, Descartes's *Discours de la méthode* (1637) and the works of Voltaire and Diderot, as well as the ENCYCLOPÉDIE (1751–72) which they edited along with others, exhibit the same belief in reason. Leibniz's philosophical optimism and Kant's *Critiques* (1781, 1788, 1790) are further German examples of Enlightenment philosophy. In religion the rational view was manifested in DEISM. *See also* NEOCLASSICISM, ROMANTICISM.

Énoncé and *Énonciation.* What is said (the 'enounced') and the act of saying it (the 'enunciation'). These are perceived as having different 'subjects'. The subjects of the enounced are the 'I', 'you', 'they','he', 'she', and so on, of the text. The subject of the act of enunciation is the inferred authorial presence, or it may be a non-presence, like Joyce's image of the artist in *A Portrait of the Artist as a Young Man* (1916), who 'like the God of the creation remains within or behind or beyond or above his handiwork, invisible, refined out of existence, indifferent, paring his fingernails'. In autobiographical writing it is common to find the mature narrator (the subject of the enunciation) writing through a childish 'I' (the subject of the enounced). In third-person narratives these two separable subjects still exist but can be heavily disguised from the reader. *See also* IMPLIED AUTHOR, NARRATIVE, PERSONA.

In the psychoanalytic theories of Jacques Lacan this distinction is used to help define the consequences of a child's entry into the world of language. Self-realisation is inherent in the act of saying 'I': a split occurs, in that the subject of the enunciation (the 'I' that speaks) is different from the subject of the enounced (the 'I' that is spoken in language), which is defined by the prevailing social attitudes towards self and identity inherent in language.

Entelechy. (Gk. 'in a state of ending') A philosophical term for actuality, or realisation (in the sense of making real) rather than potentiality. The concept is sometimes invoked in DECONSTRUCTIVE CRITICISM to imply the attempt to imprison language into fixed meanings, the opposite of a proper PLURALISM which leaves language constantly in a state of potentiality.

Envoi. See BALLADE.

Épater les bourgeois. (Fr. 'shock the bourgeois') The expression is attributed to Baudelaire, who argued that one purpose for art should be to shock the entrenched, smug, rich and conventional middle classes. AVANT-GARDE artistic movements of the late nineteenth and early twentieth century (for example, DECADENCE, DADA and aspects of MODERNISM) have frequently sought and achieved this effect. In this century artistic expression has often seemed so far from the 'norms' of 'public taste', that a rift of mutual contempt has grown between some artists and their potential audience. See also BOHEMIAN.

Ephebe. The Greek word for a young citizen in arms, used by Wallace Stevens in 'Notes Towards a Supreme Fiction' (1942) for the poetic disciple whom he addresses in the poem, and taken up in this sense by the critic Harold Bloom. See also ANXIETY OF INFLUENCE.

Ephemera. (Gk. 'diary') Minor jottings of a writer, of no significance; or the printed products of a throw-away society, the innumerable leaflets, advertisements, pamphlets, tickets, labels and wrappings that are consigned to the wastepaper basket unless someone chooses to collect them.

Epic. (Gk. 'speech, word, song') An epic is a long narrative poem in elevated style, about the exploits of superhuman heroes. 'Traditional epics', also called 'primary epics', are part of the oral tradition of a nation, and involve myths and legends of nationhood. The oldest example is the Sumerian epic *Gilgamesh* (c.2700BC). In European literature the *Odyssey* and *Iliad* (c. eighth century BC), traditionally ascribed to Homer, and in O.E. literature *Beowulf* (eighth century AD) are primary epics. The *Chanson de Roland* (c.1100), one of the many French *chansons de geste*, is almost certainly also a primary epic. The 'secondary' or 'literary epic' is a work modelled on the primary epic and including many of its characteristic features, but written by a single individual for a literate audience. Virgil's *Aeneid* (c.30–20BC) and

Milton's *Paradise Lost* (1667) are two clear examples of the literary epic, as are Camoëns's *The Lusiads* (1572) from Portugal, and Dante's *Divine Comedy* (c.1304-21) and Tasso's *Jerusalem Liberated* (1575) from Italy. Many long poems from the fourteenth century onwards, for example, Spenser's *The Faerie Queene* (1590, 1596), in some respects resemble the epic, but include elements of the ROMANCE or other kinds of literature: such works are often still called epics. The term can also be applied loosely to suitable novels or films, though in this popular sense no more may be meant by 'epic' than 'long and ambitious'.

Virgil studied Homer's epics and wrote the *Aeneid* with them in mind; Milton studied both Homer's and Virgil's works, and constructed *Paradise Lost* according to certain conventions that were thought to be essential to the form.

Some of the conventions of the epic are as follows: the hero represents a nation or race (in the case of the *Aeneid*, Aeneas is the founder of Rome, and his journeys all lead to this end; in the case of *Paradise Lost*, Adam represents the human race); the epic hero performs superhuman deeds, with the help of the gods and other supernatural helpers (called the MACHINERY in the eighteenth century), and the arena for these deeds is vast in scale, ranging from the battlefields of the Trojan Wars (Achilles's battles in the *Iliad*) to the Mediterranean, around which Odysseus and Aeneas journey, both of them also visiting the underworld, to the universal cosmic setting of *Paradise Lost*; the style of the epic is grand and formal, including traditional EPIC SIMILES, CATALOGUES and EPITHETS.

For Aristotle the epic was a less significant literary form than the tragedy. But from the seventeenth century onwards the epic ranked as the most ambitious form a poet could attempt. The NEOCLASSICAL age reverted to the epic, yet though Dryden translated the *Aeneid* and Pope the *Iliad* and the *Odyssey*, many eighteenth-century poets found their talents better suited to the **mock epic**: Pope's *The Rape of the Lock* (1712, 1714) and the *Dunciad* (1728, 1743) in their different ways are perfect examples of mock-epic writing.

Nineteenth- and twentieth-century literature has produced nothing that can be classified as pure epic, but many works that at least invite comparison with the form. Wordsworth's *The Prelude* (1850) might be described as an epic autobiography. Several poems are more clearly attempts at epic grandeur, for example, Arnold's *Sohrab and Rustum* (1853), but they are not works of a cosmic or even national significance. Pound's *Cantos* (1930-69) or W.C. Williams's *Paterson* (1946-58) are modern works with epic aspirations; yet neither is really a narrative poem, with a story: both are COLLAGES, *Paterson* giving an account of Williams's home town, while the *Cantos* are an encyclopaedia of allusions to European, American and Chinese culture and history.

David Jones's account of a battle in the First World War, set in a historical context, *In Parenthesis* (1937), is in some respects closer to being a modern version of epic.
Perhaps the novel has taken over as the medium for epic ambitions. Tolstoy's *War and Peace* (1863–9), for example, is epic in theme and scope; yet the fact that the novel is essentially a work of realism denies it the epic element of supernatural machinery. This is also, of course, lacking from Joyce's ironic masterpiece *Ulysses* (1922), in spite of the constant parallels with the *Odyssey*.

Epic simile. A long SIMILE, sometimes over twenty lines, which typically interrupts the narrative in an EPIC poem, allowing the poet to make detailed comparisons. Milton in *Paradise Lost* (1667) provides many examples, such as, at the end of Book 1, lines 780–7, in which he describes the council of the fallen angels:

> like that pygmean race
> Beyond the Indian mount, or faerie elves,
> Whose midnight revels, by a forest side
> Or fountain, some belated peasant sees,
> Or dreams he sees, while overhead the moon
> Sits arbitress, and nearer to the earth
> Wheels her pale course; they, on their mirth and dance
> Intent, with jocund music charm his ear . . .

Epic theatre. An influential style of theatrical presentation and dramatic writing developed in Germany in the late 1920s. Erwin Piscator and Bertolt Brecht were its originators. Epic theatre presents a series of episodes in a simple, direct way, with the possible accompaniment of a narrator, poetic fragments, summaries of the plot, songs, projection of slides on to a screen, music, and so on. Many of these techniques were to remind the audience that they were watching a play, forcing them to use their reason rather than being swept away by feeling for an illusion: this was Brecht's deliberate ALIENATION EFFECT. His *Threepenny Opera* (1928) and *Mother Courage* (1941) are notable examples of this kind of writing, which he used to expound his MARXIST political views. *See also* BRECHTIAN.

Epideictic. (Gk. 'showing upon') (*adj.*) Used of rhetorical language which is specially intended for display, as in a set speech praising a famous person on some ceremonial occasion.

Epigram. (Gk. 'inscription') Originally an inscription on a monument; now used of witty sayings in general but particularly of any short poem which has a sharp turn of thought or point, be it witty, amusing or satiric. The Roman poet Martial specialised in caustic and obscene epigrams, and gave the form its characteristic sting-in-the-tail. In English poetry epigrams have been a popular form from the seventeenth century onwards. Donne, for example, wrote several, some in the manner of Martial, like 'A Self Accuser' (1633):

> Your mistress, that you follow whores, still taxeth you;
> 'Tis strange that she should confess it, though it be true.

Here are two more examples of the form, both by Pope:

> You beat your pate, and fancy wit will come;
> Knock as you please, there's nobody at home!

> Sir, I admit your general rule,
> That every poet is a fool:
> But you yourself may serve to show it,
> That every fool is not a poet.

The eighteenth century was particularly rich in epigrams. The HEROIC COUPLET, with its clipped lines, imparts an epigrammatic quality even to narrative poems. Though the heroic couplet was no longer fashionable in the nineteenth century, epigrams were still popular. The complete works of most poets will include epigrams which may have been written as JEUX D'ESPRIT. Landor wrote many epigram-like poems, substituting a romantic flourish for the witty turn, as in 'Dirce' (1831):

> Stand close around, ye Stygian set,
> With Dirce in one boat convey'd!
> Or Charon, seeing, may forget
> That he is old and she a shade.

In the twentieth century the epigram is still popular: the word now embraces witty sayings in prose as well as verse. *See* APOPHTHEGM, PROVERB, WIT.

Epigraph. (Gk. 'written upon') A word with several meanings, synonymous with 'inscription'. However, it is most often used to denote the quotations or fragments that writers place at the beginning of poems, novels or chapters as a clue or hint, often somewhat indirect or obscure, towards their meaning. T.S. Eliot places an epigraph under the title of his poem 'The Hollow Men' (1925) which is a quotation from Conrad's *Heart of Darkness* (1902): 'Mistah Kurtz – he dead.' George Eliot puts epigraphs at the head of the chapters of *Middlemarch* (1871-2): some she wrote herself; some are quotations.

Epilogue. (Gk. 'speech on') A concluding speech or passage in a work of literature, often summing up and commenting on what has gone before. In plays, the epilogue is often a request for applause, like Puck's final speech in Shakespeare's *A Midsummer Night's Dream* (c.1595-6).

Epiphany. (Gk. 'manifestation') A manifestation of God's presence in the world was called an 'epiphany' by Christians. James Joyce uses the word to describe moments of sudden meaning or insight, 'sudden spiritual manifestations', as he describes them in *Stephen Hero* (published 1944), the early version of his *A Portrait of the Artist as a Young Man* (1916). Any object, he asserts, however trivial, may be 'epiphanised' (*see* the INSCAPE of G.M. Hopkins). Certain epiphanies, or MOMENTS, recur throughout Joyce's works; for example, the vision of a girl wading in the sea, given to Bloom in *Ulysses* (1922), and first used in *A Portrait* (Chapter 4):

> A girl stood before him in midstream, alone and still, gazing out to sea. She seemed like one whom magic had changed into the likeness of a strange and beautiful seabird. Her long slender bare legs were delicate as a crane's and pure save where an emerald trail of seaweed had fashioned itself as a sign upon the flesh. Her thighs, fuller and softhued as ivory, were bared almost to the hips where the white fringes of her drawers were like feathering of soft white down . . .
> – Heavenly God! cried Stephen's soul, in an outburst of profane joy.

The word is now used generally of any sudden moments of understanding or sense of revelation (associated with a particular object or scene) described in a poem or novel. Wordsworth's 'spots of time' in *The Prelude* (1850) are similar.

Episode. (Gk. 'coming in besides') Originally the name for a dialogue between two choric songs in Greek theatre; later used of 'incidental narrative'. Now an episode is a single event or incident from within some long narrative, such as an epic or a novel. The sections of a serialised work are also called 'episodes'.

Episodic. Denoting a NARRATIVE which is written in the simple form of a series of more or less separable or discrete episodes or incidents, rather than a complicated and involved PLOT.

Episteme. (Gk. 'knowledge') The accepted patterns in which knowledge is thought to be obtained and arranged at a particular time, and which have varied throughout history. The French historian Michel Foucault uses the term in his analysis of cultural change.

Epistemology. (Gk. 'knowledge study') The philosophical theory of knowledge, how it is acquired and of what it consists.

Epistemology was a central concern of eighteenth-century EMPIRICISM. In the early nineteenth century, one aspect of ROMANTICISM was a turning away from the notion that writers should aspire towards expressing UNIVERSAL TRUTHS. Instead, individual experience and feeling came to be seen as the proper source of knowledge. Seen from this perspective Wordsworth's *The Prelude* (1850), subtitled *The Growth of a Poet's Mind*, and many of his other poems, can be seen as epistemological studies in the form of a poetic self-analysis.

Epistle. (Gk. 'message') A letter: especially one of the apostolic letters in the New Testament. The word is also used of poems on moral or semi-philosophical themes addressed to a friend or patron, in the manner of an informal, well-argued letter. From the Renaissance onwards Horace's *Epistles* (*c.* 20BC) have been the model for this kind of poem. Pope casts many of his satires in this form, for example his *Epistle IV: To Richard Boyle, Earl of Burlington* (1731), which discusses taste in art and architecture.

Epistolary novel. A common form for the eighteenth-century NOVEL: the story is told entirely through letters sent by those participating in or observing the events. Richardson's *Pamela* (1740-1) and *Clarissa* (1747-8) are both epistolary novels. So too is Smollett's comic travel novel *Humphry Clinker* (1771). Richardson makes use of the special features of the form to concentrate on the characters' psychologies and moral judgment. This manner of narration is occasionally revived, as in Saul Bellow's *Herzog* (1964). *See also* NARRATIVE.

Epitaph. (Gk. 'on a tomb') An inscription on a tomb, or a piece of writing suitable for that purpose. Yeats wrote his own at the end of 'Under Ben Bulben' (1939):

Cast a cold eye
On life, on death.
Horseman, pass by!

Wordsworth wrote three essays on epitaphs, the first of which was published as a note to *The Excursion* (1814). *See also* LAPIDARY.

Epithalamion, epithalamium. (Gk. 'at the bridal chamber') A poem celebrating a marriage, traditionally sung outside the bedroom of the newly-weds. There are a few Greek and Latin examples, but the form was particularly popular during the late sixteenth and seventeenth centuries. The most famous is Spenser's 'Epithalamion' (1595), written for his own marriage. There are some more modern instances: for example, Tennyson's *In Memoriam* (1850) finishes with a description of a wedding that suggests the form.

Epithet. (Gk. 'something added') An adjective, or adjectival phrase, such as the 'heather-covered hills', which defines a special quality or attribute. The characteristic POETIC DICTION of the eighteenth century was full of epithets in which fish were called 'the finny tribe', and every noun was qualified by an adjective, like the 'lowing herd', 'solemn stillness' or 'incense-breathing morn'.

In Homer's epics there are certain recurrent adjectival expressions, such as 'the wine-dark sea' or 'rosy-fingered dawn'; these are called **Homeric epithets**, and are probably FORMULAE which result from the method of composition, half-improvised, half-memorised, typical of ORAL literature.

Epitome. (Gk. 'cut short') A short ABRIDGEMENT or SUMMARY of a longer work.

Epoché. See PHENOMENOLOGY.

Epode. See STROPHE.

Eponymous. (Gk. 'given as a name') Originally denoting persons whose names were reputed to have been used to form a place-name: as, for example, Brutus was thought to have been the founder of Britain. Now 'eponymous' is commonly used of a personage in a book whose name is used as the title: it would be possible, therefore, to refer to Tom Jones as 'the eponymous hero of Fielding's *Tom Jones* (1749)'.

Epyllion. (Gk. 'little poem') A rare term for a short narrative poem, or 'brief epic'.

Equivocate, equivocation, equivocal. (Lat. 'equal name') To 'equivocate' is to use words in a double sense, sometimes with the intention of deceiving. An 'equivocation' in literature is an AMBIGUITY, a play on words involving a double meaning, even possibly a PUN. 'Equivocal' is used almost synonymously with 'ambiguous' to refer to a word or words suggesting a double meaning, not so much an obvious and deliberate ambiguity as possible alternative interpretations.

Equivoque. A PUN: sometimes used of a whole sentence or statement with a double meaning, such as the end of MacDiarmid's poem 'At My Father's Grave' (1931) which is open to opposite interpretations:

A livin' man upon a deid man thinks
And ony sma'er thocht's impossible.

In one way of reading this, the poet states that it is impossible to imagine a less significant activity than thinking about a dead person; or to read it otherwise, thinking about a dead person is of such major significance that it excludes all other, smaller activities.

Erziehungsroman. (Ger. 'novel of education') Another word for BIL-DUNGSROMAN: a novel concentrating on the protagonist's upbringing, such as Joyce's *A Portrait of the Artist as a Young Man* (1916).

Escapist. A criticism levelled at some kinds of writing, on the grounds that they do not confront 'reality' but allow the reader to dwell temporarily in a pleasant world of illusion or fantasy. 'Romantic' novelettes are deliberately escapist; but the charge is also sometimes made against more serious kinds of literature.

Eschatology. (Gk. 'last-study') The depiction in art, the study and the theology of the end of the world, and the four last things: Death, Judgment, Heaven and Hell.

Essay. (Lat. 'to weigh, to balance') The *Essais* (1580) (in the sense of 'attempts') of the French writer Montaigne gave this form its name, and established many of its conventions. An essay is a short prose discussion of any subject, which tries to persuade the reader to adopt a particular way of looking at the subject. Apart from the occasional exception, such as the philosopher Locke's *Essay Concerning Human Under-*

standing (1690), the essay is aimed at a general audience, unlike the THESIS, TREATISE or DISSERTATION which are for specialists. Even 'formal' essays are relatively casual in their use of example and development of their argument. Francis Bacon's *Essays* (1597) are essays in the manner of Montaigne; some of the titles suggest his range of topics: 'Of Death', 'Of Love', 'Of Cunning', 'Of Plantations', 'Of Masques and Triumphs', and so on.

The PERIODICAL literature of the eighteenth and nineteenth centuries provided vehicles for several great essayists, including Addison and Steele in *The Tatler* and *The Spectator*, and Hazlitt, Lamb and De Quincey in the proliferating literary magazines of the early nineteenth century, such as *Blackwood's* or the *London Magazine*.

The prose essay is a flexible and lively form in the modern age. The study of literature as a university subject has led to poets and critics publishing collections of critical essays: T.S. Eliot's *Selected Essays* (1932), for example, have been widely influential. Whimsical **informal essays**, in the manner of Lamb's 'A Dissertation Upon Roast Pig' (1822) or 'Old China' (1823), are now confined to humorous magazines such as *Punch*, but in the daily and weekly papers there are hundreds of outlets for journalistic essays on all subjects.

Estrangement. *See* DEFAMILIARISATION.

Ethos. (Gk. 'character') The prevalent emphasis or character of a culture, community or work of art. Aristotle used the word in his writing about RHETORIC to describe the character or impression of a character which an orator will build up implicitly during a speech. Therefore a word for PERSONA or TONE.

Etymological fallacy. The pedantic insistence that the oldest meaning of a word is its proper meaning, rather than a present-day use. An ordinary example is offered by the word 'aggravate' which means 'make heavier' but, to some people's disapproval, is commonly used to mean 'irritate'.

In general, however, words have to be used without any sense of their old and now esoteric meanings. 'Admiral', for example, comes from the Arabic *emir al* meaning 'chief of – ', the final word in the Arabic expression (for a fleet of ships) having been lost; the 'd' was then added through false association with 'admire'. To insist on using a word with such a muddled provenance in any etymologically 'accurate' way would clearly be fruitless.

Etymology. (Gk. 'study of original forms') The study of the history and origins of words, and their changing forms and meanings. When studying an old text it may be necessary to investigate particular words in the full *Oxford English Dictionary*, originally in thirteen volumes, the second edition (1989) in twenty volumes, which lists all the historical meanings of words, with examples of usage. Even key words may have been used in ways quite different from their contemporary meanings.

Knowledge of the former meanings of a word may enrich its possible range of present meaning, and many writers like to make use of this semantic possibility. Milton, for example, alludes in his poetry to the Hebrew, Greek or Italian origins of words. Hopkins had an etymologist's interest in the history of words, and dialect meanings, as do Geoffrey Hill and Seamus Heaney amongst contemporary poets. Critics also like to savour the historical traces contained in words, as a way of revealing nuances of meaning, or to justify and explain some particular emphasis they want to give to a word. 'Character', for example, originates from the name for a Greek writing instrument. This is linked with its present meanings as (1) a graphic mark, and (2) the sum of a person's qualities (what 'marks' the person). Thus the word's etymology can suggest, to those who are made aware of it, the extent to which 'character' is artificially 'marked out' or 'written in'.

Euphemism. (Gk. 'speaking fair') Unpleasant, embarrassing or frightening facts or words can be concealed behind a 'euphemism': a word or phrase that is less blunt, rude or terrifying. Thus death is dealt with euphemistically: to die is to 'pass away' or 'kick the bucket'. References to sexuality, bodily functions and parts of the body are also commonly disguised: we are asked if we wish 'to wash our hands' in the 'cloakroom' as a polite way of discovering if we want to urinate. *See also* DYSPHEMISM.

Euphony. (Gk. 'well sounding') Language which sounds pleasantly smooth and musical, like the following extract from Tennyson's 'The Lotos-Eaters' (1842):

There is sweet music here that softer falls
Than petals from blown roses on the grass,
Or night-dews on still waters between walls
Of shadowy granite, in a gleaming pass . . .

As in the case of ONOMATOPOEIA, it is more the meaning of the lines which creates an agreeable impression, than the sound of the words themselves, though some combinations of vowels and consonants are more pleasurable and easy to articulate smoothly than others. Clashing, awkward and ugly combinations of sounds, whether deliberately organised to reflect the words' meaning, or created by mistake, are called CACOPHONY. *See also* ALLITERATION, ASSONANCE.

Euphuism. *Euphues: the Anatomy of Wit* (1578) by John Lyly gave the name to a kind of prose writing in vogue in the late sixteenth century. 'Euphuism' is a style which is exaggeratedly elaborate, full of ANTITHESES, ALLITERATION, balanced constructions, prolonged ornate SIMILES and learned ALLUSIONS. Shakespeare's *Love's Labour's Lost* (*c*.1594–5) includes parodies of this BAROQUE style. As an example of the style here is Euphues's reply to his rival in love, Philautus:

I remember *Philautus* how valiantly *Ajax* boasted in the feats of arms, yet *Ulysses* bare away the armour, and it may be that though thou crake of thine own courage, thou mayest easily lose the conquest. Dost thou think *Euphues* such a dastard that he is not able to withstand thy courage, or such a dullard that he cannot descry thy craft. Alas good soul. It fareth with thee as with the Hen, which when the Puttock hath caught her Chicken beginneth to cackle: and thou having lost thy lover beginnest to prattle. Tush *Philautus*, I am in this point of *Euripides* his mind, who thinks it lawful for the desire of a kingdom to transgress the bounds of honesty, and for the love of a Lady to violate and break the bands of amity.

Evaluation. (Lat. 'estimation of worth') One purpose of literary CRITICISM is the judgment of the value of a literary work: is it good or bad? DESCRIPTIVE CRITICISM, however, aims only to describe, and is not concerned to judge. In discussing literature it is necessary to discriminate between those interpretations and comments which are 'evaluative' (suggesting the relative success or failure of the work) and those which merely seek to explain or describe.

Excursus. (Lat. 'out-running') A weighty digression or separate discussion of some point in a piece of writing, usually a scholarly work.

Exegesis. (Gk. 'interpretation') Explanation and interpretation of a text, often of the Bible, but also now used of the critical analysis of literature.

Exemplum. (Lat. 'copy, pattern, example') A short tale used to exemplify a moral in a SERMON. Chaucer's *Pardoner's Tale* (late fourteenth century) is such a narrative cast in literary form. In the Middle Ages there were many books of exempla from which priests could select appropriately: the fourteenth-century *Gesta Romanorum* is one such collection. *See also* FABLE, GESTA, PARABLE.

Existentialism. Most philosophies and theologies have supposed that man's actual existence in the world is less significant than some pre-existing essence. Existentialism is a philosophical trend which stresses the importance of existence. It originates with the works of the Danish philosopher Sören Kierkegaard and finds full expression in the works of the German philosopher Martin Heidegger and the French philosopher and novelist Jean-Paul Sartre.

Though Kierkegaard elaborated a Christian version of the philosophy, in general existentialism takes the view that the universe is an inexplicable, meaningless and dangerous theatre for the individual's existence. Everyone has to assume the responsibility of making choices that determine the nature of this existence. This freedom puts human beings into a state of anxiety (ANGST), surrounded as they are by infinite possibilities, while remaining ignorant of the future, except for the fact that life is finite, and will finish, just as it began, in nothingness.

Existential thinkers differ about whether it is possible for individuals to transcend their particular situations. They argue whether some kinds of existence may be more 'authentic' than others. In his succinct guide to existentialist doctrine, *Existentialism and Humanism* (1947), Sartre expresses the view that man can become committed (ENGAGÉ) to political and social action by an act of will. His novel *Nausea* (1938) is fictionalised autobiography, focusing on his concern with the freedom of the will and nature of existence, which is given full philosophical expression in *Being and Nothingness* (1943).

Another French exponent of existentialism was the writer Albert Camus, whose short novel *L'Étranger* ('The Outsider', 1942) is a famous expression of the absurdity of life. The depiction of the ABSURD, especially in the theatre, almost amounts to a literary movement in the mid-twentieth century; its protagonist was Samuel Beckett, whose celebrated play *Waiting for Godot* (1953) is considered another key work of existentialism: two tramps wait in a waste place for 'Godot', who may or may not exist, but with whom they think they may have an appointment. The action, or lack of action, is absurd both in its irrationality and in the grotesque comedy occasioned by the tramps' dialogue and slapstick. *See also* MODERNISM.

Exordium. (Lat. 'beginning') A rhetorical term for the introductory section of a speech or essay.

Explication. (Lat. 'unfolding') A French word for the kind of CLOSE READING and PRACTICAL CRITICISM adopted by the NEW CRITICS as the standard procedure for discussing a text: a rigorous examination of a text's meaning and explanation of the way the resources of language have been used to create that unique meaning. *See also* CRITICISM.

Explicit. *See* IMPLICIT.

Explicit metaphor. *See* METAPHOR.

Exposition. (Lat. 'explaining') The explanation, often necessary at the beginning of a narrative, of the events leading up to the start of the narrative. In Shakespeare's *The Tempest* (*c*.1611), I.2, for example, Prospero recounts to Miranda the story of his having been betrayed by his brother and cast away on an island: these events are essential for understanding the plot, but happened far back in time before the point at which the play starts.

Expressionism. A European artistic movement which started *c*.1900 in Germany. Expressionism was a revolt against REALISM. Instead of attempting to represent the world conventionally and objectively, Expressionist writers and painters show reality distorted by an emotional or abnormal state of mind, even by madness. Van Gogh's famous violent landscapes with whirls of thick paint representing cornfields and menacing v-shaped black crows are examples of this kind of distortion. In literature the Swedish dramatist Strindberg is a notable exponent of Expressionism. His *Dream Play* (1902) dislocates the ordinary sequence of time and conveys a view of the unreality of man's existence through a collection of dream-like fragments. This departure from the rigidities of realism in the theatre has been highly influential in twentieth-century dramatic writing, though the Expressionist Movement as such was short-lived.

The Cabinet of Dr Caligari (1919), directed by Robert Wiene, was an early film in the Expressionist manner which has been very influential. *See also* DADA, SURREALISM, SYMBOLISM.

Expressive criticism. Examining a text as an expression of the writer's feelings, imagination and personality. It tends to judge the work by its sincerity or the extent to which it has successfully revealed the author's state of mind. Romantic writers such as Coleridge and Wordsworth were expressive critics in this sense. The NEW CRITICISM of the 1920s regarded expressive criticism as mistaken. *See also* CRITICISM.

Expurgate. (Lat. 'purify out') To remove offensive words or passages from a text. School editions of some of Shakespeare's plays which contain the occasional rude word or allusion used to be BOWDLERISED or expurgated. The *Index Expurgatorius* is a list of writings forbidden to Catholics unless certain passages have been excised.

Extempore. (Lat. 'out of time') A Latin phrase meaning 'on the spur of the moment' used of music (especially jazz), poetry or stories composed at the moment of recital or delivery, rather than worked upon before the event. Much ORAL poetry was composed in an extempore manner (though the units out of which it was put together might have been traditional and predetermined). *See also* FORMULAE.

Extradiegetic. *See* DIEGESIS.

Extradiscursive. Outside the established terms of reference of a particular DISCOURSE.

Extravaganza. (It. 'wandering around') A sumptuous and elaborate theatrical entertainment, mixing music and dance in the light-hearted treatment of some traditional tale; popular in the nineteenth century. Now the word refers to any expensive and varied stage performance.

Eye rhyme. Words placed in a position where a RHYME is expected, and which are spelt similarly but pronounced differently, creating HALF-RHYMES: flow/now, home/come.

F

Fable. (Lat. 'discourse') A short TALE conveying a clear moral lesson in which the characters are animals acting like human beings. The stories attributed to the Greek slave Aesop (sixth century BC) are the earliest and most famous fables; some have entered the language as clichés or proverbial expressions (the fox and the sour grapes, for example).

George Orwell's political satire *Animal Farm* (1945) is a modern example of an extended fable. *See also* ALLEGORY, PARABLE, PROVERB.

Fabliau. (Fr., from Lat. 'discourse') A short satirical or comic TALE in verse, characterised by bawdiness. Fabliaux deal with low- or middle-class life in a realistic, earthy, even obscene manner, and are thus the genre most distant in tone and subject-matter from COURTLY LOVE. They were popular in France during the twelfth and thirteenth centuries. Chaucer's *The Miller's Tale* (late fourteenth century) is a good example in English literature.

Fabula. *See* NARRATOLOGY.

Fabulation. A modern term to categorise certain kinds of novel or ANTI-NOVEL which are characterised by the self-conscious creation of fictions within fiction, elaborate forms, and manipulation of the reader's beliefs and expectations, so that the reader is led into an abstruse maze of fiction rather than a traditional story.

Facticity. ('Fact-ness') The quality and nature of being factual; used in discussing the nature of historical writing of all kinds, which may manifest different degrees of facticity. It should not be confused with 'factitious', meaning 'invented, artificial, sham'.

Faction. Novels and other forms that are based on actual events; also called the **non-fiction novel**. The words 'fact' and 'fiction' are combined together in a portmanteau word that indicates the confusing combination of invention and factuality that the form can assemble. Thomas Keneally's *Schindler's Ark* won the Booker Prize for fiction in 1982, in spite of protest that, based as it was entirely on historical fact, it was not a fiction at all. Other examples are Truman Capote's *In Cold Blood* (1966), a novel describing an actual murder, and the very different journalistic histories of political events by Norman Mailer, that began with *The Armies of the Night* (1968).

The term is also used of the television drama-documentary, which confuses or conflates two forms which had previously been perceived as entirely contradictory, one investigative and factual, the other patently fictional and inventive. Many such programmes have seemed controversially unbalanced in their manipulation of the sympathies of the audience, in a manner quite unlike the apparently judicious balancing of opinion in the conventional documentary (which may of course be equally false). *See also* FACTOID.

Factoid, factoidism. Often used to mean the same as FACTION, but different in emphasis: it is a coinage by the American novelist and journalist Norman Mailer, to indicate untrue information which is presented and repeated in such a way that it comes to be taken as truth.

Fairy tale. Originally a variety of folktale (*see* FOLKLORE), concerning fairies, magic, witches, giants and other supernatural agents, in their contacts with the world of ordinary people. The famous collections by the brothers Jakob and Wilhelm Grimm, *Kinder- und Hausmärchen*, were made between 1812 and 1822. The fairy tales of Hans Christian Andersen, published in 1835, are mostly literary inventions rather than traditional stories.

Fallible narrator. *See* NARRATIVE.

Falling action. *See* FREYTAG'S PYRAMID.

Falling rhythm. TROCHAIC or DACTYLIC metres in both of which strongly stressed syllables are followed by weak ones, thought to sound like 'falling', unlike the RISING RHYTHM of IAMBIC and ANAPAESTIC metres. *See* METRE for further discussion of these terms.

Fancy. (A contraction of fantasy, Gk. 'a making visible') Originally synonymous with IMAGINATION and FANTASY, referring to the faculty of forming in the mind representations of things not actually present. While 'imagination' has come to refer to the purposeful and coherent exercise of this faculty in artistic organisation or creation, 'fancy' is reserved for its more arbitrary, insubstantial, decorative and whimsical manifestations. Coleridge is probably responsible for this distinction between fancy and imagination, as he was at pains to contra-distinguish the terms in Chapter 13 of his *Biographia Literaria* (1817).

Fantastic, The. Writings that present unreal happenings that hover between supernatural and psychological explanation, thereby leaving the characters in the book and the reader in a particular state of suspended understanding. Todorov classifies this kind of literature in his study *The Fantastic* (1970). The uncertain status of Cathy's ghost, which Lockwood convinces himself is a dream, is an example from *Wuthering Heights* (1847).

Fantasy. (Gk. 'appearance, phantom, mental process, perception, imagination') Though, like FANCY, 'fantasy' originally applied generally to the mind's perceptual and imaginative processes, it is now used to denote the most playful kind of imagining, divorced from any contact with the real world of things and ideas. 'Fantasy' literature deals with imaginary worlds of fairies, dwarves, giants and other non-realistic phenomena. A fantasy world may be an entirely consistent parallel with the ordinary world, as in the fairy-tale trilogy *The Lord of the Rings* (1954–5) by J.R.R. Tolkien which makes use of many Nordic myths; or it may have a dream-like illogicality and episodic structure, as in Lewis Carroll's *Alice's Adventures in Wonderland* (1865). Both kinds of fantasy are open to ALLEGORICAL or SYMBOLIC interpretation. *See also* FANTASTIC, IMAGINATION, NONSENSE.

Farce. (Lat. 'to stuff') A kind of drama intended primarily to provoke laughter, using exaggerated characters and complicated plots, full of absurd episodes, ludicrous situations and knockabout action. Mistaken identity is frequently an element in the plot. 'Bedroom farce' concentrates on marital infidelity and sexual escapades: the typical stage setting involves a large number of doors through which the characters pop in and out at moments inconvenient to each other.

Farce is obviously related to COMEDY, but it has no apparent intention other than rumbustious entertainment and the good-natured depiction of folly. Unlike satire, it is not censorious.

Farcical episodes date back to Aristophanes and occur alongside serious drama in all ages. The derivation of the word is suggestive. The Latin term *farsa* was first applied to passages of medieval French inserted in the Latin text of the Mass; then it came to be used to describe impromptu additions to religious plays (INTERLUDES in the English MYSTERY PLAYS), and from this use its modern meaning has developed.

Though elements of farce emerge in the work of all great comic playwrights, pure farce, unmixed with other comic styles, appears as a common genre only in the nineteenth century. The French writer Georges Feydeau is often cited as having brought the form to a state of perfection. In English literature Brandon Thomas's *Charley's Aunt* (1892) is often cited as an example of all that is best and worst about farce. *See also* ABSURD, BURLESQUE, VAUDEVILLE.

Faust theme. A sixteenth-century legend about a magician who sold his soul to the devil in return for knowledge and power: the story has come to be an ARCHETYPE of the man of learning who is prepared to suffer the torments of hell in return for intellectual satisfaction and access to ultimate truths. Marlowe's *Tragical History of Dr Faustus* (*c*.1588) is an early version of the story. The German poet Goethe's *Faust* (1808, 1832) and Byron's *Manfred* (1817) are two examples of the strong eighteenth- and nineteenth-century interest in this theme: many writers and musicians have used the Faust story to symbolise the way in which the artist's obsessive pursuit of the truth often leads to misery.

Feign. (Lat. 'form, contrive, conceive') A word which can mean simply 'to imagine' or 'to invent' in the sense of writing poetry. But more often 'feign' suggests dishonest invention, concealment or dissembling. Since Plato banned poets from his ideal state in Book 10 of *The Republic* (*c*.360BC), critics have always had to contend with the view that poets are liars, and poetry 'mere feigning' in the sense both of creation and lying. Carlyle sums up the paradox nicely in his essay on 'Biography' (1832), which ironically makes the comment through the PERSONA of a fictional German Professor Sauerteig: 'Fiction, while the feigner of it knows that he is feigning, partakes, more than we suspect, of the nature of *lying*; and has ever an, in some degree, unsatisfactory character.'

Feminine ending. A line of poetry which ends with an extra lightly stressed syllable; common in lines of IAMBIC PENTAMETER:

What is/more gen/tle than/a wind/in summ/er.

See also METRE.

Feminine rhyme. Rhymed words of two or more syllables, when the last syllable is not stressed: finding/grinding, ladle/cradle. *See also* RHYME.

Feminist criticism. Since the late 1960s feminist theories about literature and language, and feminist interpretations of texts have multiplied enormously. Feminist criticism is now a significant area of literary study and discussion, to the point of being a subject for study in itself. The changes in perspective involved in some feminist concepts have been revolutionary, and, as many have observed, the passion with which feminist points of view have been adopted has resembled a religious awakening, sometimes fundamentalist in its energy. Since this feminist revolution, no critic, even if unconvinced by feminist arguments, can write or speak without being to some extent conscious of the role that gender may have in the creation or production of literature or the reader's response to it.

Feminism had a considerable history before its burgeoning in the 1970s. Early texts include Mary Wollstonecraft's *A Vindication of the Rights of Women* (1792), J.S. Mill's *The Subjection of Women* (1869) and, in this century, Virginia Woolf's influential *A Room of One's Own* (1929), which examines the disadvantages of being a woman writer in a 'patriarchal society'. Simone de Beauvoir's *The Second Sex* (1949) investigates female sexuality and the cultural construction of gender in terms of male dominance. Kate Millett's *Sexual Politics* (1969) defines the way men manipulate power in order to keep women subordinate. Both these last two writers explore writing by men as a means of illustrating their arguments.

Within feminist criticism there are numerous different positions and controversies. Many of these are part of the wider range of feminist thinking in relation to society as a whole, and are not specific to literature. On the other hand, literature is seen as a particular focus for the preconceptions and prejudices that can be discovered by feminist analysis, and an array of special terms and concepts have been defined to aid these investigations, in addition to the critical vocabularies provided by STRUCTURALISM, DECONSTRUCTION, MARXIST and PSYCHO-ANALYTIC CRITICISM.

A tenet of feminist thought is that male ways of perceiving and ordering are 'inscribed' into the prevailing IDEOLOGY of society. This can be disclosed by studying language itself, and texts, in order to discover the characteristic assumptions which are inherent in them. In patriarchal societies (also called 'androcentric' (Gk. 'man-centred') or 'phallocratic' (Gk. 'penis-ruled')), language contains BINARY OPPOSITIONS of qualities such as active/passive, adventurous/timid, or reasonable/irrational, in which, it is argued, the feminine is always associated with the less desirable words in the listed pairs. Women are subordinated because they are perceived through this constantly repeated framework of negative perceptions which are inherent in language. Areas of human achievement are defined in terms of male ideas and aspirations, and the presumption that advances in civilisation have always been brought about by men. Women are thus conditioned to enter society accepting their own inferiority, and even co-operating in and approving its perpetuation. Femininity is regarded as a construction of society. In a famous sentence, de Beauvoir separates sexual identity from gender: 'One is not born, but rather becomes, a woman.'

One task of feminist criticism is to examine and re-evaluate literature in the light of this perception. Texts may be revealed as built on intrinsically male value-structures, by depicting women in terms of STEREOTYPES of womanhood (polarised into Madonnas or Magdalens) or marginalising female characters (and readers) by subscribing chiefly to masculine endeavours and interests. **Images of women criticism**, the first phase of feminist criticism, traced the depiction of women in the literary CANON. This has been followed by **gynocriticism**, a coinage of Elaine Showalter in *A Literature of Their Own* (1977), which is the study of women writers and the female imagination. This involves the discovery and recovery of writers and texts ignored by the masculine-orientated canon, and the establishment of a female or feminine literary tradition, and defining particular feminine subject matter and sensibilities. **Gynotexts**, texts written by women, are not necessarily gynocentric, according to some theorists who argue that gynocriticism confuses biological sex with gender (the female with the feminine). Indeed the polarisation of male and female essential to the gynocritics' enterprise can be seen as a perpetuation and tacit acceptance of the masculine/feminine dichotomy which 'metaphysical feminism', the abstract theorising branch of the subject, would prefer to deny.

Festschrift. (Ger. 'celebration writing') A collection of ESSAYS presented to a distinguished scholar or writer by friends and colleagues to celebrate a notable career.

Ficelle. (Fr. 'string, trick') Henry James uses this term to describe a minor character in a novel whose conversations with the PROTAGONIST are used as a device to impart background information to the reader.

Fiction. (Lat. 'fashioned') The action of feigning, lying or inventing; that which is feigned or invented; things imagined as opposed to fact. 'Fiction' is nowadays used of NOVELS and stories collectively, to distinguish imaginative literature from 'non-fiction', for example, biography or history. The American poet Wallace Stevens used the word to mean the coherent arrangements which the human mind apprehends amidst the chaos of reality; art creates fictions through which we interpret and organise the world about us. For Stevens, 'poetry is the supreme fiction' ('A High-Toned Old Christian Woman', 1923). *See also* IMAGINATION.

Figural interpretation. Another name for the typological interpretation of the Bible. *See also* ALLEGORY.

Figurative language, figures of speech. (Lat. 'to shape, form or conceive', compare FICTION, FEIGN) Any form of expression or grammar which deviates from the plainest expression of meaning is designated a 'figure of speech'. Departures into more decorative language are further defined by a large number of terms such as APOSIOPESIS, ALLITERATION, ELLIPSIS, HYPERBOLE and LITOTES: most of these classifications originated in the ancient study of RHETORIC. METAPHOR is probably the figure of speech which most clearly characterises literary language: hence 'figurative language' can specifically refer to metaphorical language as well as to language abounding in other figures of speech.

Fin de siècle. (Fr. 'end of the century') The kind of DECADENCE that occurs at the end of a historical era, in particular the literary atmosphere of the late nineteenth century in France. *See also* AESTHETICISM, SYMBOLISM.

First-person narrative. Stories told in the first person singular. J.D. Salinger's *The Catcher in the Rye* (1951), for example, is narrated by its hero, the adolescent Holden Caulfield:

> If you really want to hear about it, the first thing you'll probably want to know is where I was born, and what my lousy childhood was like, and how my parents were occupied and all before they had me, and all that David Copperfield kind of crap, but I don't feel like going into it.

See also AUTOBIOGRAPHY, NARRATIVE.

Fit. (O.E. 'juncture') The Anglo-Saxon word for a division of a poem. The long, late fourteenth-century poem *Sir Gawain and the Green Knight* is divided into four fits.

Fixation. *See* PSYCHOANALYTIC CRITICISM.

Fixed forms. Metrical forms and STANZA patterns, such as the BALLADE, RONDEAU, SONNET, VILLANELLE, and so on, which are fixed and (except within certain limits) unvariable in line length and RHYME SCHEME.

Flashback. A term borrowed from films. A sudden jump backwards in time to an earlier episode or scene in the story of a novel, play or film. Increasingly common as a technique in novels, no doubt due to its familiarity from the cinema and television.

Flat character. *See* ROUND CHARACTER.

Fleshly school of poetry. *See* PRE-RAPHAELITES.

Flyting. (O.E. 'wrangling') Versified abuse: a quarrel in poetry between warriors about to do combat, as in the O.E. poem *The Battle of Maldon* (late tenth century); or between poets, as in the *Flyting of Dunbar and Kennedy* (*c*.1508) by Dunbar, a combat of virtuoso scurrility, which may owe something to Gaelic BARDIC scolding contests.

Foil. (Lat. 'leaf') A thin sheet of metal placed under a gem to improve its brilliance. In novels and plays a minor character may be introduced simply to illuminate by contrast aspects of a more significant character.

Folio. (Lat. 'leaf') A large page size, formed by a single fold in a sheet of printer's paper, giving four pages (or sides). Shakespeare's plays were first collected by Heminges and Condell in the volume called the First Folio (1623). Before this only nineteen of his plays had been published, all of them in unauthorised Quarto editions (a QUARTO page being half the size of the folio page, formed by another fold in the printer's sheet). Bibliographical discussion of Shakespeare's plays refers continually to different Quarto and Folio texts. *See also* DUODECIMO, OCTAVO.

Folk drama. *See* FOLKLORE.

Folklife. *See* FOLKLORE.

Folklore. The traditional customs and sayings handed down by word of mouth in societies not yet dominated by the written word are called collectively 'folklore'. Since the middle of the nineteenth century such materials have been carefully collected: they include BALLADS, folksongs, LEGENDS, TALES, superstitions, PROVERBS, RIDDLES, magic spells, sayings about the seasons, marriage and funeral rituals, and so on. Such customs are found alongside written 'literature' in modern Western societies as well as in Africa and other areas where literacy has arrived comparatively recently.

Special criteria for the examination of ORAL LITERATURE are being forged during the twentieth century: too often the artistic products of oral societies have been subjected to false comparisons with written literature. A modern term for the study of such societies and their art form is **folklife**, which combines anthropology, sociology and literary criticism.

Folktales are short, pithy stories of unknown authorship, which have been transmitted orally. They are a worldwide phenomenon and they encompass MYTHS, legends of superheroes, beast-FABLES, FAIRY TALES and stories of monsters, ghosts and giants, and jokes of all kinds. Similar themes and MOTIFS crop up in the folktales of different societies, giving some evidence to Jung's theories of ARCHETYPES and the COLLECTIVE UNCONSCIOUS. Elements of folklore and the folktale appear in the most sophisticated literature: in Shakespeare's *King Lear* (c.1605), Lear's testing of the love of his daughters, and the fact that only one of the three is sincere, is a typical folktale situation, not unlike the story of Cinderella and the ugly sisters.

Communal singing and dancing is common in most oral societies, celebrating social occasions such as marriages and funerals, or the passage of the seasons. Sometimes this may develop into **folk drama**. A few examples (the MUMMING PLAY) survive in English literature: such a play is described in Hardy's *The Return of the Native* (1878).

Folk poetry and **folksongs** are also common, and include ballads, work-songs, long narrative poems which are improvised, religious and love songs, children's rhymes. Many collections of such material have been made, from the eighteenth century onwards. Early collectors often rewrote the poems in a more literary form: much of Bishop Thomas Percy's influential *Reliques of Ancient English Poetry* (1765) consisted of 'restored' versions of folk material. At the end of the eighteenth century the Scottish poet Robert Burns and Sir Walter Scott also collected and sometimes modified many Scottish ballads and songs. Many of Burns's famous poems, such as 'Auld Lang Syne', are remodelled folksongs. Traditional ballads in many variant forms are still being collected from folksingers in Britain and America. Anthropologists and scholars of oral literature are also collecting folksongs and folk-materials in Africa and many other parts of the world.

Folksong. *See* FOLKLORE.

Folktale. *See* FOLKLORE.

Folly literature. A form of literature popular in the sixteenth century which examined fools and folly in a fantastical or satirical manner. The major example is Sebastian Brant's *Das Narrenschiff* ('The Ship of Fools', 1494), in which 112 different kinds of fool are described in rough poetry: this went through innumerable editions, translations, adaptations and copies. Erasmus's *Encomium Moriae* ('In Praise of Folly', 1511) is another example of a popular book about folly.

Delight in folly manifests itself in other types of literature, from Pope's *Dunciad* (1728, 1743) to Edward Lear's *A Book of Nonsense* (1846). *See also* BURLESQUE, NONSENSE.

Foot. In order to work out the metre of a line of verse, it is necessary to divide it into 'feet', which are certain fixed combinations of weakly and strongly stressed syllables into which the line is divided. The names for the various 'feet', such as the IAMB, TROCHEE, ANAPAEST and DACTYL, are borrowed from Greek metrical analysis. *See* METRE for further discussion of these terms.

Foregrounding. A concept much used in STYLISTICS. Foregrounding occurs when any deviation from the normal resources of language is found in a literary text; the deviation may be a matter of grammar, metaphor, or any other figure of speech; its effect is to push the relevant part of the text into the reader's attention, to place it as if in the foreground of a picture. 'Foregrounding' provides a point at which literary criticism and linguistics can meet. Some theorists have argued that 'foregrounding' is the essential element that distinguishes literature from non-literary texts. *See also* DEFAMILIARISATION, FORMALISM.

Form. (Lat. 'mould, shape') 'Form' is something of a jargon word in literary criticism, and its meaning is vague. It is a word readily understood in the plastic arts: a piece of pottery, for example, has a form or shape which is easily discerned by the eye. A defined metrical form, such as a SONNET, is also clearly comprehensible: the poet has, as it were, a pattern of sounds to which he or she must conform, as if filling an empty mould with words of the right shape. 'Form' can refer to METRE in this way. Such a form as the sonnet is called MECHANICAL to discriminate it from the kind of growing, developing and changing form favoured by early nineteenth-century Romantic writers such as Coleridge, called ORGANIC FORM. For Coleridge the ideas and images of a poem give it its own appropriate form or shape, like that of a plant growing from seed.

'Form' may also be used interchangeably with GENRE or literary type: TRAGEDY or the SHORT STORY are 'forms'.

Each individual example of genre also has a unique 'form' or shape or PATTERN. STRUCTURE is a word also used in this sense as a synonym for form.

The 'form' or 'structure' of a complex literary artefact like a novel may be a consequence of a large number of factors, such as its PLOT, its closeness to some ARCHETYPE, patterns of parallel incidents, thematic imagery (*see* IMAGERY), or the manner of its narration. Any repeated element will give a sense of pattern which can be considered an aspect of form. Different critics will stress different elements in defining form. *See also* CONTENT.

Formal, formality. 'Formal' in literature suggests the opposite of personal and emotional: a formal address means one which is dignified, impersonal and carefully ordered, suitable for a solemn public occasion. A formal essay is also a serious and ordered work intended to deploy a convincing argument in an authoritative and impersonal manner, without the intrusion of intimacy or whimsicality.

Formalism. A short-lived literary movement in Russia starting about 1917 which concentrated on form, style and technique in art, excluding other considerations, such as its social, political or philosophical aspects. Formalist critics, such as Viktor Shklovsky, classified and evaluated a work of art in terms of its formal devices alone.

In the 1930s this kind of criticism was suppressed as bourgeois reactionary IDEOLOGY by the Soviet SOCIALIST REALISTS; various critics connected with formalism, including René Wellek and Roman Jakobson, moved first to Prague and then to America. Ultimately formalism has become an influential critical movement, partly because of its connection with STRUCTURALISM and STYLISTICS.

The principal tenet of formalist criticism is that the language of literature is different from ordinary language, and that the critic's task is to define this 'literariness'. Literary language is constantly FOREGROUNDING the qualities of language itself, and 'backgrounding', or minimising, the DENOTATIVE aspects of language. In this general view of literature the Formalists are not far from the American NEW CRITICS, except that they concentrate more on refining the critic's methods of discussing technical matters, such as metre, rhyme and plot-construction. Formalist critics have used the discoveries and terminology of linguistics to help to define the artistic devices which make literary language 'deviate' from the 'norm'.

Format. The size and design of a book: its physical appearance and features. *See also* DUODECIMO, FOLIO, OCTAVO, QUARTO.

Formulae. Groups of words traditionally used in ORAL poetry, which is supposed to have been composed extemporally. Rather than starting afresh at every performance, it is thought that the poets made use of pre-existent blocks of phrases, sentences and verses, which were already part of the poetic tradition that they had memorised and were able to re-combine into new arrangements. This method is called the oral formulaic system.

An individual work can be 'formulaic' if it conforms to the patterns typical of its genre. More generally, any STOCK CHARACTERS, situations, scenes, phrases, ideas, EPITHETS, and so on, can be called 'formulaic' in a derogatory way.

Fourteener. A verse line of fourteen syllables, an iambic HEPTAMETER. Not uncommon in the verse of the fifteenth and early sixteenth centuries. It tends to break down into lines of four and three feet (BALLAD METRE). *See* METRE for further discussion of these terms.

Frame narrative or **frame story.** In NARRATIVES that contain a story within a story, this is the term for the outer, containing story, which is often just a pretext for the larger and more significant narrative, or narratives, embedded within it. The ruse by which Scheherazade saves her life, telling story after story to her murderous husband, is the 'frame narrative' for *The Thousand and One Arabian Nights*. In Conrad's novel *Heart of Darkness* (1902) Marlow's story is contained in a frame, told as it is to a fellow sailor while waiting in the Thames estuary for the tide to turn.

Free indirect style or **free indirect discourse.** A technique of narrating the thoughts, decisions or speech of a character through a special blend of THIRD- and FIRST-PERSON NARRATIVE. Here is an example from Jane Austen's *Emma* (1816):

> She had been thinking of him the moment before, as unquestionably sixteen miles distant. – There was time only for the quickest arrangement of mind. *She must be collected and calm.*

This last sentence in the direct style of speech or thought would read, 'I must be collected and calm'; indirect style would be, 'she thought that she ought to be collected and calm'. The free indirect style is a collapsing of the two in a way that allows the impression of access to Emma's thoughts, combined with some detachment. Flaubert used *le style indirect libre* to renowned effect in *Madame Bovary* (1857). It is a very common means of portraying the consciousness of characters in modern fiction.

Free verse. Sometimes called by the French term *vers libre*, free verse is verse released from the convention of METRE, with its regular pattern of stresses and line lengths. It is printed in broken-up lines like verse (not continuously like prose), and it is often very rhythmical, even containing patches of metrical regularity; but overall a poem in free verse cannot be resolved into the regular lines of repeated feet that characterise traditional versification.

Free verse was developed and used extensively by MODERNIST poets, like T.S. Eliot, Ezra Pound and W.C. Williams. Both Pound and Eliot asserted that it is not easier to use properly than traditional metre. Eliot's influential *The Waste Land* (1922) is one of the masterpieces of free verse.

Various writers had experimented with non-metrical verse in the nineteenth century, for example, the French SYMBOLISTS, and the American poet Walt Whitman, whose *Leaves of Grass* (1855) used lines of variable length but frequently recurring syntax and patterns of description, not unlike the Psalms in the Bible.

In free verse the variation between RUN-ON and END-STOPPED LINES is just as significant as in metrical poetry. Variation of line length and lines that break up sentences and even words, are also common features. A fragment of 'The Fox' (1966) by the contemporary poet Charles Tomlinson will illustrate some of these effects:

> The wind
> had scarped it into a pennine wholly of snow, and
> where did the hill go now?

> There was no way round:
> I drew booted legs
> back out of it, took to my tracks again,
> but already a million blown snow-motes were
> flowing and filling them in.

Freytag's pyramid. Gustav Freytag (1816–95), a German critic, in *Die Technik des Dramas* (1863), argued that the typical PLOT of a five-act play is like a pyramid in shape, consisting of introduction, rising action, climax, crisis or turning point, falling action and catastrophe.

Fricative. (Lat. 'rubbed') A phonetic classification of sounds produced by the friction of the passage of air between parts of the mouth held close together: 'f', 'v', 'th', 's', 'z' and 'h' sounds.

Fugitives. A group of poets from the Southern states of America who contributed to the *Fugitive*, a magazine appearing between 1922 and 1925. The best known were John Crowe Ransom, Allen Tate, Robert Penn Warren and Laura Riding. Most were connected with the Vanderbilt University in Nashville, Tennessee. Ransom and Cleanth Brooks became the founders of the NEW CRITICISM. The Fugitives supported the idea of a rural south and (like Eliot in England) were reacting against industrialisation and many other social and cultural manifestations of modern life. Most of their poetry tends to be formally disciplined, wittily intelligent and sophisticated in its condemnation of the imperfect human condition.

Function. (Lat. 'perform') Something of a jargon word in literary critical discourse, like 'device', derived from Russian FORMALISM, which emphasises that texts can be seen as a collection of inter-related parts which 'function' together (like a machine, perhaps) to produce identifiable effects. Often used in essay questions, such as 'What is the function of the Fool in *King Lear*?'. This asks the student not simply to describe the character or actions of the Fool, but to explain his character and actions in relation to the patterns and organisation of the play as a whole.

In linguistics 'function' offers a means of defining language in terms of what utterances are doing: for example, the functions of greeting, apologising, regretting, and so on, are a means of analysing verbal use, and allow description of the language system to be widened and extended beyond grammar.

NARRATOLOGISTS have used a similar conception in their analysis of the development of a story, so that a 'function' is an action that propels the events of a story forwards. Attempts have been made to define and isolate the basic forms that these functions can take. *See also* ACTANT, PLOT.

Fustian. A coarse kind of cloth (the name is derived from a suburb of Cairo where it originated): it is often used to describe pretentious, BOMBASTIC or dull, turgid writing.

Futurism. A short-lived European artistic and literary movement, centred originally in Italy. Its main advocate was the poet and publicist Filippo Marinetti who contributed to the Futurist manifesto in 1909. Futurists advocated the destruction of museums and the rejection of all grammatical and artistic conventions and rules in their search for new media, and perfect freedom for their unconscious creative minds without the 'rheumatisms of logic'. They espoused speed, war and Fascism: though apparently revolutionary, the consequence of their views was highly reactionary and isolationist.

In Russia the poet Vladimir Mayakovsky led a Futurist movement from *c*.1913 onwards, which found novel poetic forms consonant with the needs of a revolutionary situation, and he continued experimenting until his suicide in 1930. *See also* DADA, SURREALISM.

G

Galley proofs. *See* PROOF.

Gathering. A group of printed pages (**signatures**), folded and gathered together in preparation for the binding of a book.

Generalisation. (Lat. 'pertaining to the whole kind') A large and all-encompassing idea or statement, as opposed to 'particularisation', the study of detailed fragments. To generalise is to utter general truths which apply to all relevant cases. It is difficult to generalise adequately and validly on any subject, and, so the word has acquired a common pejorative force: to say that a statement is 'just a generalisation' implies that it is untrue in many of the cases in which it is supposed to apply. In *A Vision of the Last Judgment* (1810) Blake writes the following:

> General Knowledge is Remote Knowledge; it is in Particulars that Wisdom consists & Happiness too. Both in Art & in Life, General Masses are as Much Art as a Pasteboard Man is Human. Every Man has Eyes, Nose & Mouth; this Every Idiot knows, but he who enters into & discriminates most minutely the Manners & Intentions, the Characters in all their branches, is the alone Wise or Sensible Man, & on this discrimination All Art is founded.

Geneva school of criticism. A group of critics who follow the philosophy of PHENOMENOLOGY and are **critics of consciousness**. In phenomenology all consciousness is 'intentional' in the sense that it is always meaningful and part of a pattern. The aim of the reader is to absorb the created vision of the writer, and recount it in his or her own words. Thus, the whole work of a writer is analysed as an expression of a unified consciousness. All aspects of the writing – style, images, characters, direct statements – as well as personal habits and relevant biographical facts, are composed by the critic into an overall vision. In building up this picture of a writer's unique consciousness the critic may ignore the writer's explicit intentions, in order to reveal patterns of meaning of which the writer may have been unconscious or only partially conscious. The best-known exponent of this approach in English-language criticism is the American J. Hillis Miller (later a DECONSTRUCTIONIST).

Genre. (Fr. 'type') The term for a kind or type of literature. The three major genres of literature are poetry, drama and the novel (prose); these kinds may be subdivided into many other genres, major and minor, such as LYRIC (incorporating ELEGY, EPIC, ODE, SONG, SONNET), NARRATIVE VERSE, TRAGEDY, COMEDY, SHORT STORY, AUTOBIOGRAPHY, BIOGRAPHY, and so on.

Up until the end of the eighteenth century genres were regarded as relatively fixed entities, which ought to be written according to certain rules. Also genres were ranked in order of difficulty and seriousness of purpose: Milton's poetic career, for example, shows him trying out various kinds of poetry, such as the sonnet and the elegy ('Lycidas',

1637) in preparation for the most ambitious project of all, his epic *Paradise Lost* (1667).
   The NEW CRITICS tended to disregard generic considerations in their concentration on the text as AUTONOMOUS and self-sufficient. Recent criticism, however, has paid much more attention to this aspect of literature, not least in the attempts by critics like Northrop Frye to analyse literature in its totality in terms of different genres.

Georgian poetry. Though historically speaking the 'Georgian period' refers to the period covered by the four successive Georges (1714–1830), the term 'Georgian poetry' usually refers to poets who wrote during the reign of George V (1910–36). Between 1912 and 1922 Edward Marsh published four anthologies called *Georgian Poetry*, including poets such as W.H. Davies, Walter de la Mare, Ralph Hodgson and Rupert Brooke. The poems Marsh selected tended to be metrically conventional lyrics on rural themes; they were criticised as minor and unadventurous by those who had created (or espoused) MODERNISM, like T.S. Eliot. Two of the best poets who are often labelled as 'Georgian', Edward Thomas and Wilfred Owen, did not in fact appear in Marsh's anthologies.

Georgics. (Gk. 'to do with farmers') Agricultural poetry written in the spirit of the Roman poet Virgil's *Georgics* (37–30BC), which are practical, DIDACTIC poems on rural matters like growing crops and vines, bee-keeping, care of cattle, etc. Thomas Tusser's *Hundred Good Points of Husbandry* (1557) is an example.

Gesta. (Lat. 'deeds') Collections of heroic incidents, legends and adventures. The *Gesta Romanorum*, for example, is a fourteenth-century compilation of chivalric romances and stories of the saints, all with a moral; it was printed by Wynkyn de Worde in the early sixteenth century.

Gestalt. (Ger. 'form, shape') A philosophical term for an organised, coherent whole, whose parts are not randomly juxtaposed, but are ordered by laws intrinsic to the whole. In this sense it is used occasionally to discuss the overall STRUCTURE of a literary work.

Ghostwriter. Celebrities will sometimes employ a 'ghostwriter' to help them write their life-stories. The fact that a book has been 'ghosted' is usually concealed.

Gloss. (Lat. 'word needing explanation', from Gk. 'foreign language') Explanations of difficult words or phrases written in the margin or between the lines of a text. Greek manuscripts were often glossed in Latin. Modern editions of Middle English poems often have glosses on the page, or collected into a glossary at the back of the book. Coleridge's 'The Rime of the Ancient Mariner' is a relatively rare example of a poem usually printed with an explanatory gloss alongside it, though the glosses were added after its original publication in 1798. *See also* MARGINALIA.

Glossary. A collection of explanations of difficult words in alphabetical order.

Gnomic verse. (Gk. 'to do with opinion, judgment') Verse containing MAXIMS of popular wisdom, that is, short, impressive statements of general truths, also called *gnomes*. The word 'gnomic' is derived from early Greek poetry (sixth century BC) of this type, but many ancient cultures embodied wisdom in poetry. The Book of Proverbs in the Old Testament is an example. *See also* APHORISM, APOPHTHEGM, PROVERB.

Goliardic verse. Goliards were wandering scholars of the twelfth and thirteenth centuries: the verse named after them consists of uproarious songs about drinking and love, and rough satire against the Church. The *Carmina Burana* is a collection of such poems in a CODEX of thirteenth-century songs in Latin, Old German and Old French, found in the German monastery of Benediktbeuren: they are well known because the twentieth-century composer Carl Orff gave them a musical setting.

Gongorism. The Spanish poet Góngora developed an extremely difficult poetic style, full of word-play, elaborate METAPHORS, difficult ALLU-SIONS, obscure LATINATE vocabulary and dislocated word-order. This style, also called CULTERANISMO, dominated Spanish literature during the seventeenth century, then fell into disrepute, but (like METAPHYSICAL POETRY) its popularity was revived in the twentieth century. Similar manifestations of BAROQUE use of language are EUPHUISM and MARINISM.

Gothic novel. The word 'Gothic' originally referred to a Germanic tribe, but came to be used to mean 'medieval'. Nowadays the word refers to the art and architecture of the Middle Ages, in particular the pointed arch typical of medieval architecture. The 'Gothic revival' in architecture, harking back to the medieval style, started in the eighteenth century but flourished in the nineteenth.

'Gothic NOVELS' are fictions (originating at the same time as the revival of interest in the Middle Ages) which deal with cruel passions and supernatural terrors in some medieval setting, such as a haunted castle or monastery. Famous examples are Walpole's *The Castle of Otranto* (1764), Ann Radcliffe's *The Mysteries of Udolpho* (1794), 'Monk' Lewis's *The Monk* (1796) and Charles Maturin's *Melmoth the Wanderer* (1820). In their depiction of wild feelings they are both precursors and part of the literary movement called ROMANTICISM.

Works with a similarly obsessive, gloomy, violent and spine-chilling atmosphere, but not necessarily with a medieval setting, are also called Gothic: Mary Shelley's *Frankenstein* (1818), for example. Indeed any work concentrating on the bizarre, the macabre or aberrant psychological states may be called Gothic. In this sense Gothic elements are common in much nineteenth- and twentieth-century fiction.

Grammar. (Gk. 'concerning letters') Traditional grammar is the study of the way words combine to form sentences. *See also* MORPHOLOGY and SYNTAX.

In linguistics the term has a very wide range of specific uses beyond this simple definition. Descriptive grammar, theoretical grammar, comparative grammar, competence and performance grammars, all represent different ways of approaching and analysing language. In general 'grammar' in linguistics does not imply the framework of 'correctness' and 'wrongness' that was essentially part of the pre-scientific formulation of grammatical 'rules'.

Universal grammar attempts to define the characteristics of human language in general. As yet the existence of such a grammar is speculative.

'Grammar' is sometimes used metaphorically to denote an attempt to classify and order a subject.

Grammatology. The theory of writing put forward by Jacques Derrida, the originator of DECONSTRUCTION, in *De la grammatologie* ('Of Grammatology', 1967), in which he argues against the usually assumed primacy of speech (as opposed to writing).

Grand Guignol. Originally 'Guignol' was the name of a French puppet invented in Lyon in the eighteenth century. Like Punch and Judy, Guignol inhabited a world of brutality and infantile violence. Presumably because of this association, in the nineteenth century, Paris theatres specialising in MELODRAMATIC and macabre stories were called the 'Théâtre du Grand Guignol'. Nowadays *Grand Guignol* refers to any play which features sensationally gruesome or bloodthirsty effects.

Grand style. A phrase used by Arnold in his essay 'On Translating Homer' (1861). Homer, Virgil, Dante and Milton in their epics are all exponents of the 'grand style' which results when a gifted and noble poet 'treats with simplicity or severity a serious subject'.

Graveyard poets. Several eighteenth-century poets wrote mournfully pensive poems on the nature of death, which were set in graveyards or inspired by gloomy nocturnal meditations. Examples of this minor but popular genre are Thomas Parnell's 'Night-Piece on Death' (1721), Edward Young's *Night Thoughts* (1742–6) and Robert Blair's *The Grave* (1743). Gray's 'Elegy Written in a Country Churchyard' (1751) owes something to this vogue.

Great Chain of Being. The American scholar Arthur O. Lovejoy's famous study, *The Great Chain of Being* (1936), examines this concept in detail. The Great Chain of Being is the ladder-like hierarchy of life on earth, extending from the lowest animals up to God, with humankind somewhere in the middle. The idea goes back to Plato and was popular in the Renaissance; it became a central aspect of a view of life for the German Leibniz and other eighteenth-century philosophers, who regarded the universe as a vast proof of God's creativity and bountifulness. Their philosophical optimism ('Everything is for the best in this best of all possible worlds') was mocked by Voltaire in *Candide* (1759). Two famous poetical accounts of the 'Great Chain' are Ulysses's speech on 'degree' (I.3) in Shakespeare's *Troilus and Cressida* (*c*.1602) and Pope's *An Essay on Man* (1733-4), Epistle I, Section 8:

> Vast chain of Being, which from God began,
> Natures aethereal, human, angel, man,
> Beast, bird, fish, insect! What no eye can see,
> No glass can reach! from Infinite to thee,
> From thee to Nothing!

Grotesque. (Lat. 'like rocky caves') A common word in art criticism, referring originally to a particular kind of decoration used in architectural grottoes, to the fantastic interweaving of human and vegetable forms in BAROQUE decoration, and then to any extravagant and incongruous embellishment.

In the eighteenth century the word came to be used of all bizarre aberrations from the norms of good taste. Sometimes the grotesque might be sought for its own sake; for example, the desire to view wild natural scenery, such as the Alps, which strengthened during the eighteenth century, was a commonplace nineteenth-century taste.

Nowadays the word is used of deliberate distortions and ugliness, in the plastic arts or literature, intended to shock, satirise or amuse.

Grub Street. The name of a London street (now called Milton Street) which, during the eighteenth century, was populated by poor authors prepared to write anything for money. Hence the word applies to needy authors and HACK writers, and the kind of work they do. George Gissing's semi-autobiographical novel *New Grub Street* (1891) describes the life of such writers in the nineteenth century. *See also* POT-BOILER.

Gusto. (Lat. 'taste') A word used by the early nineteenth-century critic Hazlitt. His essay 'Gusto' (1816) begins: 'Gusto in art is power or passion defining any object.' Hazlitt uses the term to signify the artist's aesthetic pleasure in his subject, whether it be good or evil. Keats's idea of NEGATIVE CAPABILITY is similar. Both concepts look forward towards the AESTHETICISM of the late nineteenth century.

Gynocritic. (Gk. *gyne*, 'woman') 'Gynocritics' is the study of women's writing; a 'gynotext' is a text produced by a female, which may be studied by a gynocritic. *See also* ÉCRITURE FEMININE, FEMINIST CRITICISM.

H

Hack. A bad writer, or someone who writes just for money. The word is derived from 'hackney', a horse for hire. *See also* GRUB STREET, POT-BOILER.

Hagiography. (Gk. 'holy writing') Pious literature concerning the lives of Christian saints and martyrs. A common form of literature in the Middle Ages.

Haiku. (Jap. 'amusement verse') A Japanese lyric form. Exactly seventeen syllables are used in three lines: 5/7/5. Each *haiku* is a complete idea or observation: their common method is to describe a natural scene or object as a way of implying feeling. Several twentieth-century English and American poets have experimented with the form, including Ezra Pound, whose interest in the form coincided with his theories of IMAGISM. Many translated *haiku* do not conform to the exact syllable count. In the following example a mistaken perception offers an implicit metaphorical comparison:

> The fallen blossoms
>   seemed to fly up to their branch!
> They were butterflies.

Half-rhyme. An imperfect RHYME. Half-rhymes are common in twentieth-century poetry; poets wish to create some sense of pattern, without the possibility of irritating the reader with the chiming effect of full rhymes. These examples are from 'Steam' (1987) by Derek Walcott:

> A window cracked can thin the temperature
> of a steaming bath, a mirror's wisping hair;
> the zeros bubbling in bald, cobbled water
> with the plug pulled will gurgle and disappear,
>
> but the fog from potato fields, the error
> John Webster called 'a general mist,' condensed
> in the stubborn clouding of a bathroom mirror,
> cannot be cleaned by faster circling hands.

Hamartia. (Gk. 'error') Aristotle, in his *Poetics* (fourth century BC), uses this word to denote the error of judgment which tragic heroes make and which leads to their downfall. It is often translated as 'fatal' or 'TRAGIC FLAW', a significant if apparently small shift of emphasis, suggesting that TRAGEDY is a question of character rather than actions. *See also* HUBRIS.

Hapax legomenon. (Gk. 'once said') A word in a dead language, like Ancient Greek or Old English, of which only one use is recorded.

Happening. A fashionable concept of the 1960s in which some popular event, such as might take place in the streets of a city, bringing together a large crowd, is viewed as if it was a kind of theatrical entertainment, with the participants being both the actors and the audience. Anything might turn into a 'happening', from a political demonstration to a pop concert.

Harlem Renaissance. Also called the Black Renaissance, this was a flowering of literary activity by black writers in the 1920s, centred on Harlem, a district of New York. The anthology *The New Negro* (1925), edited by Alain Locke, collected together various artists in a way that was new in black culture. The African heritage of black Americans (at this time under enlightened scrutiny by anthropologists), and their folk traditions, were emphasised in poetical works like Countee Cullen's *Color* (1925) and Langston Hughes's *The Weary Blues* (1926), and in the novels of Zora Neale Hurston, such as *Mules and Men* (1935).

Hellenist, Hellenistic, Hellenism. 'Hellas' is Greece; therefore 'Hellenistic' refers generally to Greek culture. The more specific 'Hellenistic age' lasted from the death of Alexander the Great in 323BC to the subjugation of the Mediterranean world by the Romans towards the end of the first century BC; its centre was Alexandria.

In *Culture and Anarchy* (1869) Matthew Arnold elaborated a special meaning for 'Hellenism' in an extended contrast with 'Hebraism', which he saw as complementary human energies summed up by the different attractions of, on one hand, the pagan Classical past, and on the other, the Bible. The former aims at beauty and intellect, and 'to see things as they really are'; the latter stands for 'conduct and obedience'.

Hemistich. (Gk. 'half-line') Half of a section of a metrical line (divided by the CAESURA). Also denotes a line of less than the normal length.

Hendecasyllable. (Gk. 'eleven syllables') A verse line of eleven syllables.

Hendiadys. (Gk. 'one through two') Usually two nouns brought together into a single meaning by 'and': 'time and tide' or 'root and branch'.

Heptameter. (Gk. 'seven measures') A line of seven feet in English versification. Chapman's translation of the *Iliad* (1611) is written in iambic heptameter, also called 'FOURTEENERS'. The following example is from Macaulay's 'Virginia' in *Lays of Ancient Rome* (1842):

> When Appius Claudius saw that deed, he shuddered and sank down,
> And hid his face some little space with the corner of his gown,
> Till, with white lips and bloodshot eyes, Virginius tottered nigh,
> And stood before the judgment-seat, and held the knife on high.

Heptameters tend to break down into BALLAD METRE of alternating three- and four-stress lines. *See also* METRE, POULTER'S MEASURE.

Hermeneutic circle. A philosophical conundrum in interpretation: how can we understand a part of a work without first having some idea of the whole, yet how can we have a view of the whole without first understanding the part? *See also* EMPIRICISM.

Hermeneutics. (Gk. 'science of interpretation') Originally a word applied to interpretation of the Bible; now applied generally to the theory of how, to what extent and by what principles and procedures we can interpret literary or indeed any texts. The NEW CRITICISM stressed the impossibility of examining a work by reference to its writer's intention (the INTENTIONAL FALLACY), and the modern critical theories of STRUCTURALISM and DECONSTRUCTION equally deny the possibility of discovering a determinate reading of a text. By contrast, RECEPTION THEORY analyses the conditions which control textual interpretation.

Hermetic, Hermeticism. Poetry which is obscure to the point of seeming to have its meaning sealed in some secret symbolic code may be dubbed Hermetic. The term is often applied to the work of the nineteenth-century SYMBOLIST poets, such as Baudelaire and Mallarmé. The word originates from the body of writings attributed to 'Hermes Trismegistus' ('Hermes the Thrice-Greatest'), the Greek name for the Egyptian god Thoth, mythical inventor of writing and all the arts connected with it, and the name given to the author of various mystical, alchemical and occult writings dating from the first to the third centuries, which were revered by the NEOPLATONISTS and certain seventeenth-century writers, such as the poet Henry Vaughan and his brother Thomas.

Hero, heroine. (Gk.) The chief character in a work of literature. Tragedy usually focuses on a single figure; in comedy the interest is usually dispersed over several characters. *See also* PROTAGONIST.

Heroic couplet. Lines of IAMBIC PENTAMETER rhymed in pairs. A common metre, especially in the eighteenth century. Pope brought the metre to a peak of polish and wit, using it in satire, in verse-essays, in MOCK-HEROIC and descriptive verse. His *Epistle II: To a Lady. Of the Characters of Women* (1735) begins thus:

Nothing so true as what you once let fall,
'Most Women have no Characters at all.'
Matter too soft a lasting mark to bear,
And best distinguish'd by black, brown, or fair.
How many pictures of one Nymph we view,
All how unlike each other, all how true!
Arcadia's Countess, here, in ermin'd pride,
Is there, Pastora, by a fountain side.
Here Fannia, leering on her own good man,
And there, a naked Leda with a Swan.

The regular, obtrusive and exact rhymes give the form an EPIGRAMMATIC quality. In eighteenth-century verse the couplets tend to be **closed**; the syntax coincides with the metre so that each pair of lines is a sentence, as in the case of all the couplets above. In order to avoid monotony Pope arranges his grammar so that the lines are varied and broken up by several strong CAESURAE, or pauses. *See* METRE for further discussion of these terms. *See also* NEOCLASSICISM.

Heroic drama, heroic tragedy. Plays influenced by French classical drama and written mostly during the Restoration period (1660–1700) with subjects which aspired to epic grandeur, dealing with the exploits in battles and love, of great warriors, emperors and kings. Typically the demands of love and patriotic duty come into conflict. Dryden's *All for Love* (1678), a reworking in BLANK VERSE and according to late seventeenth-century taste of Shakespeare's *Antony and Cleopatra* (*c*.1607), is one of the most successful examples of this kind of drama. The high aspirations of the style led often to BOMBAST; heroic drama was easily parodied, as shown by Fielding's *The Tragedy of Tragedies, or The Life and Death of Tom Thumb the Great* (1731).

Heroic poetry. Another name for EPIC poetry.

Heroic quatrain. Lines of IAMBIC PENTAMETER rhymed *abab, cdcd*, and so on. Thomas Gray's 'Elegy Written in a Country Churchyard' (1751) is a notable example. *See also* METRE, STANZA.

Heterodiegetic. *See* DIEGESIS.

Heuristic. (Gk.'discover') An adjective applied to the process of searching for clues while trying to comprehend a puzzling phenomenon. In discussing literature, the word refers to those parts and aspects of a text on which an interpretation can be built, as well as to the process of interpreting it. 'Heuristics' is therefore the study or science of procedures for the discovery of meaning in philosophy, mathematics and literary criticism.

Hexameter. (Gk. 'six measures') In English versification, a line of six feet. A line of IAMBIC HEXAMETER is called an ALEXANDRINE. Dowson's 'Cynara' (1891) is written in six-line stanzas composed of rough iambic hexameter, except for the fifth line which is a PENTAMETER:

All night upon mine heart I felt her warm heart beat,
Night-long within mine arms in love and sleep she lay;
Surely the kisses of her bought red mouth were sweet;
But I was desolate and sick of an old passion,
    When I awoke and found the dawn was gray;
I have been faithful to thee, Cynara! in my fashion.

See also METRE.

Hiatus. (Lat. 'opening') A gap, break or pause in an argument or action.

Hidden agenda. An 'agenda' (Lat. 'things to be done') is simply a list. The term 'hidden agenda' is used in the discussion of literature to suggest that some aim or intention lies behind a work which has nothing to do with its apparent subject matter, argument or purpose. These hidden aims may be non-literary, and even apparently in opposition to the explicit aims of a work. For example, it might be argued that the 'hidden agenda' of much love poetry by men is to exclude women from male-orientated structures of reasoning and power, by idealising and mystifying womanhood. *See also* SUBTEXT.

Hierarchy of discourses. DISCOURSE, in the sense of a narrative style involving a relationship with the reader, is a complex and multiple event. An omniscient narrator will present a number of different layers of understanding of the action: some characters will be described as unknowing and insensitive to the events and unfolding morality, others as partially knowing, and perhaps a protagonist may be portrayed as fully conscious of his or her own activities. Yet the 'AUTHOR', not necessarily the NARRATOR, but the ultimate creator or producer of the text, is above all the characters and controls the reader's response to them, and is the source of all the sensitivity and wisdom (as well as knowing how the story will end). This pyramid of understanding, with the author at the apex as the privileged, ultimate author/ity, is called the 'hierarchy of discourses', and it is supposed to be the distinguishing feature of the kind of REALISM called 'CLASSIC BOURGEOIS'. *See also* ÉNONCÉ, IMPLIED AUTHOR, NARRATOLOGY.

Hieratic. (Gk. 'priestly') Sometimes used of style (in contrast with the DEMOTIC style) to denote elaborate and formal language.

High comedy. High comedy was distinguished from LOW COMEDY in Meredith's 'The Idea of Comedy' (1877): it is the comedy of wit and intellectual detachment. A comedy of manners such as Congreve's *The Way of the World* (1700) is a typical example of high comedy. *See also* COMEDY.

Higher criticism. The new rigorous, scholarly study of the Bible which originated in Germany in the late eighteenth century and flourished during the nineteenth century. It was concerned with authorship, exact dating and cultural history.

Histoire. In French the word refers to historical writing, as well as meaning 'story' in its ordinary sense. It also has a more technical meaning in NARRATOLOGY where it refers to the simplest chronological shape of a story, which is then twisted and re-ordered into the pattern of its actual narration in the text. *See also* DIEGESIS.

Historical novel. A type of NOVEL developed by Sir Walter Scott, starting with *Waverley* (1814), which is set in a particular historical period, and which describes events and manners of that period. Both real and imaginary persons may appear as characters. An extremely popular type of nineteenth- and twentieth-century fiction.

Historicism. The doctrine that all systems of thought must be judged within a historical perspective. And, going beyond this, the belief that social science, including history, should be devoted to uncovering laws of development that rule historical changes and allow forecasts to be made about the future. MARXIST social analysis, for example, is historicist.

The **new historicism** refers to the work of a loose affiliation of critics who discuss literary works in terms of their historical contexts, often minutely researched, as a reaction against both the anti-historical precepts of the NEW CRITICISM, and the equally anti-historical methods of criticism that have succeeded it, STRUCTURALISM and DECONSTRUCTION. Some new historicists make use of the terminology of POST-STRUCTURALISM. They see literature as one of many DISCOURSES that require to be separated from each other. In particular they seek to study literature as part of a wider cultural history, and often to validate Marxist critical assertions concerning the relationship of literature and society. One method is to build a historical 'counter-narrative' with which to compare a text. For example, at the time that Wordsworth wrote 'Lines Composed a Few Miles above Tintern Abbey' (1798), it is known that the ruined abbey was used as a shelter by vagrants and beggars. This fact is not mentioned by the poet, in spite of his declared concern for such people in other poems. Such an 'absence' may be used to suggest that the poem is élitist and escapist, though a critic unsympathetic to this kind of analysis would regard it as mistaken to judge a poem by what is not in it, rather than by its actual contents.

Historicity. A term for historical authenticity and validity: the historicity of an event concerns the degree to which it might actually have happened in history, and the degree to which it is a historically meaningful event.

The historicity of a novel might refer to the extent to which it deals with events that actually happened, its resemblance to a historical account or document, or the historical relevance of the events it recounts.

History play. Broadly speaking, any play which is set in a historical period. Specifically, however, the term refers to plays which are dramatisations of Holinshed's *Chronicles* of English history (1577, 1587): such works were popular in the late sixteenth century. Shakespeare wrote a large number of history plays of this kind, dealing with King John and the complete succession of English kings from Richard II to Henry VIII. *See also* CHRONICLE PLAY.

Holograph. (Gk. 'whole writing') A manuscript or typescript which includes corrections, crossings-out and additions suggesting the writer's process of composition and creation. Originally the term simply meant a manuscript entirely in its author's handwriting.

Homeric epithet. *See* EPITHET.

Homily. (Gk. 'discourse, sermon') Whether spoken or written, a homily is a sermon-like discourse, or short lecture, intended to be morally edifying.

Homodiegetic. *See* DIEGESIS.

Homology. (Gk. 'same study') The condition of being 'homologous', that is, sharing a similar structure with something else. Critics may find 'homologues' (similarly structured configurations) in different spheres of human activity: for example, patterns in a work of literature might be seen to be comparable with a prevalent social structure, or a set of psychological models.

Homonym. (Gk. 'same name') A word with two or more different meanings and derivations, e.g. 'bark', meaning 'the noise a dog makes' or 'skin of a tree'. Also a pompous word for a PUN.

Homophone. (Gk. 'same sound') A word which is pronounced identically with another word, but is spelled differently and has a different meaning, e.g. so/sew, bough/bow. Sometimes used to mean 'RHYME'.

Homostrophic. (Gk. 'same STROPHES') Using the same STANZA form throughout, as, for example, Keats's *Odes*.

Horatian ode. *See* ODE.

Horatian satire. Genial, urbane, witty and tolerant SATIRE of the kind written by the Roman poet Horace (65–8BC). Pope wrote several *Imitations* of Horace's *Satires* and *Epistles* between 1733 and 1738.

Horizon of expectations. A term from RECEPTION THEORY to describe the background network of ideas, attitudes and conventions possessed by readers, and through which they perceive the object of their studies. As such a horizon is constantly changing, readers of different eras cannot avoid interpreting works in radically different ways. *See also* COMPETENCE, CONVENTION, IDEOLOGY, PARADIGM.

Hornbook. A type of child's reading primer which was in use in poor elementary schools until the eighteenth century. The alphabet, numbers and sometimes the Lord's Prayer were mounted on wood and covered in a layer of thin, transparent horn.

Hubris. (Gk. 'insolence, pride') The self-indulgent confidence that causes a tragic hero to ignore the decrees, laws and warnings of the gods, and therefore defy them to bring about his or her downfall (NEMESIS). In Euripides's *The Bacchae* (fifth century BC) Pentheus shows *hubris* in his hostility to Dionysus and is torn to pieces by the god's worshippers.

Hudibrastic verse. Samuel Butler's *Hudibras* (1662–78) is a satire chiefly against Puritanism, but also directed against nearly all things serious. It is a MOCK-HEROIC, episodic narrative of the adventures of a ludicrously pedantic knight, Sir Hudibras. The language is grotesquely colloquial, scurrilous and at times degenerates into DOGGEREL. Its metre is rough OCTOSYLLABIC COUPLETS. Verse of this kind is called 'hudibrastic'. The poem opens with a reference to the civil war between the Royalists and Parliamentarians:

When civil fury first grew high,
And men fell out, they knew not why;
When hard words, jealousies and fears,
Set folks together by the ears,

And made them fight, like mad or drunk,
For Dame Religion as for punk,
Whose honesty they all durst swear for,
Though not a man of them knew wherefore;
When gospel-trumpeter, surrounded
With long-ear'd rout, to battle sounded,
And pulpit, drum ecclesiastic,
Was beat with fist instead of a stick:
Then did Sir Knight abandon dwelling,
And out he rode a-coloneling

See also BURLESQUE, TRAVESTY.

Humanism. The word 'humanist' originally referred to a scholar of the HUMANITIES, especially Classical literature. At the time of the RENAISSANCE (*c.* sixteenth century) European intellectuals devoted themselves to the rediscovery and intense study of first Roman and then Greek literature and culture, in particular the works of Cicero, Aristotle and Plato. Out of this period of intellectual ferment there emerged a view of man and a philosophy quite different from medieval SCHOLASTICISM: in the nineteenth century this trend of Renaissance thought was labelled 'humanism'. Reason, balance and a proper dignity for man were the central ideals of humanist thought.

Among the many humanist thinkers the Dutch priest Erasmus deserves special mention: his works (in Latin) were known all over Europe. He was an independent and anti-authoritarian thinker whose criticisms of the unreformed Church paved the way for the REFORMATION, although he opposed Luther and the various Protestant theological factions.

The kind of Christian humanism typified by Erasmus is reflected in the writing of men like Sidney, Bacon, Spenser, Milton and, possibly, Shakespeare. Their attitude to the world is anthropocentric: instead of regarding man as a fallen, corrupt and sinful creature, their idea of truth and excellence is based on human values and human experience. They strive for moderate, achievable, even worldly aims, rather than revering asceticism. Hamlet's famous speech beginning 'What a piece of work is man! How noble in reason! How infinite in faculty!' (*Hamlet*, II.2, *c.*1601) is often quoted to exemplify the humanist view, though, of course, Hamlet undercuts his praise by referring to man finally as 'this quintessence of dust'.

'Humanism' in a general sense has been revived at various times since the Renaissance. The domination of society by science and industry during the nineteenth century led many writers, notably Matthew Arnold, to stress humanist values in an attempt to define a properly rounded education as a counter to the cultural aridity they saw spreading around them. The American **New Humanism**, led by the critic and teacher Irving Babbitt during the 1920s and 1930s, was a similar assertion of humanist values in the form of 'the classical spirit . . . consecrated to the service of a high, impersonal reason'.

Nowadays 'humanism' refers vaguely to moral philosophies which reject the supernatural beliefs of religion: many twentieth-century 'humanists', in this loose sense, are actively opposed to Christianity. The word is also used as an insult by MARXIST critics, for whom it is a label that sums up all that is wrong with those who live contentedly within the 'bourgeois' IDEOLOGY.

Humanities. In the Middle Ages, grammar, rhetoric and poetry, with Greek and Latin, were *literae humaniores*, as opposed to divinity (*literae divinae*). Nowadays the word tends to refer generally to the arts subjects studied at university rather than science or the social sciences.

Cicero used the word *humanitas* to denote a liberal education.

Humour, humours. (Lat. 'liquid') In ancient medical theory (lasting until *c.* seventeenth century) there were four principal 'humours' in the human body (phlegm, blood, choler and black bile). If any one of these predominated in an individual's constitution then that person's character would be phlegmatic, sanguine, choleric or melancholic. An exact balance made a compound called 'good humour'; predomination by any one humour caused 'ill' or 'evil' humour. Ben Jonson wrote several 'comedies of humours', such as *Every Man in His Humour* (1598) in which each character is dominated by a passion or obsession.

In modern usage 'humour' can mean 'mood' or 'character', but the word also denotes 'that which causes laughter'.

Hymn. (Gk. 'song in praise of god or hero') A religious song praising God. Many examples, in Latin and, from the sixteenth century onwards, in English, have been written by poets and ecclesiastics. The eighteenth and nineteenth centuries were particularly rich periods for the writing and composing of hymns.

Hypallage. (Gk. 'exchange') A rhetorical term describing the figure of speech in which the natural relations of words are exchanged, often by placing an EPITHET in an unusual position. In Keats's 'the murmurous haunt of flies on summer eves' ('Ode to a Nightingale', 1820) it is actually the flies that are murmurous, and not the haunt. This kind of transfer is common in everyday speech, in expressions such as 'a successful day' or 'uncomfortable shoes'.

Hyperbaton. (Gk. 'step over') A learned rhetorical term for INVERSION of ordinary word order, common in poetry or statements seeking to be poetic: 'Above us the waves' or 'These you have loved'.

Hyperbole. (Gk. 'throwing too far') A figure of speech: emphasis by exaggeration. Common in everyday speech: 'There were millions of people at the cafe.' Common also in all kinds of literature, comic and serious. In Shakespeare's *Macbeth* (*c.*1606) Macbeth expresses in hyperbole his guilt at murdering Duncan (II.2):

Will all great Neptune's ocean wash this blood
Clean from my hand? No, this my hand will rather
The multitudinous seas incarnadine
Making the green one red.

Hypermetrical. (Gk. 'too many measures') A line of verse with more syllables than its metrical pattern allows. The commonest example is the FEMININE ENDING: a line of verse ending with an extra unstressed syllable.

Hypodiegetic. *See* DIEGESIS.

Hypostatisation. (Gk. 'standing under, foundation') A type of PERSONIFICATION in which an abstract quality is spoken of as if it was a substance or a person: 'Sorrow has come among us' or 'A terrible beauty is born'.

Hypotactic style. *See* PARATAXIS.

I

Iamb. (Gk. 'to assail', alluding to the use of iambic metres in satiric poetry) The commonest metrical FOOT in English verse, consisting of a weak stress followed by a strong stress, ti-tum. *See also* METRE.

Iambic hexameter. A line of six IAMBIC feet (*see* METRE for further discussion of these terms). The metre is rather ponderous in English verse. Its first extensive use was by Drayton in his topographical poem *Poly-Olbion* (1612, 1622):

When in the lower Brake, the Nightingale hard-by,
In such lamenting strains the joyful hours doth ply,
As though the other Birds she to her tunes would draw.
And, but that Nature (by her all-constraining law)
Each Bird to her own kind this season doth invite,
They else, alone to hear that Charmer of the Night
(The more to use their ears) their voices sure would spare . . .

Iambic pentameter. A line of five IAMBIC feet (*see* METRE for further discussion of these terms). The iambic pentameter is the most pervasive metrical pattern found in verse in English. Rhymed in pairs it is called the HEROIC COUPLET; the following unrhymed example (BLANK VERSE) is from Book IV of Milton's *Paradise Lost* (1667):

So hand in hand they passed, the loveliest pair
That ever since in love's embraces met:
Adam, the goodliest man of men since born

His sons; the fairest of her daughters Eve.
Under a tuft of shade that on a green
Stood whispering soft, by a fresh fountain-side,
They sat them down; and after no more toil
Of their sweet gardening labour than sufficed
To recommend cool Zephyr, and made ease
More easy, wholesome thirst and appetite
More grateful, to their supper fruits they fell.

(lines 321–31)

Iambic tetrameter. A line of four IAMBIC feet (*see* METRE for further discussion of these terms).

Tennyson's *In Memoriam* (1850) is entirely composed of poems written in stanzas of four iambic tetrameters, rhymed *abba*. The example below is from the second lyric in the sequence of 130:

Old yew, which graspest at the stones
  That name the underlying dead,
  Thy fibres net the dreamless head,
Thy roots are wrapped about the bones.

The seasons bring the flower again,
  And bring the firstling to the flock;
  And in the dusk of thee the clock
Beats out the little lives of men.

Icon. (Gk. 'image') A word borrowed from art criticism (an icon is a sacred painting, a flat portrait of a sacred personage, typically found in Russian and Greek Orthodox churches). The title of W.K. Wimsatt's critical study *The Verbal Icon* (1954) suggests the way in which the NEW CRITICS stressed the AUTONOMY of a poem, as if it was an object to be contemplated, like a religious icon.

In SEMIOTICS, an icon is one of the kinds of SIGN defined by C.S. Peirce.

Iconoclasm. (Gk. 'image-breaking') The act or habit of denying and destroying accepted ideas and conventions, perhaps in a shocking manner.

AVANT-GARDE literature has almost always been iconoclastic; iconoclasm is frequently an element in MODERNIST literature.

Ictus. (Lat. 'a blow') Another word for metrical stress. *See also* METRE.

Id. *See* PSYCHOANALYTIC CRITICISM.

Idealism. (Gk. 'notion-ism', from *idea*, 'look, form, model') Any philosophical theory which suggests that the 'external world' is created by the mind.

The eighteenth-century philosopher Bishop Berkeley adopted a philosophical position that was both EMPIRICAL and idealist. For him material objects consisted of nothing but ideas or sensations which can only be experienced in the mind, either of God or of individual humans, conscious agents created by Him. Dr Johnson's famous rebuttal of this argument consisted of kicking a large stone very hard.

Blake expresses a similar idealist philosophy in *A Vision of the Last Judgment* (1810):

> Mental Things are alone Real; what is call'd Corporeal, Nobody Knows of its Dwelling Place: it is in Fallacy, & its Existence an Imposture. Where is the Existence Out of Mind or Thought?

Blake accepted that he could perceive an 'outward Creation' with his 'Corporeal or Vegetative Eye', but he regarded this as 'dirt upon my feet, No part of Me', compared with the world of his visionary imagination.

Idée fixe. (Fr. 'fixed idea') An idea to which a writer returns repeatedly. An obsession. The French poet Paul Valéry studied the nature of the phenomenon in his *Idée fixe* (1932).

Ideology. (Gk. 'discourse about or study of ideas') The collection of ideas, opinions, values, beliefs and preconceptions which go to make up the 'mind-set' of a group of people, that is, the intellectual framework through which they view everything, and which colours all their attitudes and feelings (especially, perhaps, assumptions about power and authority). What we take to be 'reality' is controlled by the ideologies of the era in which we live.

That human consciousness is shaped or 'constituted' in this way by ideology is a concept introduced by Marx. According to Marx only those who see reality from a MARXIST point of view can see beyond the prevailing ideology, which in the present capitalist era is that of the 'bourgeoisie'. Literature is permeated by the ideology of the era and the class from which it is derived.

The word has come into general use in the weak sense of 'a body of ideas' or 'a definable way of looking at the world', usually political in emphasis, and indeed, ironically, it has tended to be used only as a label for Marxist or communist ideologies. On the other hand, when Marxist literary critics use the word, they insist that a central tenet of the bourgeois ideology is the belief that its own world-view is free of ideology, and those who refuse to admit the hidden political implications of capitalist 'freedom' do so to preserve the power structures which serve themselves and their class. *See also* COMMON SENSE, ISA, PHENOMENOLOGY.

Idiolect. (Gk. 'personal speech') A linguistic term for the individual language system of a person: his or her unique pronunciation, grammatical forms and choice of vocabulary. *See also* STYLE, STYLOMETRICS.

Idiom. (Gk. 'peculiar phraseology') A phrase or way of expressing something special to a language, sometimes ungrammatical or illogical in its signification.

Expressions like 'tough luck', 'another kettle of fish', 'spot on', 'elbow-grease', 'stuck up', 'sitting on the fence' are idiomatic expressions. *See also* CLICHÉ, PROVERB, SLANG.

Idyll. (Gk. 'little form, picture') A short poem describing a picturesque rustic scene or incident. Hence 'idyll' comes to refer to poems or parts of poems which deal with ideal states of calm, happiness or enlightenment. In Theocritus's *Idylls* (third century BC) it is synonymous with PASTORAL. Tennyson's *Idylls of the King* (1842–85) are tales of Arthurian ROMANCE.

Illocutionary act. *See* SPEECH ACT THEORY.

Illusion. (Lat. 'mockery, deception') Used in criticism to denote the writer's creation of a convincing imagined world, leading to what Coleridge called in Chapter 14 of *Biographia Literaria* (1817) 'the willing suspension of disbelief'. Writers may also deliberately break the illusion they have created by talking directly to the reader; a notable modern example of this is John Fowles's *The French Lieutenant's Woman* (1969), where the author examines the business of creating a story while he is creating it.

Illusionism. A mildly pejorative label for the 'trick' that REALISM plays on its readers, by presenting fictions as if they were true. One of the distinguishing features of 'CLASSIC BOURGEOIS' REALISM, along with CLOSURE and a HIERARCHY OF DISCOURSES.

Image, imagery. (Lat. 'copy, representation') A critical word with several different applications. In its narrowest sense an 'image' is a word-picture, a description of some visible scene or object. More commonly, however, 'imagery' refers to the FIGURATIVE LANGUAGE in a piece of literature (METAPHORS and SIMILES); or all the words which refer to objects and qualities which appeal to the senses and the feelings.

Keats in his 'Epistle to J.H. Reynolds' (1848) uses (amongst others) imagery of light and darkness and of nature, especially the sea, to advance his argument. The poem concentrates on a single image of the beach:

> 'twas a quiet Eve,
> The rocks were silent – the wide sea did weave
> An untumultuous fringe of silver foam
> Along the flat brown sand . . .

The imagery appeals not just to sight but to the ear as well ('quiet', 'silent', 'untumultuous'). There is also imagery of cloth-making ('weave', 'fringe').

In the critical description above, 'imagery' and 'image' are applied (1) to a single word-picture; (2) in a general sense to all the parts of the poem not in LITERAL or ABSTRACT language; (3) to the components of the word-picture that appeal to all the senses, not just sight; and (4) specifically to the vehicles of the metaphors in the descriptions. Though it seems confusing that the word can be used in several different ways, it is usually obvious what the word's sense is from its context.

Thematic imagery is imagery (in the general sense) which recurs throughout a work of art: for example, in Shakespeare's *Macbeth* (*c*.1606), images of animals, birds, darkness and disease are common, and they are used in such a way as to underpin the play's theme of the battle between unnatural evil and goodness.

Images of women criticism. *See* FEMINIST CRITICISM.

Imagination. (Lat. 'forming an image, representation') The mental faculty which forms images of external objects not present to the senses. In this sense the act of reading (and of writing) literature is an imaginative act.

Some writers, notably Coleridge, have sought to distinguish the imagination from other similar faculties of the mind (especially 'FANCY', which in the eighteenth century was synonymous with imagination) and define it as the principle of creativity in art. In the famous Chapter 13 of *Biographia Literaria* (1817) Coleridge describes the poetic imagination: 'It dissolves, diffuses, dissipates, in order to recreate; or where this process is rendered impossible, yet still at all events it struggles to idealise and to unify. It is essentially vital.' In Chapter 14 he explores the way in which the imagination creates harmonious wholes (poems) out of disparate experience: 'This power . . . reveals itself in the balance or reconciliation of opposite or discordant qualities: of sameness, with difference; of the general, with the concrete; the idea with the image . . . a more than usual state of emotion, with more than usual order.'

For Coleridge the imagination is a 'synthetic and magical power' (i.e. it synthesises); it is the power of creativity, a power modelled on the way in which the mind perceives, perception being itself an active and creative function.

Coleridge's value-laden view of the imagination has come to be an accepted critical meaning of the word; it usually denotes the mind's artistic creative faculty.

In a weak popular sense 'imagination' might be used pejoratively to indicate something that was not true or real: 'It's only your imagination.'

Imagism. A self-conscious movement in poetry in England and America initiated by Ezra Pound and T.E. Hulme in about 1912. Pound tired of it when it was taken over by the American poet Amy Lowell who published three anthologies called *Some Imagist Poets* between 1915 and 1917.

Pound described the aims of Imagism in his essay 'A Retrospect' (1918):

1. Direct treatment of the 'thing' whether subjective or objective.
2. To use absolutely no word that does not contribute to the presentation.
3. As regarding rhythm: to compose in the sequence of the musical phrase, not in sequence of a metronome.

Pound defined an 'Image' as 'that which presents an intellectual and emotional complex in an instant of time'. His HAIKU-like two-line poem 'In a Station of the Metro' (1916) is often quoted as the quintessence of Imagism. The following example is 'Autumn Haze' (1919) by Amy Lowell:

Is it a dragonfly or a maple leaf
That settles softly down upon the water?

Imitation. (Lat. 'copy') Three meanings may be discerned in literary criticism: (1) A work such as Pope's *Imitations of Horace* (1733-8) or Robert Lowell's *Imitations* (1961) in which a poet provides a loose translation of another work, transposed into a contemporary and personal situation: the pleasure for the reader lies in the cleverness of the adaptation rather than in the accuracy of the translation. (2) The belief that poets should in general 'imitate' the classics and other models of excellence in any genre which precedes them. 'Imitation' in this sense was a tenet of eighteenth-century NEOCLASSICISM, and of most views of poetry until the nineteenth century. Something more than merely copying is implied: the poet must catch the form and spirit of his or her models, but animate them with his or her own genius. (3) 'Imitation' is the key-word in MIMETIC views of literature which follow Aristotle in regarding poetry as an 'imitation' of human actions. Literature holds a mirror up to life, or is a 'true' model of life. Again this view was common until the end of the eighteenth century, though what literature should imitate, and how, were subjects for controversy. The CHICAGO CRITICS reintroduced 'imitation' as a significant word in their reworking of Aristotle's literary philosophy; it also underlies theories of REALISM.

Imperfect rhyme. An inexact RHYME between words, common in modern poetry.

Impersonal narrator. *See* NARRATIVE.

Impersonality. (Lat. 'not pertaining to an individual') The quality in literature of having no sense of the writer's personality and no personal tone or references. This exclusion of the self from literature has been highly valued by some critics, notably T.S. Eliot, as, for example, in his influential theory of the OBJECTIVE CORRELATIVE. In his essay 'Tradition and the Individual Talent' (1919) he argues against the view that poetry is an expression of personality: 'Poetry is not a turning loose of emotion, but an escape from emotion; it is not the expression of personality, but an escape from personality. But, of course, only those who have personality and emotions know what it means to want to escape from these things.'

Implication. (Lat. 'folding in') Words often imply, or strongly suggest, meanings beyond their literal meaning. In Shakespeare's *Othello* (*c*.1604), for example, Iago constantly implies that Desdemona has been unfaithful to Othello; he does not state it as a fact. Literary language is always replete with implication. *See also* CONNOTATION, DENOTATION, REFERENTIAL LANGUAGE.

Implicit. (Lat. 'entwined') What is implied or suggested, but not expressed; meanings that are not **explicit** (Lat. 'unfolded'). Part of the pleasure of reading all kinds of literature is following the clues that allow us to follow the writer's implicit meaning: these may be in the form of IRONY, SYMBOLS, ALLEGORY, CONNOTATION, METAPHOR, STRUCTURE, PLOT. Indeed nearly all the elements of literary composition may be means of imparting implicit meaning. *See also* IMPLICATION, INVOLUTE, SUBTEXT.

Implicit metaphor. *See* METAPHOR.

Implied author. Wayne Booth in *The Rhetoric of Fiction* (1961) defines the way in which every NARRATIVE creates a sense of a particular kind of author, which the reader infers from hints and statements in the text. This 'second self' is not the same as the author, but a product of a particular work: it may, indeed, be quite different in different works by the same author. No novelist can escape this:

> Even the novel in which no narrator is dramatized creates an implicit picture of an author, who stands behind the scenes, whether as stage manager, as puppeteer, or as an indifferent God, silently paring his fingernails.

When a novelist dramatises him- or herself as the narrator, this is still not the same as the implied author, who is the presumed arbiter of all the choices that make up the work, the mouthpiece being just one of those options. *See also* ÉNONCÉ, PERSONA.

Implied reader. In his essay 'Of the Standard of Taste' (1741) Hume describes an ideal reader, who attempts to forget his 'individual being' and 'peculiar circumstance' and consider himself as 'a man in general' in order to rid himself of the distortions of prejudice. READER-RESPONSE CRITICISM argues that all texts construct by implication an imagined reader of which Hume's ideal is only one possibility. Other similar terms are 'super-reader', 'informed reader' and 'encoded reader'. In every text a variety of features will point towards the kind of reader for which it is intended. These include the TONE, assumptions about what a reader will and will not know, difficulty or simplicity of argument, the diction, jargon, ALLUSIONS, IRONY, and so on. Very complex and difficult texts 'construct' or imply (or require) readers with a high degree of literary COMPETENCE, as well as intelligence, patience and perseverance, to the point where reading is an imaginative process not dissimilar to the creative act itself. *See also* LISIBLE.

Impressionistic criticism. CRITICISM which concentrates on the critic's personal response to a work and attempts to reproduce these feelings in words, rather than to examine a literary work in the light of some theory of literature. Much of the criticism of the nineteenth and early twentieth centuries was impressionistic. The NEW CRITICISM and PRACTICAL CRITICISM sought to bring a more exact rigour into the evaluation of response.

The term may also apply to a criticism by metaphor, like, for example, Dr Johnson's contrast in his *Life of Pope* (1781):

> Dryden's page is a natural field, rising into inequalities, and diversified by the varied exuberance of abundant vegetation; Pope's is a velvet lawn, shaven by the scythe, and levelled by the roller.

In medias res. (Lat. 'in the middle of things') A phrase describing a common technique of story-telling in which the narrator begins not at the beginning of a story or action but in the middle, going back to recount earlier events at a later stage, or letting them emerge during the course of the story. Such an opening is almost a convention of the epic. It is common also in the novel: the narrator of Emily Brontë's *Wuthering Heights* (1847) begins *in medias res. See also* FLASHBACK.

Incantation. (Lat. 'enchantment, song') Words spoken or chanted to create magic, full of repeated syntax and other hypnotic effects. The witches' spells in IV.1 of Shakespeare's *Macbeth* (c.1606) are incantations.

Incident. (Lat. 'happening') A single event in a story, or part of an action. A short story might be written about one incident; a novel will probably contain many, each one a component part of the PLOT.

Incremental repetition. The name given to a repeated REFRAIN in poems (especially BALLADS) which is altered from verse to verse so as to fit in with the story or comment on the action. In some ballads each stanza is a kind of refrain, being repeated with modifications throughout the poem. The traditional Scots ballad 'Lord Randal' is typical; two verses demonstrate the method:

> 'O where ha' you been, Lord Randal, my son?
> And where ha' you been, my handsome young man?'
> 'I ha' been at the greenwood; mother, mak my bed soon,
> For I'm wearied wi' huntin, and fain wad lie down.'

> 'An' wha met ye there, Lord Randal, my son?
> An' wha met you there, my handsome young man?'
> 'O I met wi' my true-love; mother, mak my bed soon,
> For I'm wearied wi' huntin, and fain wad lie down.'

Incunabula. (Lat. 'swaddling clothes, cradle') Very early printed books, appearing in the first half-century after Johannes Gutenberg invented movable types, up until 1500, during the 'infancy' of printing.

Indeterminacy. A point arrived at in certain texts where the reader must make a choice about possible meanings. According to DECONSTRUCTION, the philosophy of language promulgated by Jacques Derrida, all language is subject to a state of indeterminacy, in which it is impossible to choose one particular meaning.

Index. (Lat. 'forefinger') In SEMIOTICS one of the three main classes of SIGN distinguished by C.S. Peirce.

Index, The. From the sixteenth century to 1966 Roman Catholics were forbidden to read books which had been listed by the Church in the *Index Librorum Prohibitorum*. Passages which had to be excised to make certain works suitable for Catholics were listed in the *Index Expurgatorius*.

Induction. (Lat. 'leading in') An archaic word for a prologue introducing a work. The FRAME STORY involving a drunken tramp which begins Shakespeare's *The Taming of the Shrew* (c.1594) is called the 'induction'.

Inflection. (Lat. 'bending') The modification of a word according to its grammatical purpose and meaning in a sentence (a MORPHEMIC change), for example, to indicate the tense of a verb (come/came), or the plural of a noun (girl/girls, man/men). In English, word-order is a vital aspect of meaning, unlike, for example, Latin, in which so many parts of speech are inflected that often the words of a sentence can be written in any order without changing the sense.

Influence. (Lat. 'flowing into') A writer's conscious or unconscious debt to those who have written before, observable in echoes and imitation of subject matter or style, or via explicit statement or allusion. *See also* ANXIETY OF INFLUENCE, INTERTEXTUALITY.

Informal essay. *See* ESSAY.

Inkhorn term. A learned, obscure or pedantic word borrowed from another language; common in Elizabethan times. An inkhorn was a receptacle for ink fastened to the clothing. Thomas Wilson criticised the use of such words in his *Art of Rhetoric* (1553).

Inscape. A word invented by the nineteenth-century poet Gerard Manley Hopkins to denote the special tensions and forms within an object or scene which render it unique and beautiful at one particular moment. *See also* EPIPHANY, INVOLUTE.

Intentional fallacy. The American NEW CRITICS W.K. Wimsatt and M.C. Beardsley introduced this term for what they regarded as the mistaken critical method of judging a literary work according to the author's intentions, whether stated or implied. They argued that the value and meaning of each literary work resides solely in the text itself, and any examination of presumed intention is merely irrelevant, distracting the critic towards the writer's psychology or biography, rather than focusing on the use of language, imagery, tensions, and so on, within the freestanding literary artifice. Their essay on the subject is printed in Wimsatt's *The Verbal Icon* (1954).

Interior monologue. An attempt to convey in words the process of consciousness or thought (as a means of narrating a story). *See also* STREAM OF CONSCIOUSNESS.

Interlude. (Lat. 'between play') A short dramatic entertainment, probably produced during a feast, or between the acts of another play. There are many extant, dating from the late fifteenth and sixteenth centuries, and ranging in subject matter from FARCE to something close to the MORALITY PLAY. The dramatist John Heywood wrote several interludes, including courtly disputations like *The Play of the Weather* (1533) and coarser farces like *The Four P's* (*c*.1544).

Internal rhyme. A pair of words rhyming within a line of verse, rather than at the end of lines. The final two lines of Blake's 'The Garden of Love' (1794) provide a double example:

And I saw it was filled with graves,
And tombstones where flowers should be;
And Priests in black gowns were walking their rounds,
And binding with briars my joys & desires.

See also RHYME.

Interpellation. (Lat. 'pushing between') Originally 'pleading' or 'intercession' in the French parliament. 'Interpellate' has a special meaning in MARXIST critical discourse in defining the relationship between IDEOLOGY and individuals. According to the French political philosopher Althusser, subjectivity itself, that sense of a unique individuality which we are supposed to feel (but which Marxists regard as illusory), is constructed by the language system. Ideology 'interpellates' people, 'calls' upon them and creates them as subjects, so that they voluntarily take up their positions as subjected beings in the social formation, and obey the Absolute Subject of the authority above them. The concept is applied by Marxist critics to the relationship between literature and society.

Interpolation. (Lat. 'polish') An addition to a work, usually by another writer. The comic passages in Marlowe's *Dr Faustus* (*c*.1588) may have been interpolated at a later date.

Interpretation. (Lat. 'explaining') The act of explaining the meaning and effects of a literary text. Ostensibly one of the traditional aims of studying literature (or made so after literary history and textual scholarship were ousted by the NEW CRITICISM in Britain and the USA). Interpretation is now a vexed issue.

Writers in the twentieth century have often resented PARAPHRASE, and argued that the meaning of a particular work cannot be expressed with any exactness in any way other than its own unique combination of FORM and CONTENT in words. A poem, writes Archibald McLeish, should not mean but be.

Interpretation, in so far as it arrives at no more than boiled down meanings, may seem to deprive the artwork of mystery and energy, and the desire to defy this loss lies behind movements in the arts from DADA onwards. The world-wide professionalisation of literature teaching has led to incessant interpretative acts being conducted on an ever-widening body of texts. Many critics have themselves written against the consequences of this exhausting industry, as, for example, Susan Sontag in her essay 'Against Interpretation' (1964). Poets such as John Berryman and John Ashbery have adopted a deliberately impenetrable and illogical style, in order, amongst other things, to defy the neutralising and miniaturising effects of interpretation.

Since the early 1970s the possibility of interpretation has been attacked in literary and linguistic theories (STRUCTURALISM and DECONSTRUCTION), which argue that meaning is not ultimately inherent in language, and that texts are, in a philosophical sense, unknowable. Yet the critical methods which deny meaning are derived themselves from acts of interpretation, and use language that, even if it is deliberately opaque and unstable like Derrida's, is still paraphrased by his followers. And texts of all kinds, from technical manuals to literary theory, are being constantly 'interpreted' by the act of translation from one language to another.

Interrogation. (Lat. 'explaining') A vogue critical usage of the 1990s referring metaphorically to the relationships between the reader and the text, and between the text and the various topics with which it deals. Critics thus 'interrogate' the text, meaning no more than 'read with discrimination'. Texts are perceived as 'interrogating' their subject matter, other texts, or the societies in which they are generated. The political and criminal associations of the metaphor lend a glamour of violence to the usually timid activity of reading.

Intersubjective. A word sometimes used in the attempt to solve the problem of 'subjectivity' versus 'objectivity' of interpretation: objectivity may be a human impossibility, in so far as we can only ever approach a text with our judgment coloured by unique personal experience. However, a group of people sharing the same cultural background are very likely to agree about the interpretation or judgment of a text. They will arrive at a shared response which may not be 'objective', but will however be 'intersubjective', thereby (comfortingly) escaping the lonely prison of self by pooling their subjectivities.

Intertextuality. STRUCTURALISM argues that a text is a system in which language does not refer to 'reality' but only to itself and the patterns created within the text. Literature as a whole is also perceived as a self-referential system or structure. Intertextuality is a term invented by the French critic Julia Kristeva to refer to the many and various kinds of relationship that exist between texts, such as adaptation, translation, IMITATION, ALLUSION, PLAGIARISM and PARODY.

Intonation. (Lat. 'sounding') The pattern of the pitch or melody of an utterance, which marks grammatical structures, such as sentences and clauses. In English, for example, it can indicate contrasts between statements and questions: 'you are going' could be either statement or question, according to whether it is said in a rising or falling pitch. Punctuation provides a crude visual indication of intonation in writing: 'you are going?' or 'you are going!' In reading literary texts aloud, correct intonation has to be determined (like TONE and emphasis), according to context and meaning.

Intradiegetic. *See* DIEGESIS.

Introduction. (Lat. 'leading in') A piece of writing which precedes and explains in advance a work.

Intrusive narrator. *See* NARRATIVE.

Invective. (Lat. 'scolding') The brief denunciation of someone or something, in derogatory or vituperative language. A famous example occurs in Shakespeare's *King Lear*, II.2 (*c*.1605) when Kent abuses Oswald:

> A knave, a rascal, an eater of broken meats; a base, proud, shallow, beggarly, three-suited, hundred-pound, filthy, worsted-stocking knave; a lily-liver'd, action-taking knave; a whoreson, glass-gazing, superserviceable, finical rogue . . .

See also FLYTING, LAMPOON, SATIRE.

Invention. (Lat. 'come upon') Originally 'invention' was used in rhetoric to refer to the introduction of the subject in a speech or written argument. Nowadays the word signifies the writer's capacity to create a new style or subject-matter that shows originality. In this sense it is sometimes contrasted with convention.

Inversion. (Lat. 'turning in') A departure from normal word order, common especially in poetry. Milton's *Paradise Lost* (1667) is full of inversions:

> A Dungeon horrible, on all sides round
> As one great furnace flam'd, yet from those flames
> No light, but rather darkness visible
> Serv'd only to discover sights of woe.   (I.61–4)

Invocation. (Lat. 'call upon') A poet's address to a god or muse, to assist in composing a poem: Milton starts *Paradise Lost* (1667) with an invocation to the Holy Spirit, to help his 'adventurous song' to pursue 'Things unattempted yet in Prose or Rhyme'. *See also* APOSTROPHE.

Involute. (*n*.) A word coined by De Quincey in an autobiographical essay called 'The Affliction of Childhood', originally published in *Tait's Magazine*, February 1834:

> . . . far more of our deepest thoughts and feelings pass to us through perplexed combinations of *concrete* objects, pass to us as *involutes* (if I may coin that word) in compound experiences incapable of being disentangled, than ever reach us *directly*, and in their own abstract shapes . . .

Such 'involutes' become the climactic MOMENTS in De Quincey's rambling prose, moments when meaning is perceived in terms of experience like Joyce's EPIPHANY, Wordsworth's 'spots of time' and Hopkins's INSCAPE.

Involvement. (Lat. 'rolled up') In critical use this refers to the extent to which a reader is fascinated or uninterested by the subject matter and technique of a literary work.

Irony. (Gk. 'dissembling') A manner of speaking or writing that is dispersed through all kinds of literature; 'irony' consists of saying one thing while you mean another. The EIRON ('dissembler') in Greek comedy continually pretended to be stupid, while the ALAZON was a stupid and complacent braggart: irony, then, is the eiron's method of achieving meaning via UNDERSTATEMENT, concealment and ALLUSION, rather than by direct statement.

Sarcasm is an ironical statement intended to hurt or insult. It is a common form of mockery in ordinary day-to-day speech: 'Brilliant', says the schoolteacher to a child whose answer is obviously wrong; it is clear from the context that the teacher actually means the reverse.

Unfortunately ironical statements in literature are not so easily discerned or understood. In certain cases the context of an ironical comment will make clear the true meaning intended. But more often a writer will have to rely on the reader sharing values and knowledge in order for his or her meaning to be understood. Jane Austen's famous opening sentence of *Pride and Prejudice* (1813) is typical: 'It is a truth universally acknowledged that a single man in possession of a good fortune must be in want of a wife.' This 'truth' (far from true and not universal) refers ironically to the fact that unmarried women want rich husbands, and that an unmarried rich man is considered a highly desirable target for their attentions. To unravel the irony the reader must know something of Jane Austen's society: of course the novel itself provides enough information of this kind to make the meaning clear. But an ironical statement on its own is liable to confuse the non-native speaker of English or anyone not familiar with the conventional attitudes implied in a work of literature of a different period.

Certain works are totally ironic; they use some feature of their structure, such as a fallible or unreliable narrator (*see* NARRATIVE), in order to test the reader's intelligence or gullibility. Swift loved this kind of writing: his 'A Modest Proposal' (1729) suggests eating babies as an answer to Ireland's famine. The inventor of this argument is utterly logical but insensitive to the point of madness: there is no explicit evidence to suggest his unreliability as a narrator, so that to read the work ironically we need to be sure that Swift was merely finding a horrific way of pointing out the social injustice and poverty which prevailed in Ireland at that time.

Ironic literature, whether it contains structural or verbal irony, characteristically presents a variety of possible points of views about its subject matter, and equally any work which presents multiple viewpoints may be called ironic, though its narrators may not actually be unreliable, and it may contain no verbal ironies. Ironists manage to suggest many different ways of considering their material, and may conceal entirely their own attitudes. Henry James's novels (published between 1875 and 1904) are often works of this kind: the reader needs to thread a way with care through the nuances of meaning and implication, and may still be left in a state of moral doubt about some of the characters, just as might be experienced with a character in real life. Ironic literature of this sort is so complex and fascinating that irony has come to be considered almost as a criterion of excellence by some twentieth-century critics. The idea that a work should contain ironic TENSION, and an awareness of many possible points of view (perhaps unresolved), became a commonplace for the NEW CRITICS. Poetry expressing an ironic frame of mind, in which the writer shows an awareness of opposite and complementary views, became more valued than poetry committed to any single point of view, ideal or feeling. Such poetry is characteristic of the mid-twentieth century.

Cosmic irony is used of works in which God or Destiny is shown manipulating events so as to frustrate the lives of the characters. Hardy's novels, such as *Tess of the d'Urbervilles* (1891), are often demonstrations of this view of life.

Dramatic irony occurs when the audience of a play knows more than the characters and can therefore foresee the tragic or comic circumstances which will befall. *See also* PERSONA, POINT OF VIEW, ROMANTIC IRONY.

Irregular ode. *See* ODE.

ISA. An Ideological State Apparatus, as defined by the French political philosopher Althusser in an essay devoted to the topic in 1971: an ISA is any social institution which supports and affirms current ideological practices. Examples are the education system, and probably the institution of literature, in so far as it is taught in schools, polytechnics and universities, and thereby helps to reproduce the myths that maintain or sustain people in the present social formation. *See also* COMMON SENSE, IDEOLOGY, INTERPELLATION.

Italian sonnet. *See* SONNET.

Ivory tower. An expression suggesting a refuge free from the day-to-day strivings and posturings of the world, but also divorced from reality. Writers are often criticised for living in the ivory tower of their imagination.

J

Jacobean age. (Lat. *Jacobus*, 'James') The reign of James I, from 1603 to 1625, which followed Elizabeth I's long reign. Jacobean drama, comprising the works of Webster, Middleton and Massinger, as well as late Shakespeare and Ben Jonson, is often seen as a distinct kind of drama, harsh and violent in its view of life, yet skilled in technique. Poets active during this period include Donne and Drayton. The most notable achievement in prose was the King James translation of the Bible (1611), but Bacon and Robert Burton were also writing during this fertile if short literary period.

Jargon. (O. Fr. 'birdsong') The special technical language of any trade, profession or branch of scholarship. Often such a specialised language is unintelligible to an ordinary layman, so that the word is frequently used as a pejorative, though increased specialisation, and the speed at which new disciplines and technologies advance, make jargon the inevitable means of communication between experts. Literary criticism is not without its jargon.

Jeremiad. A woeful and lengthy outpouring of anguished criticism of the state of the world, perhaps full of dire warnings, like the Old Testament Lamentations of Jeremiah.

Jeu d'esprit. (Fr. 'game of the mind') A witty comment, light-hearted but cleverly expressed. Also used to describe a small and insignificant literary piece, written for fun.

Jingle. A simple, more or less nonsensical rhyme or catchy song, especially as used in advertisements on the radio and television:

> If you like to chew,
> Chew Wiggely Gum.
> Three times the flavour,
> Three times the fun.
> Wiggely, Wiggely, Wiggely Gum.

Jongleur. (Fr. 'juggler') In the Middle Ages, a professional wandering entertainer with various skills, including juggling, acrobatics and reciting poetry.

Jouissance. (Fr. 'enjoyment') A word used by the French critic Roland

Barthes in *Le Plaisir du texte* ('The Pleasure of the Text', 1973) in contrast to *plaisir* ('pleasure') to describe different kinds of reading experience. *Jouissance* is often translated as 'bliss', which suggests some of the sense of sexual pleasure that the word has in French. Such a feeling is experienced when reading texts which force the reader into some kind of creative, active participation in the act of interpretation. These difficult, thought-provoking texts Barthes calls *scriptible* ('writable' or 'writerly'). On the other hand, texts which can be read easily are *lisible* ('readable' or 'readerly'), and only provoke the less intense *plaisir*, which is merely comforting, rather than stimulating.

Feminists use the word *jouissance* to designate and celebrate the joy of being female.

Journal. (O. Fr. 'daily') Any kind of newspaper or magazine, learned or popular.

Journalistic. Written in the manner of journalists, or writers for the newspapers. Usually a pejorative word, if applied to a literary work, indicating slapdash construction, sensational effects and shallow opinions.

Juvenalian satire. See SATIRE.

Juvenilia. (Lat. 'youth-works') The youthful works of any writer, whether published during his or her life-time or collected after death. Pope's *Pastorals* (1709), written when he was sixteen, are very sophisticated juvenilia.

K

Kabuki. (Jap. 'singing-dancing art') A kind of Japanese drama, more popular in tone than the courtly NOH plays, but still highly formal and stylised, using heavy make-up, elaborate costumes and dance-like movements. Men play the female roles. *Kabuki* plays are often based on popular MYTHS and LEGENDS.

Kailyard school. A derogatory term for late nineteenth- and early twentieth-century popular novels which sentimentalised rural life in lowland Scotland. A 'kailyard' is a cabbage patch. A line from a song, 'There grows a bonnie brier bush in our kailyard', was used by 'Ian Maclaren' (John Watson) for the title of his collection of anecdotal stories, *Beside the Bonnie Brier Bush* (1894). Other Kailyard novelists were J.M. Barrie and S.R. Crockett.

Kenning. (O.N. 'know, recognise') A stock metaphoric phrase in the ORAL poetry of Scandinavia and in Anglo-Saxon verse. Old English examples are swan-rad ('swan-road') or hron-rad ('whale-road') for 'the sea', beado-leoma ('battle-light') for 'sword', or saewudu ('sea-wood') for 'ship'. See also FORMULAE.

Kind. The English word for GENRE: the eighteenth-century word for literary categories, such as TRAGEDY, the EPIC, PASTORAL ELEGY, and so on.

Kitchen-sink drama. A term applied to plays of the 1950s and 1960s which focused realistically on domestic life, family quarrels, marriage, and the problems of the ordinary bourgeois or working-class way of life. Such plays were thought to be typical of radio and television drama. On stage, some of the works of John Osborne and Arnold Wesker might be so categorised. *See also* ANGRY YOUNG MEN.

Kitsch. (Ger. 'throw together') Originally the word referred to something of little merit: rubbish. Nowadays kitsch refers to the ironical enjoyment of worthless and ugly things; to enjoy kitsch is to indulge in the perverse taste for mean, cheap and vulgar objects and art-works. *See also* CAMP.

Künstlerroman. (Ger. 'artist-novel') A novel which focuses on the development of an artist or writer: Joyce's *A Portrait of the Artist as a Young Man* (1916) is a famous example from English literature. *See also* BILDUNGSROMAN.

L

Laconic. (Gk. 'member of the Spartan race') The Lacedaemonian or Spartan people were renowned for their brevity of speech. 'Laconic' refers then to a short, pithy kind of utterance or style, full of matter in spite of its shortness. A laconic style may result in SENTENTIOUSNESS, or in the kind of gruff UNDERSTATEMENT common, for example, in the prose of the twentieth-century American novelist, Ernest Hemingway.

Lacuna. (Lat. 'pool, ditch') A gap, break or missing part in a text, often in a manuscript.

***Lai,* lay.** (O. Fr.) The *Contes* of Marie de France (*c*.1175), who wrote for the court of the English king, Henry II, are the best-known *lais*: they are short narrative poems, many of which are Arthurian ROMANCES. Poems written in the fourteenth century similarly concerning Celtic legends were called 'Breton lays': two notable poems of this kind are Chaucer's *The Franklin's Tale* and the anonymous *Sir Orfeo*.

In the nineteenth century 'lay' came to refer to any short narrative poem, for example, Macaulay's *Lays of Ancient Rome* (1842). *See also* BALLAD, CONTE, FABLIAU.

Lake poets. The three early nineteenth-century ROMANTIC poets, Wordsworth, Coleridge and Southey, who lived in the Lake District of Cumbria in northern England. This term was often applied in a derogatory way, suggesting the provincialism of their themes and interests.

Lament. A poem expressing deep sorrow for the death of a person or people, or loss of status and security. Common in many literatures;

David's lament for Saul and Jonathan is a biblical example: 'How are the mighty fallen' (II Samuel 1:17–27). *See also* COMPLAINT, CORONACH, DIRGE, ELEGY, MONODY, THRENODY.

Lampoon. (Fr. 'let us swig') A virulent SATIRE or CARICATURE. A harshly critical portrait in verse, prose (or in a drawing or painting), mocking a person's most unpleasant aspects. Pope's description of Lord Hervey as 'Sporus' in his 'Epistle to Dr Arbuthnot' (1735) is a famous example in English literature:

> Who breaks a butterfly upon a wheel?
> Yet let me flap this bug with gilded wings,
> This painted child of dirt, that stinks and stings.

See also DIATRIBE, FLYTING, INVECTIVE.

Langue. (Fr. 'language') A word given a special technical meaning in the field of linguistics in the influential teaching of Ferdinand de Saussure whose *Course in General Linguistics* (1915) has been the model for many revolutionary theories of language and culture, notably STRUCTURALIST anthropology and criticism.

Saussure defined *langue* as the system of a language, its rules and combinations, which all skilled speakers of that language share and tacitly understand. *Parole* (Fr. 'word') is a particular utterance, in speech or in writing, within the *langue*.

Lapidary. (Lat. 'stony') Suitable for inscription on a stone monument as an EPITAPH, or on a gem as a more private message. Therefore, used as a description of literary style, lapidary means elevated, concise, and aimed at posterity, though perhaps not as loftily and solemnly dignified as the MARMOREAL.

Latent content. *See* PSYCHOANALYTIC CRITICISM.

Latinate, Latinism. From the seventeenth century onwards, but during the eighteenth century especially, when Roman models were copied in prose and poetry, writers used words or grammatical constructions which originated in Latin, and which gave an impression of Latin in English. Words of Latin derivation are commonly longer and more abstract in meaning than their Anglo-Saxon counterparts: e.g. vision (Lat.) = sight (O.E.). In general Latinate diction, then, will be more abstract, and liable to be polysyllabic. The PERIODIC SENTENCE is an attempt to mimic Latin syntax, which leaves the main verb until late in the sentence. Two eighteenth-century prose-writers fond of Latinisms are Dr Johnson and Gibbon. Milton is also famous for his Latinate constructions in *Paradise Lost* (1667), as in 'Him the Almighty Power/ Hurled headlong' which twists the normal English order of subject-verb-object into object-subject-verb. *See also* POETIC DICTION.

Lay. *See* LAI.

Leaping and lingering. *See* BALLAD.

Leavisite. An adherent of the critical beliefs and methods of F.R. Leavis (1895–1978), a Fellow of Downing College, Cambridge from 1936 to 1962, and his wife Q.D. Leavis (1906–81).

Close examination of literary texts (PRACTICAL CRITICISM), and the evaluation of works and writers in terms of their status and worth, was the vital element in turning literary studies away from the dry if scholarly historical approaches that in the 1930s and 40s seemed to have prevailed in academic study since the origins of English as a university subject (in the late nineteenth century). Leavisites shared many critical beliefs with the American NEW CRITICS in their desire to reveal the complexity and seriousness of literature in terms of patterns of feeling and reason. Leavisites also believed in literature's capacity to train the feelings, sensibilities, and powers of reasoning in those who studied it. But they added to these ideas a strong moral tone, and sometimes a strident critical rectitude, combined with contempt for those kinds of literature which failed their exacting standards. This has come to be seen as a damaging élitism, expressed also in their cherishing a CANON of great works, and in the methods by which they arrived at their judgments.

To be a Leavisite in the 1940s was to adopt a thrillingly divisive position in relation to traditional scholarship; by the 1980s, after the professionalisation of criticism and tertiary teaching in the USA, and the advance of critical theory linked with this, 'Leavisite' had become an insult, to be directed at those who were lost in a critical cul-de-sac. Yet it would be difficult to over-emphasise the far-reaching influence of Leavisite views and methods in the teaching of literature at secondary and tertiary levels in Britain during the 1950s and 1960s. *See also* CAMBRIDGE SCHOOL OF CRITICS, CULTURES, THE TWO.

Legend. (Lat. 'what is read') Originally legends were collections of the lives of the saints, especially the thirteenth-century *Legenda Aurea* ('Golden Legend'). The word now means a story, or a group of stories, about a heroic personage – not a god (for such stories would be MYTHS) but a historical or semi-historical character such as King Arthur, Robin Hood or Rob Roy. Legends of this kind, in spite of the word's derivation, are part of the ORAL tradition, being the subject matter for songs and BALLADS, and developing quickly about any popular folk hero or heroine. *See also* FOLKLORE.

Leitmotif. *See* MOTIF.

Lexicography. (Gk. 'writing of words') The writing of a dictionary. Characterised by Dr Johnson as the work of 'a harmless drudge'.

Lexicon. (Gk. 'to do with words') A dictionary, especially one of Latin or Greek.

Lexie. (From Gk. *lexis*, 'word') A word invented by Roland Barthes in *S/Z* (1970) for the minimal unit of reading, the stretch of text which is separable from other parts of the text as having some specific effect or function. It could be a single word, or a phrase, or several sentences. The purpose of identifying these units is to reveal the coded meanings and assumptions that underlie ordinary prose narrative. This method of analysis, only half worked out in a study of a fragment of a story by Balzac, in which Barthes identified five lexies, enjoyed a brief fashion.

Lexis. (Gk. 'word') A term used in linguistics: the vocabulary of a language.

Libretto. (It. 'little book') The text of an opera, or any similar work involving words and music.

Light verse. A vague term for verse which does not aspire to be treated very seriously, either because it deals with trivial matters, or because it adopts a light-hearted approach to a grave subject. It is usually colloquial in tone, employing the grammar and vocabulary of the ordinary speaking voice. Often it is comic or mildly satiric. Complex and amusing rhymes are also common in light verse. Great practitioners of light verse include, in the nineteenth century, W.S. Gilbert and Hilaire Belloc, and, in the twentieth, the American poet Ogden Nash and Sir John Betjeman. *See also* BURLESQUE, CLERIHEW, LIMERICK, NONSENSE, PARODY, VERS DE SOCIÉTÉ.

Ligne donnée. (Fr. 'line given') A phrase invented by the French poet Paul Valéry, referring to a line which occurs as if 'given' to the poet by God or some other source of inspiration, and around which the rest of the poem crystallises.

Limerick. (Said to be derived from a refrain, 'Will you come up to Limerick', chanted during party games involving the invention of nonsense verse) A form of LIGHT VERSE popularised by Edward Lear in his *A Book of Nonsense* (1846). In Lear's limericks the first and last line often rhyme on the same word:

> There was an Old Man with a beard
> Who said, 'It is just as I feared! –
>   Four Larks and a Wren,
>   Two Owls and a Hen,
> Have all built their nests in my beard!'

Later versions of Lear's form vary this rhyme:

> There was a young lady from Ryde
> Who swallowed some apples and died.
>   The apples fermented
>   Inside the lamented
> And made cider inside her inside.

For the technically minded, a limerick consists of five lines, mixing ANAPAESTS and IAMBS, rhyming *aabba*, the first, second and fifth lines being TRIMETERS, with the third and fourth DIMETERS (*see* METRE for further discussion of these terms). Limericks are often anonymous and very often ribald or obscene. *See also* MACARONIC VERSE, NONSENSE.

Limited edition. Sometimes books are printed in small numbers, with the aim of creating highly priced, sought-after objects, often specially bound, each one numbered.

Limited point of view. *See* NARRATIVE.

Line. Poems are divided up into lines, which are classified according to the number of metrical feet they contain (*see* METRE). If a poem was printed as prose, without the typographical representation of it line by line, the metre would be unchanged, though the pause at the line-ending would be lost. *See also* ENJAMBMENT.

Linguistics. (Lat. 'study of tongues') The scientific study of language. The word covers a number of different approaches, including SEMANTICS, PHONETICS, description of languages and their history and geographical distribution.

Lisible. (Fr. 'readable' or 'readerly') A word employed in a particular, pejorative sense by Roland Barthes in *S/Z* (1970) as part of his sporadic attack on the tradition of REALISM. Realist texts, according to him, make no demands on the reader, because of the familiarity of their conventional aspects, notably the comforting ILLUSIONISM by which the reader is duped into forgetting that a fictional text has been created. Their fixed and closed meanings are therefore merely reassuringly consumed, and fail to challenge the reader, unlike MODERNIST, 'open' texts. *See also* 'CLASSIC BOURGEOIS' REALISM, CLOSURE, HIERARCHY OF DISCOURSES, JOUISSANCE, SCRIPTIBLE.

Litany. (Gk. 'prayer') A prayer consisting of a series of INVOCATIONS, often chanted by a choir in procession.

Literal. In typesetting and proof-reading a 'literal' is a simple error of typesetting or spelling.

Literal language. Usually opposed to the METAPHORICAL and FIGURATIVE, or IRONICAL use of language, literal language is language which is used exactly, in its most precise and limited sense. The literal meaning of a statement is its most exact, precise and limited meaning, without attention to secondary or SYMBOLIC meanings, metaphoric overtones, nuances or ironies. *See also* CONNOTATION, DENOTATION, REFERENTIAL LANGUAGE.

Literariness. According to the theories of Russian FORMALISM literary texts are distinguished from non-literary texts by a variety of special linguistic devices and features, most of them deviations from ordinary usage, which result in DEFAMILIARISATION. The object of criticism is not literature itself, but 'literariness', and its purpose is the description and definition of all those features that make a text literary rather than non-literary.

Literary ballad. A poem which imitates the BALLAD in form and subject matter, but which is not an anonymous product of the ORAL tradition or folk culture, being the word of an individual poet: Coleridge's 'The Rime of the Ancient Mariner' (1798) is a famous example.

Literary competence. *See* COMPETENCE.

Literary theory. To elaborate a theory of literature is to seek answers to fundamental questions about the nature, purpose and value of literature, and how answers to these questions can be ascertained. Such topics have been debated since the earliest Greek philosophers discussed drama, poetry and rhetoric. As a special branch of literary critical discussion, literary theory has been intellectually fashionable and a source of vigorous dispute in European and American universities, especially from the 1970s onwards. By 1990 literary theory had been institutionalised, in the sense that it is now commonly taught as an academic subject in its own right.

Literary theory may be studied historically, in order to discover what assumptions writers and critics of past ages have made about literature. More often, however, the many and various contemporary literary theories are the subject of study. Some teachers of theory argue that it is impossible to read a text without a theoretical standpoint, even though readers may be wholly unconscious of what their standpoint is. Therefore all literary study should begin with a grounding in literary theory. A counter argument is that no literary theory can be properly examined and discussed without some prior knowledge of texts.

In the twentieth century certain critical movements have tended towards the current emphasis on theory. The Russian FORMALISTS formulated views of literary language that led away from the study of individual texts and their history into defining 'literariness'. STRUCTURALISM also shifted interest away from individual texts on to the relationship between language and the world of things and the conditions by which meaning is understood or created. Critics interested in politics and sociology theorised about literature as a social institution, and its relationships with non-literary forms of artistic expression, and with the structures of power that prevail in society.

In general the development of literary theory has tended towards the demolition of many assumptions that used to prevail in relation to texts: for example, that clear boundaries exist between literature and non-literature; that literature is the repository of universally acceptable truths and values; that texts have precise and definite meanings which readers strive to ascertain; and that there are 'objective' and agreed critical values for deciding what kinds of writing are best.

Literati. (It. 'the learned') People involved in the creation or study of literature. Originally meaning simply scholars, it is now a mildly derogatory term, suggesting snobbery and remoteness from the real world, perhaps by confusion with the coinage based on literati, 'glitter-ati', journalist's shorthand for the rich and glamorous.

Literature. (Lat. 'alphabetic letters') A vague, all-inclusive term for poetry, novels, drama, short stories, prose: anything written, in fact, with an apparently artistic purpose, rather than merely to communicate information; or anything written and examined as if it had an artistic purpose. 'Literature' also is an evaluative word: to say that a novel is 'not literature' is to imply that it is badly written, or has for some other reason failed to achieve the status of art.
   Some contemporary critics refuse to accept that there is a special category of writing called 'literature'. *See also* CANON, DISCOURSE.

Litotes. (Gk. 'simple, meagre') A figure of speech akin to UNDERSTATE-MENT in which an affirmative is expressed by its contrary denied by a negative. The common everyday use of 'not bad' to mean 'good' is an example. Not uncommon in poetry or prose.

Liturgy. (Gk. 'public worship') The forms of public Christian worship, as, for example, the prayers and ceremonies in the Book of Common Prayer.

Liverpool poets. Adrian Henri, Roger McGough and Brian Patten, who utilised the fame of Liverpool as a centre of youth culture during the era of the Beatles to publicise their work by giving it a group identity. They were published in *Penguin Modern Poets 10* (1967), subtitled *The Mersey Sound.* Their collection stayed in print long after other titles in the series were defunct. All three were influenced by the BEATS, amongst other American poets, to which they added a dash of Liverpudlian SURREALISM, and the concerns of English suburban teenagers. Their work has the immediate impact and wry comedy which is typical of PERFORMANCE POETRY.

Livre à clef. See ROMAN À CLEF.

Loan word. A word borrowed from another language: most languages have increased their vocabulary in such a manner. English is particu-larly free in adopting foreign words, and a large proportion of basic English words were borrowed in this way from Scandinavian, Dutch, German, French, Greek, Latin, Arabic, Russian, etc.

Local colour. Details of a particular region or place, such as dress, customs, vegetation, dialect, foreign words, which are used in a work of fiction to create a sense of authenticity. Kipling's *Kim* (1901), for example, is full of local colour, creating the exotic atmosphere of nineteenth-century India.

Locutionary act. *See* SPEECH ACT THEORY.

Logocentricism. *Logos* (Gk. 'word') in Christianity is equated with God the Son, the second person of the Trinity, and has a special force as a centre and origin of religious belief. St John's gospel begins with the famous words: 'In the beginning was the Word.'

In philosophy 'logos' means many things, including 'reason', regarded as the essential controlling principle of human thought. For the Stoics it was God conceived as the source of all rationality.

The philosophy of language called DECONSTRUCTION regards Western culture as essentially logocentric, centred on the *logos*: that is, organised around the belief or hope that there is meaning in language, and even some ultimate final meaning, such as God or Truth, rather than the endless play of DIFFÉRANCE. *See also* DECENTRE.

Longueur. (Fr. 'length') A boring passage in a work of literature or music.

Loose sentences. Casual, conversational prose which is not grammatically highly ordered and which readily splits apart into short units of sense. *See also* PERIODIC SENTENCE.

Low comedy. Unlike HIGH COMEDY, which appeals to the intellect, low comedy is aimed at provoking laughter by the simplest of means: physical action, like falling down stairs or fighting, SLAPSTICK, ribald jokes, clowning and ridiculous clothes are all common in low comedy on the stage. It may, like the antics of Sir Toby Belch in Shakespeare's *Twelfth Night* (*c*.1600), be COMIC RELIEF from the other kinds of COMEDY, or it may be the chief component of a FARCE. 'Low comedy' may also be used to categorise non-dramatic prose or verse. Chaucer's *The Miller's Tale* (late fourteenth century) is an example. *See also* FABLIAU.

Low style. Along with High and Middle style, one of the three-fold classifications of style made common by traditional theoreticians of rhetoric: the plainest, unadorned and most basic kind of writing.

Lullaby. (Lat. 'song') A song sung to soothe a child to sleep. Several nursery rhymes are lullabies.

Lyric. In Greek verse, a song to be accompanied by the lyre, a harp-like instrument. The word 'lyrics' is still applied to the words of a song.

Lyric poetry in its widest sense encompasses a large number of other more specialised kinds of poetry, including the SONNET, ELEGY, ODE and HYMN. It is poetry which is neither narrative nor dramatic. A more particularised definition can be made: a lyric is a poem, usually short, expressing in a personal manner the feelings and thoughts of an individual speaker (not necessarily those of the poet). The typical lyric subject matter is love, for a lover or deity, and the mood of the speaker in relation to this love. Poetry of this kind seems common to many ages and societies. There were many Greek and Roman lyric poets. The earliest English poems are the Anglo-Saxon LAMENTS, which may be considered as a kind of lyric verse. The main tradition of European lyric originates in the verse of Provence and shows a steady development in the Renaissance refinement of Petrarch in Italy and Ronsard in France. Many of its forms (including the sonnet) were first used in English in the early sixteenth century by Wyatt and Surrey, after whom there followed a flowering of lyric poetry of all kinds, written by all the major writers of the day, including Shakespeare, Sidney, Campion, Spenser, Jonson, Donne, Herbert, Marvell, Herrick: the list could be extended enormously. The period (*c.*1550–1650) is marked by the variety and excellence of its lyric poetry. The Elizabethan lyrics were typically smooth and sweet in diction, against which the METAPHYSICALS reacted with their harsher and wittier argumentative verse, which often has a dramatic context. Here is an example of a lyric which returns to the smoothness of the Elizabethan, by the mid-seventeenth-century writer Waller. It is a quintessential lyric: elegant, concerning love, employing a metrical form devised specially for the poem:

> Go lovely Rose,
> Tell her that wastes her time and me,
> That now she knows
> When I resemble her to thee
> How sweet and fair she seems to be.
>
> Tell her that's young,
> And shuns to have her Graces spied,
> That hadst thou sprung
> In Deserts, where no men abide,
> Thou must have uncommended died.
>
> Small is the worth
> Of Beauty from the light retired:
> Bid her come forth,
> Suffer herself to be desired,
> And not blush so to be admired.
>
> Then die – that she
> The common fate of all things rare
> May read in thee;
> How small a part of time they share,
> That are so wondrous sweet and fair!

Simple lyric poems of this kind occur in later ages of English poetry, until the present day. However, the ROMANTIC poets expanded the lyric to include conversational and meditative poems exploring memory and the association of ideas, like Wordsworth's 'Tintern Abbey' (1798) and Coleridge's 'Frost at Midnight' (1798).

The nineteenth century was another great age of lyric poetry, with much experimentation in forms and METRES. Browning and Tennyson also refined another specialised form which comes under the general heading 'lyric', the dramatic monologue (*see* MONOLOGUE), an extension of the dramatic lyric which created a sense of a particular occasion and place.

The vast majority of twentieth-century poets are in a sense 'lyric poets', though Waller's elegance and smoothness has ceased to be a generally desired effect. Short poems or 'expanded lyrics' of the nineteenth-century variety, examining ideas and feeling in relation to the poet's mood and process of thought, are still the most common form for poetry.

The NEW CRITICISM's insistence that a poem should be discussed for itself has caused critics to be shy of assuming that the speaker of a lyric, 'the poet', is in fact the same as the poet who wrote it. Each lyric is seen as a PERSONA or mask created for a particular purpose: this is held to be the case even when circumstantial details in the poem invite us to see its relevance to the poet's life. *See also* CARPE DIEM, UBI SUNT.

M

Macaronic verse. Verse (named after the Italian food *maccheroni*) which is made up of languages muddled together for comic effect. The first examples occur in the late fifteenth century in Italy and mix Italian and Latin by applying absurd Latin endings to vernacular words. Teofilo (or Girolamo) Folengo, a renegade monk, seems to have originated the form and given it its name, in his *Baldus*, or *Maccaronea* (1517), a burlesque epic dealing with chivalry. The English poet Skelton wrote some macaronic verses. It is a common ingredient in NONSENSE poetry.

William Drummond's *Polemo-Middinia inter Vitarvum et Nebernam* (*c*.1645), from which the following extract is taken, describes a battle between two villages, in a strange mixture of Latin and Scottish dialect words:

> Battelli onsetto! pugnat muckcreilus heros
> Fortiter, et muckam per posteriora cadentem
> In creilibus shoollare ardet: sic dirta volavit.
> In qualis feirie fairie fuit, si forte vidisses
> Pipantes arsas, et flavo sanguine breickas
> Dripantes, hominumque heartas ad praelia fantas!
> O qualis hurlie burlie fuit!

Machiavel. A villainous STOCK CHARACTER in Elizabethan and Jacobean drama, so called after the Florentine writer Niccolò Machiavelli (1469-1527), author of *The Prince* (written 1513), a book of political advice to rulers that recommended the need under certain circumstances to lie to the populace for their own good and to preserve power. Embellishment of this suggestion (which was only one small part of his analysis of political power and justice) made Machiavelli almost synonymous with the Devil in English literature.

Machiavels are practised liars and cruel political opportunists, who delight in their own manipulative evil: Shakespeare's Iago in *Othello* (*c*.1604) and Edmund in *King Lear* (*c*.1605), and Bosola in Webster's *The Duchess of Malfi* (*c*.1613) are examples. The topics of dissembling and disguising one's true identity amount almost to an obsession in plays in the early seventeenth century. *See also* STEREOTYPE.

Machinery. The name given, especially in the eighteenth century, to the actions of deities and other supernatural beings in EPICS, TRAGEDIES and the like: the Olympian Gods in Homer's *Iliad* (*c*. eighth century BC) are supernatural 'machinery'.

Macspaunday. A word made up of the names of four British poets of the 1930s who were often grouped together because of their left-wing politics at that time, and who were, indeed, friends: Louis MacNeice, Stephen Spender, W.H. Auden and Cecil Day Lewis.

Madrigal. (From Lat. 'motherly', then 'simple, primitive') A LYRIC poem, mostly about love or the pastoral life, intended to be sung, usually by several singers. Extremely popular in England during the sixteenth century. There is no fixed metrical form.

Magazine. (Ar. 'storehouse') A periodical publication, especially for general readers; for example, in the eighteenth century, *The Gentleman's Magazine*.

Magic realism. Fiction which mixes and disrupts ordinary, everyday REALISM with strange, 'impossible' and miraculous episodes and powers. The hero of Salman Rushdie's *Midnight's Children* (1981) receives telepathic communications from all over India. A character in Milan Kundera's *The Farewell Party* (1976) emits a blue light after making love. Short stories and novels by Angela Carter rework folk and fairy tales to create a particular kind of magic realism that mixes the modern and the mythical.

Several South American novelists, notably the Colombian Gabriel García Márquez, are strongly identified with this kind of fiction. The conjunction of 'reality' and the FANTASTIC is of course as old as telling stories, but in spite of early examples like Günter Grass's *The Tin Drum* (1959), the term 'magic realism' is usually restricted to novels of the 1970s and 1980s, which sought to break the boundaries of realism while still engaging with political and social issues. The imaginative leaps and disruptions of magic realism serve to remind the reader of the invented nature of narratives, unlike the ILLUSIONISM of so-called 'CLASSIC BOURGEOIS' REALISM.

Magnum opus. (Lat. 'great work') A great work; a writer's greatest achievement.

Maker. In Middle English the word means 'creator' and 'poet'.

Malapropism. (Fr. *mal à propos,* 'not to the purpose') Mistaken and muddled use of long words: so called after Mrs Malaprop in Sheridan's play *The Rivals* (1775), who continually utters nonsense in her attempts to sound learned. Dogberry in Shakespeare's *Much Ado About Nothing* (*c*.1598) is another dramatic character whose language is full of errors of this kind, for example, his comment that 'comparisons are odorous' (III.5).

Manifest content. *See* PSYCHOANALYTIC CRITICISM.

Manifesto. (Lat. 'struck by hand') A written declaration of a political, religious, philosophical or literary standpoint. Many self-conscious MODERNISTIC movements in the arts during the twentieth century, such as SURREALISM, VORTICISM or FUTURISM, were defined by manifestos written by their originators.

Mannerism. A constantly recurring feature of a writer's style, especially if somewhat excessive. In the history of art Mannerism refers to the work of sixteenth-century Italian artists such as Parmigianino who distort their human figures slightly by lengthening arms, legs and neck in the interest of elegance and emotional effect.

Mantissa. (Lat. 'makeweight') A trivial addition or supplement. Used by John Fowles as the title of a short erotic METAFICTION, published in 1982.

Manuscript. (Lat. 'written by hand') A hand-written book; or the hand-written (or even typed) version of a book before it is printed and published. *See also* HOLOGRAPH, TYPESCRIPT.

Märchen. The German word for FAIRY TALES, like those collected by the Grimm brothers during the early nineteenth century.

Marginalia. Notes written in the margins of manuscripts and books. Such comments in texts owned and used by great writers may provide invaluable evidence for critics and scholars concerning matters of influence and literary taste. *See also* GLOSS.

Marinism. The elaborate and exaggerated style of the Italian poet Giovanni Battista Marini (1569–1625), comparable with EUPHUISM, and the poetry of the METAPHYSICALS in English literature. *See also* GONGORISM.

Marmoreal. (Lat. 'marble') Used of a literary style that is weightily and smoothly decorous, and perhaps a little impenetrable.

Martianism. A kind of writing identified with certain young poets of the late 1970s and 1980s who seemed to share stylistic traits. The name comes from a poem by Craig Raine, 'A Martian Sends a Postcard Home' (also the title of his second book of poems, published in 1979), in which things are described as if perceived (and misunderstood) by a visitor from another planet. Here Raine's Martian riddlingly describes a common household object:

> In homes, a haunted apparatus sleeps,
> that snores when you pick it up.
>
> If the ghost cries, they carry it
> to their lips and soothe it to sleep

with sounds. And yet, they wake it up
deliberately, by tickling with a finger.

The term is used to describe the surprising CONCEITS and metaphors
in the poetry of Raine and a few of his contemporaries. The poetry of
Christopher Reid, and some of the early prose of Martin Amis was
labelled Martian. A 'Martian' simile often has the form of a precise
visual analogy perceived between two different kinds of object (one
usually domestic), such as comparing the pink bag of an old-fashioned
upright vacuum-cleaner to a cow's udder. *See also* DEFAMILIARISATION.

Marvellous, The. The large grouping of various kinds of fiction that
construct worlds in which the non-realistic is accepted as normal.
J.R.R. Tolkien's *The Lord of the Rings* (1954–5) is probably the most
famous example. SCIENCE FICTION, FAIRY TALES and many ROMANCES are
all different branches of the marvellous. *See also* FANTASTIC, FANTASY,
UNCANNY.

Marxist criticism. Criticism that considers literature in relation to its
capacity to reflect the struggle between the classes, and the economic
conditions which, according to Karl Marx (1818–83) and Friedrich
Engels (1820–95), lie at the basis of man's intellectual and social
evolution. Marxists believe that in the present capitalist age the means
of material production are possessed by the bourgeoisie, whose IDEO-
LOGY, devised to keep power from the proletariat wage-earning class,
saturates every aspect of society, thought and culture, including literature, criticism and the education system. The aim of Marxist criticism is
to explore literature in relation to this Marxist vision, which is seen as a
scientific truth.

At its most simple, Marxist criticism leads to SOCIALIST REALISM, the
doctrine that literature ought to express directly the social realities as
perceived from the Marxist point of view. However, more subtle
analyses of the relationship of literature and society allow literature
some AUTONOMY, and find more indirect means of discussing literary
values in terms of the social, cultural and economic context which gives
rise to them. The Hungarian Georg Lukacs, for example, examined the
form and theory of the novel in *Studies in European Realism* (1950) and
The Historical Novel (1962), and argued that realist novels create
separate fictional worlds which reveal social truths of which the author
might be unconscious.

Theorising about the nature of REALISM and the MIMETIC function of
literature remains a fundamental concern for Marxist critics. Non-
realistic forms, such as modernist poetry, require special kinds of
argument. One such is the proposition that the experimentalism of
twentieth-century literature suggests a dissatisfaction, or even a decadence, which illustrates the alienation of living in a capitalist society.

Amongst the most famous of Marxist thinkers is the German

playwright Brecht, who invented a variety of theatrical techniques for breaking down the bourgeois complacency of the theatre, including his EPIC THEATRE and ALIENATION EFFECT. Another German critic, Walter Benjamin, in an influential essay on 'The Work of Art in the Age of Mechanical Reproduction' (1936), examined the diminished role of 'high art' in a world changed by new technical methods of reproduction and new media like photography and the cinema, though he also wrote extensively on 'high art' writers like Kafka and Proust.

The post-war development in France of STRUCTURALISM helped to revive Marxist approaches to literature and suggested new ways of examining and explaining the relationships between society and writing that broke the simple mimetic relationship assumed by socialist realism. Althusser's writing concentrates on describing the permeation of society by bourgeois ideology, and refines the concept of INTERPELLATION as the means by which the subservience to the prevailing authority is disguised by the illusory freedom of subjectivity. Barthes's early analyses of prose helped to define the characteristic features of 'CLASSIC BOURGEOIS' REALISM. Macherey's *A Theory of Literary Production* (1966), as well as re-defining literary creation as a kind of PRODUCTION, showed how the absences, gaps and silences in texts might reveal the ultimate incoherence of the bourgeois ideology.

POST-STRUCTURALIST views of the instability of meaning have been used to attack not only the concept of a traditional CANON of literary texts, but the very practices of INTERPRETATION and evaluation that are the staple educational methods of dealing with literature. The appointment in 1991 of Terry Eagleton, a leading British exponent of continental LITERARY THEORY, as Warton Professor of English at Oxford, marks the success of Marxist criticism even at the centre of the British academic establishment, suggesting perhaps how extremely cerebral an activity it is, and how completely divorced it is from political action. *See also* AGITPROP, AUTHOR, COMMON SENSE, CRISIS IN ENGLISH STUDIES, FEMINIST CRITICISM, HIERARCHY OF DISCOURSES, HISTORICISM, INTERROGATION, ISA, POSTMODERNISM, SUBVERSION.

Masculine ending. A line of verse which ends on a stressed syllable, as in most IAMBIC verse; TROCHAIC verse commonly loses its final weak syllable, also creating a masculine ending:

$$/ \quad (X)$$
Lay your/sleeping/head my/love /

See also METRE.

Masculine rhyme. A monosyllabic RHYME on the final stressed syllables of two lines of verse:

Humpty Dumpty sat on a <u>wall</u>;
Humpty Dumpty had a great <u>fall</u>.

Masque. (Fr. 'mask') A courtly dramatic entertainment which flourished in Europe during the late sixteenth and early seventeenth centuries. Songs, poems, dancing, drama played by masked actors, extravagant costumes and spectacular stage effects and decorations were all expensively combined in a loose plot, usually ALLEGORICAL or MYTHOLOGICAL. The aristocratic audience participated in the final dance. Ben Jonson's collaboration with the architect Inigo Jones produced some of the most celebrated masques during the first quarter of the seventeenth century, but the best-known masques are Milton's *Comus*, performed at Ludlow Castle in 1634, and the masque of Juno and Ceres in Act IV of Shakespeare's *The Tempest* (*c*.1611). *See also* ANTIMASQUE.

Matter of Britain, The. *See* ROMANCE.

Maxim. (Lat. Boethius's *Maxima propositio*, 'greatest proposition') A proposal as to how one should conduct oneself; a short, pithy statement concerning human nature and behaviour. Comparable with the APHORISM, PENSÉE or APOPHTHEGM. The French writer La Rochefoucauld's *Maximes* (1665) is one of the greatest collections of such invented sayings: they are mostly cynical and witty. Many writers have coined maxims, but collections of this kind are rare in English literature, though Oscar Wilde as a conversationalist was famous for his capacity for outrageous maxims. His plays also contain many maxims. The following example is from *A Woman of No Importance* (1893):

> Children begin by loving their parents; after a time they judge them; rarely, if ever, do they forgive them.

Measure. Another word for METRE.

Mechanic form. The name given, usually to create a distinction from ORGANIC FORM, to a poetic FORM imposed from outside, or from prescriptive rules, rather than that which 'grows' in accordance with the ideas it contains.

Medievalism. Starting with the Gothic revival and the GOTHIC NOVEL in the eighteenth century, certain writers have sought to recreate the atmosphere, sensibility and, to some extent, the literary style of the Middle Ages, the period which lasted from about AD800 until the Renaissance in the fifteenth century. Several of the ROMANTIC poets wrote 'medieval poems', such as Coleridge's 'Christabel' (1816) and Keats's 'The Eve of St Agnes' (1820). Later in the nineteenth century social critics such as Carlyle, Ruskin and William Morris wrote about the medieval world as idyllic and harmonious in contrast with their own turbulent century. Tennyson's Arthurian ROMANCE *Idylls of the King* (1842–85) is another sustained exercise in medievalism. In the novel a medieval setting was also common: some of Sir Walter Scott's HISTORICAL NOVELS, for example *Ivanhoe* (1819), were amongst the earliest works in this vein.

Medium. (Lat. 'middle, means') An artist's medium is the kind of material used in creating a work, such as oil-paint, water-colour, engraving, and so on. The primary medium of literature is language, but we may experience it aurally or on the printed page. As a literary term 'medium' focuses attention on the literary work as an intermediary between the reader and some 'message', and also on the means by which the literary work arrives before its audience. The catch-phrase 'The medium is the message', popularised by the Canadian critic Marshall McLuhan, suggests that the nature of the medium itself is fundamental in creating meaning. He argues in *The Gutenberg Galaxy* (1962) that 'the *forms* of experience and of mental outlook and expression have been modified, first by the phonetic alphabet and then by printing'. He explores the differences between the 'literature' of oral and literate societies, and what effect new media like radio and television may have on cultural expression.

Meiosis. (Gk. 'lessening') Greek term for UNDERSTATEMENT.

Melodrama. (Gk. 'play') The most common critical use of the word 'melodrama' or 'melodramatic' is to characterise any kind of writing which relies on sensational happenings, violent action and improbable events.

This usage is based on the development of melodrama as a minor genre in the nineteenth century. Originally melodrama meant a play with music, including early opera. In the early nineteenth century popular theatres in London put on plays with musical accompaniment (partly because only certain theatres were allowed by licence to produce serious drama; musical entertainments were excluded from this ban). These plays were naïvely sensational, with simple, flat characterisation, unrelentingly vicious villains plotting to trap virtuous maidens, and much bloodthirsty action, including horrible murders, ghosts and the like. The famous examples, occasionally still staged as amusing pieces, are *Maria Marten; or, The Murder in the Red Barn* (*c.*1830) and *Sweeney Todd, the Demon Barber of Fleet Street* (1842). The horror film nowadays supplies a similar kind of entertainment.

Memento mori. (Lat. 'remember you must die') An emblem of death, such as a skull, to remind us of the shortness and uncertainty of human life. Common especially in Elizabethan and Jacobean art and literature.

Memoirs. (Fr. 'memory') A species of AUTOBIOGRAPHICAL writing, stressing the people known or events witnessed by the author, rather than concentrating on personality or life. *See also* CONFESSION.

Menippean satire. *See* SATIRE.

Metacriticism. (Gk. *meta*, 'with, among, after, beyond, above', often implying change) Criticism about criticism, such as the theory or history of criticism. One of a number of coined words on the model of METALANGUAGE.

Metadrama, metatheatre. Drama about drama. The most obvious example is Pirandello's extraordinary dramatisation of the playwright's relationship with the creatures of his imagination, *Six Characters in Search of an Author* (1921), but plays have always abounded with metadramatic moments, in which the audience may suddenly be reminded of its role in watching an acted fiction, such as the common EPILOGUE at a play's end when an actor speaks half in person, half in character. Plays-within-plays, such as those in *A Midsummer Night's Dream* (*c.*1595-6) and *Hamlet* (*c.*1601), are also implicitly metatheatrical. So are many other conventions, in Elizabethan and Jacobean theatre, such as the ASIDE and SOLILOQUY, and perhaps also its obsession with disguise.

Metafiction, metanovel. Fiction about fiction, in particular novels which examine the nature of novel-writing, most often by breaking away from the illusions of REALISM and the OMNISCIENT NARRATOR and addressing the reader directly, thereby drawing attention to the act of fiction-making (and reading). A notorious example is the Italian writer Italo Calvino's *If on a Winter's Night a Traveller* (1979), which begins:

> You are about to begin reading Italo Calvino's new novel, *If on a winter's night a traveller*. Relax. Concentrate. Dispel every other thought. Let the world around you fade.

Sterne's *Tristram Shandy* (1759-67), in which the narrator constantly draws attention to his labyrinthine digressiveness, ends thus:

> L – d! said my mother, what is all this story about? –
> A COCK and a BULL, said Yorick – And one of the best of its kind, I ever heard.

Novels about novelists, which may be implicitly metafictional, are common in twentieth-century fiction: *The Golden Notebook* (1962) is a novel by a woman novelist (Doris Lessing) about a woman novelist who is writing a novel about a women novelist. John Fowles's *The French Lieutenant's Woman* (1969), with its choice of endings, places together different kinds of narrator, one of which comments throughout on the nature of novel-writing. *See also* ANTI-NOVEL, MISE-EN-ABYME, NARRATIVE.

Metalanguage. Language about language, usually the special language of linguistics, but the term can be applied to other sciences as well · The concept implies a 'higher-level' language, and an 'object language', which, in the case of linguistics, is language itself.

Metalepsis. (Gk. 'substitution') A rare rhetorical term indicating a building of layer upon layer of FIGURATIVE terms (often a METONYMY which is standing in for a word that is itself already figurative), thus distancing the TENOR from the vehicle, sometimes to an unacceptable degree. An example might be the peculiar concatenation of metaphors common in

Crashaw's poetry, for example, 'The Weeper' (1652), of which this is one stanza:

> O cheeks! beds of chaste loves,
> By your own showers seasonably dashed,
> Eyes! nests of milky doves
> In your own wells decently washed.
> O wit of love! that thus could place,
> Fountain and garden in one face!

In NARRATOLOGY metalepsis refers to points of intersection between different 'levels' of narrative, perhaps unexpected and illogically breaking through the logical structure of points of view in a text. It is also called more simply 'frame-breaking', and is common in METAFICTION. In Fowles's *The French Lieutenant's Woman* (1969) the novelist-narrator describes himself sitting opposite one of his characters on a train. *See also* DIEGESIS.

Metanovel. *See* METAFICTION.

Metaphor. (Gk. 'a carrying over') A metaphor goes further than a comparison between two different things or ideas by fusing them together: one thing is described as being another thing, thus 'carrying over' all its associations. When Shakespeare remarks in Sonnet 116 (1609) that love 'is the star to every wandering bark' he defines exactly that aspect of a star which he wants to associate with love: its constancy and secure fixedness in a world of change and danger.

I.A. Richards in *The Philosophy of Rhetoric* (1936) introduced terms for the different parts of a metaphor: the TENOR is the subject of the metaphoric combination ('love' in the example), while the metaphoric word, which 'carries over' its meaning, is called the 'vehicle' ('the star').

In many metaphorical expressions the tenor may remain unstated:

> And Winter's dregs made desolate
> The weakening eye of day.

Hardy (in 'The Darkling Thrush', 1901) clearly means us to understand that 'the weakening eye of day' is the sun, made dreary by the dull winter light and the cold weather. Such a metaphor is called **implicit** rather than **explicit**.

Parts of speech other than nouns can be used in a metaphorical way: any slight departure from LITERAL LANGUAGE is likely to impart a shade of metaphorical meaning. Shelley's 'Mutability' (1824) starts with a verb metaphorically describing the blooming of a flower: 'The flower that *smiles* today'. Wordsworth describes 'The Vale *profound*' in 'The Solitary Reaper' (1807): the scenery seems more solemn because of the adjectival metaphor, though in fact the lines go on to activate the original meaning of 'profound', which is 'deep', and the vale metaphorically is 'overflowing with the sound', the woman's song being turned into a liquid. 'Profound' in its sense of 'solemnly thoughtful, showing depth of thought' is a metaphorical extension of the word's simple meaning of 'deep'. 'Depth of thought' is also, strictly speaking, metaphorical, but the use of 'profound' and 'depth' in these senses no longer carries any strong metaphorical 'charge': they are '**dead metaphors**', like the 'leg' of a table, or the 'arm' of a chair, and they pass unnoticed. This habit of words to extend their meaning by metaphor and then cease to be metaphorical is a fact of language. Writers, however, especially poets, use metaphor to create original and thrilling new combinations of ideas, objects and sensations. Sometimes these combinations are too daring, and we feel the parts do not fuse together successfully: such a failure can be called a **mixed metaphor**. Hamlet's comments on flattery are an example (III.2):

No, let the candied tongue lick absurd pomp
And crook the pregnant hinges of the knee
Where thrift may follow fawning.

The 'hinges' of the knee are 'pregnant' because flattery successfully gains advancement: Shakespeare (or Hamlet) may be said to be in control of his mixed metaphor. The term is more commonly used in a pejorative way to point out a muddle caused by clashing dead metaphors or CLICHÉS so as to create a ridiculous combination: 'He was rushing about like a bull in a china shop, until he found himself on the horns of a dilemma.' *See also* SIMILE, SYMBOL.

Metaphysical conceit. *See* CONCEIT.

Metaphysical poets. Metaphysics is the philosophy of being and knowing, but this term was originally applied to a group of seventeenth-century poets in a derogatory manner. Dryden, in his *A Discourse Concerning the Original and Progress of Satire* (1693), remarks that John Donne 'affects the metaphysics', meaning that Donne's poetry is full of ingenious, abstruse and unnecessary argument; Dr Johnson in his *Life of Cowley* (1779) applied the term 'metaphysical' to all the seventeenth-century poets who wrote like Donne.

The other 'Metaphysicals' are Herbert, Vaughan and Crashaw (all of whose poems are mainly religious) and Cleveland, Marvell and Cowley. Each of these poets has a strongly individual style, but there are still some common features that allow the identification of something like a 'Metaphysical style'. The chief feature of Donne's poetry is his abrasive colloquiality, especially in contrast with the smooth Elizabethan LYRICS that preceded him. His poems often start with an exclamation and take the form of an argument with another person, lover or God. In these arguments Donne likes to indulge in fantastical flights of logic, bringing in an extraordinary range of discordant imagery and ideas. 'A Valediction: Forbidding Mourning' (1633), for example, compares his leaving home to a dying man, surrounded by friends; makes a blasphemous comparison between his love and religion; discusses earthquakes, astronomy and the refining of gold and finishes with a famous comparison between his love and a pair of compasses drawing a circle: all this in a love poem trying to persuade someone not to weep. It is this density and range of metaphorical association, and the witty display of ingenious comparisons and CONCEITS, clever PARADOXES and PUNS, that the other poets copied and modified into their own separate styles.

It is exactly these qualities that twentieth-century writers like T.S. Eliot and especially the NEW CRITICS admired, to the extent that the Metaphysicals have come to be regarded as major poets; former ages tended to consider them eccentric and unnecessarily difficult.

Metatheatre. *See* METADRAMA.

Methodology. The study or science of methods; the system of method and principles used in an intellectual discipline. Often used as a jargon term indicating simply 'method', or the theoretical approach to a subject.

Metonymy. (Gk. 'change of name') A figure of speech: the substitution of the name of a thing by the name of an attribute of it, or something closely associated with it. For example, 'the Crown' for the monarchy; 'the pen is mightier than the sword', in which 'the pen' stands for literature and 'the sword' for fighting and war; 'the stage' for the theatrical profession; 'Shakespeare' stands for his works ('he has read all of Shakespeare').

An influential article by the linguistician Roman Jakobson, 'Two Aspects of Language and Two Types of Aphasic Disturbances' (1956), has led to metonymy being perceived, along with METAPHOR, as a fundamental aspect of language choice and literary effect. Metaphor works by similarity, while metonymy works by plainer logical relationships. One way of expressing the distinction is to see metaphor as 'vertical', while metonymy is 'horizontal' (these terms are used in linguistics to express the opposition between the PARADIGMATIC and the syntagmatic). The tendency of realistic narrative description is to move horizontally, concentrating on items which stand representatively for more than just themselves, in other words metonymically, through causal links and the logic of contiguity (next-door-ness). The following is an example from Dickens's *Bleak House* (1852–3):

> The day changes as it wears itself away, and becomes dark and drizzly. Jo fights it out, at his crossing, among the mud and the wheels, the horses, whips, and umbrellas, and gets but a scanty sum to pay for the unsavoury shelter of Tom-all-Alone's. Twilight comes on; gas begins to start up in the shops; the lamplighter, with his ladder, runs along the margin of the pavement. A wretched evening is beginning to close in.

There are several metaphors in this: the day 'wears itself away' and Jo 'fights it out', but here they do not propel the passage forward. Instead its chief effects are metonymic. Objects which are parts of greater wholes – 'the mud and the wheels, the horses, whips, and umbrellas' – are chosen to represent the quality of Jo's life. The gas, the lamplighter, his ladder, the margin of the pavement, are less obviously metonymic, but they are still details that are representative of a whole, that fill out figuratively the general statement that 'twilight comes on', and they are contiguous and related by cause and effect to that which they represent. Moreover, this metonymic mode pervades the whole passage in more than just a locally descriptive way. This is a representative evening for Jo: it is a metonym for his whole way of life. And Jo himself is the metonymic representative of his class of street-sweepers, and the utmost poor of Tom-all-Alone's. Such effects are the staple methods of realistic prose.

Metre. (Gk. 'measure') Verse is discriminated from prose because it contains some linguistic element which is repeated, creating a sense of PATTERN. In English verse the commonest pattern is stress- or accent-based metre, which consists of the regular arrangement of strong stresses in a stretch of language.

In English every word of more than one syllable has an accent, or tonic stress, on one of its syllables. (Non-native speakers commonly mispronounce words by stressing the wrong syllable.) The stress may occur on any syllable: mispronounce, syllable. Strong stresses only exist in relation to the weaker-stressed syllables that surround them. Monosyllabic words are stressed according to their value in the organisation and meaning of the sentence. It is possible to explain the rhythm of any sentence of spoken English, or the CADENCE of any phrase, in terms of the variation in stress from syllable to syllable. Scansion is the analysis of the rhythm or metre of individual poems. Prosody is the study of the theory, practice and development of metres.

Metre and scansion are areas of study which have been extended and made more complicated by the development of linguistics in the second half of the twentieth century. By the standards of phoneticians and linguisticians, the following description of scanning verse is extremely crude; nevertheless it is still commonly used by critics and poets for defining rhythmical effects.

The terms used for describing metre are borrowed from the analysis of Ancient Greek and Latin poems, which were based on QUANTITY rather than stress. In Latin changing the length of a vowel (i.e. its quantity) in a word (e.g. *mensă/mensā*) changed its meaning and grammatical function. The metres of Latin poetry were based on patterns of long and short vowels; combinations of clusters of consonants were also considered to lengthen a syllable. As English metres are based on stress rather than quantity, it is a mistake to discuss the metre of a poem in English in terms of long and short syllables. (Though, of course, every poem will contain long and short syllables. Also some poets, such as Campion and Bridges, have tried to write quantitative verse.)

Poetry is scanned line by line: the line is the rhythmical unit. In the following examples, strongly stressed syllables are marked with a /, weaker-stressed syllables with an x.

x   /   x   /   x   /   x   /
I have/a boy/of five/years old;
x   /   x   /   x   /   x   /
His face/is fresh/and fair/to see

The rhythm of these lines is easily perceived: it consists of relatively weak and strong syllables alternating regularly. In scanning a line it is divided into small units of rhythm called feet. Note that metrical feet cut across polysyllabic words quite arbitrarily. A weak stress followed by a strong stress (x /, ti-tum) is called an iamb. The two lines above therefore are iambic tetrameters, meaning lines of four iambs.

Iambic metres (also called 'rising rhythm') are the most common in English verse. The other most common metre in lyric poems is the trochaic metre ('falling rhythm'), built from alternating strong and weak stresses (/ x, tum-ti). In trochaic lines it is common for the last weak stress to be omitted: such a line is called catalectic:

/   x   /   x   /   x   /   (X)
Lay your/sleeping/head my/love,
/   x   /   x   /   x   /   (X)
Human/on my/faithless/arm.

In scanning verse it is rarely necessary to use more than the following feet:

iamb	x /
trochee	/ x
anapaest	x x /
dactyl	/ x x
spondee	/ /
pyrrhic	x x

The following terms are used to describe lines of different lengths:

One foot:	Monometer
Two feet:	Dimeter
Three feet:	Trimeter
Four feet:	Tetrameter
Five feet:	Pentameter
Six feet:	Hexameter

Seven feet: Heptameter
Eight feet: Octameter

In determining the metre of a piece of verse, it is essential to read it out loud. Always read the whole line, and note where the major stresses fall, which is where, were it a song, you would tap your foot. Decide if it is in a duple (two-syllable foot) or triple (three-syllable foot) metre. Decide which kind of foot predominates, and how many feet there are in each line. Remember that lyrics may have lines of various lengths and different metres.

Here are examples of different metrical lines:

i) Iambic pentameter:

    x   /   x   /   x   /   x / x   /
From fair/est creat/ures we/desire/increase,

    x   / x   /   x   /   x   / x /
That there/by beau/ty's *Rose*/might ne/ver die.

ii) Iambic trimeter:

  x / x   /   x   /
It is/the eve/ning hour;

    x   / x   / x /
How si/lent all/doth lie.

iii) Trochaic tetrameter (catalectic):

  /   x / x / x   /   (x)
Come, my/Celia,/let us/prove,

  /   x / x / x /   (x)
While we/may the/sports of/love.

iv) Dactylic tetrameter:

   / x   x   /   x   x / x x   /   x x
Woman much/missed, how you/call to me,/call to me,

  /   x x   / x   x   / x x   / (x x)
Saying that/now you are/not as you/were.

v) Anapaestic tetrameter:

  x   x / x x   / x x   / x x   /
The Assyr/ian came down/like the wolf/on the fold

   x   x / x   x   / x x / x x /
And his co/horts were burn/ing in pur/ple and gold.

Whereas some verse fits easily and exactly with an imagined, abstract metrical pattern, other kinds of poetry seem only to suggest a regular metre or even to be in constant tension with it. SUBSTITUTION of another foot (breaking the metrical pattern) is common except in the most regular verse. Frequently a trochee is placed at the beginning of an iambic line for emphasis.

The commonest metre in English verse is the IAMBIC PENTAMETER. Shakespeare's plays, Milton's *Paradise Lost* (1667) and Wordsworth's

The Prelude (1850) are all examples of BLANK VERSE, that is unrhymed iambic pentameters. Rhymed pairs of lines in iambic pentameter are called HEROIC COUPLETS.

The nineteenth century was a great age of experiment in metrical forms. Saintsbury's *A History of English Prosody* (1906-10) is the most complete study of the practice of metre. *See also* DEMOTION, ENJAMB-MENT, RHYME, STANZA.

Middle English period. A crucial time in the history of the English language and literature. Middle English was the language (in a variety of different dialect forms) which resulted from the modification of Anglo-Saxon after the Norman Conquest in 1066, and which was spoken and used as a vehicle for literature until about 1500 when the London dialect (that used by Chaucer) became the standard literary language, and therefore recognisably the basis for 'modern English'. An Anglo-Norman period, in which a French dialect dominated non-Latin literature, lasted until about 1350. After that date, especially during the reign of Richard II (1377-99), Middle English literature burgeoned. Chaucer was the leading poet. His *Canterbury Tales* and *Troilus and Criseyde* rank amongst the greatest works in English literature. His contemporaries include John Gower, who wrote the *Confessio Amantis*, William Langland, author of the religious dream satire *Piers Plowman*, and the anonymous poet who wrote *Sir Gawain and the Green Knight* and *Pearl*.

In the fifteenth century several Middle Scots poets, sometimes called the SCOTTISH CHAUCERIANS, including King James I of Scotland, Robert Henryson, Gavin Douglas and William Dunbar, represented a flowering of poetic talent in Scotland. The fifteenth century was also the age of medieval drama, the MIRACLE and MORALITY PLAYS, of popular lyrics and BALLADS, and of Sir Thomas Malory's great Arthurian prose ROMANCE *Le Morte d'Arthur*.

Miles gloriosus. (Lat. 'boastful soldier') A STOCK CHARACTER, common in comedies by the Roman playwright Plautus (second century BC), which finds its way into the English drama: the soldier braggart, who boasts continually of his deeds as a warrior, but is in fact a cowardly sham. Ancient Pistol and Falstaff in Shakespeare's *Henry IV*, Parts 1 and 2 (*c*.1597, *c*. 1598) are both examples of this type.

Mills and Boon. A publishing house dedicated to producing popular 'romantic' novels for a mass market. In 1988 it published 560 titles and had a turnover of £15 million. The name has become shorthand for a particular kind of short fiction, which deals in an emotive way with women's feelings, in a variety of stereotypical situations to do with love, courtship and marriage.

Mime. (Gk. 'imitation') A kind of acting, by gesture, without words or sounds. Ancient Greek in origin (fifth century BC), it has remained an element in all kinds of drama. In modern France it is a popular form of entertainment in its own right, with Marcel Marceau its greatest practitioner. In mime the gestures and emotions portrayed are often exaggerated almost grotesquely; much skill is exercised in creating the illusion that things not present on the stage (walls, doors, ladders, furniture, etc.) are there. *See also* DUMB SHOW, PANTOMIME.

Mimesis, mimetic. (Gk. 'imitation') A word used by Aristotle in his *Poetics* (fourth century BC) when he states that tragedy is an 'imitation' of an action.

Mimetic criticism regards literature as imitating or reflecting life, and therefore emphasises the 'truth' and 'accuracy' of its representation, its REALISM in a general sense. *See also* DIEGESIS.

Minimalism. Art, music and literature reduced to their most simple and bare elemental forms. Japanese forms like the HAIKU and TANKA might be called minimalist, but they appear florid when compared to Beckett's 'play' (in both senses of the word) *Breath* (1970), which consists of nothing but a single exhalation lasting half a minute. Another minimalist work is the following poem or story, said to be an example of the shortest possible narrative: 'Frog/Pond/Plop!'.

Minstrel. (Lat. 'official') A professional reciter of poetry and a musician; minstrels flourished in the late Middle Ages (thirteenth and fourteenth centuries), singing traditional narrative poems and folk BALLADS. *See also* ORAL LITERATURE, TROUBADOUR.

Minstrel ballad. *See* BALLAD.

Miracle play. (Lat. 'wonder at') A form of late medieval drama. Dramatisations of saints' lives and miraculous events and legends (distinguished from the MYSTERY PLAY which dealt with biblical stories). The most famous example is the cycle of forty-two French plays called *Miracles de Notre Dame* (late fourteenth century).

Miscellany. (Lat. 'mixture') A collection of various kinds of writing in one book. The famous *Tottel's Miscellany* (1557) is a collection of lyric poems by various authors.

Mise-en-abyme. (Fr. 'put in the abyss') A term for a self-reflexive repetition in a text. The central character of Gide's novel *The Counterfeiters* (1926) is a novelist working on a novel which is very like the novel itself. The term also suggests infinite regression, such as the design which used to appear on the Quaker Oats packet, on which there was a picture of a man holding a Quaker Oats packet, on which there was a picture of a man holding a Quaker Oats packet, and so on.

The term has been taken up in DECONSTRUCTIVE CRITICISM for the occasional glimpses of the 'solving emptiness' that underlies the endless free-play of meanings in words, the revelations of an abyss of nothingness which is constantly covered and uncovered by the signs themselves. *See also* METAFICTION.

Mise-en-scène. (Fr. 'put on stage') The setting of a theatrical production; the scenery, properties, etc. Sometimes this phrase refers to the position of the actors at a particular moment in a play.

Misprision. (O. Fr. 'error') Misreading. In origin, a misdemeanour or neglect of duty committed by a public official, then meaning the act of mistaking one thing for another, or failing to appreciate the value of something. Oscar Wilde has a character called Miss Prism in *The Importance of Being Earnest* (1895), who muddles up a handbag, a pram, a baby and a manuscript.

The word has been taken up by the American critic Harold Bloom and others to refer to a special kind of creative 'misreading' which results in writing shaped by a reaction to some powerful (and possibly resented) influence. *See also* ANXIETY OF INFLUENCE.

Mixed metaphor. *See* METAPHOR.

Mnemonic. (Gk. 'mindful') For the purpose of helping the memory. Coleridge in Chapter 14 of *Biographia Literaria* (1817) suggests that rhyme and metre in poetry have a mnemonic function, and he cites a widely known mnemonic JINGLE to illustrate the idea:

Thirty days hath September,
April, June and November.

Mock epic. *See* BURLESQUE, EPIC, PARODY.

Mock-heroic. Refers to the style of mock epic (*see* EPIC), or to any work which treats a trivial subject with ridiculous, comic grandeur. An example is Thomas Gray's 'Ode on the Death of a Favourite Cat' (1748). The BURLESQUE and the PARODY are often mock-heroic.

Mode, modality. (Lat. 'tune, manner') A mode is a kind or manner of writing that cuts across genre, such as the ironic mode, the comic mode, the fantastic, realism, and so on. It indicates, broadly, a work's approach to its subject matter. Different kinds of discourse will employ different modes; a novelist will thus exhibit a different modality from a historian, or an advertising copy-writer. A novel of fantasy will have a different modality from a realistic work, and a single novel may contain several different modalities.

In linguistic analysis modality refers to contrasts in MOOD signalled chiefly by changes in the verb. In English the subtle use of 'modal' verbs, such as 'may', 'will', 'can', 'shall' or 'must', defines the attitudes of the speaker towards the factual content of what is being said (uncertainty, possibility, definiteness, and so on), which is often connected with modality.

Modernism, modernist. The First World War (1914–18) is generally considered to be the catalyst that initiated the modern period in literature. 'Modernism' is the label that distinguishes some characteristics of twentieth-century writing, in so far as it differs from the literary conventions inherited from the nineteenth century. It may seem ridiculous, but critics have sought to categorise twentieth-century literature with such haste that the 'modernist' phase is already over: we have entered a phase of POSTMODERNISM. Words like 'paleo-modernism' and 'neo-modernism' have so far not (yet) achieved general currency. Certainly 'modern' is not used by critics to mean 'contemporary' or 'of the present'.

The most typical 'modernist' feature of twentieth-century literature is its experimental quality, which is thought to be a response to the condition of living in a 'modern' world, that is to say, one characterised by scientific, industrial and technological change, like Europe and North America in the twentieth century. Radical technical innovations have taken place in all three of the major genres: in the novel, Proust, Kafka, Lawrence, Joyce and Faulkner all broke in some way with the broadly REALIST nineteenth-century tradition. In poetry, Pound, Eliot, Yeats and W.C. Williams, and, in the theatre, Strindberg, Pirandello, Brecht and Beckett, are all celebrated for having broken old forms and conventions.

What forms do these innovations take? A few trends can be mentioned, but with the proviso that none of them is common to more than a few writers. There are huge discrepancies in outlook: while Eliot was saying that twentieth-century poetry must be complex, W.C. Williams argued for the simplicity of the view that there are 'no ideas but in things'. Modernist writers value the AUTONOMY of the literary artefact, even to the extent of what the Spanish critic José Ortega y Gasset calls 'the dehumanisation of art'. Modernist writers throw old formal conventions away: Pound asserts in the Cantos (1930–69) that he 'broke' the pentameter. FREE VERSE in poetry is matched by the novels which depart from a simple chronology, like Faulkner's As I Lay Dying (1930), with its multiple points of view, or Proust's exploration of his memories in A la recherche du temps perdu (1913–27). Lawrence and Woolf argued that they found a new kind of characterisation, more fluid and less stable than the fixed psychologies of nineteenth-century fiction. The theatre has turned its back on reflecting reality and presents its truths through abstractions of reality like Strindberg's Dream Play (1902), Brecht's EPIC THEATRE or Beckett's Waiting for Godot (1953).

Modernist writers have been self-conscious innovators: the number of small movements and '-isms' testifies to their deliberation: SYMBOLISM, NATURALISM, EXPRESSIONISM, IMAGISM, VORTICISM, FUTURISM, DADA, SURREALISM. Many of these groups have published explanations of their programme. Similarly techniques have been labelled and explained by their practitioners: STREAM OF CONSCIOUSNESS, ALIENATION EFFECT, ANTI-NOVEL. No doubt the study of literature as a university subject and the fact that authors can earn money as teachers and critics has added to this self-consciousness. CRITICISM has been equally apt to split into self-labelling groups: the NEW CRITICS, the CHICAGO CRITICS, MARXISTS, LEAVISITES, STRUCTURALISTS. This fissiparousness amongst artists and critics is presumably an indication that there is no modern agreed convention except the need to be AVANT-GARDE; and it may be that a counter-modernist traditional reaction will come which will in the future seem to represent the twentieth century better than any of the explicitly modernist writers. In English poetry respect for the modernist influence of Pound, Eliot and Yeats has given way to some extent to a reverence for a rival, anti-experimental tradition in lyric poetry, finding its way into the twentieth century via Hardy: the popularity of the poetry of Philip Larkin during the 1960s and 1970s has much to do with this. And, of course, in order to be unconventional it is necessary to have conventions to turn against.

Moment. A non-jargon term for intensely joyful or in some other way memorable experiences which may form the basis for a poem or episode in a novel. Shelley talks of such 'moments' in *The Defence of Poetry* (written 1821), and Wordsworth organises *The Prelude* around these semi-visionary experiences; he also calls them 'spots of time' (*The Prelude*, 1850 text, Book 12, l.208). A more formal critical term for the 'moment' is EPIPHANY. *See also* INVOLUTE.

Monodrama. (Gk. 'alone-play') A dramatic piece composed for one actor only, playing one character. *Krapp's Last Tape* (1958) by Beckett is an example. Quite a common form of radio play. Tennyson called his long dramatic monologue *Maud* (1855) a monodrama.

Monody. (Gk. 'single-song') A DIRGE or ELEGY, uttered by a single person: Matthew Arnold's poem in memory of the poet Clough is entitled 'Thyrsis, a Monody' (1866).

Monologic. *See* DIALOGIC.

Monologue. (Gk. 'speaking alone') A single person speaking, with or without an audience, is uttering a monologue. (Two persons speaking together: a DIALOGUE.) Therefore lyric poems, prayers and, in the theatre, the SOLILOQUY, are all varieties of monologue.

The **dramatic monologue** is the name given to a specific kind of poem in which a single person, not the poet, is speaking. In the 1840s Browning and Tennyson seem to have perfected this form almost simultaneously as a way of expressing ideas which they wanted to explore without the reader associating such speculations with the poet's own point of view. Thus Tennyson can examine the desirability of death in 'Tithonus' (1860) or Browning can present the amoral aesthetic sensibility of a murderer in 'My Last Duchess' (1842). Both poets' earlier works had been criticised for morbid self-indulgence: the dramatic monologue was a clearly impersonal form.

As such it has been popular also with twentieth-century poets, for whom Eliot's ideas of IMPERSONALITY have been influential. Pound and Eliot both use the form, while Yeats's masks are similar denials of self-involvement.

Usually the dramatic monologue is something more than an expression of feeling: the speaker is placed in a situation which is also dramatically realised through what he says. Browning's 'Fra Lippo Lippi' (1855), for example, describes a monk's reaction to being arrested late at night when he should be in his convent.

In the twentieth-century novel the STREAM OF CONSCIOUSNESS is an internalised dramatic monologue.

Monometer. (Gk. 'one measure') In versification a line with only one FOOT (rare). *See also* METRE.

Mood. (O.E. 'mind, feeling', from O.N. 'anger') A term used synonymously with ATMOSPHERE to indicate in a literary work the prevailing feeling or frame of mind, especially at the start of a play, poem or novel, creating a sense of expectation about what is to follow.

Mood also has a grammatical sense with reference to types of sentence, especially in relation to the verbs they contain. The imperative, subjunctive and indicative use of verbs are different 'moods'.

Moral. A lesson which can be learned or abstracted from a story, fable or play. It is sometimes over-simple in its summary of what the message of a work might be: many readers feel indignant that the Ancient Mariner, in Coleridge's poem of that name (1798), after narrating a tale of extraordinary vividness and complexity, should remark somewhat tritely:

He prayeth best, who loveth best
All things both great and small;
For the dear God who loveth us,
He made and loveth all.

Morality play. *Everyman* (*c*. 1500) is the best known of the many morality plays written and performed between about 1450 and 1550. It is typical of the form: it is an ALLEGORY in which Everyman is summoned by Death, and is deserted by all his friends (Goods, Knowledge, Strength, Beauty, etc.) except for Good Deeds who is prepared to make the journey with him. The forces of good and evil, and a Christian moral lesson concerning salvation, are dramatised with simplicity and vigour.

Many morality plays contained a character called the Vice, a half-comic, half-evil tempter. Shakespeare's Falstaff is supposedly a sophisticated version of this figure. Morality plays are a development of the MYSTERY PLAYS of the late Middle Ages.

Morpheme. (Gk. 'form') The smallest unit of speech sounds in a language which is meaningful. Usually a word, though prefixes and suffixes like 'dis-', 'un-', '-ful' or '-able' are also morphemic.

Morphology. The study of the structure of words. SYNTAX explains the rules for combining words into sentences; morphology examines INFLECTIONS and other kinds of word-change and development.

Motif. (O. Fr., from Lat. 'moving') A motif is some aspect of literature (a type of character, theme or image) which recurs frequently. Encounters with tramps in lonely places is a 'motif' common in Wordsworth's poetry. The chasm and dome of Coleridge's 'Kubla Khan' (1816) are motifs common to many other nineteenth-century poets. Certain archetypal figures, such as the bewitching fairy lady, are motifs from folklore.

An individual work may have its own recurring motifs, or leitmotifs, repeated phrases, images, description or incidents. **Leitmotif** (Ger. 'leading motif') is borrowed from music where it means a repeated phrase. *See also* CARPE DIEM, TOPOS, UBI SUNT.

Movement, The. The name for a group of poets of the 1950s whose work was collected in the anthology *New Lines* (1956) by Robert Conquest. The most distinguished contributors were Philip Larkin, Thom Gunn, Ted Hughes and Elizabeth Jennings. All the poets concerned quickly sought to dissociate themselves from any idea of a shared coherent programme for poetry; but none the less 'the Movement' can perhaps be characterised as a move away from the self-indulgent 1940s wildness of Dylan Thomas and his admirers, towards the virtues, in poetry, of intelligence, control, verbal dexterity combined with wit and clarity, and a certain modesty of ambition.

Multi-accentuality. The capacity of words to have different meanings according to the contexts in which they are used. Words, far from having a fixed signification, may be the focus of conflict, and their meanings the object of controversy. In politics, for example, words like 'anti-social', 'authority', 'censorship', 'criminal', 'patriot', 'terrorist', 'traitor', and so on, have very different meanings according to who is using them and for what purpose.

Mumming play. A folk drama performed throughout Britain until the middle of the nineteenth century. Most versions of the play involve a fight between St George and a Turkish knight; the former is killed, and then revived by a doctor. Devils and clowns provide diversions from this basic theme of miraculous resurrection, suggesting that its origin is in a pagan solstice or spring festival. The actors who perform the play are called 'mummers'.

Muse. One of the nine Greek goddesses who presided over the arts: Calliope (epic poetry), Clio (history), Erato (love poetry), Euterpe (lyric poetry), Melpomene (tragedy), Polyhymnia (songs for the gods), Terpsichore (dancing), Thalia (comedy), Urania (astronomy). Poets traditionally invoke the aid of a muse to help them write, so the word has come to stand for a poet's inspiration.

Mystery play. (Lat. *mi(ni)sterium* 'handicraft, guild', from Gk. 'secret rites') Dramatisation of the Old and New Testaments which evolved steadily from about the tenth century onwards. Originally performed in Latin by priests, the form developed as it moved out of the church precinct, adopted the vernacular and was gradually taken over by the various guilds of tradesmen in the large towns. By the fourteenth century elaborate cycles had developed, played during the Feast of Corpus Christi, with each guild responsible for a biblical episode from the Creation right through to the Crucifixion and resurrection of Christ. Each scene was presented on a waggon which could be moved around the city. Comic scenes, between Noah and his wife, or the Shepherds at the Nativity, were common. The verse is rough and vigorous, but the later plays show a strong sense of character and psychology.

The chief English cycles extant are those of York (48 episodes), Coventry (42), Wakefield or Towneley (32) and Chester (25). All are anonymous. Mystery plays were performed in other European countries. *See also* MIRACLE PLAY, MORALITY PLAY.

Myth. (Gk. 'word, fable') Myths are stories, usually concerning super-humans or gods, which are related to accompany or to explain religious beliefs: they originate far back in the culture of ORAL societies. A **mythology** is a system of mythical stories which, taken together, elaborate the religious or metaphysical beliefs of a society. Such a system is likely to contain rituals. In its weakest sense the word 'myth' may mean no more than 'untruth' ('It is a myth that . . .'). With reference to religions the word suggests a certain detachment; a mythology is a religion which is no longer felt to be true. To discuss 'Christian mythology', then, is to take up a certain point of view about Christianity.

Writers of almost all ages have valued myths and used them for literary purposes long after the stories had ceased to have any religious content. Romantic PRIMITIVISM resulted in a vastly increased interest in mythology in the nineteenth century which culminated in attempts to systematise different mythologies from all over the world: Sir James Frazer's anthropological study of magic, *The Golden Bough*, started appearing in 1890, and in the twentieth century Jung's theories of ARCHETYPAL SYMBOLS and the COLLECTIVE UNCONSCIOUS rely heavily on the study of mythology. More recently STRUCTURALIST critics have seen mythology as a kind of language for communicating ideas, significant not for its content but for the structure of its systems. Another contemporary development has been **myth criticism** by (among others) the Canadian Northrop Frye, who expounded the view that all literature is based on myths, in particular myths explaining the cycle of the seasons and the different phases of the agricultural year. Different genres belong to the different seasons: comedy to spring, romance to summer, tragedy to autumn and irony to winter. Even the most sophisticated literature can be seen in this way to express recurrent archetypes and plots.

Writers have used myths in many different ways. The flexibility of the stories allows a single myth to be remodelled in many different forms. Shelley's *Prometheus Unbound* (1820) is such a reworking. Many writers, such as Blake and Yeats, have even created their own elaborate systems of mythology. Others, such as Joyce in *Ulysses* (1922) and Eliot in *The Waste Land* (1922), have placed myths alongside views of modern society in an ironic parallel or contrast.

In recent criticism the word tends to lose its connection with religion and is used to describe the complete range of systems and signs by which a society expresses its cultural values. The French structuralist Roland Barthes, for example, in his collection of essays called *Mythologies* (1957), analyses phenomena such as wrestling, strip-tease and car design, in order to reveal aspects of French culture and society.

Myth criticism. *See* MYTH.

Mythology. *See* MYTH.

Mythopoeia. (Gk. 'MYTH creation') The invention of mythological systems by poets. Many poets of the Romantic period invented myths. All Blake's long poems consist of an elaborate exercise in mythopoeia: 'I must create a system or be enslaved by another man's', he explained.

N

Naiv und sentimentalisch. (Ger. 'naïve and sentimental') In 1795 the German poet Schiller wrote an essay in which he used the two words to define different kinds of poet. The naïve poets, like Homer and Shakespeare, express in their work an immediate, instinctive reaction to nature; while the sentimental poets (like Schiller himself) seek in nature a lost ideal, and depict an imagined version of how nature might be, rather than nature as it really is. These were not simply chronological categories but an attempt to discriminate two differing poetic attitudes or premises.

Naïve narrator. *See* NARRATIVE.

Narratee. The implied, imagined figure to whom a NARRATIVE is told, not always the same as the actual reader and to be distinguished also from the IMPLIED READER. In some works there is a known narratee: Wordsworth addresses his autobiographical study *The Prelude* (1850) to Coleridge. In others it may be a character in the fiction itself: a large part of Emily Brontë's *Wuthering Heights* (1847) is told by Nelly Dean to Lockwood as narratee; it is his narration to an imagined and anonymous narratee (in this case the reader) that starts and finishes the book.

Narrative, narrator. (Lat. 'to tell') A narrative is a story, tale or recital of facts. What distinguishes a story from the flux of raw experience is that in a story a selection of incidents is made so as to suggest some relationship between them. To create a narrative or narrate a story is therefore to recount and establish some connection between a series of events. History is a narrative, though the word is more commonly associated with FICTION.

In examining any narrative, for example a novel, it is immediately clear that it is composed of a mixture of different kinds of writing in different proportions. A novel is likely to include dramatised incident, description (of people or places), dialogue, condensed report of past events, reflection by the author or by a character, generalised commentary, and figurative writing. What brings all these diverse elements together in the proportions unique to any particular narrative is the narrator. In understanding and commenting on a story, our attention is immediately focused on the narrator and his or her **point of view**. What kind of connection is being made between events? Is it a carefully wrought 'plot' or loosely related set of episodes? And how is the material being presented to an audience? The analysis and identification of point of view is one key to the discussion of methods of narration.

A simple distinction can be made between **first-person narrative**, in which the narrator speaks of him- or herself as 'I', and is generally a character in the story, and **third-person narrative**, in which the narrator describes the characters as 'he', 'she' or 'they'. Both kinds are common. Dickens's *David Copperfield* (1849-50) is a first-person narrative, beginning 'Whether I shall turn out to be the hero of my own life, or whether that station will be held by anybody else, these pages must show'. Conrad's *The Secret Agent* (1907) is third-person narrative: 'Mr Verloc, going out in the morning, left his shop nominally in charge of his brother-in-law.'

In third-person narratives it is necessary to discern the explicit or implicit nature of the narrator's approach to the audience and the events described. He or she may be a garrulous **intrusive narrator** who continually comments upon the story that is being self-consciously told (in this case, there may even be confusion with first-person narrative). Or the narrator may remain 'silent' except for the purpose of 'showing' the dramatised incidents and events which combine to make the story, being as unintrusive or **impersonal** as possible. In the case of intrusive narrators, such as Fielding in *Tom Jones* (1749), Byron in *Don Juan* (1819-24) or George Eliot in *Middlemarch* (1871-2), modern critical conventions demand that the narrator should be considered as a mask or PERSONA, a character in its own right, rather than the author's own self, and always referred to as 'the narrator'.

An **omniscient narrator** describes a story (with godlike ease) as if capable of seeing every event which concerns the characters, even to the extent of knowing their innermost thoughts and motives. On the other hand an author may choose one or a few of the characters and concentrate on depicting the events as seen from a **limited** or **restricted point of view**. Henry James called this a 'focus' or 'centre' of consciousness: *What Maisie Knew* (1897) is recounted solely from the point of view of a child (though it is still a third-person narrative). This technique shades gradually into the STREAM OF CONSCIOUSNESS in which events are related as if flowing through the perceptions of a character. In this method, characteristic of much famous twentieth-century fiction, including works by Joyce, Virginia Woolf and Faulkner, the author seems to disappear altogether, with the reader indulging in the illusion of participating in the evolving circumstances of a character.

First-person narrators, since they are characters in the story, are likely to have the limited viewpoint consonant with the part they have to play. They may be the hero of the narrative, such as Richard Hannay in John Buchan's *The Thirty-Nine Steps* (1915) or Copperfield in Dickens's *David Copperfield*. They may be only a peripheral observer, such as Marlow in Conrad's *Heart of Darkness* (1902), or a minor character, such as Nick Carraway in F. Scott Fitzgerald's *The Great Gatsby* (1925) or Jim Hawkins in Stevenson's *Treasure Island* (1883). In some cases a narrator who is also a character in a novel may be classed as **unreliable** or **fallible**. Nellie Dean in *Wuthering Heights* (1847) by Emily Brontë may be seen as an honest, no-nonsense housekeeper, but at times it is clear from her own account that she actually interferes with events in a disturbing manner: it seems, though she herself makes light of the matter, that she may be partly responsible for the death of Cathy, as she tells no one how gravely ill Cathy is, and allows her to go to sleep with the window open. A modification of this tricky relationship between narrator and reader where the reader may be left uncertain exactly what to believe or disregard, is the **naïve narrator**, whom we are more obviously supposed to view ironically. Swift's Gulliver in *Gulliver's Travels* (1726) is clearly supposed to be seen as gullible in the way he falls in with every absurd custom in the countries he visits, though Swift likes to keep us guessing by varying the extent and quality of the irony.

Another major means of discriminating between different sorts of narrative is in terms of the PLOT, or the STRUCTURE and arrangement of incidents in a book. Authors also manipulate time in different ways. Sterne's *Tristram Shandy* (1759–67) is a famous example of a distorted and disrupted time-scheme. Thematic imagery (*see* IMAGERY) may also be used as an aspect of narrative technique – for example, the many images or symbols of enclosure and imprisonment that occur throughout Dickens's *Little Dorrit* (1855–7). In the above cases, however, (as, indeed, with 'point of view') it is difficult always to distinguish narrative technique from subject matter. Probably such a distinction is unnecessary anyway, when discussing an individual work, rather than theorising about categories. *See also* DIEGESIS, FREE INDIRECT STYLE, NARRATOLOGY, SHOWING AND TELLING.

Narrative verse. Simply, verse which tells a story. The EPIC and BALLAD are two narrative verse genres, but there is a huge body of other kinds of narrative poetry. Many chivalric ROMANCES were in verse. Before the success of the novel in the eighteenth century, verse was a more common medium for story-telling than prose. The commonest metres have been BLANK VERSE, RHYME ROYAL (also called the Chaucerian stanza), and the SPENSERIAN STANZA. Many of the methods of examining NARRATIVE prose can usefully be applied to narrative verse.

Narratology. The study, analysis, categorisation and theory of NARRATIVES and the way they work. Critics from Aristotle onwards have been involved in this endeavour. Wayne Booth's *The Rhetoric of Fiction* (1961), which seeks to define the techniques by which a novelist can manipulate the reader, was highly influential during the 1960s. However, the term 'narratology' is usually restricted in reference to European STRUCTURALIST approaches to narrative, for example, the works of Gérard Genette and Paul Ricoeur. *The Morphology of the Folktale* (1958) by Vladimir Propp was a pioneering work in this field: it attempts to isolate the fundamental units of meaning in folktales, to create a 'MORPHOLOGY' or grammar (or 'POETICS') of tales.

A basic idea of narratology is that a 'STORY', the succession of events that are to be recounted, in their simplest chronological form, is manipulated in a variety of different, definable ways into a finished narrative, which is the text. (The 'story' in this sense has to be abstracted and reconstructed from the evidence of the text.) Different narratologists give different labels to the elemental story and the finished narration: for example, *fabula* and *histoire* designate the original events of the story; *discours*, **discourse** and *sjuzet* (or *sujet*) are labels for the finished narration. They also seek to define the kinds of events that are dealt with in narrative fiction and to find some order amongst the innumerable different ways in which narratives are constructed, including methods by which time is manipulated, exact discrimination of the various kinds of narrator, splitting up the narrative into multiple 'levels', and exploring the inferences and assumptions in the text about its narrator, author and reader. *See also* ACTANT, ANACHRONY, DEEP STRUCTURE, DIEGESIS, ÉNONCÉ, FRAME NARRATIVE, FUNCTION, IMPLIED AUTHOR, IMPLIED READER, METALEPSIS, NARRATEE, PLOT.

Naturalism. A more particularised branch of REALISM. Naturalism expresses a post-Darwinian view of life in which man is seen as fundamentally no more than a specialised animal, subject wholly to natural forces such as heredity and environment. Man's spiritual or intellectual aspirations are seen as meaningless. In his preface to *Thérèse Raquin* (1867) the French writer Zola calls himself a *naturaliste* and discusses his view of the novelist's role as a pathologist dissecting life, with the novel as a kind of experiment. Though naturalism makes claims to scientific accuracy, it is no different from any other literary stance; the naturalist selects and orders those materials that illustrate a world-view. Typical subject matter is the miserable and poverty-stricken, or those driven by animal appetites such as hunger or sexuality. Life is seen as a squalid and meaningless tragedy, with man in society like a caged wild animal.

Zola's *Nana* (1880) and *Germinal* (1885) are the classics of naturalism. The de Goncourt brothers, Edmond and Jules, also helped initiate the movement in France. Its influence can be seen in English literature in Hardy's *Jude the Obscure* (1895) or in the works of Gissing. The Scandinavian playwrights Strindberg and Ibsen were much affected by naturalism. Theodore Dreiser, a novelist, was one of several American naturalists.

Negative capability. A phrase used by Keats in a letter (to G. and T. Keats, 21–7 December 1817):

> It struck me, what quality went to form a Man of Achievement especially in Literature & which Shakespeare po[s]sessed so enormously – I mean *Negative Capability*, that is when man is capable of being in uncertainties, Mysteries, doubts, without any irritable reaching after fact & reason . . .

Critics often explain the phrase with reference to another letter (to Woodhouse, 27 October 1818) in which Keats discusses his own poetical character, as opposed to the 'wordsworthian or egotistical sublime': he asserts that he has no identity, or character, but is always filling some other body, and delights therefore in imagining evil as well as good: 'It has as much delight in conceiving an Iago as an Imogen. What shocks the virtuous philosop[h]er, delights the camelion Poet.'

Negative capability, then, is the artist's sympathetic imagination (which Keats possessed in large measure), the capacity to forget his or her own personality and enter imaginatively into the existence of others and other kinds of existence. *See also* EMPATHY, GUSTO.

Negritude. (Fr. 'negro-ness') A term coined in the 1930s by Aimé Césaire and Léopold Senghor to characterise what they valued in black African writing: they sought to sustain and continue traditional African culture and sensibility in modern literary forms. Senghor's *Négritude et humanisme* (1964) summed up its features. Negritude was a forerunner of the more aggressive Black Power movement which originated in America in the 1960s.

Nemesis. (Gk. 'righteous indignation, retribution') The early Greeks personified this force as a goddess who punished man's insolence (HUBRIS) towards the gods. Nemesis is the fate that overtakes the tragic hero or heroine, the deserved retributive punishment that in the end cannot be escaped. *See also* TRAGEDY.

Neoclassicism. (Gk. *neo,* 'new') The word 'Neoclassicism' refers to the fact that some writers, particularly in the eighteenth century, modelled their own writing on CLASSICAL, especially Roman, literature. Because the word refers to an explicit mode of thought, 'Neoclassicism' is perhaps a more clearly defined literary mood or period than, say, ROMANTICISM (with which it is constantly contrasted). It is still, however, a vague concept, to be used only after careful qualification. The peril inherent in all literary-historical labels like this is that they are reductive: they destroy the individuality of each writer by trapping him or her in a framework of generalised ideas. As with Romantic writers, Neoclassic writers are very varied in their styles, attitudes and aspirations.

'Neoclassicism' as a label is applied to a period of English literature lasting from 1660, the Restoration of Charles II, until about 1800. The following major writers flourished then: in poetry, Dryden, Pope and Goldsmith; in prose, Swift, Addison, Johnson and Gibbon. As the novel lacks Classical models, eighteenth-century novelists are excluded from lists of Neoclassical writers; an exception might be made for Fielding who held many views in common with the writers above.

The generalised beliefs of the Neoclassical writers are based on the premise that the world is God's carefully ordered creation, with man, midway in the GREAT CHAIN OF BEING, a rational being capable of living harmoniously in society. 'The proper study of mankind is man', wrote Pope in *An Essay on Man* (1733-4). Man's rational intelligence, common sense, was honoured and valued above all other faculties. Reason demonstrated that the great truths about the world were well known, and fixed: the writer's duty was to express these truths in appropriate language. 'True wit', to quote Pope again, is 'what oft was thought but ne'er so well expressed.' In spite of reason, man was a limited being who should not aspire beyond sensible, limited aims: pride, vulgarity, excess, extremes of all kinds, even enthusiasm (by which was meant extravagant religious fervour), were to be distrusted. BALANCE, CORRECTNESS, DECORUM, a sense of the innate rightness of the golden mean, of measure in life and art, these were the routes to human excellence.

Unlike Romantics, then, Neoclassical writers did not value creativity or originality highly. Literature reflected life; art was MIMETIC. Poetry demanded long study and practice: Pope's advice to young writers, based on Horace in the *Ars Poetica* (*c.*20BC), was to keep their peace for nine years.

Poetry demanded the polish of the craftsman's skill. Neoclassic writers valued the various genres, such as epic, tragedy, pastoral, comedy, because rules for writing in these genres could be abstracted from studying the Classical models which had already reached perfection. Not surprisingly Aristotle's views on tragedy, concerning the UNITIES, for example, were regarded as essential. Neoclassic writers accepted the fact that a rough genius like Shakespeare could disregard such rules, but felt that they could not model their own methods on such a rare and fortuitous talent.

Dryden translated Virgil's *Aeneid* (*c*.30–20BC) into verse, while Pope did the same for Homer's *Iliad* (*c*. eighth century BC). But both writers developed the branch of poetry best capable of expressing the Neoclassic reaction to the vulgarity, folly, corruption, stupidity and excess perceived in society: SATIRE. Works like Dryden's satiric narrative poem *Absalom and Achitophel* (1681) and Pope's verse epistles (based on Horace) developed satirical writing to a new level of polish and perfection. The metre for almost all these works was the HEROIC COUPLET, which, in the constant brilliant artifice and EPIGRAMMATIC quality of its rhymes, perhaps mirrors the ideal of balance and proportion.

In eighteenth-century prose writing, the Roman writer Cicero was much admired for his balanced and polished style. Johnson in his critical writings and more particularly Gibbon in his massive *The History of the Decline and Fall of the Roman Empire* (1776–88) developed a LATINATE prose style full of balanced phrases, sonorous ANTITHESES and dignified rhetoric. Addison's essays written for PERIODICALS were less weighty in style, but remained elegant models of clarity. *See also* AUGUSTAN AGE, UNIVERSAL TRUTHS.

Neologism. (Gk. 'new word') An innovation in language; an invented or newly coined word. New words are entering the language all the time. Writers will sometimes invent words for a particular purpose. Hardy's 'wistlessness' in his poem 'The Voice' (1914) is an example: it is presumably the opposite of 'wistfulness' as well as including the idea of 'unknowableness' from O.E. *witan* 'to know'. In its context it seems natural and unforced, and many readers no doubt have not noted its novelty. The poet is remembering his dead wife: 'You being ever dissolved to wan wistlessness . . .'. *See also* NONCE-WORD, PORTMANTEAU WORD.

Neoplatonism. The system of philosophy based on Plato's ideas (*see* PLATONISM), especially as modified by Plotinus and other 'new Platonists' of the third to fifth centuries, whose work was revitalised during the RENAISSANCE.

Neo-realism. A term usually referring to post-war Italian films depicting working-class life, the most famous of which is De Sica's *Bicycle Thieves*

(1948). Novels like Alberto Moravia's depiction of the life of a prostitute in *The Woman of Rome* (1947) and Cesare Pavese's study of antifascism in *The Moon and the Bonfire* (1950) are sometimes associated with neo-realism in the cinema, though SOCIALIST REALISM was not a primary interest for either of these writers.

New Apocalypse. A not very clearly defined British literary movement of the 1940s, which was in reaction against the political COMMITMENT of 1930s writers. The Apocalyptical poets valued myth and were SURREAL- ISTIC in technique and subject matter. The movement's leaders were G.S. Fraser and Henry Treece. Three anthologies were published: *The New Apocalypse* (1939), *The White Horseman* (1941) and *The Crown and the Sickle* (1945). Dylan Thomas is sometimes associated with the movement.

New Comedy. From the late fourth century BC the OLD COMEDY of Aristophanes was taken over by the New Comedy, of which the chief exponent was Menander. His plays (of which only one survives, *The Bad-Tempered Man*, 317BC) were models for the Roman playwrights Plautus and Terence. They depict a world of young men beset by difficulties caused by rich old fathers, imperious slaves and young women. P.G. Wodehouse's characters Wooster and Jeeves present a modern analogy. *See also* COMEDY.

New Criticism. A name still applied to a major critical movement of the 1930s and 1940s in America. John Crowe Ransom's *The New Criticism* (1941) fixed the label and summed up the issues. Other 'New Critics' were Allen Tate, R.P. Blackmur, W.K. Wimsatt, Cleanth Brooks and Robert Penn Warren. The last two named wrote an excellent textbook, *Understanding Poetry* (1938), which resulted in the New Critics' methods and views being taught throughout American universities and schools.

The AUTONOMY of literature is a vital tenet of New Criticism. As T.S. Eliot recommended, a poem must be studied as a poem not as a piece of biographical or sociological evidence, or literary-historical material, or as a demonstration of a psychological theory of literature, or for any other reason. New Critics defined various wrongful ways of looking at literature, for example, the INTENTIONAL and the AFFECTIVE FALLACIES. CLOSE READING of texts became the only legitimate critical procedure, seeing the work as a linguistic structure in which all the parts are held in a TENSION of PARADOX, IRONY and AMBIGUITY, words, symbols and images. Some of their ideas in this respect were taken from I.A. Richards's attempt to create a proper terminology for literary effects and his remodelling of Coleridge's ideas of form as the synthesising element of poetry. Richards's idea that literature was written in a special, non-REFERENTIAL LANGUAGE also appealed to them.

The English critic F.R. Leavis (*see* LEAVISITE) was influenced by the

New Criticism, but though he believed in the autonomy of literature he stressed its value in moral and cultural education.

The New Criticism has had a lasting effect on critical attitudes, not least because it cleared away the former amateurish historical-biographical study of literature. Probably the EXPLICATION of texts remains the centre of the undergraduate study of literature. But it is no longer at the forefront of literary study: RHETORICAL CRITICISM and an interest in plot and genre supplanted the rigorous exclusiveness of the objective critical stance. STRUCTURALISM and DECONSTRUCTION were the controversial new criticisms of the 1970s and 1980s. LITERARY THEORY is now commonly a part of a degree programme. *See also* CRITICISM.

New Englishes, english, new literatures in English. The many varieties of the English language (in East, West and South Africa, Australia, Canada, Hong Kong, India, Malaysia, New Zealand, Sri Lanka, the West Indies, to name but a few of the locations) found now all over the world, are perceived, not as derivative dialects constantly aspiring towards the correctness of Received Pronunciation and Standard English, but as vigorous and developing languages in their own right. The name for literatures in english (written by some critics with a lower case initial letter to distinguish it from the English variety of the language) has been a source of dispute, but 'new literatures in English' was for a time a common term in the 1970s. *See also* COMMONWEALTH LITERATURE, PIDGIN, POST-COLONIAL LITERATURE.

New historicism. *See* HISTORICISM.

New Humanism. *See* HUMANISM.

Nihilism. (Lat. 'nothing-ism') The rejection of all established codes of value and morality. Bazarov in Turgenev's *Fathers and Sons* (1862) calls himself a nihilist; radicals like him believed in science, materialism and revolution. It is often employed as a term of abuse for revolutionary or unorthodox philosophies.

Noble savage. The idea that man in primitive society is a more noble human type than modern urban man, corrupted by civilisation. Montaigne wrote an essay on cannibals (1580) which mentioned the idea. Aphra Behn's *Oroonoko: or The Royal Slave* (1688) sentimentally depicts a negro slave as tragic hero. But the concept was most discussed after Rousseau declared that the uncorrupted savage possessed real virtue in *Discours sur l'origine et les fondements de l'inégalité parmi les hommes* ('Discourse on the Origin and Foundations of Inequality Among Men', 1754). The concept of the noble savage recurred in many forms during the nineteenth century, and even sometimes animates a popular view of twentieth-century anthropology. *See also* PRIMITIVISM, ROMANTICISM.

Noh, Nō. (Jap. 'talent') A form of Japanese drama dating from the fourteenth century. Intended for an aristocratic audience (unlike

KABUKI theatre), and highly ritualistic and stylised, its methods and texts have been fixed since the seventeenth century. The actors wear masks; they dance and chant to a musical accompaniment, sometimes for up to seven hours at a time in a full *Noh* cycle. Several Western writers became interested in *Noh* drama in the early twentieth century, including Pound, and Yeats, who used it as a model for some of his verse plays.

Nom de plume. (Fr. 'pen-name') A false name used by an author. *See also* PSEUDONYM.

Nonce-word. (Mid. E. 'for-a-purpose-word') A word coined and used once only for a particular occasion. *See also* NEOLOGISM, PORTMANTEAU WORD.

Non-fiction novel. *See* FACTION.

Non-periodic sentence. *See* PERIODIC SENTENCE.

Nonsense. Apart from its normal application (meaninglessness or stupid absurdity in language), 'nonsense' refers to a kind of fantastical writing which is almost a minor genre in English literature. The nineteenth-century writers Edward Lear and Lewis Carroll wrote several masterpieces of nonsense: Lear wrote nonsense verse, including his LIMERICKS and narrative poems such as 'The Dong with the Luminous Nose', 'The Jumblies', 'The Owl and the Pussy Cat' and 'The Pobble Who Lost His Toes' (1846), while Carroll is well known for *Alice's Adventures in Wonderland* (1865) and *Through the Looking-Glass* (1871). Both authors wrote chiefly for children, but their works are well loved, even admired by adults. The invention of an illogical fantasy world is only a short stretch of the imagination further than the poetic worlds of SYMBOLIST poems like Coleridge's 'Kubla Khan' (1816). 'Serious nonsense', which is chiefly an English phenomenon, has its antecedents in nursery rhymes, and has been absorbed in the twentieth century into MODERNIST movements like DADA and SURREALISM.

Nouveau roman. (Fr. 'new novel') The French writer Alain Robbe-Grillet orchestrated discussion of a new kind of NOVEL during the 1950s and 1960s. He wished to dispense with many of the traditional characteristics of the ordinary novel, including PLOT, CHARACTERISATION, NARRATIVE, etc. His novel *La jalousie* (1957) is a series of disconnected and obsessive observations, mostly of apparently inconsequential things, like gravel on a drive: gradually it becomes clear that these are the perceptions of a morbidly jealous husband. Other authors of AVANT-GARDE experimental ANTI-NOVELS were Nathalie Sarraute and Michel Butor. *See also* ANGRY YOUNG MEN, NOUVELLE VAGUE.

Nouvelle vague. (Fr. 'new wave') A French artistic movement, or cultural fashion of the 1950s and 1960s. It included the NOUVEAU ROMAN by ANTI-NOVELISTS Alain Robbe-Grillet, Nathalie Sarraute and Michel Butor, and the experimental films of Alain Resnais, Jean-Luc Godard and François Truffaut. Certain very influential films like *Last Year at Marienbad* (1961) and *Hiroshima, mon amour* (1959) had screenplays by Robbe-Grillet and Marguerite Duras. Playwrights like Beckett and, in Britain, Pinter were loosely connected with this consciously experimental AVANT-GARDE movement. *See also* ABSURD, ANGRY YOUNG MEN, BLACK COMEDY.

Novel. The word comes from the Italian *novella*, 'a piece of news, tale', which was applied to the collections of short tales like Boccaccio's *Decameron* (*c*.1348–51) which were popular in the fourteenth century. Nowadays, along with poetry and drama, the novel forms the third in the trio of major genres. The category is as wide as 'poetry': novels are long prose fictions, including every kind of PLOT (tragic, comic), all styles and manners of dealing with their material (from the satiric to the rhapsodic) and showing a capacity to cover every imaginable subject matter from all points of view. They range from the popular THRILLER to the most esoteric literary artifice. The capacity of the form to absorb other literary styles, its freedom to develop in any direction and its flexibility, have made the novel the major modern literary form.

This all-encompassing quality makes accurate or succinct definition impossible. A novel is a long fiction almost always concentrating on character and incident, and usually containing a plot.

As might be expected the novel's antecedents are many and various. Something not utterly unlike the novel existed in ancient cultures, as, for example, Petronius's *Satyricon* (first century AD) and Apuleius's *The Golden Ass* (second century AD). But literary historians usually date the start of the English novel proper in the early eighteenth century. Different kinds of prose literature existed before this which are clearly forerunners: prose ROMANCES of chivalry, such as Malory's *Le Morte d'Arthur* (1485), pastoral romances, such as Sidney's *The Arcadia* (1590), the seventeenth-century vogue for CHARACTER sketches, as well as the well-developed story-telling techniques of the NOVELLA and NARRATIVE VERSE, all these point towards the novel. *Don Quixote* (1605, 1615) by the Spanish writer Cervantes is perhaps the single most significant early novel: it follows the adventure of a genial but mad knight who imagines himself in the world of chivalric ideals and adventure and continually conflicts with reality. Its anti-romantic REALISM, showing illusions in collision with experience, is a way of looking at character which recurs continually throughout the history of the novel.

Defoe's *Robinson Crusoe* (1719) and *Moll Flanders* (1722), the first the journal of a ship-wrecked sailor, the second a PICARESQUE autobiography, are always mentioned as early examples of the true novel. Both focus on the revelation of a particular character amidst a carefully depicted world of things. This kind of realism is a central novelistic convention.

Richardson took the examination of character even further in *Pamela* (1740–1), the tale of a servant girl who, not without a certain coy cleverness, manages to preserve her chastity against the advances of her young master, and eventually marries him. This is an EPISTOLARY NOVEL, the story being told entirely through letters sent by the major characters, a common method of narration in the eighteenth-century novel.

Fielding is another of the many eighteenth-century novelists worth mentioning: his mock epic *Tom Jones* (1749) is told from the POINT OF VIEW of an intrusive omniscient narrator.

The nineteenth century saw the burgeoning of the novel all over Europe. In Britain Sir Walter Scott, Jane Austen, Emily and Charlotte Brontë, George Eliot, Thackeray, Dickens and Trollope are only a few of the novelists of major significance writing in the middle of the nineteenth century. Some trends should be noted. Most of these writers wrote 'three-decker' novels, three-volume works (sometimes of considerable length), often intended for the rapidly multiplying lending libraries. The novel was immensely popular. Publication of the novels bit by bit in periodicals brought them to a mass market which thrilled at the suspense of waiting for the next episode. Many of the popular writers were women. And one of the major interests of the novel at this time was the changing role of women in society.

Two very different novelists, Thomas Hardy and Henry James, dominated the latter part of the nineteenth century, both shaping the novel to include new techniques and subject matter (James shifted the point of view to a 'centre of consciousness'; Hardy wrote REGIONAL NOVELS about rural Wessex).

During the twentieth century a mainstream of novelists has continued to write in the nineteenth-century realist tradition, while other writers have adapted the novel to express the ideas of MODERNISM. Joyce's *Ulysses* (1922) is written in a variety of literary styles, among them the STREAM OF CONSCIOUSNESS technique used by several other experimental writers in the early twentieth century, including Virginia Woolf. The French NOUVEAU ROMAN of the 1950s and 1960s, with its puzzle-like concentration on the contents of consciousness, did not have many followers in Britain. A later experimental development, in the 1960s and 1970s, is METAFICTION (or FABULATION), novels which continually toy with the business of being fiction. MAGIC REALISM, in which realistic and non-realistic conventions are mixed together in the same NARRATIVE, was a fashion of the 1980s.

At the present time the novel is still an immensely varied and popular form. Many of its specialised categories, such as the thriller, the detective story, the spy story, SCIENCE FICTION or the NOVELETTE, make large sums of money for successful authors; films and television versions of novels (nineteenth- and twentieth-century) lead to large sales of books.

Criticism of the novel is also highly developed. There are many historical studies, tracing the development of technique and subject matter, or defining the characteristics of some special form, such as the BILDUNGSROMAN, the SOCIOLOGICAL NOVEL or the HISTORICAL NOVEL. Another approach is to examine different methods of narration, via analysis of the narrator's point of view, or the use of thematic imagery (*see* IMAGERY) or SYMBOLS. Of the many historical studies, Ian Watt's *The Rise of the Novel* (1957) is a stimulating examination of the eighteenth-century novel and society; two very helpful theoretical studies are Wayne Booth's *The Rhetoric of Fiction* (1961) and David Lodge's *The Language of Fiction* (1966). *See also* NARRATOLOGY, ROUND CHARACTER.

Novelette. Usually used disparagingly to denote an insignificant and trifling kind of NOVEL, a sentimental 'romance' or adventure story. But novelette can also be used as a neutral term, much the same as NOVELLA, for a work of fiction of modest length, longer than a SHORT STORY, but shorter than a novel.

Novella. (It. 'tale, news') Originally a short tale of the kind Boccaccio wrote in his *Decameron* (*c*.1348–51). Now the word is applied to a story somewhat longer than a SHORT STORY, but not long enough to be considered a NOVEL, as, for example, D.H. Lawrence's *The Virgin and the Gipsy* (1930). The novella is not as common in English literature as it is, for example, in German: Mann's *Death in Venice* (1912) is a famous example.

Numbers. An old-fashioned way of referring to the regularity of METRE.

Nursery rhyme. Simple, often nonsensical verse sung to very young children by their parents. Part of the ORAL tradition, many are very old. One famous one, 'Ring-a-ring-o' Roses', refers to the plague which swept Europe in the sixteenth century: the roses (spots) and the sneezing were symptoms. *Mother Goose's Melody* (*c*.1765) is a famous early collection. Much research has been done on the meaning and origin of the rhymes by Iona and Peter Opie in *The Oxford Dictionary of Nursery Rhymes* (1951).

O

Obiter dicta. (Lat. 'things said by the way') A judicial expression referring to a judge's off-the-record utterances which have no legal authority. In literature the expression denotes the overheard conversation of great writers, possibly collected as APHORISMS or TABLE TALK. Dr Johnson's *obiter dicta* provide the substance of Boswell's masterpiece *The Life of Samuel Johnson* (1791).

Objective. *See* SUBJECTIVE.

Objective correlative. The term comes from an essay on 'Hamlet and His Problems' written in 1919 by T.S. Eliot:

> The only way of expressing emotion in the form of art is by finding an 'objective correlative'; in other words, a set of objects, a situation, a chain of events which shall be the formula of that *particular* emotion; such that when the external facts, which must terminate in sensory experience, are given, the emotion is immediately evoked.

Eliot argues that Hamlet's feelings are in excess of the facts provided and this unbalances the play.

The term became extremely fashionable amongst critics, as did the idea stressed by Eliot that poetry should always be objective, impersonal. The semi-scientific vocabulary ('formula', 'chain of events') was common in Eliot's criticism at the time. Nowadays the whole manner of the assertion seems over-dogmatic, and the 'objective correlative' itself presents a falsely clear-cut view of a poet's method of composition. Critical thought at that time stressed the need for a scientific exactness of approach, and was in reaction against vagueness and self-indulgent feeling in literature; this was partly responsible for the term's popularity.

Objective criticism. A term which can be applied to much of the criticism since the 1920s, including the NEW CRITICS, which examines the work of literature as an AUTONOMOUS creation, free from the poet, the reader and the world. A poem, for example, is examined for its intrinsic complexity, BALANCE, PATTERN and coherence, in order to reveal the relationships between its various parts, and not because it adds to our biographical knowledge of the poet, our understanding of literary history, or any of its other extrinsic features.

Obscurity. (Lat. 'devoid of light') Needless difficulty placed in the way of the reader in the form of contortions of grammar, rare words, private images, words from foreign languages, elliptical thought. The META-PHYSICAL POETS were disliked by Dr Johnson for their quaintness and obscurity. In the twentieth century more damaging charges have been laid against the whole direction of MODERNIST poetry as written by Eliot, Pound and others. Eliot himself remarked in his essay 'The Metaphysical Poets' (1921) that 'it appears likely that poets in our civilization, as it exists at present, must be difficult'. Some of Eliot's early verse now does look needlessly obscure. But works such as *The Waste Land* (1922) probably justify their apparent (and actual) difficulty by the ambitiousness of their subject matter and their thrillingly diverse technique. The American poet W.C. Williams remarked, however, that Eliot had 'given poetry back to the academics'.

The works of Pound and Eliot, read sympathetically and as a source of cultural reference, are an education in themselves: there is no reason why writers should limit their range of ALLUSION to that of some hypothetical 'ordinary reader'. Poetry has in fact rarely been a popular or populist art form. Since the 1970s critical theory has become the focus for an obscurity and laboured difficulty that makes the work of Eliot and Pound look easy. The writings of the French linguistic philosopher Jacques Derrida, the prophet of DECONSTRUCTION, are contrived so as to demonstrate the impossibility of stable transparency of meaning in language. In America Harold Bloom creates a kind of poetic criticism which brings together abstruse rhetorical terms, moments of insight, and a bewilderingly kaleidoscopic range of reference.

Occasional verse. A poem, common in all ages, written to celebrate or lament a particular occasion: a triumph, birth or death, anniversary, wedding, public event, and so on. POET LAUREATES often celebrate royal events with occasional verse. Many great poems have owed their origin in this way to a particular occasion. ODES and ELEGIES are traditionally connected with real events in the public world. Four very different examples give some idea of the range of occasional poetry: Milton's 'Lycidas' (1638), Tennyson's 'The Charge of the Light Brigade' (1854), Pope's 'An Epistle to Miss Blount, on Her Leaving Town' (1717) and Hopkins's 'The Wreck of the Deutschland' (written c.1875).

Occupatio. (Lat. 'seizing') A rhetorical figure by which the speaker draws attention to something by saying that he or she is not going to mention it: 'This is not the right moment to remind you that . . .'. A device much employed by politicians.

Octameter. (Gk. 'eight measures') In versification, a metric line of eight feet; only occasionally attempted in English verse. *See also* METRE.

Octave. The first eight lines of a SONNET, or a STANZA of eight lines. *See also* OTTAVA RIMA.

Octavo. (Lat. 'eighth') A book or paper size: the printer's sheets are folded three times to produce eight leaves of sixteen pages. The size smaller than QUARTO. *See also* DUODECIMO, FOLIO.

Octosyllabic couplet. A rhymed COUPLET of eight-syllable lines, usually IAMBIC (*see* METRE for further discussion of these terms). A common metre. Marvell's 'To His Coy Mistress' (1681) is a famous example:

> Had we but World enough, and Time,
> This coyness, Lady were no crime.

Ode. (Gk. 'song') The ode is a form of LYRIC poem, characterised by its length, intricate STANZA forms, grandeur of style and seriousness of purpose, with a venerable history in Classical and post-Renaissance poetry.

The Greek poet Pindar established the form. His odes were written to glorify the winners of the Olympic and other games. His poetry is marked by elevated thought, bold metaphor, and the free use of myths. He modelled his stanzas on the dramatic CHORUS, using a threefold pattern like the dance rhythm of strophe (moving to left), antistrophe (moving to right), and epode (standing still).

The Latin poet Horace admired Pindar's eloquence, the boldness of his metaphor and his use of myths, and Pindar provided a model for his own odes, especially those dealing patriotically with Roman politics. But **Horatian odes** tend to be more meditative and personal in tone than those of Pindar, and also they are usually written in repeated regular stanza forms.

Some odes in English are learned copies of Pindar's stanza form: Gray's 'The Progress of Poesy' (1757) is a good example of the regular or **Pindaric ode**. Cowley is usually credited with the invention in the 1650s of a modified form of the Pindaric ode, called the **irregular** or **Cowleyan ode**: each stanza follows its own pattern, with varied line lengths, rhyme schemes and numbers of lines. Early in the seventeenth century Ben Jonson and Marvell had also experimented with different kinds of ode.

Cowley's modified version of the Pindaric ode, with its freedom to alter the form in accordance with changing argument, subject matter and feeling, proved very influential. Dryden wrote several great poems in this form, including 'Song for St Cecilia's Day' (1687). In the 1740s the poets Gray and Collins wrote numerous odes experimenting with different forms and different kinds of subject matter. Some discuss abstractions like 'Liberty' or 'Fear' or a season such as 'Spring'; others were written in celebration of a particular event (Gray: 'Ode on the Death of a Favourite Cat', 1748) or view (Gray: 'Ode on a Distant Prospect of Eton College', 1747). Coleridge and Wordsworth use irregular ode form for their 'Dejection' (1802) and 'Intimations of Immortality' (1807) respectively. Keats's six great odes are more Horatian in form and feeling than many of his predecessors', but by 1820 the simple models of Pindaric and Horatian ode had been broken down. Keats would have been looking to models in English literature, rather than imitating the Classical forms. This is true also of modern poets. Allen Tate's 'Ode to the Confederate Dead' (1928) uses the label; but poems of considerable length, meditating on a private or public issue in solemn language are extremely common in modern poetry, and can only be called odes in the loosest sense.

Oedipus complex. *See* PSYCHOANALYTIC CRITICISM.

Oeuvre. (Fr. 'work') Either an individual work of literature, or the complete works of a writer.

Old Comedy. COMEDY as produced by Aristophanes in the fifth century BC, satirical, anarchically festive, with a CHORUS of grotesques in masks, like *The Clouds* (423BC) and *The Frogs* (405BC). *See also* NEW COMEDY.

Old English period. Old English (O.E.) or Anglo-Saxon was the language spoken in England in widely differing dialects from *c.*450, when Britain was invaded by various Germanic tribes including the Angles and Saxons, till the invasion of the Normans from France under William the Conqueror in 1066. After conversion to Christianity became general in the seventh century, some of the Anglo-Saxon poems, till then part of an ORAL culture, were written down, no doubt being modified by monks in the process. Only a handful survive, but they include vigorous ALLITERATIVE LAMENTS like 'The Wanderer' and 'The Seafarer' and also the great EPIC *Beowulf.* Some Anglo-Saxon poems are explicitly Christian, like 'The Dream of the Rood'. The prose of the period is also lively and various: Alfred the Great, King of the West Saxons (871–99), was himself a writer and a patron of the arts. The great scholar of the age was Bede (eighth century), who wrote in Latin.

Omniscient narrator. A story-teller with total, God-like knowledge of the characters and their actions. *See also* NARRATIVE, POINT OF VIEW.

Onomatopoeia. (Gk. 'name-making') Words which sound like the noise which they describe are the simplest forms of onomatopoeia: 'swish', 'cuckoo', 'smack', 'rattle', 'plonk', 'bang', etc. In prose and verse sustained onomatopoeic effects are not infrequent:

A tap at the pane, the quick sharp scratch
And blue spurt of a lighted match . . .

(Browning, 'Meeting at Night', 1845)

It is the meaning which creates the effect, not solely the sound of the words: the sounds themselves are neutral. Words very close in sound to those above give no onomatopoeic impression: 'wish', 'snack', 'pang', etc.

Onomatopoeia can be broadened to include words that, through their sound, give an impression not just of a noise, but of an action, movement, appearance, or even an object: 'flounder', 'slither', 'dollop', 'baffle'. In his *An Essay on Criticism* (1711) Pope recommends that in poetry 'the sound should seem an echo to the sense' and proves his point by mimicking different kinds of movement in the following lines:

When Ajax strives some rock's vast weight to throw,
The line too labours, and the words move slow;
Not so, when swift Camilla scours the plain,
Flies o'er th' unbending corn, and skims along the main.

See also ALLITERATION, ASSONANCE, EUPHONY, PHONAESTHEME, SYNAES-THESIA.

Oral literature, orality, oral tradition. Certain literary forms, such as the EPIC and BALLAD, have their roots in an oral culture which existed before literature, before the art of writing imposed its methods on the living word. The critical criterion brought to bear on literature may be totally wrong when applied to 'oral literature' (a term which is, of course, self-contradictory). The 'text' of a ballad, for example, cannot be fixed: the ballad may exist in many forms.

There are many parts of the world, even in Europe, where oral traditions something like those which prevailed in Ancient Greece or early Anglo-Saxon Britain can still be heard. Oral poetry is usually made up as the poet progresses, but out of a 'word-hoard' of pre-existent fragments of verse which can be re-ordered and used in different contexts. Famous research on Yugoslav oral poetry was carried out by Milman Parry and A.B. Lord, and applied to Homer's poetry by Lord in *The Singer of Tales* (1964). *See also* FORMULAE, MEDIUM.

Oration. (Lat. 'discourse, advocate's speech, prayer') A formal speech suitable for some dignified public occasion.

Oratorical. In the style suitable for an ORATION: dignified, formal, eloquent, self-consciously using RHETORICAL FIGURES; consequently also meaning pompous, exaggerated language.

Orature. A contraction of 'ORAL LITERATURE' which avoids the paradoxical aspect of that term.

Organic form. Several ROMANTIC writers, especially Coleridge, believed that poetry should create its own FORMS from within, like a plant growing. Their idea of organic form was opposed to MECHANIC FORM, in which the work of art was made to fit a rigid pre-existent shape. Coleridge's idea is something more than a metaphor: the idea that a literary work should be shaped according to its internal momentum has come to be generally accepted.

Originality. Writers who discover new forms or bring new subject matter to literature are said to be original. In some literary periods originality has been praised and sought after; in others it has been the object of suspicion and contempt. Originality breaks with CONVENTIONS, and then itself becomes a convention. *Lyrical Ballads* (1798) by Wordsworth and Coleridge seemed a work of revolutionary originality, but then became the standard taste against which younger writers strove to prove their own originality. In general, originality has become a sought-after quality in literature only in the last two centuries. A writer such as Milton in the seventeenth century wished to write perfect examples of standard conventional forms, like the sonnet, elegy, epic. Though he wished his writing to be uniquely his own, he would have sought to justify every element he used by citing the precedent of earlier examples.

Ossianism. During the early 1760s the Scottish poet James Macpherson published several works which he claimed were translations of epic poems in Gaelic by 'Ossian'. They were in fact forgeries, but their influence was still significant in disseminating Gaelic myths and a sense of Britain's ancient past. Goethe's hero in *The Sorrows of Young Werther* (1774) reads Ossian to his Lotte. 'Ossianism' and the controversy surrounding Macpherson were a typical aspect of the so-called age of SENSIBILITY which led towards ROMANTICISM.

Ostranenie. Russian for 'making strange' or DEFAMILIARISATION.

Ottava rima. (It. 'eighth rhyme') An eight-line IAMBIC STANZA, rhyming *ababababcc* (*see* METRE for further discussion of these terms). Used by various Renaissance Italian epic poets, it was introduced into English poetry by Wyatt. It is the form used in Byron's *Don Juan* (1819–24), Keats's 'Isabella' (1820) and Yeats's 'Sailing to Byzantium' (1928), amongst other famous examples. Byron wrote the following example on the back of the manuscript of Canto I of *Don Juan*:

> I would to heaven that I were so much clay,
> > As I am blood, bone, marrow, passion, feeling –
> Because at least the past were pass'd away –
> > And for the future – (but I write this reeling,
> Having got drunk exceedingly to-day,
> > So that I seem to stand upon the ceiling)
> I say – the future is a serious matter –
> And so – for God's sake – hock and soda-water!

Over-reading. The danger of ingeniously working subtleties of meaning out of a literary passage which do more credit to the critic's capacity for fantasy or pedantry than COMMON SENSE.

The critical practice of DECONSTRUCTION insists that the reader produces meanings which will always be indeterminate, and that there can be no fixed and absolute meaning in language: according to this view, over-reading is a theoretical impossibility.

Oxford Movement. Also called the **Tractarian Movement** after the *Tracts for the Times* (1833–41) through which the ideas of John Keble, Newman and E.B. Pusey were spread. The purpose of these men was to revitalise the role of the Church of England. So-called High Church views of the Sacrament led some members of the movement into the Roman Catholic Church, notably Newman, whose famous *Apologia Pro Vita Sua* (1864) was a reply to an attack on his character by Charles Kingsley. Other literary figures were drawn into these turbulent religious controversies.

Oxymoron. (Gk. 'pointedly foolish') A figure of speech in which contradictory terms are brought together in what is at first sight an impossible combination. A special variety of the PARADOX. Typical examples are poems written in the Petrarchan tradition which express the pangs of love via contradictory states: 'I fear and hope', 'I burn and freeze like ice'. The 'darkness visible' of Hell in Milton's *Paradise Lost* (1667) is a serious use of oxymoron to transcend human perception. Wordsworth describes landscape using several oxymorons in Book 6 of *The Prelude* (1850):

> The immeasurable height
> Of woods decaying, never to be decayed,
> The stationary blasts of waterfalls . . .
> Tumult and peace, the darkness and the light

See also ANTITHESIS.

P

Paean. (Gk. 'striking') A hymn to Apollo invoking his name as 'the Striker', the physician of the gods who heals with magic blows. Hence a song or poem of joy, exultation or triumph.

Paeon. (Gk. variant of paean) In Classical prosody a FOOT consisting of four syllables, one long and three short. According to which syllable is long, it is called first, second, third and fourth paeon. Rare in English, though Gerard Manley Hopkins experimented with it.

Pageant. (Med. Lat. 'scene of a play') Originally a movable stage on which open-air plays, such as the MIRACLE PLAYS, were acted. The modern meaning, however, denotes a spectacular procession, exhibition, or series of TABLEAUX, usually depicting historical events, in which the emphasis is on costume and in which there is little or no dialogue.

Page proofs. *See* PROOF.

Palaeography. (Gk. 'ancient writing') The study and knowledge of ancient methods of writing, manuscripts and inscriptions.

Palimpsest. (Gk. 'rubbed smooth again') A piece of some material, like parchment, which has been used more than once for writing on, previous inscriptions having been rubbed out. This practice was common in the Middle Ages when writing materials were expensive.

Sometimes a much-corrected and amended document is called metaphorically a palimpsest. In his *Suspiria de Profundis* (1845) De Quincey turns it into an image of the human mind:

> What else than a natural and mighty palimpsest is the human brain? Such a palimpsest is my brain; such a palimpsest, O reader! is yours. Everlasting layers of ideas, images, feelings, have fallen upon your brain as softly as light.

Palindrome. (Gk. 'running back again') A word or group of words which reads the same backwards as forwards, e.g. 'Madam, I'm Adam'.

Palinode. (Gk. 'again-song') A recantation; a poem written to contradict some earlier work by the poet. Chaucer's *The Legend of Good Women* (*c*.1380–6) was supposed to rectify the condemnatory portrait of womanhood in *Troilus and Criseyde* (*c*.1380–5).

Pamphlet. (From twelfth-century Lat. poem 'Pamphilus seu de Amore') A small prose argument or ESSAY, shorter in length than a book, and not bound in hard covers, therefore easily and speedily printed and produced. Almost always devoted to topical issues, such as religious or political controversies.

Panegyric. (Gk. 'public assembly') A public speech or poem wholeheartedly praising someone or something.

Pantomime. (Gk. 'all-imitator') (1) MIME is the art of acting without speech, by means of gestures, facial expression and bodily movement, often exaggerated and comic. 'Pantomime' sometimes means no more than mime, but it also signifies (2) a theatrical entertainment at Christmas-time intended for children, usually a dramatised fairy tale, with traditional features such as the 'principal' boy being played by a young woman, a comical dame played by a man, songs, dances and topical jokes.

Parable. (Gk. 'comparison, proverb') A short narrative devised so as to give a clear (but not necessarily explicit) demonstration of a moral or lesson. Christ's favourite method of teaching; there are many examples in the Gospels. The parable of the Good Samaritan (Luke 10:30-7), for instance, is an illustration of what Christ meant by 'Love thy neighbour'. *See also* ALLEGORY, EXEMPLUM, FABLE.

Paradigm. (Gk. 'example') A word with several different meanings. (1) In ordinary usage it designates a model or pattern, sometimes a perfect model. (2) In the history of ideas (especially science) a paradigm refers to the general foundation of scientific understanding on which a body of knowledge is built, but which may change. Einstein's theories of relativity established a new paradigm for elaborating laws of physics totally different from those of the Newtonian cosmos that preceded it; such a change of fundamental view is called a 'paradigm shift'. (3) In linguistics a paradigm is the set of all the INFLECTED forms of a word, such as would appear in a traditional grammar of a language.

Paradigmatic and **syntagmatic** (Gk. 'put in order') denote different ways of approaching a subject. In linguistics 'paradigmatic' denotes the 'vertical' examination of the part of a sentence, considering, for example, all the different inflections and tenses of a verb that could change the sentence's meaning. On the other hand 'syntagmatic' refers to the 'horizontal' relationships between the words in sequence, that is their order or syntax, which if altered also changes the sentence's meaning.

The terms may be used loosely to discriminate between critical approaches to literature. For example, a paradigmatic account of *Hamlet* (*c*.1601) might see it in relation to other tragedies, written by different writers in different periods; a syntagmatic account would relate it to other plays by Shakespeare.

Paradox. (Gk. 'beside-opinion') An apparently self-contradictory statement, or one that seems in conflict with all logic and opinion; yet lying behind the superficial absurdity is a meaning or truth. Common in METAPHYSICAL POETRY. Some of Donne's poems are extended paradoxical arguments, full of witty comparisons and unexpected reversals, as, for instance, 'Death, Be Not Proud' (1633), which argues towards the assertion that 'Death, thou shalt die'. T.S. Eliot begins *The Waste Land* (1922) with an unexpected view of spring: 'April is the cruellest month'. *See also* ANTINOMY, ANTITHESIS, OXYMORON.

Paragraph. (Gk. 'written by the side', the early method of indicating a break in sense in a passage) A coherent section or passage in a piece of writing, prose or verse, which deals with one particular point or idea. Clear subdivision of an argument or description into paragraphs is necessary to make any subject easily comprehensible.

Paraliterature. (Gk. *para*, 'by the side of, beyond') A jargon term for works deemed not to have arrived at the status of 'literature', such as some detective stories, MILLS AND BOON romances, mass-market BLOCKBUSTERS, and so on.

Parallel. (Gk. 'alongside one another') Parallels in literature are different works or parts of works that in some way resemble each other, and are therefore useful for the purposes of comparison and contrast. Their similarity may be a matter of subject matter, or an aspect of style or method. Considering in what ways they are alike and in what ways they differ may bring into sharp focus their different emphases and effects. *See also* ANALOGUE, SOURCE.

Parallelism. The building up of a sentence or statement using repeated syntactic units, as in the following critical comparison by Dr Johnson from his *Life of Pope* (1781):

> If the flights of Dryden therefore are higher, Pope continues longer on the wing. If of Dryden's fire the blaze is brighter, of Pope's the heat is more regular and constant. Dryden often surpasses expectation, and Pope never falls below it. Dryden is read with frequent astonishment, and Pope with perpetual delight.

Parallelism achieves an effect of BALANCE. It is common also in incantatory prose or verse, such as the Psalms, or the poetry of the nineteenth-century American poet Walt Whitman.

Paraphrase. (Gk. 'tell in other words') A rewriting of a passage, usually with the aim of making it more readily comprehensible. To paraphrase a difficult piece of writing is a useful and difficult task; but the word is often used pejoratively by teachers of literature to indicate critical writing which merely reproduces the basic meaning of a literary work without subtle explanation of the writer's methods. The American NEW CRITIC Cleanth Brooks argued in *The Well-Wrought Urn* (1947) that it is impossible to paraphrase a poem, and that to attempt to do so is to indulge in 'the heresy of paraphrase'.

Pararhyme. Another name for HALF-RHYME. *See also* RHYME.

Parataxis, paratactic style. (Gk. 'place side by side') The placing of clauses, sentences or propositions side by side without connecting words. Common in twentieth-century prose, such as that of the American novelist Hemingway, famous for his clipped, laconic sentences. Here, a short early sixteenth-century poem exhibits the figure:

> Westron winde, when will thou blow,
> The smalle raine downe can raine?
> Christ if my love were in my armes,
> And I in my bed againe.

The opposite kind of style, in which the relationships between ideas are constantly made explicit by connectives like 'however' or 'because', or phrases like 'with the result that' is called **hypotactic style.** *See also* IMAGISM, PERIODIC SENTENCE, UNDERSTATEMENT.

Parchment. (From Lat. *pergamina charta*, writing material invented at Pergamum, now Bergamo) The skin of a sheep or goat prepared for writing. **Vellum** (O. Fr. *vélin*, 'calf') is a fine parchment made from calf-skin. The printing of thirty vellum copies of the Gutenberg Bible, precursor of the mass-production of books, used the skins of some 5100 beasts.

Paper made from rags or vegetable fibres, probably invented in China in the second century AD, was introduced into medieval Europe by the Moors. *See also* PALIMPSEST.

Parenthesis. (Gk. 'place in besides') Material inserted into a passage (usually to qualify, clarify or explain) which grammatically is not part of the original construction, so that it is commonly indicated by dashes or brackets. The word also denotes 'bracket'.

Parnassians. A French literary movement of the second half of the nineteenth century, characterised by the doctrine of AESTHETICISM. Its two major figures were Leconte de Lisle and Théophile Gautier. English poets of the 1880s, Swinburne for example, may have been influenced by the Parnassians in their use of French verse forms like the RONDEAU and VILLANELLE.

Parody. (Gk. 'mock poem') An imitation of a specific work of literature (prose or verse) or style devised so as to ridicule its characteristic features. Exaggeration, or the application of a serious tone to an absurd subject, are typical methods. Fielding's *Shamela* (1741) is a whole novel parodying Richardson's *Pamela* (1740-1). Lewis Carroll's version of Longfellow's *Hiawatha* (1855) parodies its thumping metre and long-winded narrative style by describing in tedious detail Hiawatha's efforts at photography. It begins thus:

From his shoulder Hiawatha
Took the camera of rosewood –
Made of sliding, folding rosewood –
Neatly put it all together.
In its case it lay compactly,
Folded into nearly nothing;
But he opened out its hinges
Till it looked all squares and oblongs,
Like a complicated figure
In the second book of Euclid.

Parole. *See* LANGUE.

Paronomasia. (Gk. 'altered in naming') The rhetorical term for a PUN.

Passion play. (Lat. 'suffering') A religious drama representing the Cruci-fixion of Christ, usually performed on Good Friday, and dating far back into the Middle Ages, certainly as far back as the thirteenth century. The villagers of Oberammergau in southern Germany have produced a Passion play every ten years since 1633.

Passive. *See* ACTIVE.

Passus. (Lat. 'step') In medieval works, a section of a long poem or story, as, for example, in Langland's *Piers Plowman* (*c*.1372–89).

Pastiche. (It. 'pastry, muddle') A work of art made up of fragments of an original. It can be used in a derogatory sense, but 'pastiche' may also apply to a SATIRE or PARODY constructed in this patchwork manner. *See also* BURLESQUE.

Pastoral. (Lat. 'to do with shepherds') The pastoral describes an imagin-ary world of simple, idealised rural life, in which shepherds and shepherdesses fall in love, enjoying a life of blissful ease, singing songs, playing the flute, and so on. Marlowe's 'The Passionate Shepherd to His Love' (1599) suggests the conscious artificiality of the genre:

And I will make thee beds of Roses,
And a thousand fragrant posies,
A cap of flowers, and a kirtle
Embroidered all with leaves of Myrtle . . .

A belt of straw, and Ivy buds,
With Coral clasps and Amber studs,
And if these pleasures may thee move,
Come live with me and be my love.

No one could be mistaken into thinking this concerns the life and habits of real shepherds. Pastorals usually deal with a perfect, mythical world, set far back in time, a Golden Age of uncorrupted rural simplicity. Gods and goddesses and other supernatural beings such as nymphs are its inhabitants.

The genre originates with the *Idylls* of Theocritus, a Greek poet living in Sicily in the third century BC. These narratives about gods and shepherds were the model for the *Eclogues* (42–37BC) of the Roman poet Virgil which in turn became the model for the pastoral poetry and prose written in Europe during the Renaissance. Shakespeare uses many of the conventions of pastoral in *As You Like It* (*c.*1599): sophisticated courtiers meet rustic yokels and ardent shepherd boys in the Forest of Arden, where everything eventually ends happily. Spenser's *Shepherd's Calendar* (1579) is another example. Pastoral elements find their way into prose, for instance, Sidney's *The Arcadia* (1590). Indeed *As You Like It* is based on a pastoral ROMANCE, mainly in prose, by Thomas Lodge.

The Christian idea of Christ as a shepherd allowed the pastoral to be adapted and to develop other ALLEGORICAL associations. Its conventions remained valid till the early eighteenth century: Pope's *Pastorals* appeared in 1709. From the mid-eighteenth century onwards poems of country life began to focus more realistically on their subject. Crabbe's *The Village* (1783) declared its aim to depict the labourer's cottage 'As truth will paint it, and as bards will not'. Wordsworth's *Michael* (1800) is subtitled 'A Pastoral Poem', but only ironically: it is a realistic tale about shepherds. However, Wordsworth does hint at the artifice of the pastoral in 'Intimations of Immortality' (1807), asking to 'hear thy shouts, thou happy shepherd-boy!'. Aspects of the pastoral continue to crop up in nineteenth- and twentieth-century poetry: the PASTORAL ELEGY in particular remained in use as a poetic convention after the artifices of the ordinary pastoral had been withered by the assumptions of REALISM.

Pastoral elegy. In his *Idylls* (third century BC) Theocritus described nature mourning the death of Daphnis, a shepherd murdered by Aphrodite because of his faithful love for a nymph. This 'Lament for Daphnis' was a model for the 'Lament for Adonis' of Bion (*c.*100BC) and the 'Lament for Bion' of Moschus (*c.*150BC) which in turn have been copied by English poets, including Milton in 'Lycidas' (1638), Shelley in *Adonais* (1821) and Arnold in 'Thyrsis' (1866). Aspects of the convention include the lament of all nature, a procession of mourners, contrast between the fixity of death and the reawakening of spring, and the idea that the dead poet is immortal.

Pathetic fallacy. Used to describe the habit, common among poets, of assuming an equation between their own mood and the world about them: they are sad, therefore the weather is gloomy. Many poets go further and describe nature in terms of their feelings: the sky weeps, the wind moans. The attribution of human feelings to inanimate nature is a common form of metaphorical writing.

The phenomenon was given this name by Ruskin (in Volume III,

Chapter 12 of *Modern Painters*, 1856) who wished to discriminate between accurate depictions of nature and the distortions caused when the writer's emotions falsify the appearance of things, an effect which he regarded as 'morbid'. It is a useful term, nowadays used descriptively rather than pejoratively. Critics have since coined a number of other 'fallacies'.

Pathos. (Gk. 'suffering, grief') Moments in works of art which evoke strong feelings of pity and sorrow are said to have this quality. The death of Little Nell in Chapter 71 of Dickens's *The Old Curiosity Shop* (1840-1) is typical of the nineteenth-century taste for pathetic death scenes:

> For she was dead. There, upon her little bed, she lay at rest . . . She was dead. No sleep so beautiful and calm, so free from trace of pain, so fair to look upon. She seemed a creature fresh from the hand of God, and waiting for the breath of life . . .

Such focuses of tenderness are nowadays felt to be too blatant in their manipulation of our feelings. Tragic drama is full of moments of pathos: for example, Gertrude's description of the death of Ophelia at the end of Act IV in Shakespeare's *Hamlet* (*c*.1601). Nor is comedy without sudden flashes of pathos.

Patriarchy. (Gk. 'father-rule') An ANDROCENTRIC social and political system organised so as to give power and prestige to men, and likely to be regarded by men as the natural order of things. A term frequently used in FEMINIST CRITICISM.

Patronage. (Lat. 'protector, father') Before the modern age of printing and publishing many writers and artists were paid for their efforts and looked after by a patron, a person of wealth, standing and taste, who could afford to assist artistic endeavour. Patronage was common from Classical times right up to the seventeenth and eighteenth centuries.

The need to find a patron could be a constant source of worry to even the most talented artists. On the other hand, Pope's earnings from his successful translation of the *Iliad* (1715-20) released him from the need to flatter patrons. He is often regarded as the first professional poet. Dr Johnson discusses patronage in a famous letter to Lord Chesterfield, written in 1755 and published in 1790.

Pattern. (O. Fr. 'model', from Lat. 'father') Used in two senses in literary discourse. (1) A literary model, worthy of copying. (2) A 'pattern' can refer to those repeated elements in a literary work that gave it a shape or form. Used in this way, like many critical words it is to some extent a critical metaphor, in this case borrowed from the plastic arts.

Pattern poetry. The name for verse which is written in a STANZA form that creates a picture or pattern on the page. A precursor of CONCRETE POETRY. Here is the first stanza of Herbert's 'Easter Wings' (1633):

Lord, who createdst man in wealth and store,
Though foolishly he lost the same,
Decaying more and more,
Till he became
Most poor:
With thee
O let me rise
As larks, harmoniously,
And sing this day thy victories:
Then shall the fall further the flight in me.

See also EMBLEM-BOOK.

Pejorative. (Lat. 'making worse') An adjective or noun which denotes depreciation. Many words have both a literal and a pejorative meaning: for example, 'artificial' literally means 'made by art', but the word also has a pejorative sense of 'false and unpleasantly unnatural'. The word 'silly' originally meant 'blessed', but now only has the pejorative meaning 'foolish'.

Pensée. (Fr. 'thought') The French philosopher Pascal provided the type for this literary form in his collection of *Pensées* (1670), which consists of notes towards a defence of Christianity. The *pensée* is a single idea, expressed pithily like the APHORISM, or spelt out at some length. Occasionally writers have copied the form. *The Unquiet Grave* (1944) by 'Palinurus' (Cyril Connolly) is a good example: each reflection or description stands on its own, but there is a clearly discernible overall drift of argument.

Pentameter. (Gk. 'five measures') In versification a line of five feet. The IAMBIC PENTAMETER is the commonest metre in English verse, either rhymed (the HEROIC COUPLET) or unrhymed (BLANK VERSE) (*see* METRE for futher discussion of these terms). Gray's 'Elegy Written in a Country Churchyard' (1751) is composed of four-line stanzas of iambic pentameter with alternate rhymes:

The curfew tolls the knell of parting day,
    The lowing herd wind slowly o'er the lea,
The plowman homeward plods his weary way,
    And leaves the world to darkness and to me.

Now fades the glimmering landscape on the sight,
    And all the air a solemn stillness holds,
Save where the beetle wheels his droning flight,
    And drowsy tinklings lull the distant folds.

Performance. *See* COMPETENCE.

Performance poetry. A kind of poetry written chiefly for oral delivery before an appreciative audience. Most poetry is written to be read out loud, but the BEAT poets in the USA, in particular Allen Ginsberg, popularised poetry-reading to a new degree during the 1960s. Other groups, such as the LIVERPOOL poets, soon sprang into the limelight, and for a time poetry readings in pubs and other public places became a fashionable aspect of the new youth culture of the 1960s. The demand persists, and there are some poets (for example, Pam Ayres) who are successful entertainers, devising verse which is usually comical, whimsical or wry, and always instantly comprehensible. Even the most severely complex and inaccessible of contemporary poets can supplement their income by reading their works, which may be baffling to those in the audience who had been led to expect poetry to have the immediate impact of poetry written with performance foremost in mind.

Performative. *See* SPEECH ACT THEORY.

Period. (Gk. 'circuit, revolution') For the convenience of scholars literary history is divided into 'periods', often named after the reigning king or queen or some political event (ELIZABETHAN, JACOBEAN, RESTORATION, VICTORIAN, etc.) or after some predominant style or mode of thought (AUGUSTAN, ROMANTIC, MODERNIST, etc.). Some of these labels are precise enough names for an identifiable literary manner; others conceal large and significant changes in literary taste and practice. The medieval or Victorian periods are so long as to render the labels medieval and Victorian almost meaningless except to indicate a very general chronology. Though it is helpful and necessary to know the various 'periods' of English literature, it is also vital to be aware of the misleading and woolly inexactitude of this method of categorisation.

Period is also an old word for a sentence, or an American word for 'full stop'.

Periodic sentence. A sentence in which the words are ordered so that it achieves its full sense only in the last few words: all depends on its conclusion. The effect is LATINATE and formal. Mungo Park's *Travels in the Interior of Africa* (1799) opens thus:

> Soon after my return from the East Indies in 1793, having learnt that the noblemen and gentlemen, associated for the purpose of prosecuting discoveries in the interior of Africa, were desirous of engaging a person to explore that continent by way of the Gambia river, I took occasion, through means of the President of the Royal Society, to whom I had the honour to be known, of offering myself for that service.

Periodic sentences are particularly common in formal eighteenth-century prose. Modern writing is more often in the form of non-periodic or LOOSE SENTENCES, more conversational in construction, which can be broken up into shorter units of sense without difficulty. *See also* PARATAXIS.

Periodical. A magazine with a distinct literary or academic flavour, published at regular intervals: weekly, monthly, quarterly, etc. Periodicals date from the seventeenth century, but the eighteenth and nineteenth centuries saw their great flowering. *The Tatler* (1709–11) and *The Spectator* (1711–12) were the work of Addison and Steele, whose essays therein have entered the canons of literature. In the nineteenth century there were highly prestigious periodicals such as the Tory *Quarterly Review* (begun 1809), and also the more eclectic magazines in which essayists like Lamb, De Quincey and Hazlitt wrote, such as *The London Magazine* (1820–9) and *Blackwood's Edinburgh Magazine* (1817–1980).

Peripeteia. (Gk. 'sudden change') The 'peripety' or 'reversal' in the hero's fortunes in TRAGEDY was observed by Aristotle in his *Poetics* (fourth century BC). The term can also refer to a sudden change for the good, as in comedy. *See also* PLOT.

Periphrasis. (Gk. 'roundabout speech') An indirect manner of describing or speaking, also called CIRCUMLOCUTION, often used for comical purposes, but 'periphrastic' can also be used pejoratively to indicate unnecessary verbosity.

Certain metaphorical ways of describing are periphrastic, like the Old English KENNING in which the sea is called 'the swan's road', etc. Ideas of poetic DECORUM in the eighteenth century led poets to prefer periphrastic phrases such as 'finny tribe', rather than use a humble word like 'fish'. *See also* EUPHEMISM, JARGON, POETIC DICTION, TAUTOLOGY.

Perlocutionary act. *See* SPEECH ACT THEORY.

Peroration. (Lat. 'thorough speech') The conclusion and summing up of a highly formal speech or written work. Nowadays the word suggests pomposity.

Persona. (Lat. 'mask') A word which referred originally to the mask used by actors in the Classical theatre, but which has been taken over for a special purpose by literary critics. Many novels and poems use the POINT OF VIEW of a person who clearly is not the author for the purpose of NARRATION. The speaker (a murderous duke) in 'My Last Duchess' (1842) or Marlow in *Heart of Darkness* (1902) are personae adopted by Browning and Conrad. Since the NEW CRITICISM, critics prefer to use 'persona' to denote the first-person narrator even in works which are explicitly autobiographical, like Wordsworth's 'Tintern Abbey' (1798): they wish to free such poems from the limiting oversimplicity of biographical interpretation, and show how Wordsworth in the course of his poem constructs a particular kind of narrator for a particular poetic purpose, and how the narrators (the personae) created by Wordsworth differ from poem to poem. *See also* ÉNONCÉ, LYRIC, MONOLOGUE.

Personification. (Lat. 'person-making') A variety of FIGURATIVE or METAPHORICAL language in which things or ideas are treated as if they were human beings, with human attributes and feelings. It may be a short momentary effect, like Tennyson's trees that 'Laid their dark arms about the field', *In Memoriam*, XCV (1850), or extended like the second stanza of Keats's 'To Autumn' (1820) where Autumn is pictured in several ways as fulfilling autumnal tasks or sleeping, 'Or by a cyder-press, with patient look', watching 'the last oozings hours by hours'. Personification of abstractions is extremely common in eighteenth- and nineteenth-century poetry, especially in the form of an INVOCATION. *See also* ANTHROPOMORPHISM, PATHETIC FALLACY.

Petrarchan conceit. *See* CONCEIT.

Petrarchan sonnet. *See* SONNET.

Petrarchism. Imitating the style and subject matter of the Italian poet Petrarch (1304-74). Though he wrote various kinds of poetry, it is his *Canzoniere* (*c.* 1335), 366 LYRIC poems in the Provençal COURTLY LOVE tradition, which were so influential in shaping lyric poetry, especially during the sixteenth century, but continuing right up till the seventeenth century. The poems are dedicated to the idealised memory of a woman called Laura; they are filled with highly rhetorical expressions of his passion, including CONCEITS concerning the effects of love on his changing mood. *See also* OXYMORON, SONNET.

Phallocentric, phallocratic. (Gk. *phallos*, 'penis') Feminist terms, used comprehensively of Western culture, for societies organised according to masculine values. These terms emphasise the dominating sexuality and authoritarianism of masculine assumptions. *See also* ANDROCEN-TRIC, FEMINIST CRITICISM.

Phatic language. (Gk. *phasis*, 'utterance') In social situations words and phrases of little significance are used as signs to establish a relationship between the speakers: 'Good morning, how are you? What a wonderful day. Thank goodness the rain has stopped', and so on. Such platitudes mean almost nothing in themselves, but are necessary (and significant) as a means of keeping communication open between human beings. Dramatists sometimes load with meaning what seem no more than phatic exchanges between their characters.

Phenomenology. A phenomenon (Gk. 'appearing') is an object or occurrence perceived by the senses. Phenomenology is the method of enquiry promoted by the German philosopher Husserl, which begins with the investigation of one's own consciousness and intellectual processes. All prior conceptions, whether from philosophy or COMMON SENSE, have to be laid aside in a suspension (*epoché*) of all existing ideas about the nature of experience. Thus even the 'reality' of the objects of consciousness has to be held in doubt ('bracketed'). Husserl also argued that all consciousness is 'intentional' in that it must always be directed at an object.

Husserl's views were developed by Merleau-Ponty in France and Heidegger in Germany. Phenomenology has influenced several different approaches to literature, notably the GENEVA SCHOOL OF CRITICISM, READER-RESPONSE CRITICISM and RECEPTION THEORY.

Philistine. A biblical word used by the nineteenth-century poet and critic Matthew Arnold to denote the English bourgeois classes who, he argued, in their devotion to wealth for its own sake, were utterly uninterested in any forms of art, culture or intellectual aspiration. Many of his views on this subject were spelt out in *Culture and Anarchy* (1869). 'Philistine' has entered the language in the sense invented by Arnold.

Philology. (Gk. 'love of learning and language') The word used to refer to the study of literature; it is now used as a general term for the study of language.

Phonaestheme. Sounds which bear meaning, through associations with their use in groups of words. A term which was invented by the linguistician J.R. Firth in *Speech* (1930); though rare, it can be useful in considering relationships between sound and meaning, particularly in poetry. The term was coined in attempting to account for the pejorative meaning of the word 'sketchy' (vague and incomplete):

> . . . *sketchy* derives its 'setting' from the living suffix *y*, and from the monosyllabic phonaestheme with initial *sk*, which appears to link 'superficial' experiences, particularly those associated with superficial movements, edges, surfaces that are thin layers, or thin-shaped surfaces, and certain kinds of thinness. Such words are *skate, skedaddle, skid, skiff, skill, skim, skimp, skin, skip, skirt, skit, skull.* The etymology of these words is exceedingly various, but it is impossible to ignore the suggestive value of grouping.

Firth goes on to mention a number of phonaesthemic groupings from different European languages, including, for example, eighty pejorative Norwegian words in 'sl', and the 'diminutive' characteristic of the final 'dark' 'l' sound in words like 'bungle', 'coddle', 'nestle', 'sprinkle', 'tipple', 'wobble', 'snaffle'.

Phoneme. (Gk. 'speech sound') Every language has its basic sound units, though they vary from language to language. In Spanish, for instance, the sounds represented by 'b' and 'v' (voiced and unvoiced labial plosives) are not discriminated. In English 'b' and 'v' are phonemes: their different pronunciation leads to different meanings, for example, 'bat' and 'vat'. Phonemes are the basic sound units used to create different meanings. *See also* MORPHEME.

Phonetics. The description of the sounds of different languages, and how they are produced. The 'phonetic alphabet' is a standardised set of symbols for writing out the speech-sounds of different languages.

Phonocentrism. (Gk. and Lat. 'sound-centred') An aspect of LOGOCENTRICITY. In the view of the French linguistic philosopher Derrida, Western culture has tended to regard speech as primary and authentic, and writing as secondary and at one remove from meaning, there being no speaker to give the illusion of PRESENCE. Derrida overturns common assumptions by asserting that writing 'precedes' speech, arguing that the system of DIFFERENCE upon which speech depends originates in writing.

Phonology. (Gk. 'sound-study') The study of sound systems in individual languages, and language in general, examining not the production of the sounds themselves (which is PHONETICS), but how different sounds create different meanings, and the patterns and rules by which they do this. *See also* PHONEME.

Picaresque novel. (Sp. *picaro*, 'rogue') A kind of NOVEL which recounts the adventures of a likeable rogue. It usually has a simple plot, episodic in structure, consisting of a series of adventures happening to the hero, whose character changes little: its tone is likely to be somewhat amoral and satiric. Such narratives originated in sixteenth-century Spain. Alain-René Lesage's *Gil Blas* (1715-35) is a famous French example. Picaresque elements recur from time to time in the English novel. Defoe's *Moll Flanders* (1722) is typically picaresque, except for the fact that the main character is a female rogue, and she herself tells the story of her life as whore, five times wife, thief and penitent. Works such as Fielding's *Tom Jones* (1749) and Byron's *Don Juan* (1819-24) show aspects of the form, but their PROTAGONISTS are both innocents of the type also to be found in Voltaire's *Candide* (1759); and *Tom Jones* has a complex plot. Thackeray's *Memoirs of Barry Lyndon* (1852) is a nineteenth-century version of the picaresque autobiography. Elements of picaresque are common in twentieth-century fiction, for example, J.P. Donleavy's *The Ginger Man* (1955).

Pidgin. A hybrid language spoken in various parts of West Africa (chiefly Sierra Leone and Cameroon), in the West Indies, and in Papua New Guinea. Pidgins often contain words from many different languages, but are chiefly caused by the fusion of two languages resulting from speech communities trying to communicate with each other, and creating a new language, with simplified grammar, which is not recognisably a version of either. Groups who use pidgin as their mother tongue are called Creoles, and the tendency for this to happen is called **creolisation**. Linguisticians used to despise pidgins as infantile and incomplete languages enforced on their speakers by colonial powers, but now they recognise them as full and subtle languages in their own right. As yet there is little literature in pidgin, except for translations, but its success in West Africa suggests it may one day yield a rich and vigorous culture. The Nigerian novelist Chinua Achebe includes dialogue in pidgin in *Anthills of the Savannah* (1987):

Here is the Lord's Prayer in Cameroonian pidgin:

Our Father, whe you lif for heaven,
your name must be holy,
make your commandia i come for we,
how you want,
so i must be for ground like for heaven.
Give we chop whe enough for we this day,
and excuse we bad, like we too, we excuse the people whe them do
  we bad,
no lef we go for bad road,
but move we for bad thing. Amen.

Pindaric ode. *See* ODE.

Pirate edition. *See* COPYRIGHT.

Plagiarism. (Lat. 'kidnapping') The wrongful taking over and publication of someone else's work or ideas as your own. 'Plagiarism' always suggests dishonest intention (though this may be difficult to prove): it does not denote the practice of 'borrowing' from 'sources', which has always been a legitimate literary method. Of course there may be cases where it is difficult to distinguish between 'borrowing' and 'plagiarism'. *See also* INTERTEXTUALITY.

Plaisir. *See* JOUISSANCE.

Platitude. (Fr. 'quality of flatness') A dull, ordinary remark or idea, without originality, in speech or writing. *See also* CLICHÉ, COMMONPLACE.

Platonism. A body of ideas originating in the two dozen DIALOGUES of the Greek philosopher Plato (*c*.429–*c*.347BC). Most of these dialogues have Socrates as their principal character.

A summary of Plato's ideas and their modification throughout the history of philosophy is not possible here. Several aspects of Platonism, however, have been particularly significant with regard to literature.

Plato himself showed a famous disrespect for poets, who he felt did not assist rational thought but dealt with feelings in a muddled way: in his *The Republic* he says they should be banished from the ideal state.

Also in *The Republic* (Book VII) occurs his famous image of the cave illustrating the difference between appearance and reality. Men are chained in a cave facing a wall; a fire burning behind them projects shadows on to a wall, which they take to be real objects. Anyone escaping from the cave and seeing the real world by the light of the sun, would be unable to convince the cave-dwellers that they see only vague reflections of reality.

For Plato the world of 'reality' was an illusory world of shadows in contrast with the world of Ideas or Forms, which are eternal transcendent realities. This key idea has fascinated several poets, notably Shelley, whose poetry often refers to the perfect world beyond our day-to-day world.

Earthly beauty, for Platonists, hints at a more perfect Ideal beauty. This idea is fundamental to the complex bundle of the logical and philosophical doctrines called Platonism, and also to the recast version of Plato's ideas called **Neoplatonism**, the dominant philosophy in Europe from about AD250 to 1250, which was revived during the sixteenth century in Italy. By adoring the physical beauty of a loved one, the Platonist lover was initiating a movement up a spiritual ladder towards the ideal beauty of the soul, ultimately leading to a beatific vision of God. This notion permeated the love poetry of the Middle Ages and the Renaissance; it provided a convenient Christian context for erotic love. The modern popular meaning of 'platonic love' as 'love without sex' is a reduced and debased version of what was a serious philosophical definition and code of behaviour.

Pléiade. Ronsard gave this name (meaning a seven-star constellation) to himself and six other French poets in 1556. The group continued throughout his lifetime with occasional changes of membership; they stood for innovation based on rejection of medieval forms in favour of Classical models such as the ODE and ALEXANDRINE.

Pleonasm. (Gk. 'superfluity') Use of unnecessary extra words. Another word for TAUTOLOGY. Many CLICHÉS are pleonastic: for example, 'in the fullness of time' instead of 'eventually' or 'soon'.

Plot. (O.E. 'small piece of ground, plan, outline') The plan of a literary work, especially of dramas and novels. To reveal the plot of a novel involves something more than simply explaining the sequence of events: 'plot' suggests a pattern of relationships between events, a web of causation; this happens because of that, and so on. Novels which consist of merely a string of events happening to the same person (like the PICARESQUE) might be considered to have no proper plot, or at best only a rudimentary form of it.

Aristotle in his *Poetics* (fourth century BC) called the plot of a TRAGEDY 'the imitation of the ACTION'. He too stressed the necessity of events relating to each other. If a tyrant was killed by chance under a falling statue, such an action consisted merely of two unrelated episodes, not a proper plot. His chosen illustration reveals that he considered the revelation of character as an essential element in plotting. Though plot and character seem separable elements, in fact they are often utterly interdependent: as Henry James remarks, 'What is character but the determination of incident? What is incident but the illustration of character?'

Aristotle provided names for certain common features of the dramatic plot, which can still be useful. Reversal of the hero's or heroines's fortunes, or PERIPETEIA, in which he or she either suffers failure (in tragedy) or success (in COMEDY), usually occurs at the CLIMAX or CRISIS in the plot; at such moments the PROTAGONIST may also experience

ANAGNORISIS, the sudden discovery of the truth of an experience: Shakespeare's Macbeth discovers that the witches' seemingly impossible predictions are coming true; Fielding's Tom Jones finds out who his parents were.

Suspense is vital to make a plot entertaining: we should be made to want to know what is going to happen, and be surprised by new incidents, yet satisfied that they grow logically out of what we already know. A proper sense of an ending also is an almost indispensable part of the plot; a story which finishes without tying up the various strands of NARRATIVE can seem desperately unsatisfactory, unless (and even if) some special message is being emphasised by this omission. Works which avoid CLOSURE have been fashionable in the latter half of the twentieth century.

The SUBPLOT of Elizabethan drama, when compared with the labyrinthine interweaving of character and incident in some of the enormous nineteenth-century novels, appears incredibly simple. Complex plotting is somewhat like the orchestration of a grand symphony: a sense of unity and pattern prevails, though it may be impossible to follow each instrument of the orchestra. Critics often resort to metaphor, as above, to explain their sense of a plot; they discuss its 'shape'.

Lastly it needs to be emphasised that the whole idea of 'plot' is artificial. Because of the universal existence of stories, we accept that story-making is an essential human pastime. But discerning a pattern within the chaotic muddle of human experience is in fact a willed creative act. The plot, a story with a beginning, middle and end, with its various parts bound together by cause and effect, exhibiting a view of morality or a version of typical experience, is an artifice which has entertained and satisfied people in all ages and countries. *See also* DIEGESIS, NARRATOLOGY.

Pluralism, pluralist, plurality. A term much used in POST-STRUCTURALIST criticism to indicate the desirable openness of texts to many different interpretations which the insights of DECONSTRUCTION allow. As language has no verifiable and absolute meaning, no TRANSCENDENTAL SIGNIFIED, all texts are open to the play of innumerable meanings, rendering the search for meaning infinitely extendable and, it might be argued, therefore pointless, though deconstructionists continue to pursue their own kinds of meaning in texts.

The term 'pluralist' also applies to critics and scholars who entertain a variety of critical approaches to texts, because they claim that given the enormous variety of literature, no single critical dogma, tactic or method is likely to prove wholly appropriate for all kinds of text.

Plurisignation. (Lat. 'many signs') A jargon word for the capacity of words in literature to have many significant meanings and possible reverberations, useful because it avoids the hint of the pejorative in

AMBIGUITY, and suggests more than just two interpretations. *See also* POLYSEMY.

Poem. (Gk. 'something created') An individual composition, usually in some kind of verse or METRE, but also perhaps in heightened language which has been given some sense of PATTERN or organisation to do with the sound of its words, its IMAGERY, syntax, or any available linguistic element.

Poet laureate. A laurel crown is the traditional prize for poets, based on the myth in which Apollo turns Daphne into a laurel tree. Poet laureates have been officially named by the British monarch since Dryden's appointment in 1668 by Charles II: they are supposed to stand as the figurehead of British poetry, but in the two centuries after Dryden, with the exceptions of Wordsworth (1843–50) and Tennyson (1850–92), most were minor poets. Some indeed were poets of no significance whatever. The poets laureate in the twentieth century have been less negligible. Ted Hughes is the present incumbent.

Poetaster. ('Poet' and pejorative suffix '-aster') A bad and insignificant poet; used of would-be poets without talent who frequent literary circles in the hope of finding admirers. Always a derogatory term.

Poète maudit. (Fr. 'accursed poet') An expression taken from Verlaine's collection of essays *Les poètes maudits* (1884) which concerns writers like Rimbaud and Mallarmé, at that time not widely read. The phrase suggests a view of the poet at odds with society, indifferent to bourgeois values, lonely, poor and miserable but unrelenting in the pursuit of poetic truth.

Poetic diction. In general the phrase refers to the kinds of words selected by poets: the language of poetry. However, the phrase is most often applied to the special poetic language employed by eighteenth-century poets in accordance with the NEOCLASSICAL principle of DECORUM, which decreed that serious poetic forms such as the EPIC or ODE should employ an elevated and dignified vocabulary. The first version of Thomson's *Winter* (1726) includes the following lines (40–6):

> Now, solitary, and in pensive Guise,
> Oft, let me wander o'er the russet Mead,
> Or thro' the pining Grove: where scarce is heard
> One dying Strain, to cheer the *Woodman*'s Toil:
> Sad *Philomel*, perchance, pours forth her Plaint,
> Far, thro' the withering Copse.

Features of eighteenth-century poetic diction include ARCHAISMS, like 'guise', 'oft' and 'perchance', LATINATE vocabulary ('solitary' and 'pensive', rather than 'alone' and 'thoughtful'), a lack of direct, simple vocabulary ('dying Strain' and 'Plaint' for bird-song), and a tendency to qualify every noun with an adjectival EPITHET ('pensive Guise', 'russet

Mead', 'pining Grove', etc.). This passage avoids many of the odder eighteenth-century excesses of Latinate vocabulary or PERIPHRASIS, like 'Aetherial Nitre' for frost, 'bleating kind' for sheep, or 'feathery tribes' for seagulls.

Wordsworth attacked this kind of stilted poetic diction in his famous 'Preface' to the second edition of *Lyrical Ballads* (1800); he preferred to employ 'a selection of language really used by men', rather than what he later called 'a motley masquerade of tricks, quaintnesses, hieroglyphics and enigmas'.

In turning against the tradition of a specialised poetical manner and vocabulary, Wordsworth established for the nineteenth and twentieth centuries the idea that poetry should be related to speech. Yet it would be false to suppose that poets, including Wordsworth himself, do or should really use ordinary language, if such a thing exists: with few exceptions poetic diction is nearly always a heightened and modified version of language. *See also* DICTION, STYLE.

Poetic drama. A play written with all the dialogue in verse. The commonest form used in English is BLANK VERSE; Shakespeare's plays are the greatest example of poetic drama in this metre. HEROIC TRAGEDIES of the Restoration period were generally written in HEROIC COUPLETS. Some poetic drama is composed of a variety of different METRES and STANZA forms, for instance Shelley's *Prometheus Unbound* (1820) which is also a CLOSET DRAMA, not intended for performance. Twentieth-century examples of poetic drama include plays by T.S. Eliot and Christopher Fry.

Poetic justice. Thomas Rymer devised this term in *The Tragedies of the Last Age Considered* (1678) to describe the idea that literature should always depict a world in which virtue and vice are eventually rewarded and punished appropriately. Writers swiftly rejected the notion that they ought to fulfil the requirements of poetic justice. Yet fictions persistently tend to present a morality much more in accordance with Rymer's view than the arbitrary justice of the real world, in which the good often suffer while the bad thrive. *See also* PLOT.

Poetic licence. The necessary liberty given to poets, allowing them to manipulate language according to their needs, distorting syntax, using odd archaic or novel words and constructions, and so on. The language of poetry has always been in this respect freer than the language of prose, but the extent of the freedom has differed from age to age, and not all freedoms can be justified.

In a wider sense poetic licence can refer to the manner in which poets, sometimes through ignorance, or deliberately, make mistaken assumptions about the world they describe: a writer's vision is not significantly impaired by small departures from historical or scientific accuracy, unless the kind of work in question implies a fidelity to historical and scientific detail, as for example, a HISTORICAL NOVEL or a crime mystery.

Poetic prose. Prose which in its heightened language (i.e. use of FIGURES OF SPEECH, ornate DICTION and IMAGERY, possibly even in its RHYTHM) begins to share some of the features of poetry. There are many examples of such prose, either occurring for short stretches amidst ordinary prose, or written for its own sake: De Quincey's *The English Mail Coach* (1849) is an example of the latter.

Poeticism. Words or phrases that have come to be used only in poetry, having dropped from ordinary speech; for example, 'thee' and 'thou' survived as ARCHAISMS in verse and elsewhere after they had dropped from standard use. 'Poeticism' may also be used as a pejorative label for the kind of pampered vocabulary deemed typical of poetry. *See also* POETIC DICTION.

Poetics. Statements of the general principles of poetry and, more often, of literature as a whole. Defining the 'poetics' of the detective story, for example, would consist of defining the chief features of the form, and elaborating the critical criteria and appropriate critical approaches by which that form might best be understood and analysed.

Poetry. (From Gk. 'creator') A vague term, referring, like the word VERSE, to literary compositions which are not in prose, that is, which are given some sense of PATTERN like the individual 'poem'. 'Poetry' is also to some extent an evaluative term: we refer to 'Romantic *poetry*' but 'comic *verse*'.

Point of view. Whether we are made conscious of the fact or not in reading a story, every narrative has to have a narrator: 'point of view' refers to the way in which a narrator approaches his or her material (characters, action, setting, etc.) and the audience. Criticism of the novel has led to considerable interest in defining the many ways in which a narrative can be presented, and 'point of view' is the key to these various classifications, which are dealt with more fully under NARRATIVE.

In defining the 'point of view' of a text, the following questions may be useful. Who speaks? Is the narrator (a) an imaginary omniscient observer (third-person narrator)? or (b) a character in the story (first-person narrator)? If (a), does the narrator address the reader and comment on events (intrusive narrator) or does the narrator observe impartially and without intruding opinions? Does the narrator 'tell' the story or 'show it', letting events speak for themselves? Does the narrator limit or focus knowledge through any particular character or characters (limited point of view)? Does the narrator toy self-consciously with the business of telling a story, teasing the reader perhaps? Is the narrator reliable? If the narrative is told through a first-person narrator (b), this implies (usually) a knowledge of events; but most of the questions above can still help to define what the author (clearly standing at one remove from the narrator) is attempting to achieve. *See also* DIEGESIS, IMPLIED AUTHOR, IMPLIED READER, NARRATOLOGY.

Polemic. (Gk. 'warlike') A fiercely disputatious piece of writing, concerning religion, politics or any other controversial subject. Milton's *Areopagitica* (1644), a plea for the freedom of the press, is a famous example.

Polyphonic. (Gk. 'many voiced') A term for music in which two or more strands (instruments or voices) sound simultaneously, as opposed to monophonic music, with just a single line. The word has been borrowed in discussing literature to suggest a work in which different points of view are allowed to co-exist, rather than being organised to support a single authorial position. *See also* CLOSURE, DIALOGIC, HIERARCHY OF DISCOURSES.

Polysemy. (Gk. 'many meanings') The capacity of words to have several separable meanings. Most words are 'polysemous': 'bank', for example, has at least four quite different meanings. A literary text that is capable of being interpreted in many different ways is also 'polysemous'. *See also* DIALOGIC, POLYPHONIC.

Polysyllabic. (Gk. *poly*, 'many') Long words, with many syllables.

Polysyndeton. (Gk. 'Many bindings') A rhetorical name for the stringing together of several phrases and clauses with repeated conjunctions, such as 'and', 'or' and 'nor'. The opposite of ASYNDETON.

Pornography. (Gk. 'writing of whores') Fictional writing, pictures, films, etc. about sexuality of all types, including aberrations and perversions, which may be intended to stimulate the reader's sexual appetite, and therefore may be written without any artistic interest or purpose. On the other hand, works which deal with sexual themes, but which are intended to be read as 'literature' have been considered pornographic, even to the extent of remaining unpublished for many years. The trial of Lawrence's *Lady Chatterley's Lover* (written in 1928, published in Britain in 1960) was a watershed in the publication of sexual material, but provided no clear definition of pornography, or what should be considered obscene, perhaps illegal, and so on. Such decisions anyway are subject to violent changes in public morality and taste.

Pornography is by no means a modern phenomenon. It seems to have flourished in Ancient Rome, in the Renaissance, and in the eighteenth and particularly in the early nineteenth century. Examples are also common in literatures other than European.

Portmanteau word. (Fr. *porter*, 'to carry', *manteau*, 'cloak') An invention of Lewis Carroll's. Humpty Dumpty in *Through the Looking-Glass* (1871) explains to Alice that the new word 'slithy' is a combination of 'lithe' and 'slimy': 'You see it's like a portmanteau – there are two meanings packed up into one word.' A portmanteau word is thus a word formed by combining two words. Joyce's punning dream-narrative *Finnegans Wake* (1939) is full of examples. *See also* NEOLOGISM.

Post-colonial literature. The very varied literatures of the many countries whose political existence has been shaped by the experience of colonialism are seen by some critics to share basic characteristics, especially in relation to their use of the language of the colonial power, and the cultural and literary associations attached to that language. According to scholars of post-coloniality, the literature of post-colonial nations commonly starts by developing distinctive variant forms of the language of the colonial power. In the case of English, clearly there are many distinct and vigorous versions of the language operating in different parts of the world: some critics mark the English as used in England from the englishes used elsewhere by the use of the lower-case initial letter.

Language variation is followed by processes of **abrogation**, in which writers deny the assumptions and claims to centrality of the colonial literary framework in which they find themselves, and **appropriation**, the use and modification of its forms for their own purposes. Characteristic forms and methods of post-colonial writing are explained in terms of the tensions between the 'metropolitan centre' and the supplanting and subverting of its authority by the 'margins'. These metaphors of centre and margin are used to describe the literary relationship between ex-colonial power and ex-colony rather than the intrinsically patronising metaphors of parent and child.

'Post-colonial' has become the common label bringing together the many literatures in english from Africa, Australia, Canada, India, Singapore and the West Indies. As such it is more useful in some respects than referring to them as COMMONWEALTH LITERATURE (though many nations where english is a literary language are members of the Commonwealth), allowing as it does fruitful comparison with other non-Commonwealth english literatures (North American, Irish, South African) with which they may have much in common, and also with non-english literatures that share a similar colonial heritage (for example, those of francophone African nations). However, a problem with the term is that it is all-inclusively vague, forcing together for consideration literatures that may have little in common. It also fixes cultures permanently into some relation with their colonial past, which may eventually have little to do with the facts of their artistic production.

Postmodernism. A vague term, but much in vogue in the late 1980s, and of disputed meaning and value, not least because it refers both to intellectual concepts and to style. Cultural philosophers involve themselves in arguments of bewildering abstraction about the nature of the 'postmodern condition', while a fashion writer may breezily refer to a pair of shoes as 'postmodern'.

MODERNISM broke with the artistic traditions and conventions that had prevailed for many centuries. But in time the experiments of modernism itself came to look familiar and even conventional, and often to endorse very traditional attitudes to society under the guise of experimental forms. Given the thoroughness of the modernist experiment, in the search for new styles what can contemporary artists do? One method is to go back to pre-modernist writings and reshape them in new ways. Magpie borrowings of former styles are a characteristic of postmodern style. Such borrowings can be witty and clever, and make a statement about PLURALISM, tolerance and eclecticism, as well as revealing limitations in the assumptions inherent in former literary conventions and methods.

Some literature is postmodern in this sense of knowingly making use of methods and techniques of former ages in the spirit of serious PASTICHE. Novels like Barth's *Giles Goat-Boy* (1966), written in the form and style of an eighteenth-century work, predated the invention of the term 'postmodern'. Fowles's *The French Lieutenant's Woman* (1969) self-consciously recreates aspects of the nineteenth-century novel, mixed with experiments (a double, indeterminate ending), and authorial intervention. Carey's *Oscar and Lucinda* (1988), by mingling figures from history with unbelievable action ripe with symbolic meaning, similarly confuses and delights, manipulating the reader's contrasting expectations of nineteenth- and twentieth-century novels. MAGIC REALISM creates bewildering mixtures of the plausible and the impossible. Salman Rushdie's *Midnight's Children* (1981) gives the same status to the historical and the whimsically fantastic. All these approaches might be labelled 'postmodernist'. In literary discussion the term has tended to be restricted to the novel.

One conclusion inherent in this intersection of different literary styles and modes is the insight common to many strands of POST-STRUCTURALISM, that meaning is neither inherent in language, nor in the world of things, but is 'constructed' by conventional frameworks of thought and language. Even our most cherished concepts, such as individuality, human character, freedom, are subject to the dissolving perspective that far from being UNIVERSAL TRUTHS, they are constructs of a particular culture and time, and therefore have no absolute authenticity. According to the philosophy of DECONSTRUCTION language itself is doomed to perpetual non-meaning in the endless play of DIFFERENCE. This challenge to meaning in the second half of the twentieth century, as well as social and political factors, such as the persistence of war, the constant possibility of nuclear holocaust and a new sense of the despoiling of the environment and the planet, have all combined to create a sense of despair and disillusion. In the face of meaninglessness we can only play with styles and values that used to have meaning. In this respect postmodernist style shares and extends aspects of the modernist movement called the ABSURD. Postmodern texts are often organised to reveal the instability of language, and to show the reader how particular meanings and values are temporary and self-generated constructions. Judgment may be suspended, for example, between multiple narrative possibilities.

In capitalist society the multiplicity of images and signs, now equally perceived as disconnected and empty of meaning, in advertisements, television and other media, adds to a sense of being bombarded with reminders of our inauthenticity. The new disciplines of cultural and media studies have analysed these phenomena from post-structuralist perspectives. Many intellectuals rejoice in the freedom of interpretation that postmodernist ideas allow, particularly the promise of pluralism. The distinctions between 'high' and 'low' art have been thrown aside, allowing graffiti to be examined with the same scrupulosity as *King Lear*, since both are cultural and social constructs and may be equally revealing about the nature of meaning and the political and cultural realities of our existence, or about the nature of non-meaning and inauthenticity.

As a means of re-examining the nature and history of present-day capitalist and consumerist society in terms of post-structuralist attitudes to meaning, the concept of 'postmodernism' has been defined and re-defined by cultural historians and political philosophers such as Jean-François Lyotard in *The Postmodern Condition* (1986) and Frederic Jameson in essays like 'Postmodernism, or the Cultural Logic of Late Capitalism' (1984).

Post-structuralism. A term covering the bundle of different approaches to language and literature (and other fields) which share the common feature of building and refining the attitudes to knowledge and culture initiated by the linguistic theories of the Swiss linguistician Saussure, which led to the development of the network of ideas called STRUCTURALISM. A basic and shared tenet is that meaning is not inherent in words, but depends on their mutual relationships within the system of language, a system that is based on DIFFERENCE. The single most significant post-structuralist development is the linguistic philosophy developed in the 1970s and 1980s in France, chiefly by Jacques Derrida, called DECONSTRUCTION, which has had a strong influence on literary and critical theory. Post-structuralism is a part of the wider, more general, and vaguer trend called POSTMODERNISM. *See also* FEMINIST CRITICISM, MARXIST CRITICISM.

Post-structuralist criticism. *See* DECONSTRUCTION.

Pot-boiler. A work written with the chief purpose of earning money, therefore usually a derogatory term.

Poulter's measure. Rhyming COUPLETS consisting of an IAMBIC HEXAMETER followed by an iambic HEPTAMETER. An unwieldy metrical form common in sixteenth-century verse. *See* METRE for further discussion of these terms.

Practical criticism. A way of studying that is concerned not to theorise about literature, but to examine and analyse particular works, working from the particular towards understanding of writers and periods. Two books were particularly influential, both by I.A. Richards: *Principles of Literary Criticism* (1924) and *Practical Criticism* (1929). The latter book consists of a large number of evaluative exercises performed by Richards's pupils, illustrating the disorganisation of their critical procedures.

The tenets of 'practical criticism' were taken up and disseminated with fervour by the English critic and teacher F.R. Leavis: most British universities and schools still are dominated by this approach. 'Practical criticism' became almost the shibboleth of Leavis and his followers, who saw themselves in opposition to the woolly-minded literary-historical approach, which paid insufficient attention to the words on the page, the texts. The periodical *Scrutiny* (1932–53) was very influential as a means of disseminating reassessments of English literature by Leavis and his followers. In fact, Leavis's own approach to literature was less concerned with explaining texts: he valued literature as the focus for moral and cultural perspectives which it was the business of education to provide. *See also* CAMBRIDGE SCHOOL OF CRITICS, CRITICISM, LEAVISITE, NEW CRITICISM.

Pragmatic criticism. 'Pragmatic' may be applied to those kinds of CRITICISM which see literature as designed to achieve effects on its audience (instruction, aesthetic pleasure, etc.) and judge it according to the successful achievement of this assumed aim. *See also* AFFECTIVE FALLACY, INTENTIONAL FALLACY, RHETORICAL CRITICISM.

Praxis. (Gk. 'doing, action') Aristotle's term in his *Poetics* (fourth century BC) normally translated as the 'action' of a play. The word is also used to indicate the practice of, say, the craft of writing, as opposed to the theory.

Précis. (Fr. 'exactly expressed', from Lat. 'cut short') A concise account or version of some longer text or passage. An ABRIDGEMENT, SYNOPSIS or SUMMARY.

Preface. (Lat. 'speak before') An explanatory introduction to a literary work.

Pre-Raphaelites. Originally a group of artists (including John Millais, Holman Hunt and Dante Gabriel Rossetti) who organised the 'Pre-Raphaelite Brotherhood' in 1848: their aim was a return to the 'truthfulness' and simplicity of medieval art (Raphael was a Renaissance artist). D.G. Rossetti was a painter and poet, and other poets became associated with the movement, including Christina Rossetti, Algernon Swinburne and William Morris. MEDIEVALISM, ARCHAISM and lush sensuousness combined with religious feeling are typical aspects of their poetry, which came also to be given the derogatory title of the **'fleshly**

school of poetry', a term invented by Robert Buchanan in *The Contemporary Review* (October 1871).

Prescriptive criticism. CRITICISM which knowingly or by implication attempts to prescribe or advocate rules for how works should have been written, rather than examining them as they are. Sometimes adverse criticism of literature is a consequence of the bias of the critic towards certain literary forms which he or she feels *ought* to be discernible in the work under review, when in fact such an expectation is illogical or presumptuous.

A new emphasis is placed on the reader's role in creating meaning in some contemporary literary theories, such as DECONSTRUCTION and READER-RESPONSE criticism. The encounter with the text can only illuminate the prescriptive beliefs of the reader, and can never arrive at any exact, stable or unprejudiced truth about the text, and so prescriptive criticism is an inescapable condition. For MARXISTS, all criticism (even, to some extent, their own) takes place within the parameters of the prevailing IDEOLOGY, and therefore will always contain hidden prescriptions which must be made apparent, if that is possible.

Presence. The notion or feeling, mistaken in the view of STRUCTURALIST and POST-STRUCTURALIST critics, that meaning is inherent in words and utterances. By his theory of the meaning of signs depending on DIFFERENCE the Swiss linguistician Saussure is deemed to have put in question the 'metaphysics of presence' which has dominated Western culture. *See also* DECONSTRUCTION, TRANSCENDENTAL SIGNIFIED.

Presupposition. Those ideas and feelings about the nature of things which the reader brings to a text (and indeed to all understanding): what the world is supposed to be like. In the methodology of NEW CRITICISM a reading was supposed to be divested of prejudices and presuppositions, in the interests of replacing subjectivity with a more scientific objectivity. Contemporary views of language suggest that objectivity is an impossible aim, since reality cannot be approached outside the confines and principles which are inherent in and imposed by language itself. *See also* HERMENEUTIC CIRCLE, HORIZON OF EXPECTATIONS, STRUCTURALISM.

Pretentiousness. (Lat. 'stretching forth') To judge a speech or writing as 'pretentious' is to assert that it has failed to achieve its ambitions, that it has 'pretended' to be something more significant or beautiful than it is. Such an assertion, unless carefully explained and qualified, is liable to indicate as much about the person who makes it as it claims to indicate about its object.

Primitivism. The taste or intellectual preference for nature rather than society, for the idea that civilisation, society and urban life have destroyed a more wholesome and worthwhile mode of existence. Such a view may be allied to a nostalgic yearning for some past Golden Age, an Eden from which modern humanity is banished. Primitivism is a mood which occurs in different ages and in different kinds of writing and at different times in the careers of individual writers; it is a vague general concept rather than a literary movement, but some literary movements contain strong 'primitivist' elements. The bundle of views called ROMAN-TICISM, for example, included many typical aspects of primitivism, including valuing childhood, peasant life, intuition rather than reason, and so on. The French writer Rousseau, whose writings include many typical Romantic concepts, elaborated the theory of the NOBLE SAVAGE, which holds that humans enjoyed a natural and noble existence till civilisation turned them into slaves to unnatural wants, and betrayed their freedom.

In the twentieth century we find writers such as D.H. Lawrence putting forward not dissimilar views, of humans being spoilt by society and needing to regain contact with an elemental animal existence.

In the history of art 'primitivism' has a different emphasis. 'Primitive' refers to some Dutch or Italian painters of the late fourteenth and fifteenth centuries, or to painters in any age who exhibit a naïvety of vision, perhaps because they were self-taught.

Privileging. A jargon word much used in POST-STRUCTURALIST critical discourse. Texts are perceived as containing different possible arguments and points of view, either organised into a HIERARCHY OF DISCOURSES, or, in a DIALOGIC or POLYPHONIC text, allowed equal play. To select one of these arguments as the text's meaning is to 'privilege' it.

For those critics who use the word, it carries all the semantic weight of 'privilege' in a class-based society, but its change from noun to verb suggests the way privilege is the result of an active process rather than a fixed and unchangeable entity. It hints that to select one meaning in a text is characteristic of the undemocratic élitism that is deemed to have characterised the study of books prior to the DECENTRING of 'literature' by post-structuralists. Such critics also maintain that to believe in a CANON of 'great works' is also falsely to 'privilege' some texts at the expense of others. If all interpretations of a text have equivalent validity, then all texts have equal validity as objects of study, and so to study Shakespeare rather than *Star Trek*, for example, is falsely to 'privilege' the Bard. But to choose any text and to make any statement about it, must be to 'privilege' certain meanings. Any use of language is to 'privilege' certain words from the chaos of non-meaning. The concept thus contains the causes of its own ineffectuality.

Problem play. A play which explores a specific sociological problem. Usually the playwright provides an unconventional slant on the question involved, and also takes sides, exhibiting a personal point of view through a suitable mouthpiece. Ibsen's many plays about the lack of proper opportunities for women, especially *A Doll's House* (1879), are early problem plays. Problem plays dealing with race relations, class and family conflict, and social and political ills, are common material for television drama. Problem films are also common.

Shakespeare's 'dark comedies' are also grouped together as 'problem plays' because of their difficult mixture of comedy and cynicism. They are *Troilus and Cressida* (*c.*1602), *All's Well That Ends Well* (*c.*1602) and *Measure for Measure* (*c.*1604).

Problematic. As a noun, a jargon term for a framework of ideas and the problems that are involved with them. An example is the 'empiricist-idealist problematic' attacked in MARXIST POST-STRUCTURALIST critical theory.

Production. A jargon word, used in MARXIST and POST-STRUCTURALIST literary criticism since Pierre Macherey's *A Theory of Literary Production* (1966). Macherey examines the relationship between literature and IDEOLOGY, taking up ideas initiated in the political philosophy of Althusser, and evolves a 'materialist' theory of literary 'production' in which the writer is a 'workman' who 'produces' texts. These metaphors are supposedly less mysterious than those of the writer as a 'creator' (with all the mythological attachments that word has), and the idea that the literary work is a 'creation' made out of nothing.

Proem. (Gk. 'prelude') A preface or introductory section.

Projective verse. *See* BLACK MOUNTAIN SCHOOL.

Prolepsis. (Gk. 'take forward') A rhetorical term referring to an anticipation of future events in narratives. *See also* ANACHRONY, NARRATOLOGY.

Prologue. (Gk. 'pre-speech') The introductory section of a work, or, in the case of a play, the speaker of such an introduction.

Promotion. (Lat. 'moving forward') A term for the effect which occurs when the metrical stress in a verse line falls on a syllable which would normally be unstressed, leading to its being accentuated in a reading. *See also* DEMOTION, METRE.

Proof. A stage in the preparation of a book for printing. Normally after books are set in type the author receives first the **galley proofs**, in which the text appears in a continuous stream chopped up arbitrarily according to the size of paper it is printed on. After these have been corrected the typesetters produce **page proofs**, which resemble the final text in being divided into numbered pages, allowing the organisation of the index and cross-referencing.

Propaganda. The word is derived from the Lat. title *Congregatio de propaganda fide*, the committee of cardinals charged with the missionary business of the Roman Catholic Church. 'Propaganda' can still be used to describe literature designed to persuade towards particular religious views, but the term is now much more commonly used of political literature, designed to convince people, or uphold the value, of a political system or creed, and perhaps even move them to political action, to join a party, support a pressure group, or cure a specific social evil. Harriet Beecher Stowe's novel about slavery in the southern states of America, *Uncle Tom's Cabin* (1851–2), is an example of the last type.

The German playwright Brecht, in plays such as *The Caucasian Chalk Circle* (1948), presents a clear case for some aspects of MARXIST thought: propaganda may be perceived as a duty for Marxists, of which they are proud. However, the term may also be used in a derogatory way, to indicate the failure of a work of art to present a balanced point of view: 'It's just propaganda.' *See also* COMMITMENT, DISTANCE.

Properties. In theatrical language the furniture and movable bits and pieces (such as drinks, cigarettes or ornaments) that are part of a stage setting.

Proscenium. (Gk. 'in front of the scene') In the ancient theatre, the space between the back of the stage and orchestra. In the modern theatre, the proscenium arch is that which is filled by the curtain; some of the stage juts out towards the audience: this is the traditional nineteenth- and early twentieth-century method for staging plays, as if in a room with one of its walls missing.

Prose. (Lat. 'straightforward, direct') Prose is any language that is not made patterned by the regularity of some kind of METRE. It is contrasted with VERSE (from Lat. *vertere*, 'to turn'): prose moves 'straightforward', without turning back on itself, while verse contains some element of repetition, creating a pattern.

Prose is capable of infinite variety: from the most exquisite and exact description, to the interrupted inarticulacy of everyday speech; from the lush emotive passion of a syrupy love story, to the clear directness of a scientific report.

Adjectives from 'prose' ('prosaic', 'prosy') are employed derogatorily, signifying dullness.

Prose poem. A short work of POETIC PROSE, resembling a poem because of its ornate language and imagery, and because it stands on its own, lacks narrative, like a LYRIC poem, but is not subjected to the patterning of METRE. The French poet Baudelaire's *Petits poèmes en prose* (1869) are the most famous examples and have been copied by many modern writers.

Prosody. (Lat. 'accent of a syllable') The science of versification: the study of the theory and development of METRES and STANZA forms, and the practice of SCANSION (the analysis of individual examples of verse).

Prosopopoeia. (Gk. 'face making') Another word for PERSONIFICATION.

Protagonist. (Gk. 'first actor, first combatant') In Greek drama the principal character and actor. Now used almost synonymously with 'hero' to refer to the leading character in a play, novel or narrative poem. Strictly speaking, plays and novels can have only one protagonist, clearly the focus of major interest, perhaps in conflict with an ANTAGONIST.

Prothalamion. (Gk. 'before the marriage chamber') A marriage poem by Edmund Spenser, celebrating the weddings of the Ladies Katherine and Elizabeth Somerset in 1596. The word is a modification of EPITHALAMION.

Proverb. (Lat. 'a set of words put forth') A short popular saying embodying a general truth, sometimes in metaphorical language: for example, 'A rolling stone gathers no moss', 'A stitch in time saves nine', 'Look before you leap', etc. In modern Britain the stock of well-known proverbs has been turned into a bunch of lamentable CLICHÉS, but in rural societies with a strong sense of regional feeling, proverbial sayings still have vigour. The proverbs of other cultures are always fascinating. Here are some Italian examples: 'Love doesn't boil a saucepan', 'A bearded woman is always popular', 'Lies have short legs and a long nose'.

Proverbs seem common to most cultures and ages. They represent homely wisdom, transmitted orally. There is a Book of Proverbs in the Bible. *See also* APHORISM, APOPHTHEGM, MAXIM.

Psalm. (Gk. 'song sung to the harp') A sacred song or HYMN, especially one from the Book of Psalms in the Bible.

Psalter. A book of PSALMS.

Pseudonym. (Gk. 'false name') A book published under a name other than that of the author is 'pseudonymous': the use of a pseudonym, pen-name or NOM DE PLUME is quite common. Famous examples include Voltaire (real name: François-Marie Arouet), Stendhal (Henri Beyle), George Eliot (Mary Ann Evans), Mark Twain (Samuel Clemens), Saki (H.H. Munro).

Pseudo-statement. A term invented by I.A. Richards (*see* PRACTICAL CRITICISM) to denote the kind of 'truth' expressed by poetry which is neither necessarily logical nor accurate, unlike statements of scientific truth. Pseudo-statements represent an ordering of feelings and ideas, and are thus to be valued. Aristotle in the *Poetics* (fourth century BC) put forward a similar idea, that poetry is more valid than history because it distils general truths in a way that history cannot, and because its truths are full of limitless possibility, rather than being tied down to limited facts.

Psychoanalytic criticism. Freud developed the theory of psychoanalysis as a means of curing neuroses in his patients, but its concepts were expanded by him and his followers as a means of understanding human behaviour and culture generally. Literature and the creative process always figured largely in his accounts of the human mind, as both example and inspiration: he asserted that many of his ideas had been anticipated in great literary works, and the terms he devised for his concepts (such as the Oedipus complex), illustrate his reliance on literary models. Also, on several occasions he devoted himself to analysing literature according to his understanding of the functioning of the human mind.

Literature, for Freud, is produced by the same mechanism as dreams. Desires, mainly sexual, in conflict with social norms, are censored and pushed into the subconscious ('repressed'), from which they emerge in forms that are modified, disguised and all but unrecognisable to the conscious mind. Later in his career Freud developed terms for these conflicting aspects of human personality. The **ego** is conscious mediator of the unconscious struggle between the **id**, the unruly bundle of instincts, compulsions and desires, and the **superego**, the censor prohibiting and obstructing the id, according to the strictures imposed by reality.

There are various common forms for this distortion in dreams and literature. **Sexual symbolism** is the most widely recognised: the objects of sexual desire are represented by things that resemble them, thus giving rise to the popular concept of the 'Freudian symbol', by which anything vaguely cylindrical can be understood to be an image of the penis. Less well-known are **condensation**, the blending together of various unconscious elements into a new whole, and **displacement**, by which a socially acceptable object stands for the forbidden desire. The **latent content** of the dream or literary work is the repressed desire; its public form to the conscious mind is the **manifest content**. The artist possesses a special.capacity for **sublimation**, by which the unconscious drives and **fixations** (incidents from the individual's early psychosexual development which obsessively return even in the mature mind) are turned towards non-sexual goals, like writing and painting. Writer and audience alike can partially overcome psychological conflict and thereby be consoled in their experience of the complicated wish-fulfilments created in art. The critic's task is to reveal the true latent content of literature, the psychological realities that underlie the work of art. It will readily be seen that literary criticism, even if not explicitly in any way psychoanalytic, owes much to Freud, who provided a theory of symbolism and hidden meaning which has been exceptionally influential at a basic level, asserting that literature has to be approached as a repository of essential truths which may be wholly concealed underneath its surface, and requiring expert analysis for their revelation.

Freudian approaches to literature have abounded. His follower and biographer Ernest Jones wrote *Hamlet and Oedipus* (1949), a direct application of the Freudian theory of the **Oedipus complex** (that adult men retain repressed infantile desires for their mothers) to Shakespeare's play. Jung, though an early follower of Freud, developed an approach that has its adherents in practitioners of ARCHETYPAL criticism. More recently Jacques Lacan has reworked Freud's psychological insights in terms of STRUCTURALISM, arguing that the unconscious is organised around a system of DIFFERENCES, like language.

Psychobiography. A BIOGRAPHY that pays particular attention to its subject's psychological development as demonstrated in both life and writings, and that attempts to reveal hidden patterns of behaviour, often in line with Freud's analysis of human consciousness.

Psychological novel. A loose, general term referring to NOVELS which concentrate on the inner lives of their characters, their ideas, feelings, mental and spiritual development, rather than their external actions.

Psychomachy. (Gk. 'soul-fighting') A battle for the soul between vice and virtue, as in Prudentius's *Psychomachia* (*c.* AD400). MORALITY PLAYS reflect the pattern established in this work, as do many other medieval works of ALLEGORY.

Ptolemaic system. The description of the universe in the *Almagest* of Claudius Ptolemaeus of Alexandria (second century AD), the Greek astronomer and geographer. Ptolemy believed the Earth to be the centre around which the moon, sun, planets and stars revolve. Elaborate calculations were devised to predict the positions of the planets, which were perceived as moving stars with small cycles of their own. This system prevailed till it was ousted by Copernicus's solar system in the mid-sixteenth century. *See also* COPERNICAN THEORY.

Puff. A short, uncritical account of a book, praising its merits, with the purpose of helping it to sell well.

Pun. (Possibly from It. 'fine point') Usually defined as 'a play on words': two widely different meanings are drawn out of a single word, usually for comic, playful or witty purposes. Puns are common in good and bad jokes: 'the trouble with monks is that they never get out of their dirty old habits'; or in comic verse, like that of Thomas Hood's 'Faithless Nelly Gray' (1826):

> O, Nelly Gray! O, Nelly Gray!
>   Is this your love so warm?
> The love that loves a scarlet coat,
>   Should be more uniform.

Elizabethan and METAPHYSICAL POETS liked to pun, sometimes with gravely witty effect. In Marvell's 'The Garden' (1681) he describes a flower sundial made, we understand, of the herb, thyme:

> And, as it works, th'industrious Bee
> Computes its time as well as we.

Christ punned on Peter's name, when he remarked that he was the rock (Gk. *petra*) on which he was going to build his Church. These last two examples show that puns can also have a serious context and purpose, although this is rare after the seventeenth century. In some respects the pun shares the attributes of METAPHOR and AMBIGUITY.

Puritan interregnum. Another name for the COMMONWEALTH PERIOD, 1649 to 1660, when England was governed by Parliament, led by Oliver Cromwell.

Purple patch. A translation of Horace's phrase '*purpureus . . . pannus*' in *Ars Poetica* (*c*.20BC); it denotes a passage of heightened writing in prose or verse, standing out of context because of its intensified use of figures of speech, rhythms, imagery, diction, like a patch of purple cloth on a white garment. The term is nearly always used pejoratively to indicate a false and incongruous attempt at grandiloquence or overblown rhetoric.

Pyrrhic. (Gk. 'war dance') A metrical FOOT consisting of two short (or unstressed) syllables. As with the SPONDEE, from a linguistic point of view it is doubtful if the pyrrhic is necessary in English scansion, as two successive syllables are unlikely to bear exactly similar levels of stress. Examples of pyrrhics and spondees may be found in the following line from Marvell's 'The Garden' (1681), but it may also be interpreted as IAMBIC TETRAMETER:

x x / / x x / /
To a green thought in a green shade

See METRE for further explanation of these terms.

Q

Quadrivium. (Lat. 'place where four roads meet') Four of the seven liberal arts were so called in the Middle Ages: arithmetic, astronomy, geometry and music. *See also* TRIVIUM.

Quantity. (Lat. 'how-much-ness') The 'length' of a syllable; the duration of its sound. 'M<u>oo</u>n' is a long syllable, with a long vowel; 'měn' or 'măn' are short syllables with short vowels. Greek and Latin verse used quantity (rather than STRESS) as the basis for their METRES. Certain English poets have tried to write quantitative verse in imitation of the Classics, notably Campion in the early seventeenth century and Robert Bridges in the twentieth century. In stress-based English verse, quantity is not metrically significant, though, of course, it is a vital element amongst the variety of linguistic resources making up the effect of a line of poetry.

Quarto. (Lat. 'fourth') A paper and book size; a printer's sheet is folded twice to make four leaves (eight pages). Several of Shakespeare's plays were printed in quarto size, and these editions are known as First Quarto, Second Quarto, etc. Ordinary modern hardback books are more or less quarto-sized. *See also* DUODECIMO, FOLIO, OCTAVO.

Quatrain. (Fr. 'of four') A STANZA of four lines. A very common form in English, used with various METRES and RHYME SCHEMES. *See also* BALLAD METRE.

Quintain. (Lat. 'of five') A five-line STANZA, of any METRE or RHYME-SCHEME. Also known as **quintet** (Lat. 'little fifth').

R

Rabelaisian. Exuberant, humorous and shamelessly bawdy writing. The word derives from the French writer Rabelais (*c*.1494–*c*.1553), author of the fantasy narrative *Gargantua and Pantagruel* (1532–52). *See also* CARNIVALISATION.

Readable. (*Lisible* in French) Usually a term of praise for a book, suggesting willingness and delight on the part of the reader. However, amongst adherents of the criticism of Roland Barthes it has a special meaning: a text which is readable (or sometimes '**readerly**') is one which is easily and worthlessly assimilated, because it reflects a conventional and anodyne IDEOLOGY that does not stimulate the reader. *See also* JOUISSANCE, SCRIPTIBLE.

Reader-response criticism. A general label for a number of different literary approaches and theories common in the 1980s which share a focus on the active relationship of the reader with a text. Aspects of PSYCHOANALYTIC CRITICISM and STRUCTURALISM can be assimilated under this umbrella term, in so far as they consider the reader's role in interpreting literature (*see* COMPETENCE and JOUISSANCE). What is shared amongst all these different approaches is a rejection of the assumptions of the NEW CRITICISM about the AUTONOMY of the text, and the fixity and 'objectivity' of evaluation and meaning. Rather they see the meaning of a text as 'created' or 'produced' by readers, and therefore as an unstable or changeable entity. The many exponents of reader-response criticism differ in the emphases that they place on aspects of the reading process, and in the degree to which they allow any 'objectivity' in an interpretation of a text: is it possible, for example, to prove that a reading is wrong?

The German critic Wolfgang Iser (*The Act of Reading*, 1978) examines the writer's control of the reader's responses particularly in terms of the 'indeterminate elements' in texts, the gaps and absences which the reader must fill in, in a process of anticipation, guesswork, creation, frustration and reconstruction. In the USA Stanley Fish has developed a close examination of developing reader-response which he calls 'affective stylistics'. He also examines the nature of 'mistakes' critics have made in dealing with texts to suggest that different reading strategies are adopted by different 'interpretive communities', and that no single reading can be authoritative (*Is There a Text in This Class?*, 1980). *See also* IMPLIED AUTHOR, IMPLIED READER, INTERSUBJECTIVE, RECEPTION THEORY.

Realism. (Lat. *res*, 'thing') A word of confusingly varied applications; its uses range from the apparently categorical label for a particular style of nineteenth- and twentieth-century writing, to the vaguest kind of assertion that a particular literary approach is more 'realistic', more 'like reality', in other words a more accurate depiction of things as they 'really' are. As no two people need agree exactly about what 'reality' is, terms like 'really', 'realistic' and 'realism' have come to have an evaluative or merely personal meaning.

Realism amounts to a general trend or drift in the focus of literature, rather than a coherent literary movement. Many writers in the middle of the nineteenth century, especially novelists such as George Eliot and Balzac, saw themselves as confronting, describing and documenting new truths about people in society. No doubt the increasing relevance of scientific investigation in understanding the world was connected with this new 'realism'. 'Realism' comes to denote the kind of point of view and material common in such writers.

The attempt to portray events realistically is common in the novel before the nineteenth century. Defoe's confessional manner of narrating the life of *Moll Flanders* (1722) or the shipwrecked sailor's journal in *Robinson Crusoe* (1719) are famous early instances of fictions which aim to be realistic narratives, full of haphazard detail like authentic experience. Novels composed of journals or letters are clearly attempts at a realism of narrative POINT OF VIEW when compared with the convention of the omniscient narrator.

More problematical is the relationship of realism with subject matter. It is easier to discern what is not realistic (FANTASY, for example, or idealistic writing) than what is. Road-sweepers, doctors and royal families are all literally 'real' – their actuality is not disputed; but writers who attempt to be 'realistic' tend to prefer the proposition that 'reality' exists more completely in the life of ordinary people in ordinary situations, 'Middlemarchers', to adopt the term implicit in George Eliot's novel of provincial life, *Middlemarch* (1871–2). Often such 'realistic' writers seek to show up the false hopes and fanciful aspirations of their characters: 'realistic' novels may be contrasted with romantic or ESCAPIST fiction which depicts life as full of thrilling adventure and gratified desire.

But if realism deals with ordinary life, obviously 'ordinary' is as much a relative and evaluative term as 'reality'. Realism for Balzac and George Eliot consists of depicting bourgeois life; for a MARXIST, reality or 'truth' is to be discerned in the struggle of the working class for power, and consequently SOCIALIST REALISM deals with working-class realities. Clearly 'realism' as applied to subject matter is an exceptionally elastic and elusive term, to be used with care. Suffice it to say that realism is most frequently thought of as concerned with exploring the humdrum, dreary and often disappointing side of day-to-day existence, sometimes illuminated by a stoical heroism; and that as a descriptive label it is best used for writers who show explicit concern to convey an authentic impression of actuality, either by their narrative style, or by their serious approach to their subject matter. NATURALISM was a more coherent literary movement of the late nineteenth century, more sharply concerned to illustrate a particular kind of realism based on a view of man as inextricably and tragically dominated by the forces of nature within him, sexual drives, hunger, selfishness, and so on. Eric Auerbach's *Mimesis* (1946) is a famous study of the development of realism in world literature. *See also* ROMANTICISM, VERISIMILITUDE.

Realism, 'classic bourgeois'. *See* 'CLASSIC BOURGEOIS' REALISM.

Reception theory. A specific branch of READER-RESPONSE CRITICISM developed by Hans Robert Jauss which focuses on the changing history of the reaction to texts by readers ('Literary History as a Challenge to Literary Theory', 1967). Readers bring to the text the 'aesthetic horizon' of their time – a collection of expectations, prejudices and tolerances, that is constantly shifting and evolving, not least because it encompasses and absorbs into itself the tradition of interpretations that build up in relation to a particular text, and become a part of its meaning. There is no fixed value or meaning in texts, but only that which is produced by the 'dialogue' between the horizons of different generations of readers and the text.

Recognition. *See* ANAGNORISIS.

Recto. (Lat. 'right') The right-hand page in a book when open; VERSO is the left-hand page.

Redactor. (Lat. 'collect, reduce, bring back') Another word for an editor. A 'redaction' is an edition of a work for publication.

Reductive. (Lat. 'bringing back') An adjective which can be used to describe an interpretation of a piece of literature which, rather than exploring and revealing every possible meaning inherent in the piece, reduces and limits its meaning in a damaging way. A 'reductive' view of a work is one which diminishes and narrows its possible significance and meaning.

Referential language. The language of simple, exact and neutral description, such as is used by scientists; it is usually opposed to the **emotive language** of literature which is designed to affect and guide the reader's feelings. Compare the plain language of an extract from a handbook to birds, with a verse of Shelley's 'To a Skylark' (1820):

> Larks (family *Alaudidae*) are rather dull-looking, small to medium-sized brownish birds of open country. They sing in flight, sometimes high above the ground.

> Higher still and higher
> From the earth thou springest

Like a cloud of fire;
The blue deep thou wingest,
And singing still dost soar, and soaring ever singest.

See also CONNOTATION, DENOTATION.

Reformation. A historical term referring to the intellectual and political upheavals caused by the new Protestant religion which originated in the early sixteenth century with Martin Luther's breakaway from the Roman Catholic Church. Apart from its attack on the institutions of Catholicism, Protestantism in general placed new stress on the individual's state of mind in the spiritual struggle between doubt and faith: the individual is alone before God, and only faith will lead to salvation. The Bible became the one true source of Christianity, rather than the teaching of the Church, and hence translation became a matter of urgent significance: Luther's German translation was begun in 1521 and published in 1534. Tyndale's English translation was smuggled into England in 1526, but banned. The work of various translators, working from the 1530s onwards, culminated in the great Authorised Version of 1611.

In Britain the Reformation was initiated by Henry VIII's political break with the papacy in 1534; Protestantism steadily gained ground during the sixteenth century in spite of the setback of Mary's attempts to return to Catholicism' (1553–8). *See also* RENAISSANCE.

Refrain. (Lat. 'to break') Words or lines repeated in the course of a poem, recurring at intervals, sometimes with slight variation, usually at the end of a STANZA. Refrains are especially common in songs or BALLADS. They may consist of a single word, part of a line, a whole line, or even a whole stanza. Refrains in songs where the audience is expected to join in are called the 'chorus'.

As an example, here are some stanzas from a lyric by Sir Thomas Wyatt (written *c*.1535):

Forget not yet the tried intent
Of such a truth as I have meant,
My great travail so gladly spent
    Forget not yet . . .

Forget not yet, forget not this,
How long ago hath been and is
The mind that never meant amiss,
    Forget not yet.

Forget not then thine own approved,
The which so long hath thee so loved,
Whose steadfast faith yet never moved,
    Forget not this.

Regional novel. A NOVEL which emphasises and documents the geography, customs and speech of a particular place, with a more serious explanatory focus than for mere background information. The environment is often used to explain the character and actions of its inhabitants. Examples are Mrs Gaskell's *Mary Barton* (1848), with its description of Manchester life, or the many 'Wessex' novels of Thomas Hardy.

Register. (Lat. 'list') Apart from its ordinary use (a list of names), literary critics use 'register' to denote 'a kind of language being used', especially the kind of language appropriate to a particular situation. For example, an author of books for infants will use language of a different 'register' from a writer of technical manuals.

Reification. (Lat. 'thing-making') To reify an abstraction is to treat it as a thing. A vogue word of the 1980s, used occasionally in literary criticism to describe the way in which a hypothetical way of looking at things can come to be treated as a permanent, concrete and 'true' perspective, with resulting distortions.

MARXISTS believe that capitalism is perpetually recreating its structures and the social relationships that go with them, so as to invest them with a seeming authority and inevitability. This process was called 'reification' by Lukacs in *History and Class Consciousness* (1923).

Renaissance. (Fr. 'rebirth') The period following the Middle Ages in European history. A vital flowering of the arts and sciences, accompanied by thrilling changes in religious and philosophical thought, the Renaissance started in Italy in the late fourteenth century and spread throughout Europe, reaching England during the reigns of Elizabeth I (1558–1603) and James I (1603–25).

Naturally such a widely diffused shift in values and ideas is conceptually rather vague, and, not surprisingly, some historians doubt whether the label 'Renaissance' is useful, or describes an identifiable phenomenon. Some aspects of the intellectual changes are worth noting, however. Religion changed radically with the new Protestant reforms (*see* REFORMATION). The revival of interest in Greek literature lead to a new breed of Classical scholars called HUMANISTS, of whom Erasmus is one of the most famous. In 1543 Nicolas Copernicus put forward his new and accurate astronomical view of the solar system (*see* COPERNICAN THEORY), displacing eventually the old PTOLEMAIC SYSTEM, according to which the stars and sun revolved around the earth. Scientists like Galileo Galilei and William Harvey explored the world about them and man's physiology, in such a way as to discredit for ever the astrological and semi-magical pseudo-sciences which had prevailed in the medieval world. Last, but very significant, the new technology of printing with movable type, developed in the fifteenth century, facilitated and quickened the spread of new ideas and knowledge.

The term 'Renaissance' was a nineteenth-century invention, coined by looking back at the period. It is doubtful whether those participating in the burgeoning of the arts and ideas had such a clear view of the significance of their own intellectual endeavours, although they were conscious of the intellectual ferment around them.

The word 'Renaissance' can be applied to any equivalent flowering of the arts and scholarship, as occurred, for instance, in twelfth-century Europe; the revival of Scottish literature in the early twentieth century is called the Scottish Renaissance.

Repartee. (Fr. 'reply swiftly') A witty, swift reply, often mildly insulting. Frequent in comic drama.

Repetend. (Lat. 'what is repeated') A word or phrase that is repeated irregularly throughout a poem, rather than regularly in the manner of a REFRAIN.

Repetition. (Lat. 'saying again') Repetition is a vital part of the language of literature both in verse and prose. Repetition creates the sense of PATTERN or FORM in a work of literature, though it may be difficult to discern immediately which elements are repeated; it may be the repetition-with-variation of sound patterns as in the METRE of poetry or the repetition-with-variation of incidents or symbols as in a drama or novel; or any feature of language.

At a more particular level, repetition is used for AMPLIFICATION and emphasis. Consider Wordsworth's wearily haunting opening to 'Tintern Abbey' (1798), where the word 'five' occurs three times in one-and-a-half lines, and 'length' is modified into 'long':

Five years have passed: five summers, with the length
Of five long winters!

Re-reading. The so-called CRISIS IN ENGLISH STUDIES has given a particular gloss to the simple operation of re-reading a book, so that it means, in certain contexts, 're-reading in the light of STRUCTURALIST and POST-STRUCTURALIST literary theory, so as to reveal FEMINIST, MARXIST or DECONSTRUCTIVE critical readings'.

Restoration. The forty-year period after the restoration of the monarchy in England in 1660: Charles II came to the throne, bringing to an end the COMMONWEALTH which had existed since the execution of his father, Charles I. Restoration literature is characterised by the WIT and control of Dryden's poetry and the licentiousness of Rochester's satires. Having been banned by the Puritans since 1642, the theatre flourished: RESTORATION COMEDY and HEROIC DRAMA were forms special to this period.

Restoration comedy. A comedy of manners (*see* COMEDY) which flourished in the late seventeenth century. Its main preoccupations were sexual intrigue, the cuckolding of stupid husbands by clever, if immoral, young men-about-town, and the rarity of fidelity or love in a sophisticated urban society. Its polished, witty dialogue, full of REPARTEE, is often provocatively licentious. Two celebrated examples are Wycherley's *The Country Wife* (1675) and Congreve's *The Way of the World* (1700). Etherege, Vanburgh and Farquhar are other notable Restoration playwrights.

Restricted point of view. *See* NARRATIVE.

Revenge tragedy. A special form of TRAGEDY which concentrates on the PROTAGONIST's pursuit of vengeance against those who have done wrong. These plays often concentrate on the moral confusion caused by the need to answer evil with evil.

In English literature the Elizabethan interest in SENECAN TRAGEDY gave rise to many examples of this minor genre. Thomas Kyd's *The Spanish Tragedy* (*c*.1589) is a well-known example, not least because of its influence on Shakespeare's use of the form in *Hamlet* (*c*.1601). Other celebrated examples are Tourneur's *The Revenger's Tragedy* (1607) and Webster's *The Duchess of Malfi* (*c*.1613). The character of Bosola in the latter play, a treacherous and amoral ex-galley slave, is an interesting example of the way in which the instrument of vengeance turns upon those who use it: he kills those who have employed him to kill others. Bloodthirsty scenes, graveyards, ghosts and every kind of sensational horror typify the revenge tragedy from its beginnings, but in the Jacobean period playwrights seem to have competed with each other to present more devious methods of murder and torture, and more bodies littering the stage at the end of the play.

Reversal. The final turning point in the hero's fortunes in tragic or comic drama. *See also* PERIPETEIA.

Review. In journalism, a review is a short critical and descriptive account of a book, appearing in a newspaper or magazine. 'Review' is also a name for a serious magazine discussing the arts and culture.

Revision. (Lat. 'looking back at') An altered version of a text; or the process of altering a text.

Revue. (Fr. 'see again') A species of theatrical entertainment made up of sketches (short, dramatic, comic episodes), songs, jokes, dances. Revues usually take a satirical look at current affairs.

Rhapsody. (Gk. 'stitch song') In Ancient Greece a rhapsody was an EPIC poem recited by a minstrel, who 'stitched' together his performance out of remembered or improvised fragments.

Nowadays the word refers in literature to a wild outpouring of emotion, usually also broken up into different fragments: the feeling spills out of control and dominates the form. T.S. Eliot's 'Rhapsody on a Windy Night' (1917) is an example.

Rhetoric. (Gk. *rhetor*, 'public speaker') The art of speaking (and writing) effectively so as to persuade an audience. Rhetoric was the subject of several textbooks by Greek and Roman scholars, including Aristotle and Cicero, and was studied at universities during the Middle Ages.

Elaborate rules were devised to aid the composition and delivery of speeches, and the various devices by which an orator can help convince or sway the audience were analysed. In this respect the study of rhetoric was a forerunner of modern criticism.

Nowadays the term 'rhetorical' is often used pejoratively, to imply empty or false attempts at persuasion.

Rhetorical criticism. A term sometimes used for the work of critics of the 1960s and 1970s who analysed literature in terms of the many authorial devices used by the NARRATOR to develop a particular relationship with the reader. The American Wayne Booth's study of the novel, *The Rhetoric of Fiction* (1961), was a seminal study of this kind.

Rhetorical figure. A decorative departure from the grammar or syntax of ordinary speech in order to achieve special effects. For example, the APOSTROPHE or INVOCATION, the RHETORICAL QUESTION, CHIASMUS and ZEUGMA.

Rhetorical question. A question asked not for the sake of enquiry, but for emphasis: the writer or speaker expects the reader or audience to be totally convinced about the appropriate reply. Or, as in the following example, from Arnold's 'The Scholar Gipsy' (1853), there is no need for any reply:

> And once, in winter, on the causeway chill
> Where home through flooded fields foot-travellers go,
> Have I not passed thee on the wooden bridge,
> Wrapped in thy cloak and battling with the snow . . . ?

Rhyme. (O.H. Ger. 'number') Though by no means all verse is rhymed, rhyme is one of the most striking and obvious differences between verse and prose, and the most easily identified common aspect of English versification. It consists of chiming or matching sounds at the ends of lines of verse, which create a very clearly audible sense of pattern. Herrick's 'To the Virgins, to Make Much of Time' (1648) is a straightforward example:

> Gather ye Rose-buds while ye may,
> Old time is still a-flying:
> And this same flower that smiles today,
> Tomorrow will be dying.

Most rhymes in English verse chime on the last syllable of a line, and that syllable also bears a final stress: these strong, one-syllable rhymes are called **masculine rhymes**; lines 1 and 3 (may/day) above are an example. A different effect is created when the final syllable (or syllables) of a line is unstressed: in which case the preceding stressed syllable has to chime as well as the final syllable, as in lines 2 and 4 above (flying/dying). This is called a **feminine rhyme**. Rhymes may also be made with more than two syllables, though this chiming effect is so strong that it occurs chiefly in comic verse: it is common in Byron's *Don Juan* (1819–24), for example:

> I've got new mythological machinery,
> And very handsome supernatural scenery.

All the examples so far have been **end-rhymes**. **Internal rhyme**, words rhymed within a line, is not uncommon, as in Blake's 'The Lilly' (1794):

> The modest Rose puts forth a thorn,
> The humble Sheep a threat'ning horn;
> While the Lilly white shall in Love delight,
> Nor a thorn, nor a threat, stain her beauty bright.

Obviously exact rhymes create the clearest audible pattern, but the ear also catches inexact rhymes and incorporates them into the sense of order created by rhyme, as in Byron's lines (1830):

> So, we'll go no more a-roving
>   So late into the night,
> Though the heart be still as loving,
>   And the moon be still as bright.

Rhymes like a-roving/loving, which appear exact because of their spelling, but which are pronounced differently, are called **eye-rhymes**.

Inexact or **imperfect rhymes** are variously called **half-rhyme**, **slant rhyme** or **pararhyme**. They have always existed as a POETIC LICENCE, but are exceptionally common in twentieth-century verse, becoming a special feature of the verse of certain poets, such as Wilfred Owen, Dylan Thomas and Ted Hughes. Owen's 'Strange Meeting' (1920), for example, consists of half-rhymed COUPLETS:

> It seemed that out of battle I escaped
> Down some profound dull tunnel, long since scooped
> Through granites which titanic wars had groined.
> Yet also there encumbered sleepers groaned,
> Too fast in thought or death to be bestirred.
> Then, as I probed, one sprang up, and stared . . .

The half-rhymes and the internal half-rhyme, like down/profound, profound/groined, etc., help to accentuate the poem's dream-like, incantatory effect.

Rhyme (in conjunction with METRE) helps create an audible pattern in verse which is one of its ancient and basic pleasures. The **rhyme scheme** of a poem may be an essential aspect of its STRUCTURE and is expressed by a simple alphabetical labelling. The rhyme scheme of the following Wordsworth lyric (1807) is *abccabcdd*:

My heart leaps up when I behold
  A rainbow in the sky:
So was it when my life began;
So is it now I am a man;
So be it when I shall grow old,
  Or let me die!
The Child is father of the Man;
And I could wish my days to be
Bound each to each by natural piety.

The rhyme scheme of a poem can help to give a sense of developing argument as above (*see also* SONNET). Rhyme can also bring a pair of words or ideas into a pleasing relationship with each other, as in the play of contrasts in the couplets at the end of Pope's 'To Mrs M.B. on Her Birthday' (1723):

Let day improve on day, and year on year,
Without a Pain, a Trouble, or a Fear;
Till Death unfelt that tender frame destroy,
In some soft Dream, or Extasy of joy,
Peaceful sleep out the Sabbath of the Tomb,
And wake to Raptures in a Life to come.

The sense of controlled and witty intelligence in the HEROIC COUPLET is entirely a consequence of the precision of its end-rhymes which organise the verse into a series of pithy, EPIGRAMMATIC statements.

The significance of rhyme in English versification can be judged from the fact that the word (sometimes spelt 'rime') has often been used as a synonym for poetry.

Rhyme royal. A STANZA of seven ten-syllable lines rhymed *ababbcc* used by James I of Scotland in the *Kingis Quair* (*c*.1425), and by Chaucer in several poems, including *Troilus and Criseyde* (*c*.1380–5). Not infrequently employed by other poets.

Rhyme scheme. The pattern of RHYMES in a STANZA or section of verse, usually expressed by an alphabetical code.

Rhythm. (Gk. 'flowing') In English verse and prose the chief element of rhythm is the variation in levels of STRESS accorded to the syllables, in any stretch of language. The play of long and short syllables may also be a factor in creating variation in enunciation. *See also* QUANTITY.

In verse the rhythm is more or less controlled and regular (*see* METRE). In prose it is varied, though it may also have patches where regularity is established. *See also* CADENCE.

Ribald. (O.H. Ger. 'whore') Originally a noun meaning a scurrilous and indecent knave; the word is now an adjective denoting speech or literature which treats in a comic way subjects such as bodily functions and sexuality, which are often considered indecent. Ribaldry is usually considered more innocently comical than obscenity or PORNOGRAPHY.

Riddle. (O.E. 'opinion, counsel') A deliberately puzzling way of referring to an object or idea, with the purpose of tricking, testing or amusing. The Sphinx's riddle solved by Oedipus in the Greek legend is typical: what goes on four legs in the morning, two legs at noon and three legs in the evening? (answer: a human being in the three stages of life).

There are many riddling poems in Anglo-Saxon, some of which remain unsolved. The fact that the riddle expresses something in an odd, intriguing manner makes it akin to the METAPHOR. Riddles occur in many different ages and cultures. *See also* MARTIANISM.

Rime. *See* RHYME.

Rime riche. (Fr. 'rich rhyme') A complete RHYME, in the sense that the rhymed syllable is repeated in its entirety, including the initial consonant, as in the case of rhymed HOMOPHONES, words with the same sound, such as shake/sheik or through/threw. Uncommon, even avoided, in modern English poetry, but found in medieval English verse and common in French couplets.

Rising rhythm. A name for IAMBIC and ANAPAESTIC metres, in both of which the stress pattern is 'rising' (ti-tum) rather than 'falling' (tum-ti). *See* METRE for further discussion of these terms.

Risqué. (Fr. 'risky') Bordering on or hinting at sexual matters, usually in a frivolous context where impropriety or indecency is not likely to cause offence, as with a *risqué* joke.

Robinson Crusoe myth. Alexander Selkirk (1676–1721), a Scottish sailor, quarrelled with his captain while in the South Seas as a buccaneer. At his own request, he was put ashore on the island of Juan Fernandez, where he lived for five years until he was discovered in 1709, and brought back to Britain. Daniel Defoe's version of this story, *Robinson Crusoe* (1719), has gained the status of a modern myth. The idea of an individual surviving alone on an island has appealed in a variety of ways, and been used to express a number of different versions of human nature. It has been seen as an image of the virtues of a sober and thrifty Protestant self-sufficiency, of the loneliness of the artist, and finally in Crusoe's relationship with Man Friday, of colonial assumptions of superiority.

Cowper's poem 'The Castaway' (1803) is a poetic version of the stereotype (though not actually based on Selkirk). In this century the poets Elizabeth Bishop and Derek Walcott have reworked the Crusoe story in different ways. Wyss's *The Swiss Family Robinson* (1813-14), Ballantyne's *The Coral Island* (1857) and Golding's *Lord of the Flies* (1954) are children's books describing, with very different emphases, survival on desert islands. *See also* NOBLE SAVAGE.

Rodomontade. An extravagant boast, or a ridiculously inflated, BOMBASTIC style of speaking or writing. The word is derived from a boastful character Rodomonte (It. 'roll-mountain') in comic fifteenth- and sixteenth-century Italian epics by Boiardo and Ariosto.

Roman à clef. (Fr. 'novel with a key') A NOVEL in which some of the characters are thinly disguised portraits of real, famous people. D.H. Lawrence and Sir Oswald Mosley both appear thus in Aldous Huxley's *Point Counter Point* (1928). Also known as *livre à clef* (Fr. 'book with a key').

Roman à thèse. (Fr. 'thesis novel') A DIDACTIC NOVEL in which the resources of fiction are used to discuss and confirm a particular thesis or idea, concerned, for example, with politics, society, morality or philosophy. Also known as the 'sociological novel'. Dickens's *Hard Times* (1854) might be so designated in its attack on the effects of industrialisation, or Charles Kingsley's *Alton Locke* (1850), written to draw attention to the miseries of life in the clothes-making sweat-shops of London. Another kind of example is Sir Herbert Read's *The Green Child* (1935), in which the protagonist moves from revolutionary politics to a final state of non-involvement in the world, symbolised by turning into a green crystal.

Romance. (Med. Lat. 'in the Romanic language') Primarily medieval fictions in verse or prose dealing with adventures of chivalry and love.

'Romance' originally meant a work written in the French language. The form developed in twelfth-century France and spread to other countries. Verse gradually gave way to prose as the popular medium.

Romance characteristically describes a sophisticated courtly world of chivalry, distinct from the heroic EPIC which concentrates on war. Typical stories concern knightly quests, tournaments, magic, and contests with monsters for the sake of a heroine who is the focus for COURTLY LOVE, but many of the tales have a strong moral content, establishing codes and ideals of chivalric behaviour.

The works of the late twelfth-century French poet Chrétien de Troyes were very influential. Notable English romances include the late fourteenth-century *Sir Gawain and the Green Knight*, in ALLITERATIVE VERSE, and Malory's *Le Morte d'Arthur*, a prose work which was printed by Caxton in 1485. All the above are concerned with the semi-historical King Arthur of Britain, and with his legendary knights of the Round Table. Scholars call this 'The Matter of Britain'. Other subjects were 'The Matter of France' (exploits of Charlemagne), and 'The Matter of Rome' (Classical tales).

An interest in chivalric romance has cropped up regularly in English poetry since its medieval origins. Spenser's *The Faerie Queene* (1590, 1596) and Tennyson's *Idylls of the King* (1842–85) are both reworkings of the genre. Another famous work which is a kind of mock romance is Cervantes's *Don Quixote* (1605, 1615), the mad adventures of a knight who believes the world of chivalry still to exist, and constantly comes into absurd conflict with reality.

Finally it is perhaps worth pointing out that even the oldest romances describe chivalric behaviour in a magical world of long ago. Romances were never realistic, and did not directly imitate contemporary society.

Roman-feuilleton. (Fr. 'novel-literary article') A serialisation of a NOVEL in a French newspaper, a common means of publication in France as in Britain during the 1840s and 1850s. Balzac and Dumas *père*, amongst many others, produced works of this kind. Television soap-operas, with their huge casts of characters and inconsequential but melodramatic plots, are sometimes compared to these works.

Roman-fleuve. (Fr. 'novel-river') A series of NOVELS, each complete in itself, but all following the development of the same characters; a notable example is Proust's *A la recherche du temps perdu* (1913–27).

Romantic, Romanticism. (Fr. *romaunt*, 'romance') 'Romantic' is a word which is bafflingly vague and used in an appallingly large number of different ways in different contexts. It might be best to do away with it altogether as a critical term: it should certainly not be used carelessly in critical writing. Yet for the last two centuries, since its first rather casual use as a literary term by the German philosopher-critic Schlegel, it has been constantly redefined by writers and critics. This fact alone means that it is necessary to try to attach some kind of meaning, or bundle of meanings, to the word.

(1) 'Romantic' in its weakest, vaguest and popular sense means 'to do with love', especially idealised, glamorised and facile love. (2) The **Romantic period**. This is a convenient term in English literary history for the period dating from 1789, the French Revolution, to about 1830. The writers of this period are many and various, but they tend to share some of the features which might be said to be part of the general literary atmosphere called 'Romanticism'. Novelists of the period include Sir Walter Scott and Jane Austen. Essayists such as Lamb, Hazlitt and De Quincey are notable for their contributions to the fast-developing literary magazines. There are two 'generations' of 'Romantic poets': ironically many of the first generation, which includes Blake, Wordsworth, Coleridge and Southey, outlived their younger contemporaries, the second generation, Byron, Shelley and Keats, who all died young. (3) Romanticism: there are a large number of literary interests and attributes which might loosely be labelled 'romantic', often in contrast to literature labelled NEOCLASSICAL. These attributes and interests were common well before and long after the Romantic period designated above. They are: (i) A concern to value feeling and emotion rather than the human capacity to reason. Logical thought and understanding, often connected with a scientific, investigative manner of understanding the world, are abandoned in favour of instinctive and immediate

feeling, or intuition, or the mind's capacity to discover through ASSOCIA-
TION, rather than forced thought. (ii) This concern with feeling leads
directly to some of the topics typical of so-called romantic literature:
natural, 'primitive' human existence, whether in the form of the NOBLE
SAVAGE, the peasant or the outcast from society; children who, like man
in a state of nature, are uncorrupted by society's rigid way of compre-
hending the world of things; ghost stories, legends, myths and dreams.
(iii) The self. As wisdom and morality are conceived in terms of an
individual's response to the world outside rather than as a coherent
collection of reasoned ideas and opinions, the writers turn in on
themselves and try to explain and evaluate their living relationship with
the world about them. Wordsworth's poem on the growth of a poet's
mind, his autobiographical study called *The Prelude* (written from 1798
onwards but published in 1850), is the foremost text of this aspect of
'Romanticism', which points directly to the modern, psychological age.
(iv) Corresponding with the investigation of the self is a new detailed
interest in nature, not for its own sake necessarily, but as a way of
coming to understand the self. Many so-called 'nature poems' by
Romantic writers are studies in EPISTEMOLOGY: by examining the
individual's perception of the world of things outside, they try to
explore the complicated relationships between things, feelings and
ideas. Wordsworth and Shelley go so far as to attempt to connect the
development of moral values with the act of looking at landscape. (v)
IMAGINATION, a key word for understanding 'Romanticism'. For many
of the poets of the Romantic period the imagination represents the
mind's power to create harmonious meaning out of the chaos of
impressions, ideas, feelings and memories which inhabit it at any one
moment. It is a shaping and creative power: its visitation gives joy, and
its waning and loss are a cause for lamentation. A poem is the
expression in words of the shaping power of the imagination. (vi) A
yearning aspiration towards something beyond the ordinary world, not
necessarily religious, is a typical aspect of 'Romanticism' and often
gives rise to SYMBOLISM, both as a way of looking at the world and as a
poetic or literary technique. (vii) The sense of departure from the 'rules
of poetry' that had come to dominate Neoclassicism. Wordsworth's
'Preface' to the second edition of *Lyrical Ballads* (1800) is a manifesto
against POETIC DICTION, and defines poetry as the 'spontaneous overflow of powerful feelings', both points being a blow against the
DECORUM of his poetic forerunners. Spontaneity, creativity and the need
to allow poems to shape themselves 'organically' (naturally rather than
mechanically according to rules or reason) are all valued ideals. It is
worth pointing out, however, that this did not lead to poor, careless
writing: the Romantic poets were also superb poetic craftsmen. (viii)
Rebellion not only against poetic stultification, but against outmoded

political institutions. Many of the writers of the Romantic period were inspired by the apparent idealism of the French Revolution (1789); some, like Blake, Shelley and Hazlitt, never lost their enthusiasm for revolutionary politics.

Romanticism, in the sense of a bulky baggage-load of ideas and interests as outlined in the interconnecting eight sections above, was an international European phenomenon. The roots of many of these ideas can clearly be seen in the eighteenth-century cult of SENSIBILITY. The German STURM UND DRANG literature is also an early form of Romanticism.

Many values and interests of the Romantic period remain alive right through the nineteenth century and are absorbed into modern literature: poets such as Wallace Stevens and W.B. Yeats can be seen in many ways as 'Romantic' poets, though they were writing a century later than Coleridge or Shelley, whose work influenced them.

Romantic comedy. An Elizabethan style of COMEDY. Shakespeare's *As You Like It* (*c*.1599) is typical. Its major concern is love, especially the relationship between an idealised young couple (Orlando and Rosalind) who, after a number of scrapes and difficulties, are eventually happily united. The escape from the real world into the half-magical forest of Arden, and Rosalind's disguise as a boy, are also typifying features.

Romantic irony. An eighteenth- and nineteenth-century German term for the kind of narrative in which the author constantly breaks the illusion that is being created in order to comment on characters, explain his or her own deficiencies as a writer, and reveal the playful arbitrariness of the creative process. Sterne's *Tristram Shandy* (1759-67) and Byron's *Don Juan* (1819-24) are famous examples. The Italian novelist Italo Calvino is a modern exponent. *See also* METAFICTION, SELF-CONSCIOUS NARRATOR, SELF-REFLEXIVE.

Romantic period. *See* ROMANTIC.

Rondeau. (Fr. 'round') An elaborate verse form, French in origin and usually playful in subject matter. Typically a rondeau consists of thirteen lines, employing only two rhymes, plus a REFRAIN: the first word or opening phrase is repeated after the eighth and the thirteenth. It is commonly divided into three STANZAS: *aabba, aabR, aabbaR*. Dobson's 'A Greeting' (1890) is an example of the form:

> But once or twice we met, touched hands.
> To-day between us both expands
>   A waste of tumbling waters wide, –
>   A waste by me as yet untried,
> Vague with the doubt of unknown lands.
>
> Time like a despot speeds his sands:
> A year he blots, a day he brands;

> We walked, we talked by Thamis' side
>> But once or twice.
>
> What makes a friend? What filmy strands
> Are these that turn to iron bands?
>> What knot is this so firmly tied
>> That naught but Fate can now divide? –
> Ah, these are things one understands
>> But once or twice!

Rondel. An elaborate French verse form like the RONDEAU and the VILLANELLE, though less fixed in form. A common version is fourteen lines long, making use of only two rhymes, and repeating the first and second line as lines seven and eight, and again as lines thirteen and fourteen.

Round character. A term invented by E.M. Forster in *Aspects of the Novel* (1927) to describe a character who changes and develops in the course of a novel, as opposed to the **flat character** which does not. A round character in a drama or novel will be presented with as much complexity and detail of motivation and behaviour as someone met with in real life. Flat characters will be built around 'a single idea or quality'. Forster cites Becky Sharp from Thackeray's *Vanity Fair* (1847–8) as a round character, and Mrs Micawber, from Dickens's *David Copperfield* (1849–50), as a flat character.

Roundel. An eleven-line version of the RONDEAU invented by Swinburne in *A Century of Roundels* (1883), rhymed *abaR, bab, abaR*. The REFRAIN is a repetition of the poem's opening words.

> A roundel is wrought as a ring or a starbright sphere,
> With craft of delight and with cunning of sound unsought,
> That the heart of the hearer may smile if to please his ear
>> A roundel is wrought.
>
> Its jewel of music is carven of all or of aught –
> Love, laughter, or mourning – remembrance of rapture or fear –
> That fancy may fashion to hang in the ear of thought.
>
> As a bird's quick song runs round, and the hearts in us hear
> Pause answer to pause, and again the same strain caught,
> So moves the device whence, round as a pearl or tear,
>> A roundel is wrought.

R.P. (Received Pronunciation) *See* DIALECT.

Rune. (O.N. 'magical sign') An old Germanic kind of writing used in Britain; a rune is one of the twenty-four letters in the runic alphabet, used by the early Anglo-Saxons for carving on wood and stone.

Run-on lines. Lines of verse in which the grammar does not coincide with the metrical line – in other words, is not END-STOPPED. *See* ENJAMBMENT for an example.

Russian formalism. *See* FORMALISM.

S

Saga. (O.N. 'saying, narrative') Medieval Scandinavian and Icelandic stories in prose concerning the heroic exploits of warriors. They started to be written down in the twelfth century, but presumably existed as an ORAL tradition before this. Sagas continued to be written till the early fourteenth century. William Morris's poem *Sigurd the Volsung* (1876) is closely based on one of the most famous sagas.

Salon. (Fr. 'large reception room') An informal meeting, usually in a private house, where writers, artists and intellectuals gather. *Salons* were popular in France, especially in the eighteenth century. Very often they were organised by women, sometimes, like Madame de Staël, themselves writers.

Samizdat. (Russ. 'self-publishing') From the 1960s onwards, the word has been used of secret, private 'publishing' of banned material in the Soviet Union. Works by political dissidents like Solzhenitsyn were typed on carbon copies, or copied in other ways (though photocopying machines were forbidden), and circulated amongst trusted sympathisers. Some reached the West in this form, and were then publicly published outside the USSR.

Sapphic ode. An ODE named after the poetess Sappho (seventh century BC), consisting of QUATRAINS, mixing TROCHEES, SPONDEES and DACTYLS (*see* METRE for further discussion of these terms). Because of its difficulty in English such a metre is chiefly to be found in the work of experimental versifiers like Tennyson, Swinburne or Pound.

Sarcasm. (Gk. 'rend the flesh, speak bitterly') An extreme form of IRONY, intended to hurt. A bitter, or wounding remark.

Satanic school. The poet Southey coined this description of the second generation of Romantic poets, especially Byron, but also probably Shelley, in the preface to his poem *A Vision of Judgment* (1821). He complained of the immorality and irreligious attitudes, 'those monstrous combinations of horrors and mockery, lewdness and impiety, with which English poetry has, in our days, first been polluted!' Though Southey mentioned no names, Byron replied with his triumphantly savage parody, *The Vision of Judgment* (1822).

Satire. (Lat. 'mixture, medley', from *satis*, 'enough') Literature which exhibits or examines vice and folly and makes them appear ridiculous or contemptible. Though the distinction is not always clear, satire differs from the comic in having a purpose: it is directed against a person or a type, and it is usually morally censorious. It uses laughter to attack its objects, rather than for mere evocation of mirth or pleasure. Satirical writing has been common in most literatures, but its greatest age in English literature was undoubtedly during the late seventeenth and early eighteenth centuries.

'Formal satire' uses the first person singular in a direct address to the reader or to some second person who may draw out the speaker, as, for example, in Pope's 'Epistle to Dr Arbuthnot' (1735). 'Indirect satire' is dramatic or narrative; the objects of satire themselves, the characters, are made to illustrate folly or evil by their behaviour.

Three kinds of satire, based on Classical models, are frequently to be distinguished. **Horatian satire** is urbane, witty, informal, and tends to enjoy rather than loathe human follies. (The Roman poet Horace lived from 65 to 8BC.) **Juvenalian satire**, on the other hand, adopts a dignified public stance, and scourges mankind for its errors: it is self-consciously and seriously moral. (Juvenal (c.AD60–c.130) was also a Roman poet.) The **Menippean** or **Varronian satire** goes back to the derivation of the word and is not necessarily satirical in the usual sense: it is a rag-bag of prose and verse loosely relating to some topic but making use of all kinds of literary modes, including conversations, digressions, lists and so on. Another name for this is the ANATOMY. (Menippus was a Greek Cynic philosopher of the third century BC; Varro was a Roman poet (116–27BC).)

Dryden and Pope are the two major satirical poets in English literature, though Dryden died in 1700, at the start of the period of great satirical writing, the first half of the eighteenth century. His *Absalom and Achitophel* (1681) and *MacFlecknoe* (1682) include satirical portraits of his contemporaries couched in the HEROIC COUPLETS typical of AUGUSTAN satire. Dryden also translated Juvenal's satires and prefaced them with a long critical essay, *A Discourse Concerning the Original and Progress of Satire* (1693).

Pope's *Epistles* (1731–5) are straightforward examples of formal Horatian satire, though they are often harsh in their condemnation of human frailty. They deal with subjects such as the folly of women ('To a Lady'), the nature of good and bad taste ('Epistle to Burlington') and the life of the poet ('Epistle to Dr Arbuthnot'). This last example includes the famous LAMPOON on Lord Hervey. Pope also wrote versions of Horace's satires. Dr Johnson's *London* (1738) and *The Vanity of Human Wishes* (1749) are imitations of Juvenal's third and tenth satires from the first century AD.

Much satire exists in English literature before and after the age of Dryden and Pope. There are satirical elements in Chaucer's and Langland's poetry (both late fourteenth century), and the seventeenth-century poet Donne wrote satires; many of Ben Jonson's plays are satirical, notably *Volpone* (1605–6).

Byron introduced a special kind of satire in *Don Juan* (1819–24), which could be called 'romantic satire': he mocks the folly of his contemporaries, but erects no kind of foundation of morality from which to judge them: he ridicules the hypocritical morality of his contemporaries from a position of urbane cynicism.

Satire in prose is also common. Swift's epitaph mentioned the *saeva indignatio* (savage indignation) which caused him to write works such as his caustically ironic 'A Modest Proposal' (1729) in which he solemnly advocates eating babies as a cure for the problems of poverty in Ireland. *Gulliver's Travels* (1726) is also a satire on man's folly, though on the surface it appears whimsical.

What satire has been written since Byron has mostly been in prose. Many of the novels of Evelyn Waugh are satirical studies of life in the 1920s, such as *Vile Bodies* (1930). Possibly the modern age lacks a sense of the stability of values which might be necessary for the burgeoning of satirical writing.

Satiric comedy. *See* COMEDY.

Satyr play. The fourth play in the groups of four plays (the TETRALOGY) during the period of classic Greek drama. Satyr plays were grotesque and comic versions of the tragedies, with the CHORUS dressed to represent satyrs, creatures in the main human but with goat's legs and a horse's tail. The *Cyclops* of Euripides (fifth century BC) is the only complete play extant.

Scansion. (Lat. 'climbing, measuring') The examination and analysis of the metre of a piece of verse. The practical aspect of PROSODY, including the ability to recognise and label both the pattern of STRESS in a line, usually in terms of the Classical metrical FEET, and also the kind of STANZA employed by the poet. *See* METRE for further discussion of these terms.

Scatology. (Gk. 'dung knowledge') In medicine, diagnosis by the faeces. 'Scatological' is often applied to bawdy or obscene books.

Scenario. A summary of a film or play, sketching out its plots and characters.

Scene. (Lat. 'stage') Subdivision of an ACT in a play; a small unit of action and time in the development of a play. Some plays, for example, those of the modern German playwright Brecht, consist only of a sequence of scenes or episodes.

Scenery. The decorations on the stage of a theatre which help create the illusion that it is a particular place, inside a house or in the countryside, for example. Scenery is not necessarily realistic, and plays may be performed with very little or no scenery.

Scholasticism. An overall term for the philosophical systems prevalent in Western Europe during the twelfth, thirteenth and fourteenth centuries. The preoccupations of scholasticism are often summarised as tedious speculations as to how many angels can be balanced on the head of a pin. Renaissance HUMANISTS were to deride the intellectual efforts of the medieval 'schoolmen' as muddled, abstract and over-reliant on authority. However, in their interest in the study of language (the educational system focused on the *trivium* of logic, grammar and rhetoric), scholastic philosophers anticipated many contemporary intellectual debates. Their deductive methods of argument, by means of the *quaestio*, the systematic questioning and reconciling of authorities, led to rigorous disputations in the universities, and to the influential syntheses and encyclopaedic commentaries such as Aquinas's *Summa contra Gentiles* ('Against Errors of Infidels') and his *Summa Theologiae* (*c*.1250), a complete theological and ethical system.

There was little distinction between philosophy and theology in scholastic thought, but the main impetus for debate was the need to reconcile two opposing systems, the logical approach to knowledge as exemplified in the works of Aristotle (whose works in their entirety were finally available to Western scholars from Arab sources in the twelfth and thirteenth centuries), and the traditional wisdom thought to be inherent in the Bible and the many interpretations with which it was surrounded. The scholastic philosophers of the twelfth century included Bernard of Clairvaux, Anselm and Peter Abelard, whose *Sic et Non* contrasted inconsistent passages in the Bible. Thirteenth-century debate was characterised by the split between the Thomists and Scotists, followers of Thomas Aquinas and Duns Scotus.

Science fiction. Often abbreviated to **S.F.** Literature about the imaginary marvels or disasters created by scientific and technological discoveries and inventions of the future. The nineteenth-century French writer Jules Verne wrote several adventure stories, notably *Journey to the Centre of the Earth* (1864), which might loosely be called science fiction. H.G. Wells also wrote many early examples, including *The Time Machine* (1895) and *The War of the Worlds* (1898).

During the second half of the twentieth century S.F. writers have been prolific and popular. Ray Bradbury, Arthur C. Clarke and Isaac Asimov are amongst the most famous. The immense popularity of S.F. both in novels and in the cinema indicates that it fulfils a vital role in the modern imagination, providing scope for a sense of scientific realism in various combinations with mild flights of fantasy. It is not yet often considered as a 'serious' literary form, however.

Scottish Chaucerians. The name given to several Middle Scots poets who might have been influenced by Chaucer, especially in their use of RHYME ROYAL. The most famous are William Dunbar, Gavin Douglas and Robert Henryson. They flourished at the end of the fifteenth and start of the sixteenth century.

Screenplay. The dialogue of a film written out like the text of a play but including details of camera movements and other cinematic information.

Scriptible. (Fr. 'writable') Translated either as '**writerly**' or 'writable', the word was used by the French critic Roland Barthes to indicate a special kind of complex, open-ended text that requires the reader's constant and active participation in order to be comprehensible, to the point of having to 'write' the text. This is contrasted with the *lisible* or 'readable' text, which can be read in a passive and inert way. *See also* JOUISSANCE.

Self-conscious narrator. Self-conscious narrators refer continually to the fact that they are creating a work of art for the purpose of explaining or exploring the conventions of narrative, like John Fowles in *The French Lieutenant's Woman* (1969), or to mock them, like Byron in *Don Juan* (1819–24). Wordsworth's *The Prelude* (1850) explores the nature of the self, and is a study in intense self-consciousness. *See also* AUTOBIOGRAPHY, ROMANTIC IRONY, SELF-REFLEXIVE.

Self-reflexive. A word for a text that refers to itself, in which the writer discusses the origin and processes of composition. Sterne's *Tristram Shandy* (1759–67) is the most famous example, but many texts are less ostentatiously self-reflexive. Common, obviously, in AUTOBIOGRAPHIES, such as Wordsworth's *The Prelude* (1850). *See also* METAFICTION.

Semantics. (Gk. 'significant', from *sema*, 'a sign') The study of the meanings of words: how words express their meanings, and how their meanings have changed in time.

Semiology. (Gk. 'sign-writing') Ferdinand de Saussure in his *Course in General Linguistics* (1915) remarks:

> *A science that studies the life of signs within society* is conceivable; it would be a part of social psychology and consequently of general psychology; I shall call it *semiology* (from the Greek *Semeion* 'sign'). Semiology would show what constitutes signs, what laws govern them ... Linguistics is only a part of the general science of semiology.

The twentieth-century French philosopher Roland Barthes follows the guide-lines of Saussure's projected science in his analysis of patterns of social behaviour (fashion, architecture, etc.) as communicative 'codes' or 'languages'. Semiologists perceive literature as a kind of CODE or institution which transmits and formalises meanings and values. *See also* LANGUE, SIGN, SIGNIFIER, STRUCTURALISM.

Semiotics. A philosophical term for the theory or logic of SIGNS. Now 'semiotics' is a synonym for SEMIOLOGY, the study of all patterned communication systems.

Senecan tragedy. Seneca was a first century AD Stoic Roman philosopher who is credited with adapting nine TRAGEDIES from the Greek. His plays are characterised by concentration on imparting atmosphere and action through the language (probably because they were not performed on stage), by declamatory passages, by STICHOMYTHIA, by the theme of revenge, and by certain STEREOTYPED figures, such as the messenger reporting disasters, the ghost and the nurse. The traditional dramatic five-act structure is based on the Senecan model.

These plays were translated into English in 1581, but exerted a strong influence on English drama before and after that date. Thomas Norton and Thomas Sackville's *Gorboduc* (1561) and Thomas Kyd's *The Spanish Tragedy* (*c*.1589) are notable examples of the influence of Senecan tragedy. Shakespeare and Webster also wrote REVENGE TRAGE-DIES owing something to this influence, for example, *Hamlet* (*c*.1601) and *The Duchess of Malfi* (*c*.1613). Unlike Seneca, the Elizabethan and Jacobean playwrights preferred to show the blood-curdling horrors of revenge on the stage, though they learned much from his concentration on the spoken word.

Sense. Apart from its standard meanings, 'sense' in the eighteenth century stands for a special kind of intellectual stolidity and balanced intelligence, as suggested, for example, by Jane Austen's *Sense and Sensibility* (1811) in which it is contrasted with over-indulgence in feeling.

Sensibility. The capacity to feel; to allow literature and experience to bring forth feelings. It is sometimes used in a neutral manner as in T.S. Eliot's phrase DISSOCIATION OF SENSIBILITY, or in discussing the characteristic sensibility of a literary figure or age, but it also defines a special kind of literature popular in·the eighteenth century, which was designed to describe and evoke a specially tender susceptibility to feelings which later generations have often labelled mawkish or SENTIMENTAL. In reaction to the harshness of seventeenth-century stoicism, manifested in Thomas Hobbes's view of man as innately selfish, writers took to extolling the necessity of benevolence, sympathy and instinctive virtue. The Earl of Shaftesbury's *Characteristics of Men, Manners, Opinions, Times* (1711) provided a philosophical status for this shift in taste. The capacity to weep over the sufferings of others was extolled as a proof of moral worth. Sentimental comedies replaced the cynical RESTORATION COMEDY. In the novel, Richardson's *Pamela, or Virtue Rewarded* (1740–1) explored sensibility. Henry Mackenzie's *The Man of Feeling* (1771) is the most extreme example: the hero dies in declaring his love for a young lady. In *The Sorrows of Young Werther* (1774), in which the hero commits suicide, Goethe satisfies the taste for sensibility and implicitly criticises its excesses.

Some critics define the period from Pope's death in 1744 to the publication of Wordsworth's and Coleridge's *Lyrical Ballads* in 1798 as the '**Age of Sensibility**'. Certainly the poetry of Thomas Gray, William Collins, William Cowper and Robert Burns shows an interest in extremes of feeling, and the SUBLIME. But Dr Johnson's tempered NEOCLASSICISM also characterised this period.

Sensibility, Dissociation of. *See* DISSOCIATION OF SENSIBILITY.

Sententiousness. (Lat. *sententia*, 'mental feeling, judgment, opinion') The word 'sentence' can be used in its Latin meaning of an opinion, pronounced judgment or MAXIM (its normal modern meaning is 'a grammatically complete expression'). 'Sententious' therefore means given to the use of maxims, or APHORISTIC, which is to say using a pithy, short but impressive style; and it can be used pejoratively, to suggest the habit of pompous moralising or a pretentiously formal style of speaking or writing.

Sentimental comedy. *See* SENSIBILITY.

Sentimental novel. *See* SENSIBILITY.

Sentimentality. (Lat. 'feeling') The capacity to feel for a person, thing or predicament; usually used pejoratively to define an excess of feeling being bestowed inappropriately on an unworthy object. Thus, false, superficial or inadequately expressed feeling detected in a literary work.

What one person or age will find deeply moving another will label 'sentimental' as a show of false feeling. The novels of SENSIBILITY of the eighteenth century are now considered mawkish in their interest in tender feeling. Fashion has also gone against lingering over the death scenes of children, such as the death of Little Nell in Dickens's *The Old Curiosity Shop* (1840–1), which were highly regarded in the nineteenth century. *See also* PATHOS.

Septet. A seven-line STANZA. *See also* RHYME ROYAL.

Serenade. (It. 'evening') A song or song-like poem to lull a loved one to sleep in the evening. Not as common or clear a LYRIC form as the AUBADE or dawn song.

Sermon. (Lat. 'talk') Extempore or written discourse on a moral or religious subject, as delivered from the pulpit of a church as exhortation or instruction. A significant literary form throughout the history of the Christian Church, producing fine prose works, particularly in the seventeenth and nineteenth centuries.

Sestet. (It. 'sixth') The last six lines of a Petrarchan SONNET which should be separated by rhyme and argument from the preceding eight lines, called the OCTAVE.

Sestina. (It. 'little sixth') A rare and elaborate verse form, Provençal in origin, consisting of six STANZAS, each consisting of six lines of PENTAMETER (usually), plus a three-line envoi (*see* BALLADE). The end words for each stanza are the same, but in a different order from stanza to stanza. Ezra Pound's 'Sestina: Altaforte' (1909) is an example. In this poem each stanza uses, in a different order, the following words at the line endings: 'peace', 'music', 'clash', 'opposing', 'crimson' and 'rejoicing'. The envoi uses 'crimson', 'clash' and 'peace'. The final words of the last and first lines of each successive stanza are the same, as are the final words of the first line of the first stanza and the last line of the last stanza. The form manifests a high degree of order and repetition, but without any chiming rhymes. Here is the pattern of repetition: *abcdef*, *faebdc*, *cfdabe*, *ecfbad*, *deacfb*, *bdfeca*, *eca*.

Setting. The time and place in which a play takes place. Suitable scenery, costume and props should assist the audience to recognise the setting straightaway.

In novels and short stories, the setting, the time and place in which the characters are created, may also be crucially significant, not least because writers may use it to convey information about the mood or temperament of the characters themselves, either symbolically or by adopting the characters' POINT OF VIEW towards it. *See also* ATMOSPHERE.

Sexual symbolism. *See* PSYCHOANALYTIC CRITICISM.

S.F. *See* SCIENCE FICTION.

Shaggy dog story. A joke, the main feature of which is that the story leading up to the climax or punch-line (often weak) is filled with digressive and extraneous details.

Shakespearean sonnet. *See* SONNET.

Shamanism. (Russ., from San. 'religious exercise') The activity of priest-figures in a variety of Asian and Native American cultures, who are thought to be able to dissociate themselves from their bodies and, by communication with spirits, discover the causes and cures of illness and other misfortunes. The shaman has been used as an image of the poet (for example, in relation to Ted Hughes), who has special powers to descend into the world of the unconscious, and bring back truths concealed from normal humankind.

Shibboleth. (Heb. 'ear of corn') The word used by Jephthah to distinguish the Ephraimites, who were unable to pronounce it, from his own men, the Gileadites (Judges 12:4–6). The term now denotes a word or a catch-phrase adopted by any party or group, and regarded by them as being of special significance.

Short metre. A QUATRAIN made up of two lines of TRIMETER (three stresses in each line), one of TETRAMETER (four stresses) and a fourth of trimeter; it is rhymed *abab* or *abcb*, and is usually IAMBIC (*see* METRE for further discussion of these terms). Common in songs and especially hymns, the following example, often sung as a hymn, is from Herbert's 'The Elixir' (1633):

> A man that looks on glass,
> On it may stay his eye;
> Or if he pleaseth, through it pass,
> And then the heav'n espy.

Short story. It is easy to categorise the wide variety of small prose fictions which may be considered as 'short stories', even if it is difficult to define exactly at what point a short story turns into a NOVELLA or NOVEL. Certain features emerge as characteristic of the form: concentration on few characters, often one single character; lack of complicated PLOT and leisurely description; swift DÉNOUEMENT; economical, dense writing, usually organised so as to focus on the exposition of a single incident or character. Most of these qualities are simple consequences of the one defining factor of the short story: that it should be short.

The short story emerged as a form in its own right in the nineteenth century, though many earlier forms, such as the FABLE, LAI, FABLIAU and folktale (*see* FOLKLORE), are clearly its precursors. Amongst many long narratives that could be broken down into stories not unlike the modern short story, the Bible and Chaucer's *The Canterbury Tales* (*c*.1387–92) might be mentioned.

The American Edgar Allan Poe is often designated as the originator of the modern short story. In an 1842 review of stories by the novelist Hawthorne he defined 'the prose tale' as a narrative that can be read at one sitting in less than two hours and which, he said, was concentrated on 'a certain unique or single effect'.

Critics nowadays tend to use TALE to define a story of incidents which concentrates on the outcome of action, as opposed to stories focused on revelation of character.

Most novelists from the mid-nineteenth century onwards have written some short stories. Some writers deserve mention for concentrating on or developing the form. The Russian Chekhov is famed for brilliant studies of character. Tales by the American O. Henry nearly always include a sharp and surprising twist of events at the end. Joyce's *Dubliners* (1914) concentrates on EPIPHANIES, moments of revelation in a character's experience.

Short-Title Catalogue. A bibliography, published by the Bibliographical Society in 1926, consisting of a list of all British books published between 1475 and 1640.

Showing and telling. In any NARRATIVE the narrator can choose between the dramatic portrayal of characters, 'showing' how they behave by simply describing incidents and reporting dialogue without authorial intervention, or 'telling' readers what to think about the characters, exploring their psychology, motivation and morality. Most novelists use both methods of narration, but the distinction still remains a useful method of categorising different authorial styles. *See also* POINT OF VIEW.

Sibilance. (Lat. 'hissing') Sibilants are 's', 'z' and 'sh' sounds, and their repetition is a particular kind of ALLITERATION. In these lines from Keats's *Lamia* (1820) sibilants are mixed with 'f' and 'th' sounds (also part of the larger group called FRICATIVES), moving towards a crescendo of sibilance, which is contrasted with the final non-sibilant phrase:

Left to herself, the serpent now began
To change; her elfin blood in madness ran,
Her mouth foam'd, and the grass, therewith besprent,
Wither'd at dew so sweet and virulent;
Her eyes in torture fix'd, and anguish drear,
Hot, glaz'd, and wide, with lid-lashes all sear,
Flash'd phosphor and sharp sparks, without one cooling tear.

Sick verse. A twentieth-century label for humorous verse which derives its comic effects from the flippant use of cruelty, misfortune, sickness and death; or the term may be used of verse which can be viewed as comic because of its violent excesses, its bad taste or ridiculous lugubriousness. In Hood's poem 'Faithless Nelly Gray' (1826) humour is intentional, and only very mildly 'sick' (in the first sense):

Ben Battle was a soldier bold,
    And used to war's alarms:
But a cannon-ball took off his legs,
    So he laid down his arms!

Examples of the second kind of 'sickness', where a poet's style or subject matter inspires a shiver of disgust mixed with laughter, can be found in Keats's curious poem 'Isabella' (1820), in which the heroine, with the help of her old nurse, digs up the body of her murdered lover, cuts off his head with a blunt knife, and keeps it in a flower pot in which she grows the herb, basil:

In anxious secrecy they took it home,
    And then the prize was all for Isabel:
She calm'd its wild hair with a golden comb,
    And all around each eye's sepulchral cell
Pointed each fringed lash; the smeared loam
    With tears, as chilly as a dripping well,
She drench'd away: and still she comb'd and kept
Sighing all day – and still she kiss'd, and wept.

See also KITSCH.

Sign. (Lat. 'mark') An action, noise, gesture or object that is intended to convey information: the study of the different ways in which signs function is called SEMIOTICS. The American semiotician C.S. Peirce distinguished three main classes of sign: **icon**, **index** and **sign proper** (or 'symbol'). The 'sign proper' refers to the kind of sign which has no connection at all with that which it signifies other than through convention: the use of a red light to mean 'stop' at traffic lights, and green for 'go', is an obvious example. An 'icon' functions by means of similarities with what it signifies (rather than by convention or causality), as, for example, a map shares features with the area which it describes. An 'index' has a direct causal relationship with what it signifies, as, for example, smoke indicates a fire, in a way that is not simply a matter of convention or similarity.

Language itself works through signs, whether written or spoken. In dealing with language, Saussure's distinction between the SIGNIFIER (the sign or word itself) and the signified (what the sign or word means) is another fundamental insight of semiotics. Saussure stressed the arbitrariness of linguistic signs.

Sign proper. *See* SIGN.

Signature. *See* GATHERING.

Signified. *See* SIGNIFIER.

Signifier. A crucial distinction introduced by the Swiss linguistic theorist Ferdinand de Saussure in his *Course in General Linguistics* (1915). Words considered as SIGNS are made up of two elements, the 'signifier' (Fr. *signifiant*), which is the noises, or marks on the paper, which constitute the sign, and the '**signified**' (Fr. *signifié*), which is the meaning to which the sign refers. *See also* SEMIOLOGY.

Silver-fork novel. A mildly derisive term used of a kind of NOVEL common from about 1810 to 1840 (by, amongst others, Susan Ferrier, Benjamin Disraeli and Frances Trollope) which focused particularly on the manners and etiquette of high society.

Simile. (Lat. 'like') A figure of speech equally common in prose and verse: a species of metaphorical writing in which one thing is said to be like another. Similes always contain the words 'like' or 'as'. Whereas METAPHOR merges the two things being compared into a new non-literal conceptual compound, simile keeps the comparison explicit: for example, 'the soldier was like a lion in battle' (simile), as opposed to 'the soldier was a lion in battle' (metaphor). Sometimes this may be a crucial difference, as it allows a writer to draw out a comparison with things that are not apparently alike, as, for example, Donne's famous comparison of lovers' souls and 'stiff twin compasses' in his 'Valediction: Forbidding Mourning ' (1633). Shelley uses a list of similes in his 'Hymn to Intellectual Beauty' (1817) in an attempt to suggest the evanescent quality of this ideal, an unusual use of simile to conjure up an abstraction:

> It visits with inconstant glance
> Each human heart and countenance;
> Like hues and harmonies of evening, –
> Like clouds in starlight widely spread, –
> Like memory of music fled, –
> Like aught that for its grace may be
> Dear, and yet dearer for its mystery.

Here is a straightforward example of a descriptive simile from 'A Painful Case', in Joyce's *Dubliners* (1914):

> Beyond the river he saw a goods train winding out of Kingsbridge Station, like a worm with a fiery head winding through the darkness, obstinately and laboriously.

Sincerity. As with SPONTANEITY, critics in some periods have used the appearance of sincerity in literature as a criterion for its evaluation. That a poem should actually be the honest, direct, personal statement of belief that it may appear to be is usually impossible to prove (and perhaps of no significance), though the appearance of sincerity is an essential aspect of some kinds of literature, especially LYRIC or meditative poetry.

The nineteenth-century critic Arnold praised the 'high seriousness which comes from absolute sincerity' as a test of greatness in literature. In this he followed Romantic critics: De Quincey, for example, complained that Pope 'was incapable of a sincere thought or a sincere emotion'. Modern critics, suspicious of the INTENTIONAL FALLACY, tend to avoid speculating about a writer's state of mind, and stick to explaining the text as it is on the page.

Sjuzet. See NARRATOLOGY.

Skald. (O.N.) A Scandinavian BARD: skalds were poets or singers of the ninth to the eleventh centuries, many of whom are known by name, who composed verse in the ORAL tradition at the courts of the Scandinavian chieftains and kings.

Skeltonics. Verse of the kind written by John Skelton (*c*.1464–1529). Vigorous, colloquial verse, with short lines and plentiful rhymes and ALLITERATION, occasionally lapsing into DOGGEREL or rumbustious insult. The following is from 'Colin Cloute' (1519–20):

> His heed is so fat
> He wottyth never what
> Nor whereof he speketh;
> He cryeth and he creketh,
> He preyeth and he preketh,
> He chydeth and he chatters,
> He prayeth and he patters,
> He clyttreth and he clatters,
> He medleth and he smatters,
> He gloseth and he flatters.

See also FLYTING.

Slang. (Norw. 'offensive language') Colloquial language of a racy, informal kind; sometimes offensive or abusive language. Slang changes its forms quickly; it is the everyday, conversational usage of working people, but it is often elaborate and metaphorical, rather than simple in construction. Different classes of person and age-groups all have their own kind of slang. *See also* CANT, DIALECT, JARGON.

Slant rhyme. Another name for HALF-RHYME, i.e. an inexact RHYME.

Slapstick. Broad comedy with knock-about action, fighting, clowning, people falling over each other, and so on. So called after the stick carried by the Harlequin (in the COMMEDIA DELL'ARTE) which was constructed out of two pieces of wood which slapped together to produce a loud crack when used in mock fights.

Slave narrative. An autobiographical account of slavery by a former slave, not uncommon in American literature both before and after the Civil War. A celebrated example is the *Narrative of the Life of Frederick Douglass, an American Slave* (1845), later rewritten and enlarged twice, as *My Bondage and My Freedom* (1855) and *The Life and Times of Frederick Douglass* (1881).

Socialist realism. A phrase applied to the state-approved art of the Communist bloc. Literature and painting which is dedicated to the depiction of the struggle of the working classes for power as understood in a MARXIST view of history. Many of the twentieth-century Russian writers well known in the West, for instance, Boris Pasternak and Aleksandr Solzhenitsyn, rebelled against this view of art as subservient to IDEOLOGY and to political expediency.

Sociological novel. A NOVEL with a political or sociological argument concentrating on some aspect of society which needs reform, or on the social and economic conditions of its characters. Charles Kingsley's study of the 'sweat-shops' where clothes were made, *Alton Locke* (1850), is an early example.

Also known as **roman à thèse**.

Socratic dialogue. *See* DIALOGUE, EIRON.

Socratic irony. *See* EIRON, IRONY.

Solecism. (Gk. referring to the corruption of the Attic dialect by colonists at Soloi, 'using incorrect syntax') A transgression of the rules of polite grammar (or behaviour). In a literary context a grammatical or lexical error revealing the ignorance of the perpetrator. *See also* MALAPROPISM.

Soliloquy. (Lat. 'to speak alone') A curious but fascinating dramatic convention, which allows a character in a play to speak directly to the audience, as if thinking aloud about motives, feelings and decisions. The psychological depth which the soliloquy gives to Shakespeare's tragedies, particularly *Macbeth* (*c*.1606) and *Hamlet* (*c*.1601), is inestimable. Part of the convention is that a soliloquy provides accurate access to the character's innermost thoughts: we learn more about the character than could ever be gathered from the action of the play alone.

Many of the striking villains of Jacobean tragedy are also addicted to soliloquising about their horrific deeds, for example, Bosola in Webster's *The Duchess of Malfi* (*c*.1613). The soliloquy thus creates special effects of DRAMATIC IRONY, as the audience is given advance warning of the malevolent machinations leading towards the DÉNOUEMENT of the plot.

In later ages of drama the soliloquy becomes much rarer, though some contemporary plays, such as Beckett's *Play* (1963), might be considered as employing a dream-like technique somewhere between soliloquy and STREAM OF CONSCIOUSNESS. *See also* MONOLOGUE.

Son of Ben. *See* TRIBE OF BEN.

Song. A short LYRIC poem intended to be set to music, though often such poems have no musical setting. In English literature the late Elizabethan age, towards the end of the sixteenth century, is considered the great age of song writing, though Sir Thomas Wyatt was an earlier writer of excellent songs. The plays of Shakespeare and his contemporaries contain many examples of songs. Thomas Campion and John Dowland wrote both words and music in several *Books of Ayres*. Campion's 'Rose-cheek'd Laura' (1602) is typical of the genre in its intricate metrical structure and its allusions to the act of singing:

> Rose-cheek'd Laura, come;
> Sing thou smoothly with thy beauty's
> Silent music, either other
> Sweetly gracing.
>
> Lovely forms do flow
> From concent divinely framed;
> Heaven is music, and thy beauty's
> Birth is heavenly.
>
> These dull notes we sing
> Discords need for helps to grace them;
> Only beauty purely loving
> Knows no discord;
>
> But still moves delight,
> Like clear springs renew'd by flowing,
> Ever perfect, ever in them-
> Selves eternal.

Several seventeenth-century poets, including Herrick, Lovelace, Waller and Dryden, continued to produce many exquisite songs. The fashion for MASQUES from about 1620 to 1640 also kept the song alive. On the other hand the decrease in verse drama after the Restoration led to songs becoming less common in the theatre.

Two later poets made notable contributions to their national literatures with their songs: in Scotland, Robert Burns, and, in Ireland, Thomas Moore.

Many modern poets write song-like lyrics and there are many excellent modern popular songs, but according to some scholars and critics, the fusion of poetry and music during the Elizabethan age has never been matched. *See also* BALLAD, FOLKLORE.

Sonnet. (It. 'little song, sound') A LYRIC poem of fixed form: fourteen lines of IAMBIC PENTAMETER rhymed and organised according to several intricate schemes. The fourteen lines can be divided variously into a mixture of OCTAVE (eight lines) and SESTET (six lines) or three QUATRAINS (of four lines each) and a COUPLET. In general the ideas developed in a sonnet accord loosely with these divisions, which are marked by rhyme. Three patterns predominate: (1) The **Petrarchan** or **Italian sonnet**: octave and sestet, rhymed *abbaabba, cdecde* (or *cdcdcd*). (2) The **Spenserian sonnet**: three quatrains and a couplet, rhymed *abab, bcbc, cdcd, ee*. (3) The **Shakespearean** or **English sonnet**: similarly divided, but usually rhymed *abab, cdcd, efef, gg*.

The sonnet form probably originated in Sicily in the thirteenth century. Various medieval Italian poets used it for love poetry, but it was Petrarch who established the sonnet as a major poetic form in his *Canzoniere* (*c*.1335), a sonnet cycle concerning his love for the idealised Laura, which was a major influence on European literature. The form arrived in England, via France, in the sixteenth century: Sir Thomas Wyatt and the Earl of Surrey are credited with first using it. In the last years of that century there were many large collections of sonnets written, including Sir Philip Sidney's *Astrophel and Stella* (*c*.1582) and Spenser's *Amoretti* (1595). Shakespeare's cycle of 154 sonnets was published in 1609.

Love was the dominant theme of sixteenth-century sonneteers. Since then the history of the form has been somewhat disjointed. In the seventeenth century Milton revived the sonnet, but for occasional poems on political and personal themes. The next revival was by the nineteenth-century Romantic poets Wordsworth, Shelley and Keats, who used the sonnet for a variety of different subjects. During the remainder of the nineteenth century and in this century the form has retained its popularity and all-purpose use. George Meredith's *Modern Love* (1862) is a cycle of sixteen-line sonnet-like poems.

As an example of the sonnet form here is Wordsworth's sonnet 'Upon Westminster Bridge, 3 September 1802' (1807):

Earth has not anything to show more fair:
Dull would he be of soul who could pass by
A sight so touching in its majesty:
This City now doth, like a garment, wear
The beauty of the morning; silent, bare,
Ships, towers, domes, theatres, and temples lie
Open unto the fields, and to the sky;

All bright and glittering in the smokeless air.
Never did sun more beautifully steep
In his first splendour, valley, rock or hill;
Ne'er saw I, never felt, a calm so deep!
The river glideth at his own sweet will:
Dear God! the very houses seem asleep;
And all that mighty heart is lying still!

The octave/sestet division is observed by Wordsworth. In general the Petrarchan form has been more popular with poets after the sixteenth century, in spite of the considerable difficulty of finding rhymes in English (compared with Italian). Keats observed that the final couplet of the Shakespearean form was apt to have a trivialising effect.

Sound poetry. A kind of AVANT-GARDE poetry dating from the 1960s onward and intended chiefly for performance at poetry readings: sound poets have abandoned the logic of sentence-structure and meaning, and concentrate on sounds only. Examples include a prolonged attempt to reproduce the sound of a sneeze, or the word 'Napoleon' spoken many times in different ways. Sound poetry is a kind of oral equivalent of CONCRETE POETRY.

Source. A work from which an author has taken images, ideas, or a complete story. Unlike PLAGIARISM, the word usually has no derogatory associations, and merely indicates the way in which many authors make new use of old materials. *See also* ALLUSION, ANALOGUE, INTERTEXTUALITY, PARALLEL.

Spasmodic school. Alexander Smith, Sydney Dobell and P.J. Bailey: a group of minor nineteenth-century poets given their derogatory name by William Aytoun, who satirised their efforts in his mock-tragedy *Firmilian* (1854). Bailey's *Festus* (first published in 1839, and rewritten and enlarged until the fiftieth anniversary edition in 1889 contained 794 pages) was a verse-play of enormous pretension, filled with grand themes (universal salvation) but incoherent, bombastic and considered to have no literary merit. Dobell's chief works were also 'dramatic poems', *The Roman* (1850) and *Balder* (1853). Smith was a Scottish working-class poet who published *A Life Drama* (1853) and *City Poems* (1857), after which he wrote novels. Aytoun intended the term 'spasmodic' to imply uncontrolled verbosity.

Speech act theory. A way of thinking about language initiated by the philosopher John Austin (*How to Do Things with Words*, 1962), and extended by, amongst others, John Searle (*Speech Acts*, 1969). Speech act theory considers the relationships between speakers and listeners and the context of statements, instead of treating statements in isolation and from the point of view solely of their being false or true (as former philosophies of language tended to do). Far from being abstractly logical activities, speaking or writing actually involve a number of different kinds of definable 'speech act', some of which are described below.

A **locutionary act** is an instance of communicative activity. It needs to be defined also as an **illocutionary act**, in terms of the force of the intentions of the speaker, and as a **perlocutionary act** in terms of the effects on the listener. Without such knowledge, a simple statement like 'I will go' could be a promise, an assertion, or a threat. Thus an utterance may be considered both as an illocutionary act and a perlocutionary act. Some utterances are also **performative**, that is to say they are verbal actions that accomplish what is stated: for example, 'I promise' or 'I pronounce you man and wife'.

Speech act theory made some impact in linguistics, but to a lesser extent in examining literature, though its significance as a counter to the INTENTIONAL FALLACY, and in the analysis of IRONY is obvious.

Spenserian sonnet. *See* SONNET.

Spenserian stanza. A form invented by Edmund Spenser for *The Faerie Queene* (1590, 1596). Eight lines of IAMBIC PENTAMETER are followed by one line of IAMBIC HEXAMETER (an ALEXANDRINE), rhymed *ababbcbcc* (*see* METRE for further discussion of these terms):

> The waves come rolling, and the billows roar
> Outrageously, as they enragéd were,
> Or wrathful *Neptune* did them drive before
> His whirling chariot, for exceeding fear:
> For not one puff of wind there did appear,
> That all the three thereat waxed much afraid,
> Unwitting, what such horror strange did rear.
> Eftsoons they saw an hideous host array'd,
> Of huge Sea monsters, such as living sense dismay'd.
>
> (Book II, Canto 12, 22)

Several of the Romantic poets borrowed the form, notably Byron in *Childe Harold's Pilgrimage* (1812, 1816, 1818), Keats in 'The Eve of St Agnes' (1820) and Shelley in *Adonais* (1821). *See also* RHYME, STANZA.

Spondee. (Gk., from 'libation', used in verse to accompany libations) A metrical FOOT consisting of two long syllables or two strong stresses, giving weight to a line. The second line of Donne's 'Batter My Heart' (1633) might be scanned so as to include a spondee:

> Batter/my heart,/three-pers/oned God/, for you
>
> As yet/but knock,/breathe, shine/, and seek/to mend.

Linguisticians argue that in English the level of stress in two consecutive syllables is never entirely the same, and that therefore in stress-based English verse the spondee is technically an impossibility, though in this example the two syllables are separated by a CAESURA. *See also* METRE.

Spontaneity. (Lat. 'of one's own accord') In certain kinds of literature an effect of immediate naturalness (as if a poem, for example, was jotted down at the instant of inspiration) is valued as a proof of authenticity. Japanese HAIKU were apparently composed in spontaneous response to a situation. The American BEAT novelist Jack Kerouac claimed to have written *On the Road* (1957) in one long burst of creative energy.

Poets of the Romantic period prized the inspirational aspect of their craft. Wordsworth called poetry 'the spontaneous overflow of powerful feelings', and Keats remarked that 'poetry should come as naturally as leaves on a tree'. Yet both poets worked hard to master the technical problems of verse writing. And many poems which appear spontaneous are actually the product of years of labour. *See also* SINCERITY.

Spoonerism. Transposition of (usually) the initial consonants of two words, resulting in a different or nonsensical meaning; so called after Rev W.A. Spooner (1844–1930), an Oxford don. Among many examples he is alleged to have said, 'We all know what it is to have a half-warmed fish within us' (meaning 'a half-formed wish').

Spots of time. *See* MOMENT.

Sprezzatura. (It. 'studied carelessness, disdain') The nonchalant grace and ease which characterises the ideal Renaissance gentleman, as described in Castiglione's *Il Libro del Cortegiano* ('The Book of the Courtier'), published in 1528. The courtier had to be a soldier, statesman, athlete, philosopher, artist and conversationalist, but he had to be all these things as if naturally and without effort. *See also* COURTESY BOOK.

Sprung rhythm. A term invented by Gerard Manley Hopkins to explain his own metrical system. The basic idea is to accentuate a certain number of syllables per line very strongly, and not to worry how many weakly stressed 'slack' syllables intervene. Hopkins annotated some of his poems with strong stresses, pauses and 'quivers' (drawn-out syllables), 'slurs' and 'outrides' (extra slack syllables), marked so as to facilitate reading. Sometimes his desired reading seems to go against the natural speech rhythm. The 'Preface' to his *Poems* (1918) explains sprung rhythm in detail.

Squib. (Probably an onomatopoeic word for a firework) In its literary sense a LAMPOON or satirical sketch directed against an institution or individual. A small piece of writing giving vent to irritation or intended to annoy.

Stage. (Lat. *stare*, 'to stand') The space in which actors perform a play, usually a raised platform. In traditional theatres the stage is an area like a room, of which one of the walls has been removed, allowing the audience to see the action therein. An apron stage juts out towards the audience. *See also* PROSCENIUM, THEATRE-IN-THE-ROUND.

Stage direction. Advice about the requisite movements, gestures and appearance of actors incorporated into the text of a play. In early plays such advice was non-existent or minimal, and modern editors have often inserted their own ideas, often helpful but not necessarily reliable, about the exits and entrances of characters.

Many modern writers, for example, Shaw or Tennessee Williams, give elaborate stage directions which may be significant in interpreting the play.

Stanza. (It. 'stopping place, room') A unit of several lines of verse; a repeated group of lines of verse. Much verse is split up into regular stanzas of three, four, five or more lines each. The lines may be of different lengths or the same length; they may be rhymed or not; their METRE may be constant throughout or varied from line to line. What distinguishes the stanza from merely a 'section' of verse is the fact that it is a regular and repeated aspect of the poem's shape. Examples of stanza forms include OTTAVA RIMA, QUATRAIN, RHYME ROYAL, SPENSER-IAN STANZA, TERZA RIMA.

Stereotype. (Gk. 'solid type') The word for a printing-plate cast in some solid form from a piece of printing composed in a movable type. The normal use of the word is now its figurative meaning; a stereotype is a standard, fixed idea or mental impression. The word can be used pejoratively to indicate a CLICHÉ, an ordinary, commonplace perception made dull by constant repetition. Or it may be used neutrally to signify the kind of STOCK CHARACTERS, ideas and situations that are the typical material of literature.

Stichomythia. (Gk. 'lines of talk') Dialogue in alternate lines, often in verse, giving a sense of rapid but controlled argument.

> QUEEN: Hamlet, thou hast thy father much offended.
> HAMLET: Mother, you have my father much offended.
> QUEEN: Come, come, you answer with an idle tongue.
> HAMLET: Go, go, you question with a wicked tongue.
>
> (*Hamlet*, III.4, *c*.1601)

Stock character, stock situation. All genres make use of recurrent elements of PLOT, CHARACTERISATION and situation which indeed may become an integral defining aspect of that genre, part of its CONVENTIONS. Drama is full of stock characters, such as the innocent female heroine, the handsome prince, the crafty servant, the ignorant country bumpkin, the stupid 'gull', the jealous husband, the villain. Stock situations, such as overhearing and misunderstanding conversations, or the final unveiling of a character hitherto disguised, are also common. Novelists and playwrights continually revitalise stock characters and situations: to remark that Falstaff in Shakespeare's *Henry IV*, Parts 1 and 2 (*c*.1597, *c*.1598) or Casaubon in George Eliot's *Middlemarch* (1871–2) are examples of the bragging, deceitful soldier and the dry scholar out of touch with his feelings, two common stock characters, is not to demean either writer's achievement in any way, nor does it imply that either characterisation is unsubtle.

Stock response. Unthinking and uncritical response to a work of art; usually used in a pejorative sense to label a crude reaction unilluminated by sensitivity, intelligence or understanding.

Story. (Lat. 'history', from Gk. 'narrative, knowing by enquiry') Any sequence of events told so as to entertain is a 'story'. But the word now has a specific meaning in NARRATOLOGY: it is the list of events that represent the bare, chronological framework, out of which the narrator builds the PLOT, that organised (but not necessarily chronological) arrangement that is the actual NARRATIVE, full of glimpses backwards and forwards, and other shifts in the treatment of time. Although narratologists have mostly worked with prose fictions, the most obvious contrast between story and plot occurs in drama, in which we often learn the events which have led up to the action depicted in the play by piecing together information provided, usually piecemeal, by the characters. For example, the 'story' of Ibsen's *Ghosts* (1891) begins before the marriage of Captain and Mrs Alving, and continues with the many events surrounding that relationship, but the play actually starts with the return of their adult son from Paris, long after the death of Captain Alving.

This distinction goes by a number of other names in narratological description, taken from Russian or French: the 'story' is also called the *fabula* or *histoire*; the narrative or the act of narration is *discours*, discourse or *sjuzet* (or *sujet*). *See also* DIEGESIS.

Strategy. (Gk. 'a piece of generalship') A jargon word in modern criticism; strategy suggests the overall plan or artifice invented by a writer which dominates the ordering of material or the relationship between the reader and writer. A writer's strategy may be implicit or explicit. The word is used particularly of writers as self-conscious artists manipulating or playing with their readers' expectations and attitudes. Critics also have 'strategies' in the different ways they approach texts.

Stream of consciousness. A common NARRATIVE technique in the modern novel: the attempt to convey all the contents of a character's mind – memory, sense perceptions, feelings, intuitions, thoughts – in relation to the stream of experience as it passes by, often at random. Much of James Joyce's *Ulysses* (1922) is narrated through the stream of consciousness of its hero, Bloom:

> Grafton street gay with housed awnings lured his senses. Muslin prints, silk, dames and dowagers, jingle of harnesses, hoofthuds lowringing in the baking causeway. Thick feet that woman has in the

white stockings. Hope the rain mucks them up on her. Country bred chawbacon. All the beef to the heels were in. Always gives a woman clumsy feet. Molly looks out of plumb.

Stream of consciousness narrative is anticipated in the thought-associations of meditative CONVERSATION POEMS such as Coleridge's 'Frost at Midnight' (1798), and in the narrative methods of writers such as Henry James who tell their story chiefly from the POINT OF VIEW of one individual. Famous exponents, apart from Joyce, are Dorothy Richardson in *Pilgrimage* (1915–38), Proust in *A la recherche du temps perdu* (1913–27) and Virginia Woolf in *To the Lighthouse* (1927). It is commonplace in twentieth-century fiction.

The term 'stream of consciousness' was coined by William James in *The Principles of Psychology* (1890). Some critics distinguish between 'stream of consciousness' and INTERIOR MONOLOGUE, preferring to use the latter to refer to the strict attempt to reproduce the flow of consciousness in a character's mind, without intervention by the author, and perhaps even without grammar or logical development. In practice the terms are usually interchangeable. *See also* ASSOCIATION, FREE INDIRECT STYLE, NOUVELLE VAGUE.

Stress. In any word of more than one syllable, more emphasis or loudness will be given to one of the syllables in comparison with the others; for example, in 'emphasis' and 'loudness' the first syllable bears a stronger stress than the following syllables. In any stretch of English language there will be a discernible rhythm of strongly and weakly stressed syllables. More significant words, such as nouns and verbs, tend to bear strong stress. English verse exploits this fact to create regular patterns of relatively weak and strong stresses which are pleasant to hear. It is often difficult for non-native speakers of English to be certain of how to stress individual words or arrangements of words. Certain words change their meaning or use, according to a change of stress: e.g. convict (*v.*), convict (*n.*). *See also* METRE.

Strophe. (Gk. 'turning') A STANZA of a Greek choral song sung as the CHORUS moved to the right, followed by the **antistrophe**, as they moved to the left, and the **epode**, sung standing still. The Greek poet Pindar modelled his ODES on this symmetrical pattern. 'Strophe' is also loosely used to refer to any metrical unit, such as a stanza or a VERSE PARAGRAPH.

Structural irony. This is found in a literary work which continuously presents more than one POINT OF VIEW because of some element in its structure, such as a naïve hero or fallible narrator like Gulliver in Swift's *Gulliver's Travels* (1726), who persistently adopts the ridiculous local perspectives of all the countries which he visits. *See also* IRONY, NARRATIVE.

Structuralism, structuralist criticism. Structuralism examines aspects of human society, including language, literature and social institutions, as integrated structures or systems in which the parts have no real existence on their own, but only derive meaning and significance from their place within the system. For example, the basic unit of meaning in language, the PHONEME, is seen to derive its meaning not from any inherent qualities in itself, but because of its DIFFERENCE from other sounds. The task of the structuralist critic or scholar is to reveal the implicit rules of the systems in which cultural phenomena take place; this allows a degree of theorising which PRAGMATIC and DESCRIPTIVE CRITICISM and anthropology had not allowed, concentrating as they did on exploring the nature of individual phenomena.

Structuralist critics often explore individual works of literature by analysing them in terms of linguistic concepts, like the phoneme or MORPHEME, or as if the structure of a work resembled the SYNTAX of a sentence. Others concentrate on examining the conventions and expectations which a knowledgeable reader understands implicitly when reading the work (literary COMPETENCE), with the ultimate aim of building up a kind of grammar or ground-plan of the whole system of literature and its place in society.

Certain aspects of structuralist thought run counter to ordinary notions about the relationship between language, the writer and the reader. Writing (ÉCRITURE) is conceived as an activity governed solely by its own CODES and conventions, and these have no reference to any reality beyond or outside the system. Many structuralists, notably the French critic Roland Barthes, deny that there is any communication between author and reader: the PERSONA projected by the writer is merely a literary construction, and reading itself is merely an impersonal 'making sense' of the literary conventions within the system. Barthes admires the capacity of MODERNIST literature to expose the conventions which govern literature by breaking away from them, thereby revealing also the nature of language and the conventions through which we perceive society itself. Structuralism has now been superseded by the even more radical POST-STRUCTURALIST theories of Jacques Derrida known as DECONSTRUCTION.

The works of Roland Barthes constitute the classics of structuralist criticism; they include *Writing Degree Zero* (1967), *S/Z* (1970) and *The Pleasure of the Text* (1975). Jonathan Culler's *Structuralist Poetics* (1975) is a more general introduction to the subject. *See also* AUTHOR, FORMALISM.

Structure. (From Lat. 'to build') The overall principle of organisation in a work of literature. Literature may be shaped by many different factors, such as: NARRATIVE; PLOT; repeated IMAGES, SYMBOLS or MOTIFS; logical argument. A work's structure may be dependent on any of these, in any combination. Indeed any element of language may be used to create a sense of structure, of meaningful shape or PATTERN in literature. To some extent 'structure' was a jargon word of the NEW CRITICS, a replacement for the word FORM which had been made vague by constant redefinition.

'Structure' is also used by linguists to replace the word 'grammar'. They analyse the 'structure' of a single sentence, the way it is built up, or the 'structure' of a whole language. A language can be seen as a structure which contains and creates a particular way of looking at the world, by its vocabulary, and even by its grammatical forms. Examination of the relationship between a writer, readers, the work of art, language and society also gives rise to a 'structure' which may impose certain conditions on the nature of literature and culture. The study of 'structures' in this sense of the word has led to the modern phenomenon of STRUCTURALISM.

Sturm und Drang. (Ger. 'storm and stress') A late eighteenth-century revolutionary German literary movement, which included the early writings of Goethe and Schiller. Friedrich Klinger's play *Der Wirrwarr* (1776), re-titled *Sturm und Drang*, gave its name to the movement, which cultivated inspiration and passion rather than Classical DECORUM and reason. *See also* GOTHIC NOVEL, ROMANTICISM, SENSIBILITY.

Style. (Lat. 'writing instrument') The characteristic manner in which a writer expresses him- or herself, or the particular manner of an individual literary work. Each writer's style is unique, but it may be a combination of many different factors, such as typical syntactical structures, a favourite or distinctive vocabulary, kinds of imagery, attitude to subject matter, kind of subject matter, and so on. Criticism often consists of an attempt to describe a writer's style by analysis of SYNTAX, TONE, IMAGERY, POINT OF VIEW and, indeed, every characteristic linguistic feature.

Simple judgments of style are often cast in the form of metaphors, such as smooth, rough, high or low, etc. The purpose of a work of art may dictate a certain style, such as expository, emotive, journalistic, poetic. Individual writers or groups of writers have also given their names to identifiable styles: METAPHYSICAL, AUGUSTAN, Johnsonian, Dickensian, etc. Because in each literary work the combination of linguistic factors which characterise a writer's style is different, it is often a difficult task to define a particular style.

Stylistics. The exact analysis or description of STYLE in writing and speech, using a specialised vocabulary developed in the field of linguistics.

Stylometrics. The computer-aided analysis of STYLE. Recurrent patterns, often involving apparently insignificant words, or syntactical structures, are counted, in a passage known to be by a particular writer, so that a detailed map of characteristic word-use, a kind of stylistic 'fingerprint', can be drawn up, against which doubtful passages can be tested. Stylometrics is used in trying to decide whether parts of works (the Bible and Shakespeare, for example) are INTERPOLATIONS by different authors. The technique is also used by the police to trace the authorship of anonymous letters.

Subgenre. A definable category of writing which is part of a large GENRE. For example, the SONNET and ODE are both subgenres within the wide generic grouping of the LYRIC.

Subject. (Lat. 'throw under') In some modern critical analysis 'subject' is used in a specialised way to signify the individual as understood in Western capitalist society. Individuals are 'subjective' or possess subjectivity, in the sense of apparently feeling and thinking freely and independently, but they are also 'subjected', in the sense of being in abeyance to authority: they are politically 'subject'. Thus adherents of the MARXIST philosopher Althusser discuss the way in which certain kinds of DISCOURSE or IDEOLOGY 'construct' or 'address' the subject, and 'construct people as subjects'. This ambiguity perceived within the word 'subject' and its derivations is unravelled to suggest that the vaunted freedom of capitalist culture is illusory. *See also* INTERPELLATION.

Subjective. (Lat. 'thrown under') Often used in contrast to '**objective**' to distinguish two methods of perception, meaning the private and personal point of view, as opposed to the explicit, verifiable and agreed objective treatment of things. The subjective is the inner, biased, visionary world, rather than the outer 'real' world. Various critics, notably R. Langbaum in *The Poetry of Experience* (1957), have argued that such a distinction, though apparently clear and helpful, in fact represents an oversimplification of the way literature apprehends the world, and that all writing, whatever its appearance, is neither simply objective nor subjective, but is in fact a meeting point between the outer and inner worlds.

Sublimation. *See* PSYCHOANALYTIC CRITICISM.

Sublime. (Lat. 'high, exalted') That which is most dignified, grand and powerfully emotive in literature. A Greek critical work of the first century defines sublimity in literature; formerly it was thought to be by Longinus, the first-century rhetorician, and it is still commonly referred to as 'Longinus on the Sublime'. Its ideas were much admired and discussed by eighteenth-century writers. Edmund Burke's *Philosophical Enquiry into the Origin of Our Ideas on the Sublime and Beautiful* (1757) is an aesthetic and psychological theory of the sublime which influenced the German philosopher Kant. Aspirations towards sublimity suggest an affective view of literature. *See also* AFFECTIVE FALLACY.

Subplot. A subsidiary ACTION running parallel with the main PLOT of a play or novel. The plot and subplot may be almost separate in their development, but more often they interpenetrate, and the subplot provides parallels and contrasts with the main plot. A famous example is the way the fortunes of Gloucester and his two sons reflect the plight of Lear and his daughters in Shakespeare's *King Lear* (*c*.1605). Subplots are a very common feature of Elizabethan and Jacobean drama.

Substitution. (Lat. 'setting up in place of') In prosody the replacement of one kind of metrical FOOT by another. Perhaps the commonest example is the use of a TROCHEE at the start of an IAMBIC line:

> Like as/the waves/make towards/the pebb/led shore
> So do/our min/utes has/ten to /their end.

(Shakespeare, Sonnet 60, 1609)

One way of scanning the first line would be to see the third foot as an ANAPAEST, which in conjunction with the effect of the opening trochee followed by an iamb, mimics the sound of waves on the shore.

AUGUSTAN poets developed elaborate rules to allow substitution of feet, but in most English verse it is common and an essential means of creating the sense of repetition-with-variation that gives pleasure to the listener. *See* METRE for further discussion of these terms.

Subtext. A word for the situation that lies behind the behaviour of characters in a play, but to which no one refers explicitly and which may never be fully explained. Many of the plays of Harold Pinter revolve around this kind of situation: the audience has to work out the aims and intentions of the characters from indirect references and nuances. It may be, as for example in *Old Times* (1971), that not even the characters themselves understand the struggle for power in which they are participating.

The word can also be used to refer to any implicit assumptions or situation that can be discerned behind the manifest and explicit plot of a narrative or poem. 'Subtext' was something of a vogue word of the 1970s and 1980s, until taken over by the concept of the HIDDEN AGENDA.

Subversion. (Lat. 'turning below, overturning') The attacking and under-mining of some texts by other texts. Literature has often been perceived as divisible into different strands, with particular kinds of writing regarded as more valuable and meritorious than others. A collection of 'great works', the CANON, is established. Some critics argue that this canon is liable to express the values of the ruling classes, and therefore tends to exclude other kinds of writing, especially those that are unsympathetic to the present authority. Texts that attack the prevailing values of 'canonical' literature are labelled 'subversive', in so far as they seek to overturn the 'hegemonic' power of the traditional texts. In this way FEMINIST writing can be seen as subverting the PHALLOCENTRIC literary tradition, or African novels can be read as subverting Eurocentric attitudes to fiction.

On the other hand, literary history often suggests that the AVANT-GARDE and 'subversive' is quickly absorbed and can soon become canonical in its own right. The substitution of a traditional canon by a new canon of subversive works still subscribes to a model of literature as composed of different factions in competition with each other, a model which may in itself be distorted.

Succès d'estime. (Fr. 'success in esteem') A work praised by the critics is so described, usually to suggest some compensation for its lack of commercial success.

Succès de scandale. (Fr. 'success of scandal') A work successful in spite of (or perhaps by means of) some scandal related to its contents, its author, or the circumstances of its publication.

Suggestion. (Lat. 'bringing up') The ideas and meanings of language other than its bare literal meaning. Whereas the ASSOCIATIONS inherent in a word or phrase should be demonstrable, its evocative, suggestive qualities may be more insubstantial, perhaps even dependent on personal reaction. *See also* CONNOTATION, DENOTATION, LITERAL LANGUAGE, REFERENTIAL LANGUAGE.

Sujet. The French version of Russian *sjuzet*. *See* NARRATOLOGY.

Summary. (Lat. 'pertaining to the most important points') A short account or plan of the main features of a work.

Superego. *See* PSYCHOANALYTIC CRITICISM.

Supplement. That which supplies a deficiency; often used of extra, special editions of periodicals.

In *Of Grammatology* (1967) Derrida points out that if a body of knowledge (for example, a dictionary) requires a supplement, this suggests a lack or absence in what had been formerly perceived as complete. All systems and descriptions, not least the interpretation of texts, are capable of being supplemented. The concept of supplementarity thus provides another way of casting doubt on assumptions about the sufficiency and stability of meaning in language, suggesting that INTERPRETATION, for example, is liable to continual qualification, and that no interpretation can be complete, absolute and authoritative. *See also* DECONSTRUCTION.

Surface structure. *See* DEEP STRUCTURE.

Surrealism. (Fr. 'beyond realism') An artistic and literary movement starting in France in the 1920s which drew upon some of the concepts of Freudian psychology. The poet André Breton drew up his *Manifeste du surréalisme* in 1924.

Surrealism was anti-rational and anti-realist. It advocated the liberation of the mind from logic: instead, art should grow out of confrontation with the unconscious mind. Dreams, hallucinating states, AUTOMATIC WRITING, and even nonsense are the inspiration and subject matter of art.

Especially in the art world, surrealism has been widely if diffusely influential. In Britain, the first International Exhibition of Surrealism in 1936 resulted in the poetry of the so-called NEW APOCALYPSE of the 1940s. Several modern American writers have also experimented with surrealism (notably Edward Albee in the drama, and John Ashbery in poetry). Here is a short extract from a surrealist poem by David Gascoyne:

> These scattered tresses make the passers-by turn pale
> then hurry home to disinfect their wells
> They glitter faintly like the dust of poisoned stars
> and hypnotize the gaze of the last birds still to remain
> in that seaside-town as black as a burnt cake
> where the dead are sitting propped-up in the windows robed in
>   flags
> of all the nations – where the homeless night
> is kept awake by Autumn's chill aurora in the sky
> and silence lolls like smoke along the disused harbour-quays . . .
>   ('Phantasmagoria', 1942)

See also ALEATORY, DADA, PSYCHOANALYTIC CRITICISM.

Suspense. (Lat. 'hung up') The condition of wanting to know what will happen or expecting something to happen in a NARRATIVE, especially in a narrative of swift action.

Suspension of disbelief, Willing. *See* ILLUSION.

Syllabic verse. Verse written not in the pattern of stresses per line usual in English poetry, but simply according to a count of syllables per line. The American poet Marianne Moore was noted for her unusual syllabic verse STANZAS, often made of lines of markedly uneven length; here is the first stanza of 'Critics and Connoisseurs' (1935):

> There is a great amount of poetry in unconscious
>   fastidiousness. Certain Ming
>   products, imperial floor-coverings of coach-
> wheel yellow, are well enough in their way but I have seen
>   [something
>   that I like better – a
>   mere childish attempt to make an imperfectly ballasted
>   [animal stand up,
>   similar determination to make a pup
>   eat his meat from the plate.

The next three stanzas follow (not exactly) the same syllable count per line (14/8/12/16/6/20/12/6). Such patterns are difficult to discern by ear, but give the poem a sense of precision and exactitude.

Syllable. (Gk. 'take together') Sounds in language uttered with a single effort of articulation. Easy to define in practice but not in theory: enunciation of syllables is regulated by breath-control in the chest. 'Asp' is a monosyllable; 'aspic' is two syllables; 'aspersion' is three syllables; 'aspidistra' is four syllables.

Syllepsis. (Gk. 'taking together') Another word for ZEUGMA.

Syllogism. (Gk. 'reckoning together') A method of argument in logic, in the form of two propositions called premisses which allow a third proposition to be made, the conclusion: (1) All Scotsmen wear kilts. (2) Angus is a Scotsman. (3) Therefore Angus wears a kilt. Needless to say the truth of the conclusion is entirely dependent on the truth of the premisses.

Symbol. (Gk. 'mark, sign, token', originally 'put together') A symbol is something which represents something else (often an idea or quality) by analogy or association. Thus white, lion and rose commonly symbolise or represent innocence, courage and beauty. Such symbols exist by convention and tradition. A serpent may stand for evil or wisdom, according to different conventions. Writers use these conventional symbols, but also they invent and create their own.

A symbol may be seen as a species of METAPHOR in which the exact subject of the metaphor is not made explicit, and may even be mysterious. A whole poem may be a symbol of this kind. Blake's 'The Sick Rose' (1794) is typical:

> O Rose, thou art sick!
> The invisible worm,
> That flies in the night,
> In the howling storm,
>
> Has found out thy bed
> Of crimson joy,
> And his dark secret love
> Does thy life destroy.

The sickness of the rose, along with the suggestiveness of 'dark secret love' and 'bed/Of crimson joy' prevent a simple interpretation of the rose in its common role as a symbol of beauty destroyed by time. Sexuality, secrecy and guilt all seem drawn in by the implications of these words. A variety of readings is possible, and the emotional situation which the poem defines is subtle and complicated. In this a symbol is different from ALLEGORY, which draws out a series of clear relationships between an object or person and the abstractions for which they stand, as if, for example, Blake had written explicitly of the Worm of Sexuality destroying the Rose of Beauty. In symbolic writing the symbol itself (the vehicle (*see* TENOR AND VEHICLE) of the metaphor) is dwelt upon as the subject matter for the poem: meaning lies beyond it.

For some writers the whole of the outside world becomes a source of symbols for their states of feeling: Coleridge writes in his notebook in 1805:

> In looking at objects of Nature while I am thinking, as at yonder moon dim-gleaming through the dewy window-pane, I seem rather to be seeking, as it were *asking* for, a symbolic language for something within me that already and for ever exists, than observing anything new. Even when that latter is the case, yet still I have always an obscure feeling as if that new phenomena were the dim awakening of a forgotten or hidden truth of my inner nature. It is still interesting as a word – a symbol.

Clearly even natural description in Coleridge's poetry is liable to have symbolic overtones. This is true of all Romantic poetry and much nineteenth- and twentieth-century poetry.

Some writers return almost obsessively to the same subjects or images from poem to poem, so that gradually these recurrent MOTIFS gain special symbolic weight and depth of meaning. In the poetry of W.B. Yeats, objects, such as trees, birds, a winding staircase, and a tower, gather symbolic significances unique to Yeats but readily understood.

Novelists also commonly use symbols. The particular objects, scenes or episodes that come to stand for the major themes of the work may be repeated or mirrored in many different ways so as to give the work a symbolic structure. *See also* ARCHETYPE, METONYMY, PATHETIC FALLACY, SYNECDOCHE.

Symbolism, Symbolist Movement. Several English Romantics, notably Blake and Shelley, used both conventional and private SYMBOLS persistently in their poetry, and they might loosely be called symbolist poets. But the Symbolist Movement usually refers to French poets of the second half of the nineteenth century (Baudelaire, Rimbaud, Verlaine, Mallarmé and Paul Valéry), whose poems exploit the mysterious suggestiveness of private symbols; they concentrated on achieving a musical quality in their verse and believed that through blurring the senses and mixing images they depicted a higher reality. A Symbolist manifesto was published by Jean Moréas in 1886.

Many modern American and British poets, such as Yeats, Pound, Eliot, Stevens and Hart Crane, were deeply influenced by French symbolism, and many of the most famous works of the MODERNIST movement, such as Eliot's *The Waste Land* (1922) and Joyce's *Ulysses* (1922), are symbolist in technique. *See also* CORRESPONDANCES.

Sympathy. (Gk. 'suffering together') Often used in literary discussion to express the reader's feelings towards a character in a book: a writer may be said to manipulate the reader's sympathies by the depiction of a good or bad character.

Synaeresis. (Gk. 'seizing together') A contraction to preserve the METRE of a line, in which two vowels are run together, as in 'th'end'.

Synaesthesia. (Gk. 'feel together') The description of a sense impression in terms more appropriate to a different sense; the mixing of sense impressions in order to create a particular kind of METAPHOR. Not uncommon in poets who dwell on sensuousness, like Keats. The following example from his 'Ode to a Nightingale' (1820) describes the taste of wine in terms of colour, action, song, sensation and feeling:

> O, for a draught of vintage . . .
> Tasting of Flora and the country green,
> Dance, and Provençal song, and sunburnt mirth!

Synchronic. (Gk. 'same time') The treatment of a subject at a single moment in time, rather than in terms of its historical development (which is a DIACHRONIC approach). A term invented by Saussure to refer to the study of a language system.

Syncreticity, syncretism. (Gk. 'alliance, as between Cretan towns') The merging together of different religions, beliefs and cultures into a single, hybrid system. As a specifically literary term, syncretism refers to the way in which different cultures and forms can be mixed in a literary text. Early novels written in Bengali, or an African language, for example, in which there was no prior tradition of novel-writing, illustrate the syncretic use of a distinctively European literary form for the description of a non-European society, and may incorporate oral story-telling techniques or poetic language. Some critics argue that even the most sophisticated of English-language novels that contain or describe aspects of traditional non-European literature and society, such as Achebe's *Things Fall Apart* (1958) (which is full of the 'palm-oil' of Ibo proverbs), should still be treated as examples of syncreticity.

Synecdoche. (Gk. 'taking up with, interpreting together') A figure of speech in which a part is used to describe the whole of something, or vice versa. Common in everyday speech, as in the use of the word 'hand' in the phrase 'all hands on deck' to refer to sailors. Common also in poetry, as a kind of METAPHOR. *See also* METONYMY.

Synonym. (Gk. 'similar name') A word with a meaning identical to that of another word.

Synopsis. (Gk. 'view together') A very short plan or description of the argument of a longer work.

Syntagmatic. *See* PARADIGM.

Syntax. (Gk. 'arrangement') The arrangement of words in their appropriate forms and proper order, in order to achieve meaning.

Synthesis. (Gk. 'place together') In Hegelian DIALECTIC the synthesis grows out of the opposition between THESIS and ANTITHESIS, and then becomes itself a new thesis, for the process to begin again.

Coleridge in Chapter 14 of *Biographia Literaria* (1817) discusses the IMAGINATION as a 'synthetic and magical power' which blends, fuses and reconciles opposite and discordant qualities.

In general a synthesis is a new compound idea or object which is created by the bringing together of two elements.

T

Table talk. A collection of sayings and record of the conversational opinions of a famous person: a casual form of literary BIOGRAPHY. A celebrated early example in English literature is the Scottish poet William Drummond's record of Ben Jonson's visit to him in 1618. There was a vogue for table talk in the eighteenth century, especially in France. *See also* ANECDOTE, APHORISM, APOPHTHEGM, OBITER DICTA.

Tableau. (Fr. 'picture painted on wood') A picture; especially a pictorial grouping of persons in a drama. A *tableau vivant* is a living picture, a silent and motionless group of persons arranged so as to represent a dramatic or melodramatic scene. A set piece describing such a picture – like a grouping of people in a novel or poem – would also be called a tableau. *See also* VIGNETTE.

Tale. (O.E. 'list', from O.N. 'talk, number') A short NARRATIVE in prose or verse. It may be distinguished from the SHORT STORY because of its concentration on incident and action rather than character and atmosphere. A tale is less self-consciously literary than a short story, closer perhaps to the oral origins of literature, whereas the short story develops after the NOVEL and strives for a special kind of focus and intensity.

Tall story. An obviously exaggerated and unlikely tale. Famous examples are found in the *Narrative of Baron Munchausen's Marvellous Travels* (1785) by Rudolf Erich Raspe.

Tanka. (Jap. 'short verse') A traditional Japanese lyric form, consisting of thirty-one syllables in lines of 5/7/5/7/7 syllables. *See also* HAIKU.

Taste. (Lat. 'appraise') During the eighteenth century 'taste' meant 'critical and aesthetic judgment', but since then the word has been demoted, and refers now to the vagaries of fashionable or personal choice, as opposed to presumed or accepted standards of excellence. 'Good and bad taste' imply what is in or out of conformity with the self-conscious politeness of a social élite.

Tautology. (Gk. 'saying the same') The unnecessary repetition of ideas in different words or phrases: 'The enormous, elephantine man was very large', or 'I myself personally think'.

Taxonomy. (Gk. 'ordering, arrangement') The scientific classification of a subject. One task of criticism is the taxonomy of literature, understanding the way it can be divided into different categories, such as historical movements, genres, modes of writing, and so on, so that it can be properly understood in terms of its variety and range.

Technique. (Gk. 'art, craft') The method, craft and skill of writing. Many literary terms are attempts to categorise and detail the innumerable methods by which writers create patterns, meanings and effects out of language. Every element in a literary work, other than its theme or message, is organised according to technical considerations. Often a belief in the naturalness or spontaneity of literary utterance leads to 'technique' becoming a pejorative term, suggesting artificial and decorative effects. But though some FIGURES OF SPEECH are merely decorative, it is false to divide technique and meaning: there can be no utterance, no meaning of any kind, without technique of some sort, however rudimentary or invisible. For example, it would be absurd to say that a poet 'uses imagery' in a particular poem (making 'imagery' sound like an additional, occasional device available to the poet) when that poem consists chiefly of its own imagery.

Teleology. (Gk. 'end-study'). The perception of phenomena in terms of their ultimate purposes and functions, suggesting that things are not simply mechanistically related or contingent, but part of some overall design. To adopt a teleological view of the universe is to see it as filled with evidence of design, and possibly therefore of the existence of a Designer.

Interpretation of a text can be said to be based on the assumption of a teleology; in other words, interpretation is based on the belief that the parts of the text function coherently towards some final and comprehensible end-purpose.

Telling. *See* SHOWING AND TELLING.

Tenor and vehicle. I.A. Richards in *The Philosophy of Rhetoric* (1936) introduced these two words to distinguish the components of a META-PHOR. 'Tenor' is the subject of the metaphor; 'vehicle' is the metaphoric word itself. Thus in 'the deep, wide sea of Misery', 'Misery' is the tenor and 'the deep, wide sea' the vehicle.

Tension. (Lat. 'straining') A sometimes vague but much used critical metaphor to describe the effect of paradoxical or difficult relationships between words, feelings and ideas, especially in poetry. The American poet Allen Tate gave special significance to the word in his essay 'Tension in Poetry' in *On the Limits of Poetry* (1948). By 'tension' Tate meant a running together of the technical logical terms 'intension' and 'extension', meaning (roughly) the abstract attributes (the metaphorical meaning) and the particular reference (literal meaning) of a word. For the NEW CRITICS, to experience the 'tension' of a poem was to respond to all the available meanings and see how they are inter-related and harmonised; specially valued were poems which resolved and contained all kinds of apparent opposites.

Tercet. (It. 'little third') In verse, a STANZA, or section, of three lines.

Terza rima. (It. 'third rhyme') A RHYME SCHEME as used by Dante in his *Divine Comedy* (*c*.1304–21). TERCETS are interlocked in the following manner: *aba, bcb, cdc,* and so on. The form is not uncommon in English poetry: Shelley, for example, uses it in *The Triumph of Life* (1824) and, with a final COUPLET after every four tercets making in effect a repeated SONNET form, in 'Ode to the West Wind' (1820).

As an example of *terza rima,* showing the lacing together of the STANZAS by the rhyme scheme, here are the first four tercets of Browning's 'The Statue and the Bust' (1855)

> There's a palace in Florence, the world knows well,
> And a statue watches it from the square,
> And this story of both do the townsmen tell.
>
> Ages ago, a lady there,
> At the farthest window facing the East
> Asked, 'Who rides by with the royal air?'
>
> The bridesmaids' prattle around her ceased;
> She leaned forth, one on either hand;
> They saw how the blush of the bride increased –
>
> They felt by its beats her heart expand –
> As one at each ear and both in a breath
> Whispered, 'The Grand-Duke Ferdinand.'

Tetralogy. (Gk. 'four speeches') A series of four related plays or novels. Shakespeare's HISTORY PLAYS (listed here in the order in which they were written) are sometimes considered as forming two tetralogies: (a) *Henry VI,* Parts 1, 2 and 3, and *Richard III* (1590–3) and (b) *Richard II, Henry IV,* Parts 1 and 2, and *Henry V* (1595–9).

Tetrameter. (Gk. 'four measures') In prosody a line of four feet. IAMBIC and TROCHAIC tetrameter are common in all ages of English verse (*see* METRE for further discussion of these terms). Christina Rossetti's 'A Birthday' (1862) provides an example of iambic tetrameter:

> My heart is like a singing bird
>   Whose nest is in a watered shoot;
> My heart is like an apple tree
>   Whose boughs are bent with thickset fruit;
> My heart is like a rainbow shell
>   That paddles in a halcyon sea;
> My heart is gladder than all these
>   Because my love is come to me.

Text. (Med. Lat. 'version', from Lat. 'tissue, composition') The actual wording of a passage, rather than any paraphrase made thereof; a passage of the Scriptures, chosen as the subject of a sermon; a work of literature ready, as it were, to be analysed and discussed by a literary critic; any piece of writing which is the subject of critical examination and discussion. *See also* DISCOURSE, ÉCRITURE, LITERARY THEORY, PRACTICAL CRITICISM.

Textual criticism. The study of the various printed versions of a literary work with the aim of discovering what the author actually wrote. Many of Shakespeare's plays, for example, exist in widely differing forms, and the texts of the plays in normal use are the result of many years of scholarly research. *See also* BIBLIOGRAPHY, FOLIO, QUARTO.

Texture. The surface qualities of the words in a passage, considered apart from their meaning, can be called their texture: 'texture' may depend on the kinds of words used (harsh, violent, peaceful, etc.) or on the sounds of the words themselves. 'Texture' is often used to introduce a critical metaphor to describe the atmosphere or effect of a piece of writing: a line of poetry might thus be called 'fragile' or 'energetic' or 'liquid', and so on. *See also* IMPRESSIONISTIC CRITICISM, STYLE, TONE.

Theatre-in-the-round. Theatre arranged so as to allow the audience to surround the actors on all sides (instead of the normal confrontation between players and audience). Not uncommon in the experimental theatre during this century; it is probable that some of the MYSTERY PLAYS of the Middle Ages were also performed in this way, a cart providing an impromptu stage.

Theatre of cruelty. The French playwright Antonin Artaud argued in *Le Théâtre et son double* (1938) that plays should shock the audience in order to release subconscious truths. These theories gave rise to a theatre in which vivid lighting effects, mime, and sensational, even horrific action and spectacle predominated. The German playwright Peter Weiss's *Marat/Sade* (1964) is a well-known example.

Theatre of the Absurd. *See* ABSURD.

Thematic imagery. *See* IMAGERY.

Theme. (Gk. 'proposition, deposit') The abstract subject of a work; its central idea or ideas, which may or may not be explicit or obvious. A text may contain several themes or thematic interests. For example, it can be argued that Shakespeare's *King Lear* (*c*.1605) touches upon all the following themes: rashness, evil, the nature of truth, appearance and reality, kinship, sexuality, ingratitude, selfishness, and so on.

Thesaurus. (Gk. 'treasure') A list of words arranged according to their meanings rather than alphabetically as in a dictionary. *Roget's Thesaurus of English Words and Phrases*, first published in 1852, is a famous example.

Thesis. (Gk. 'placing') This has several meanings with regard to literature. (1) A scholarly or critical study written for the purposes of achieving a degree in higher education. (2) The basic argument of a literary work. (3) A preposition as in logic, to be countered by its ANTITHESIS.

Thesis novel. *See* ROMAN À THÈSE.

Third-person narrative. A way of telling a story about people who are described in the third person ('he', 'she' or 'they'), by a narrator who does not write as 'I', but as an unseen observer of events. The opening paragraph of a story by Katherine Mansfield, 'Life of Ma Parker' (1922), provides an example:

> When the literary gentleman, whose flat old Ma Parker cleaned every Tuesday, opened the door to her that morning, he asked after her grandson. Ma Parker stood on the doormat inside the dark little hall, and she stretched out her hand to help her gentleman shut the door before she replied. 'We buried 'im yesterday, sir,' she said quietly.

See also NARRATIVE.

Threnody. (Gk. 'wailing ode') A lamentation, especially on someone's death. *See also* ELEGY.

Thriller. A type of modern novel intended for a popular audience, with the emphasis on speedy development of the action and suspense. Crime and espionage form the typical subject matter. Many thrillers, such as those of John Buchan, Eric Ambler and John le Carré, are extremely well written, with intricate plots and taut description. But the genre also includes many books written only for sensational effect.

Tone. As well as representing the IMAGERY and argument of a literary work the words the author chooses may also impart a sense of a particular manner or mood in which a passage or sentence should be read: angrily, imploringly, monotonously, suspiciously, pompously, wittily, and so on through the whole range of behaviour. Tone is thus a critical concept which implies that literature is like speech, requiring a speaker and a listener, tone being the attitude adopted by the speaker to the listener, gathered and understood from the kind of syntax and vocabulary used. For the full understanding of a work it is essential to recognise its tone or range of tones, however difficult that may be, especially for non-native speakers of English. IRONY, for example, in which an author does not mean what he or she says, may pass unnoticed if the tone of a passage is misunderstood.

Topical. (Gk. *topos*, 'place') Because of its derivation from the Greek word for 'common-place' (as well as 'place') this word has a variety of possible meanings to do with 'topic', the argument or subject for discussion of a piece of writing or speech. But most of these meanings have fallen into disuse. The word is now commonly used to refer to literature which deals with contemporary current affairs. A 'topical' play is concerned with the subjects everyone is presently discussing (today's commonplace 'topic').

Topographical poetry. A minor tradition of poems written about specific places: the poet presents general reflections in relation to a description of the surrounding countryside. Sir John Denham's 'Cooper's Hill' (1642) is an early model for the form. Gray's 'Elegy Written in a Country Churchyard' (1751) and Wordsworth's 'Tintern Abbey' (1798) are two famous examples of this genre.

Topos. (Gk. 'place') A common and recurrent MOTIF in literature, such as the UBI SUNT or CARPE DIEM themes in LYRIC poetry.

Touchstone. A kind of stone used for detecting the purity of gold. Matthew Arnold in 'The Study of Poetry' (1880) uses the term to denote short passages of literary excellence, which can be used to test the true worth of other literary works, a procedure he considered more objective than merely valuing a work on personal or historical grounds.

Tract. (Lat. 'treatment') A short PAMPHLET or ESSAY on a controversial subject, usually political or religious.

Tractarian Movement. *See* OXFORD MOVEMENT.

Tradition. (Lat. 'hand over, deliver') Implicit and explicit beliefs concerning the practice and function of literature are handed down within every society, and these constitute that society's literary tradition. A writer may seek to emulate or rebut that which is regarded as the dominant literary tradition of the time: either way the resulting work will be absorbed into the tradition. T.S. Eliot's influential essay 'Tradition and the Individual Talent' (1919) sought to revivify a sense of the continuity of the European literary tradition. Critics may seek to identify specific trends and movements in literature and call them traditions. F.R. Leavis's *The Great Tradition* (1948) sought to demonstrate the coherent development of the nineteenth-century British novel. *See also* CLASSICISM, INFLUENCE, INTERTEXTUALITY, NEOCLASSICISM.

Tragedy. (Gk. 'goat song') Possibly the most homogeneous and easily recognised genre in literature, and certainly one of the most discussed. Basically a tragedy traces the career and downfall of an individual, and shows in this downfall both the capacities and the limitations of human life. The PROTAGONIST may be superhuman, a monarch or, in the modern age, an ordinary person. It is possible to imagine a tragic action involving a group of people, but unless they were seen as in some way outside the rest of society, some of the essential quality of tragedy, which seems to include an element of the scapegoat or sacrifice (implicit in the derivation of the word 'tragedy'), would be lost.

Aristotle in his *Poetics* (fourth century BC) began the debate about what made true tragedy, or what factors made it most compelling. He based his observations on the study of the tragedies performed annually at Athens from the sixth century BC onwards. These occasions were partly religious rites and partly competitions for dramatists. Greek tragedy was performed by professional actors who wore masks and high shoes called BUSKINS, and by a CHORUS of citizens who also danced.

The greatest fifth-century BC Greek tragedians whose works are known to us are Aeschylus, Sophocles and Euripides; of the many plays they wrote only a few survive. Aristotle analysed tragedy in his *Poetics*. He observed that it represented a single action of a certain magnitude, that it provoked in the audience the emotions of pity and terror which were then resolved or dissolved by CATHARSIS at the play's climax, and that certain features of the plot were common, notably the existence of some connection between the protagonist's downfall and preceding behaviour (HAMARTIA, 'error') and the process of the 'reversal of fortune' (PERIPETEIA) and the moments of 'discovery' (ANAGNORISIS) by which the protagonist learned the truth of his or her situation. Many of Aristotle's terms and ideas are still accepted as valuable insights into the nature of tragic drama. However, his theory of the UNITIES of time and space and some of his other ideas came to be regarded as prescriptive formulae for the construction of true tragedy, especially in France during the seventeenth century, and in this respect his influence has also been constricting, though the *Poetics* itself does not make claims to be authoritative, and the unities are not a specially significant part of Aristotle's argument.

Seneca (*see* SENECAN TRAGEDY) was the most influential Roman tragedian: his plays were probably not meant to be performed on stage, though he borrowed his subjects from the Greek playwrights.

In the Middle Ages tragedy was regarded simply as the story of an eminent person who suffers a downfall. The Classical tragedies and theories of Aristotle were unknown.

In English literature the Elizabethan and Jacobean periods are the great age of tragedy. Seneca provided the model both for the formal Classical tragedy with five acts and elaborate style, for example, Sackville and Norton's *Gorboduc* (1561), and for the popular REVENGE TRAGEDIES or tragedies of blood, full of horrific violent incidents and sensational elements, in which a quest for vengeance leads to a bloodthirsty climax. Kyd's *The Spanish Tragedy* (*c*.1589) and Webster's *The Duchess of Malfi* (*c*.1613) and *The White Devil* (*c*.1612) are notable examples of this form, though Shakespeare's *Hamlet* (*c*.1601) is the most famous revenge tragedy.

Shakespeare's tragedies are characterised by their variety and freedom from convention, in contrast with those of the slightly later classical French tragedians, Racine and Corneille. Shakespeare's lack of concern for preserving the texts (the plays were collected from a variety of sources by two of his friends, Heminges and Condell) suggests that he regarded them primarily as plays for the stage, and undervalued their literary pretensions. Shakespearean tragedy concentrates on the downfall of powerful men and often illuminates the resulting deterioration of a whole community around them. The protagonists are not necessarily good: *Richard III* (*c*.1592–3) is a punitive tragedy in which evil is justly punished. Often the extent to which the tragic fall is deserved is left richly ambiguous: when Lear wails that he is a man 'more sinned against than sinning' we may remark that this is not true at that point in the play. Also in *King Lear* (*c*.1605) when Gloucester reaches the nadir of cynical disbelief in providential justice ('as flies to wanton boys are we to the gods') we know that he is in fact being helped by his son. The relationship between human evil and the justice of fate is at the core of Shakespeare's tragic interests, as are the morality and psychology of his characters: unlike, for example, Sophocles's Oedipus, whose fate is determined before his birth, Shakespeare's protagonists are shown to be responsible for the choices that result in their downfall. This free will is obviously a Christian element which differentiates Renaissance tragedy from Classical models. In order to achieve the great goodness of Christ's crucifixion, which redeems man, the evil of Judas and the Roman soldiers is necessary. The paradoxical interdependence of good and evil in Christian thinking contributes to the special success of tragedy as a genre.

Dryden's *All for Love* (1678) is an English attempt at Classical tragedy, written according to Aristotle's views as to what made a perfect tragedy.

The modern age has seen a revival of tragedy. The nineteenth-century Scandinavian dramatists Ibsen and Strindberg depict life as a state of ruthless conflict and corrupt hypocrisy. Their NATURALISM shows ordinary bourgeois people, rather than kings and generals, as the protagonists. Mid-twentieth-century writers have also concentrated on the tragic fate of ordinary people, though not with the same bitter indictment of human failings, for example, the Americans Tennessee Williams in *A Streetcar Named Desire* (1947) and *The Glass Menagerie* (1944), and Arthur Miller in *Death of a Salesman* (1949) and *A View from the Bridge* (1955).

The ABSURD plays of Samuel Beckett, especially *Waiting for Godot* (1953), mix tragedy with comedy, but still knowingly contain many aspects which can be directly compared with the tragedies of the past: Pozzo's downfall, for example. Beckett's tragic world is populated by tramps and clowns. Pinter's *The Caretaker* (1960), dealing naturalistically with tramps and the mentally disturbed, can also be seen as a modern version of tragedy, in which the good Aston is rebuffed in his attempt to befriend Davies.

From Pinter's tramp to the gods and heroes of Greek drama, the idea of tragedy as a genre provides a clear model with which to compare and contrast the most varied kinds of literary experience. Though the most famous tragedies are all plays, other kinds of literature can also be used as vehicles for tragedy, notably the novel, for example, Hardy's *Tess of the d'Urbervilles* (1891), or Malcolm Lowry's *Under the Volcano* (1947) which even adheres to the tragic unities.

Tragedy of blood. Another name for REVENGE TRAGEDY.

Tragic flaw. Aristotle's observation in the *Poetics* (fourth century BC) that the downfall of a tragic hero should be caused not by evil but by HAMARTIA (Gk. 'error') has become a common insight into the way tragedies work. 'Tragic *flaw*' suggests imperfection of character, rather than a mistake of action, as implied by 'error'. Shakespeare's tragic heroes do often manifest a flawed character of this kind (e.g. Othello's jealousy), but not all tragedies adopt this psychological approach, which is typical of the late nineteenth- and early twentieth-century interpretation of drama, as found, for example, in A.C. Bradley's *Shakespearean Tragedy* (1904).

Tragic irony. DRAMATIC IRONY as manifested in tragedies, when the audience knows the eventual fate of the protagonist, and watches him or her struggling towards the truth in a process of painful discovery. Sophocles's *Oedipus Rex* (*c*.430BC) is a famous example. *See also* IRONY.

Tragicomedy. As the word implies, 'tragicomedy' is a mixture of TRAGEDY and COMEDY. The playwright John Fletcher defined it in his Preface to *The Faithful Shepherdess* (*c*.1610): 'A tragicomedy is not so called in respect of mirth and killing, but in respect it wants deaths, which is enough to make it no tragedy, yet brings some near it, which is enough to make it no comedy.' For the Elizabethan and Jacobean theorists the fact that in tragicomedy both upper- and lower-class people might be depicted together on the stage was also significant, and made it a problematic form, to be avoided. Shakespeare as usual heeded the theorists little, and several of his plays have tragicomical aspects, notably *The Merchant of Venice* (*c*.1596), in which a tragic ending is surprisingly avoided, and *The Winter's Tale* (*c*.1611). Various modern plays, such as Beckett's *Waiting for Godot* (1953) or Chekhov's *The Cherry Orchard* (1904), may also be termed tragicomedies, though the tragedy and comedy may be blended throughout the play, rather than existing as separable strands in the plot.

Transcendentalism. (Lat. 'climb over') The word describes modes of thought which emphasise the intuitive and the mystical powers of the mind, and the possibility of some higher world or realm of existence beyond the world of the senses.

More particularly, the Transcendentalists were a group of American writers and thinkers in the early nineteenth century who developed a common philosophy: they believed God was immanent in nature and man, that the Soul was present in all things, and that the physical senses needed to be transcended through the truth of intuition. The writers

Emerson and Thoreau were members of the group. Emerson's Transcendentalist essay 'Self-Reliance' appeared in 1841.

Transcendental signified. That which language signifies, an ultimate meaning that lies behind or beyond words; or does not, according to the philosophy of DECONSTRUCTION. *See also* LOGOCENTRISM, PRESENCE.

Travesty. (Fr., from It. 'disguise') A grotesque and ludicrous imitation. From the title of a verse BURLESQUE by the French dramatist Paul Scarron, *Virgile travesti* (1648). *See also* CARICATURE, PARODY.

Treatise. (To treat = to deal with) Extended, systematic and careful examination of a subject, often philosophical, as Hume's *Treatise of Human Nature* (1739–40).

Tribe of Ben. Seventeenth-century followers and admirers of the poet and playwright Ben Jonson. Their lyric poetry tended to be clear, witty, satiric and Classical in tone. Herrick, Carew, Suckling and Lovelace have been designated members of the 'Tribe'. Jonson himself discussed the label in his poem 'An Epistle Answering to One that Asked to be Sealed of the Tribe of Ben' (1640).

Trilogy. (Gk. 'three speeches') A group of three connected literary works, such as Shakespeare's *Henry VI* (*c.*1592), which is in three parts. Tragedies were presented in threes at the drama festivals in Athens in the fifth century BC. (Aeschylus's *Oresteia* is the only extant Greek trilogy.) Novels are also sometimes grouped in trilogies, for example, Evelyn Waugh's *Sword of Honour* (1965).

Trimeter. (Gk. 'three measures') In prosody a line consisting of three feet. Tennyson's 'Break, Break, Break' (1842) interestingly starts with three heavily stressed monosyllables in the first lines, and thereafter mixes IAMBS and ANAPAESTS (*see* METRE for further discussion of these terms):

> Break, break, break,
>> On thy cold gray stones, O Sea!
> And I would that my tongue could utter
>> The thoughts that arise in me.

Triolet. (Fr. 'little three') A fixed verse form, French in origin. Eight lines, often of TETRAMETER, are rhymed *abaaabab*: the first, fourth and seventh lines are identical (or similar), as are the second and last. A short form used chiefly in the late nineteenth century. Here is an example by Robert Bridges (1890):

> When first we met we did not guess
> That Love would prove so hard a master;
> Of more than common friendliness
> When first we met we did not guess.
> Who could foretell this sore distress,
> This irretrievable disaster,

When first we met? – We did not guess
That Love would prove so hard a master.

See also METRE, RHYME.

Triple metre. A METRE based on any three-syllable foot, such as the ANAPAEST or the DACTYL. Less common than duple metre, based on two-syllable feet, such as the ubiquitous IAMB, but nonetheless quite common, especially in nineteenth-century verse.

Triple rhyme. A RHYME on three syllables, as quivering/shivering, comparison/garrison. Most often used for comic effect.

Triplet. A STANZA of three similar lines, or three consecutive rhymed lines; HEROIC COUPLETS are sometimes diversified by the appearance of occasional triplets: for example, there are several at strategic points in Pope's *An Essay on Criticism* (1711). The following example is from a poem in heroic couplets written privately by Lady Mary Wortley Montagu in protest at a scandalous trial for adultery in 1724, the 'Epistle from Mrs Yonge to Her Husband', not published until 1972:

Nature with equal fire our souls endued,
Our minds as haughty, and as warm our blood;
O'er the wide world your pleasures you pursue,
The change is justified by something new;
But we must sigh in silence – and be true.

Triteness. (Lat. 'rubbed') In speech or writing the expression of tired dull ideas, descriptions or stylistic traits which have been worn out by too much use. CLICHÉS are trite. *See also* COMMONPLACE, STEREOTYPE.

Trivium. (Lat. 'place where three roads meet') In the Middle Ages the seven liberal arts were divided into the upper QUADRIVIUM (arithmetic, astronomy, geometry and music) and the lower *trivium* (grammar, logic and rhetoric). The word 'trivial' comes from this division.

Trochee, trochaic. (Gk. 'running') In English prosody a trochee is a FOOT consisting of a strongly stressed syllable followed by a weakly stressed syllable: tum-ti. Trochaic METRES are quite common in English poetry. Trochaic lines often omit the last weak syllable, as does this example, from W.H. Auden's 'Lullaby' (1940):

Lay your/sleeping/head, my/love,
Human/on my/faithless/arm.

Trope. (Gk. 'turn') FIGURATIVE LANGUAGE; a word or phrase used in a sense not proper to it, and thus a departure from LITERAL LANGUAGE. Common tropes include METAPHOR, SIMILE, METONYMY, SYNECDOCHE, PERSONIFICATION. Tropes are sometimes distinguished from figures of speech (in which the departure from ordinary speech is a matter of the order or rhetorical effect of the words, rather than of extension of their meaning), but the word is also applied to all decorative and rhetorical effects in language.

Troubadour. (Pr. 'composer') Troubadours were twelfth- and thirteenth-century poets in southern France who wrote in Provençal. Their lyric poetry was the origin of many of the traditional attitudes and forms associated with COURTLY LOVE. The twentieth-century poet Ezra Pound wrote several early poems about troubadours, such as Bertrand de Born and Pierre Vidal, and translated the poetry of Arnaut Daniel, whom Dante called 'il miglior fabbro' ('the better workman').

Trouvère. French for TROUBADOUR.

Turn. The name for a twist in the argument of a poem, or change of mood, especially the change of approach and subject matter that by convention often occurs between the OCTAVE and SESTET of a SONNET.

Type. (Lat. 'figure', from Gk. 'blow, impression, image') 'Type' has several uses with reference to literature. Most commonly it is another word for GENRE. More specifically in discussing Biblical allegory it is a sign or symbol of some future event (*see* 'typological allegory' *under* ALLEGORY).

In narratives 'type' refers loosely to a character that is representative of a social group or class, encompassing both one-dimensional STOCK CHARACTERS and more complex examples of CHARACTERISATION. For example, it might be argued that Casaubon in George Eliot's *Middlemarch* (1871-2) is a type-study of the desiccated scholar-clergyman.

Typescript. A word replacing MANUSCRIPT, indicating the typewritten but not yet printed and published version of a book or poem.

Typography. (Gk. 'type-writing') The organisation of words on the printed page. The most apparent difference between verse and prose, for example, is typographical: lines of verse are printed separately, while prose fills out the page. Some poets, like the twentieth-century American e.e. cummings, have given form to their poems by means of typographical experiments and tricks. *See also* CONCRETE POETRY.

Typological allegory. *See* ALLEGORY.

U

Ubi sunt. (Lat. 'where are they?') A common MOTIF in lyric poetry. The poet grieves at the loss of the pleasures, comforts and security of youth or the past, and laments the transitory nature of life on earth. A famous example is the fifteenth-century French poet Villon's 'Ballade des dames du temps jadis' with its refrain 'Mais où sont les neiges d'antan?' ('But where are last year's snows?').

Uncanny, The. (From O.N. *kunna*, 'know') The strange and weird. In the definition of FANTASTIC literature drawn up by the Bulgarian narratologist Todorov (*The Fantastic*, 1970), the 'uncanny' refers to descriptions of unnatural events which can ultimately be ascribed to the psychological state of those who have witnessed the events, be they characters in the story or the narrator. The reader knows them to be dreams, delusions or mistakes, though no less frightening, perhaps, that they are products of the human mind. A clear example is offered by the humdrum explanations which Sherlock Holmes discovers to be the cause of the (till then) terrifying supernatural phenomena in Conan Doyle's *The Hound of the Baskervilles* (1902). Todorov contrasts this kind of phenomenon with the 'MARVELLOUS', in which supernatural events are inexplicable, and in a sense taken for granted, and the 'fantastic', which hovers between the marvellous and the uncanny.

Understatement. A species of IRONY where the true magnitude of an idea, event or fact is minimised or not stated: 'It is sometimes a bit cold at the North Pole.' Wordsworth often underlines his strength of feeling by understatement, suggesting the inadequacy of language itself, as in 'She Dwelt among the Untrodden Ways' (1800):

> But she is in her grave, and, oh,
> The difference to me!

Unities. In his *Poetics* (fourth century BC) Aristotle observed that Greek TRAGEDIES concentrated on one complete action, or events which took place within a single day and night. These descriptive comments became known as the 'dramatic unities' of action and time (the unity of space was added by later critics), and from the late sixteenth century onwards scholars came to regard them as rules for the proper construction of tragedies. From the seventeenth until the nineteenth century French playwrights followed these prescriptions. Following the example of Shakespeare, whose tragedies have multiple actions, and spread themselves over many years and many different countries, English dramatists tended not to treat the unities as anything but occasional guide-lines.

Unity. The coherence and completeness of a literary artefact. The wholeness of its structure, from which nothing should be taken away or added to without disturbing its unity.

Universal truths. Truths that are common to all humanity, from whatever era, culture, gender, or racial, national, class or religious grouping. That such truths exist was a commonplace confidence of former ages. Dr Johnson incorporates the idea into this description of the poet's business in *Rasselas* (1759):

> He must divest himself of the prejudices of his age and country; he must consider right and wrong in their abstracted and invariable state; he must disregard present laws and opinions, and rise to general and transcendental truths, which will always be the same.

Some twentieth-century approaches to knowledge assume similar cross-cultural consistencies: for example, PSYCHOANALYTIC CRITICISM proceeds from the notion that the organisation of consciousness and psychosexual development is generally shared. Similarly MARXIST analyses often imply that the philosophy of materialism deals with absolute truths. A more common modern view, however, is that all cultures are relative, and are created in a particular time and place, and are therefore only 'true' locally, and not universally. This is not simply the tendency of STRUCTURALIST and POST-STRUCTURALIST thought, though these intellectual systems have challenged age-old assumptions about the basis of meaning. Even the Christian critic C.S. Lewis, while presumably believing in some religious absolutes, mocked what he called 'The Doctrine of the Unchanging Human Heart', by which he meant the assumption that human feelings and sympathies will be expressed in the same forms from age to age (*A Preface to Paradise Lost*, 1942). *See also* COMMON SENSE, IDEOLOGY.

Universality. The quality which makes the best art or literature transcend its circumstances of time and place and appeal to all mankind. Modern critical attitudes doubt that such a quality can be found in literature, which is seen as culture-bound. The existence of UNIVERSAL TRUTHS is also decried. *See also* ARCHETYPE.

University wits. The name given to a group of Elizabethan poets and playwrights who had all been educated at Oxford or Cambridge. Their leader was John Lyly, originator of EUPHUISM. Other members include George Peele, Robert Greene, Thomas Lodge and Thomas Nashe. Marlowe is sometimes considered one of the group. They are reputed to have met at the Mermaid Tavern in London in the 1590s.

Unreliable narrator. *See* NARRATIVE.

Urbanity. (Lat. 'of the town') The quality, in speech or written works, of civilised politeness and polished common sense. To be urbane is to be witty, well-mannered and knowledgeable in a worldly way, without showing off, and without pedantry.

Urtext. (Ger. *ur-*, 'primitive, earliest') The earliest and original version of a text, which may no longer exist, in which case its existence and characteristics have to be guessed at through careful TEXTUAL CRITICISM. Some scholars, for example, think that Shakespeare's *Hamlet* (*c*.1601) is based on an *Ur-Hamlet*, an earlier version of the story of which no trace remains, not even the title, but which can be guessed at from examining the play in relation to other known and existing SOURCES.

Usage. (Lat. 'use') Habitual, ordinary use of language, referring to an individual writer's typical traits, or to customary linguistic practice.

Ut pictura poesis. (Lat. 'as painting so is poetry') A comment made by Horace in his *Ars Poetica* (*c*.20BC), suggesting that poetry and painting are fundamentally similar kinds of art.

Utilitarianism. (From Lat. *utilitas*, 'usefulness') The ethical doctrine in which choices are made according to what result will most benefit the common good. An *act* utilitarian would pick a daffodil in a park, on the grounds that it would give pleasure, and one would not be missed. A *rule* utilitarian would reply that if everyone picked a daffodil, then there would be none left to enjoy.

Jeremy Bentham (1748–1832) was a leading exponent of utilitarian ideas. The utility or usefulness of individual decisions and social laws should be based on what gives 'the greatest happiness to the greatest number'. From this point of view 'push-pin [a nineteenth-century table game like bagatelle] was as good as poetry', since it gives people as much pleasure.

J.S. Mill (1806–73) was educated according to strictly defined utilitarian principles that excluded literature as fictitious and insufficiently useful. He describes in his *Autobiography* (1873) the sudden failure of the philosophy for him as a young man, because it had left him ignorant of human feelings; his first reading of the poetry of Wordsworth and Coleridge, which introduced him to the range of human emotions, had the force of a spiritual revelation.

Utopia. (Gk. *outopia*, 'no place', with a pun on *eutopia*, 'good place') Sir Thomas More's *Utopia* (1516) is a description (in Latin) of an imaginary and perfect commonwealth. The name now refers to all fictional, philosophical or political works depicting imaginary worlds better than our own. Plato's *The Republic* (*c*.360BC) is an early example. St Augustine's *City of God* (*c*.AD413–27) shows the Christian paradise as a heavenly city.

Utopian fiction can be satirical, like Book Four of Swift's *Gulliver's Travels* (1726); visionary, like William Morris's *News from Nowhere* (1890); or a serious attempt to imagine the future, like H.G. Wells's *A Modern Utopia* (1905). Many works of SCIENCE FICTION include Utopian elements.

The opposite of a Utopia is a 'dystopia', an imaginary world which is even worse than our own, like Aldous Huxley's *Brave New World* (1932).

V

Valediction. (Lat. 'saying farewell') A farewell speech; often, but not necessarily, filled with forebodings about the future of both the traveller and those who stay behind. In 'A Valediction: Forbidding Mourning' (1633) Donne discourages weeping at his departure by exercising his playful wit.

Vanity press. A small publisher of books by writers who are prepared to pay for the pleasure of seeing their work in print.

Variorum edition. (Lat. 'of various') An edition of a work including the observations of different commentators, and/or all the different textual variations in an author's manuscripts and subsequent editions of his or her work.

Varronian satire. *See* SATIRE.

Vatic. Poetry which is divinely inspired; *vates*, the Latin word for a BARD or prophetic poet, was also applied by the Romans to a class of druid.

Vaudeville. (From Fr. 'Valley of Vire', name of a region in Normandy, the songs of which had a vogue in the fifteenth century) Light stage performance, usually comic, with songs. The American equivalent of the British music hall; popular entertainment, comprising songs, comic sketches and acrobatics, flourishing from about 1890 to 1930.

Vehicle. *See* TENOR AND VEHICLE.

Vellum. *See* PARCHMENT.

Verfremdungseffekt. *See* ALIENATION EFFECT.

Verisimilitude. (Lat. 'truth-likeness') The property in a work of literature of resembling the 'truth' in its depiction of the appearance of things. An attribute of REALISM. Verisimilitude depends not on any direct relationship with 'reality', but more on a collection of literary conventions, consisting of the choice of certain kinds of material and approach, and the avoidance of obvious improbabilities.

The theory of language and literature as MIMETIC, as an imitation of the world, has been attacked by many twentieth-century philosophies, notably STRUCTURALISM. *See also* ILLUSIONISM.

Verism. (It. 'true-ism') A jargon term for the critical doctrine that supposes REALISM to be the most authentic literary form.

Verismo. A late nineteenth-century Italian version of literary NATURALISM. Its most notable exponent was the Sicilian writer Giovanni Verga, whose mature novels, short stories and dramas focused on rural poverty. His story and play *Cavalleria Rusticana* ('Rustic Chivalry', 1884) was turned into an opera by Mascagni in 1890 and translated by D.H. Lawrence in 1928.

Vernacular. (Lat. 'domestic, indigenous') The language of one's homeland. Often used to distinguish literature in English from that in Latin, but also applicable to DIALECTS, or even rough, earthy speech.

Vers de société. (Fr. 'society verse') Light, sophisticated, witty, often gently satirical poetry, frequently in intricate verse forms, dealing with frivolous social attitudes, events and relationships. *Vers de société* is elegant and complimentary rather than serious or profound.

Vers héroïque. *See* ALEXANDRINE.

Vers libre. *See* FREE VERSE.

Verse. (Lat. 'turn of the plough') Commonly refers to poetry in general, especially to denote metrical writing rather than PROSE. It is also a synonym of STANZA, indicating a regular section of metrical writing.

Old-fashioned prosodists call a single line of metrical writing a verse. Chapters of the Bible are also divided into short sections called verses. *See also* METRE.

Verse paragraph. Division of long poems, especially in BLANK VERSE, into large, irregular syntactic units, usually indicated typographically by a break in the lines. Often Wordsworth's long sentences in *The Prelude* (1850) are verse paragraphs.

Versification. The act of composition of verse; or the study of the art of writing metrically.

Verso. (Lat. 'turned') The left-hand page of a book when open: the back of the RECTO.

Vice, The. (Lat. 'defect') A figure in MORALITY PLAYS of the fifteenth and sixteenth centuries who tempts mankind in a half-comic, half-unpleasant manner. Shakespeare's Falstaff in *Henry IV*, Parts 1 and 2 (*c.*1597, *c.*1598) is thought to be partly modelled on this STOCK CHARACTER.

Victorian period. The reign of Queen Victoria, lasting from 1837 to 1901. Often spoken of as a homogeneous literary period, in fact these six decades saw huge changes in society, outlook and literary output. Among the many writers who flourished during Victoria's reign were the novelists Dickens and George Eliot, the poets Tennyson and Browning, and the essayists Arnold and Carlyle.

Viewpoint. *See* POINT OF VIEW.

Vignette. (Fr. 'small vine') Originally the ornamental design in the blank space of a book between chapters, often a picture of leaves and branches, or a country scene. The word is now also applied to descriptive passages in prose works which resemble little pictures.

Villain. (Fr. 'feudal serf') A character in a story on whom evil is focused: often the instigator of an evil plot. The STOCK CHARACTER of the villain was developed in the drama of the fifteenth and sixteenth centuries, especially in tragedy where figures such as Iago in *Othello* (*c.*1604) combine Machiavellian cunning with diabolic malice. Even the PROTAGONIST of a tragedy (e.g. *Richard III*, *c.*1592-3) can be a villain. Milton's Satan in *Paradise Lost* (1667) is a tragic villain on a grand scale. In later literature the villain's evil qualities tend to be diluted, trivialised or glamorised. The type seems to thrive at a meeting point between Christian piety and psychology: though there are many unpleasant characters in Classical literature, they do not have the full evil of the villain. *See also* ANTAGONIST, MACHIAVEL.

Villanelle. (It. 'rustic') An elaborate verse form probably originating in France in the sixteenth century. Five three-lined STANZAS are followed by a QUATRAIN; only two RHYMES are used; the first and last line of the first stanza recur alternately at the end of each stanza throughout the poem, both together in the quatrain.

James Joyce describes the composition of the following villanelle in *A Portrait of the Artist as a Young Man* (1916):

Are you not weary of ardent ways,
Lure of the fallen seraphim?
Tell no more of enchanted days.

Your eyes have set man's heart ablaze
And you have had your will of him.
Are you not weary of ardent ways?

Above the flame the smoke of praise
Goes up from ocean rim to rim.
Tell no more of enchanted days.

Our broken cries and mournful lays
Rise in one eucharistic hymn.
Are you not weary of ardent ways?

While sacrificing hands upraise
The chalice flowing to the brim.
Tell no more of enchanted days.

And still you hold our longing gaze
With languorous look and lavish limb!
Are you not weary of ardent ways?
Tell no more of enchanted days.

Dylan Thomas's 'Do Not Go Gentle into That Good Night' (1951) is another famous example.

Voice. A word sometimes used in a semi-technical sense to denote the authorial PERSONA in a NARRATIVE. The fundamental characteristics of narrative can all be traced to the art of story-telling, and the word 'voice' reminds us that the basic relationship between narrator and audience is like hearing an individual speaking, and deciding what kind of person we are listening to, what TONE is being used, and what is the narrator's attitude to the story being told.

T.S. Eliot distinguishes between private, public and dramatic poetry in his essay 'The Three Voices of Poetry' (1953):

The first voice is the voice of the poet talking to himself – or to nobody. The second is the voice of the poet addressing an audience, whether large or small. The third is the voice of the poet when he attempts to create a dramatic character speaking verse; when he is saying, not what he would say in his own person, but only what he can say within the limits of one imaginary character addressing another imaginary character.

See also MONOLOGUE.

Volta. (It. 'turn') The change in mood and argument which occurs between the OCTAVE and SESTET of a SONNET.

Vorticism. (From Lat. *vortex*, 'whirlpool') A short-lived, self-consciously MODERNISTIC movement in art and literature instigated by Wyndham Lewis and Ezra Pound in a magazine called *Blast* (1914–15). In this, Pound redefined his idea of the image in more dynamic terms than his former statements as an IMAGIST.

Vraisemblance. French for VERISIMILITUDE: the commitment to depict 'reality' in a work of art, or to maintain the illusion of depicting reality. *See also* REALISM, VERISM.

Vulgate. (Lat. 'common') The Vulgate is a Latin translation and organisation of the Scriptures, completed by St Jerome *c*. 405. From the seventh century onwards this version was regarded as the authoritative version of the Bible, and it was viewed as such during the Middle Ages. It was authorised as the official Latin text of the Roman Catholic Church at the Council of Trent in 1546.

In general (and as a biblical label), 'vulgate' simply means 'the most commonly used text'. The Vulgate Cycle of chivalric ROMANCES is a collection of French prose tales of Arthur and his knights, dating from the thirteenth century, used as a source by many later writers, including Malory in *Le Morte d'Arthur* (1485).

W

Weak ending. A weakly stressed syllable placed after the final metrical stress at the end of a line of IAMBIC verse. Also called FEMININE ENDING. *See also* METRE, PROMOTION.

Well-made play. A play which exhibits a neatness of PLOT and smooth-functioning exactness of action, with all its parts fitting together precisely. As a term of praise it originated in France: a *pièce bien faite* was likely to be a nineteenth-century comedy. Later works which display strongly manipulative plots are also called 'well-made plays'. J.B. Priestley's *An Inspector Calls* (1945) is such a work: it works through an interlocking series of unexpected disclosures, leading up to a final revelation that is almost a trick ending.

NATURALISM effected a revolution in drama that led in the twentieth century to the expression becoming a term of mild contempt, indicating superficiality and blandness.

Weltanschauung. (Ger. 'world survey') A philosophical view of the world, perhaps expressed by a single writer, or typical of a whole period.

Weltschmerz. (Ger. 'world ache') Yearning discontent with life.

Wertherism. Part of the European revaluation of sentiment and feeling at the end of the eighteenth century. A fashion for imitating and admiring the morbid sentimentalism of Werther following the publication of

Goethe's *The Sorrows of Young Werther* (1774) in which the hero commits suicide after an unhappy love affair.

Wit. (From O.E. 'to know') Originally meaning 'sense', 'understanding' or 'intelligence', during the seventeenth century the word came to refer specifically to that kind of highly valued poetic intelligence which combines or contrasts ideas and expressions in an unexpected and intellectually pleasing manner. This quality of verbal ingenuity and surprise was sought after by the METAPHYSICAL POETS. For writers in the eighteenth century the word referred to exactness and aptness of literary expression, rather than the ostentatiously PARADOXICAL. Pope provides a famous definition in *An Essay on Criticism* (1711):

> What oft was thought, but ne'er so well express'd.

Nineteenth-century writers valued feeling and imagination more than verbal polish: Hazlitt, for example, contrasted the truth of the imagination with the artificiality of wit.

Nowadays wit would specifically be used to describe intellectual and verbal brilliance of the EPIGRAMMATIC kind, to be distinguished from broader comedy or humour. *See also* CONCEIT, PARADOX, PUN.

Wrenched accent. An effect occurring when the metrical STRESS in a line of verse alters the natural stress of a word. Here, in a Scottish ballad, 'The Douglas Tragedy', the wrench occurs on 'sister' in the third line:

> 'Rise up, rise up, my seven bold sons,
> And put on your armour so bright,
> And take better care of your youngest sister,
> For your eldest's awa the last night.'

Normally 'sister' is pronounced with the stress on the first syllable, but here the METRE tends to force the reader to pronounce it with the accent on the second syllable. *See also* DEMOTION, PROMOTION.

Writerly. *See* SCRIPTIBLE.

Y

Yellow Book, The. An illustrated magazine which appeared in 1894–7. Its title evoked cheap yellow-backed French novels considered shocking in England. Many of the so-called DECADENT writers of the nineties contributed to this quarterly; Aubrey Beardsley, the artist, was the art editor of the first four volumes.

Z

Zeitgeist. (Ger. 'time spirit') The spirit or intellectual atmosphere of an age or period.

Zeugma. (Gk. 'yoking') A figure of speech in which words or phrases with widely different meanings are 'yoked together' with comic effect by being made syntactically dependent on the same word, often a verb, as in the following example from Dickens's *The Pickwick Papers* (1836–7):

> Miss Bolo rose from the table considerably agitated, and went straight home, in a flood of tears, and a sedan-chair.

Dates of writers and historical figures mentioned in the text

Unless otherwise indicated, the person is English.

ABELARD, Peter, French, scholastic philosopher: 1079–1142

ABRAMS, Meyer Howard, American, literary critic: *b*.1912

ACHEBE, Chinua, Nigerian, novelist: *b*.1930

ADDISON, Joseph, essayist: 1672–1719

AE (George William Russell), Irish, poet: 1867–1935

AESCHYLUS, Greek, tragic dramatist: *c*.525–456BC

AESOP, Greek, author or collector of fables: sixth century BC

ALBEE, Edward, American, dramatist: *b*.1928

ALEMBERT, Jean Le Rond d', French, mathematician and philosopher: 1717–83

ALEXANDER, Michael, translator and critic: *b*.1941

ALFRED THE GREAT, King of Wessex (871–99): 849–99

ALTHUSSER, Louis, Algerian and French, political theorist: *b*.1918

AMBLER, Eric, novelist: *b*.1909

AMIS, Kingsley, novelist and poet: *b*.1922

AMIS, Martin, novelist: *b*.1949

ANACREON, Greek, poet: sixth century BC

ANDERSEN, Hans Christian, Danish, writer of fairy tales: 1805–75

ANSELM, Saint, Italian, theologian: 1033–1109

APOLLINAIRE, Guillaume, French, poet and prose-writer: 1880–1918

APULEIUS, Roman, prose-writer and rhetorician: second century AD

AQUINAS, Saint Thomas, Italian, theologian: *c*.1225–74

ARBUTHNOT, Doctor John, Scottish, physician, mathematician and miscellaneous writer: 1667–1735

ARIOSTO, Ludovico, Italian, poet: 1474–1533

ARISTOPHANES, Greek, comic dramatist: *c*.450–*c*.385BC

ARISTOTLE, Greek, philosopher and critic: 384–322BC

ARNOLD, Matthew, poet and critic: 1822–88

ARP, Hans, French, sculptor: 1887–1966

ARTAUD, Antonin, French, dramatist: 1896–1948

ASHBERY, John, American, poet: *b*.1927

ASIMOV, Isaac, American, science-fiction writer: 1920–92

AUDEN, Wystan Hugh, poet: 1907–73

AUERBACH, Eric, German/American, critic and scholar: 1892–1957

AUGUSTINE, Saint, North African, Christian writer and autobiographer: AD354–430

AUSTEN, Jane, novelist: 1775–1817

AUSTIN, John, philosopher: 1911–60

AYRES, Pam, poet: *b*.1947

AYTOUN, William Edmonstoune, Scottish, academic and miscellaneous writer: 1813-65

BABBITT, Irving, American, critic and teacher: 1865-1933

BACON, Francis, essayist: 1561-1626

BAILEY, Philip James, poet: 1816-1902

BAKHTIN, Mikhail, Russian, literary theorist: 1895-1975

BALL, Hugo, German, cultural historian: 1886-1927

BALLANTYNE, Robert Michael, Scottish, writer of adventure stories: 1825-94

BALZAC, Honoré de, French, novelist: 1799-1850

BARNES, William, poet: 1801-86

BARRIE, Sir James Matthew, Scottish, dramatist and novelist: 1860-1937

BARTH, John, American, novelist: *b*. 1930

BARTHES, Roland, French, linguist, philosopher and literary theorist: 1915-80

BAUDELAIRE, Charles, French, poet: 1821-67

BAUMGARTEN, Alexander Gottlieb, German, philosopher: 1714-62

BAXTER, Richard, autobiographer and theologian: 1615-91

BEARDSLEY, Aubrey, artist: 1872-98

BEARDSLEY, Monroe, American, literary critic: *b*.1915

BEAUVOIR, Simone de, French, essayist and novelist: 1908-86

BECKETT, Samuel, Irish, dramatist: 1906-89

BEDE, Cuthbert (Edward Bradley), novelist and clergyman: 1827-89

BEDE, the Venerable, Saint, Anglo-Saxon, theologian, historian and chronologer: 672/3-735

BEERBOHM, Sir Max, essayist and parodist: 1872-1956

BEHN, Mrs Aphra, novelist and dramatist: 1640-89

BELL, Clive, art critic: 1881-1964

BELLOC, Hilaire, essayist and poet: 1870-1953

BELLOW, Saul, American, novelist: *b*.1915

BENJAMIN, Walter, German, aesthetician: 1892-1940

BENTHAM, Jeremy, philosopher: 1748-1832

BENTLEY, Edmund Clerihew, writer of detective fiction and light verse: 1875-1956

BERKELEY, George, Bishop, philosopher: 1685-1753

BERNARD OF CLAIRVAUX, Saint, French, theologian: 1090-1153

BERRYMAN, John, American, poet: 1914-72

BETJEMAN, Sir John, poet: 1906-84

BION, Greek, poet: third or second century BC

BISHOP, Elizabeth, American, poet: 1911-79

BLACKMUR, Richard Palmer, American, literary critic: 1904-65

BLAIR, Robert, Scottish, poet: 1699-1746

BLAKE, William, poet and artist: 1757-1827

BLOOM, Harold, American, literary theorist: *b*.1930

BOCCACCIO, Giovanni, Italian, poet and story-writer: c.1313–75
BOETHIUS, Roman, philosopher: AD480–524
BOIARDO, Matteo, Italian, poet: c.1441–94
BOOTH, Wayne Clayson, American, literary critic: b.1921
BORN, Betrand de, Provençal, poet: c.1140–c.1215
BOSWELL, James, Scottish, biographer and diarist: 1740–95
BOWDLER, Thomas, editor: 1754–1825
BRADBURY, Malcolm, novelist and critic: b.1932
BRADBURY, Ray, American, science-fiction writer: b.1920
BRADLEY, Andrew Cecil, literary critic: 1851–1935
BRAINE, John, novelist: 1922–86
BRAKELOND, Jocelin de, chronicler: c.1155–1215
BRANT, Sebastian, German, poet and satirist: 1457–1521
BRAQUE, Georges, French, painter: 1882–1963
BRECHT, Bertolt, German, dramatist: 1898–1956
BREEZE, Jean Binta, poet: b.1957
BRETON, André, French, poet: 1896–1966
BRIDGES, Robert, poet: 1844–1930
BRONTË, Charlotte, novelist: 1816–55
BRONTË, Emily, novelist: 1818–48
BROOKE, Rupert, poet: 1887–1915
BROOKS, Cleanth, American, literary critic: b.1906
BROWNE, Sir Thomas, prose-writer: 1605–82
BROWNING, Elizabeth Barrett, poet: 1806–61
BROWNING, Robert, poet: 1812–89
BUCHAN, John, Scottish, writer of adventure stories: 1875–1940
BUCHANAN, Robert, poet and novelist: 1841–1901
BUNYAN, John, allegorist: 1628–88
BURKE, Edmund, Irish, philosopher and politician: 1729–97
BURLINGTON, Richard Boyle, Third Earl of, architect: 1694–1753
BURNS, Robert, Scottish, poet: 1759–96
BURROUGHS, William, American, prose-writer: b.1914
BURTON, Robert, scholar and anatomist: 1577–1640
BUTLER, Samuel, satirist and comic poet: 1612–80
BUTLER, Samuel, novelist: 1835–1902
BUTOR, Michel, French, novelist: b.1926
BYRON, Lord George Gordon, poet: 1788–1824

CALVINO, Italo, Italian, novelist and short-story writer: 1923–85
CAMOËNS, Luis de, Portuguese, poet: c.1524–80
CAMPION, Thomas, poet: 1567–1620
CAMUS, Albert, French, philosopher and novelist: 1913–60
CAPOTE, Truman, American, novelist: 1924–84
CAREW, Thomas, poet: c.1594–c.1640

CAREY, Peter, Australian, novelist: *b*.1943

CARLYLE, Thomas, Scottish, prose-writer: 1795-1881

CARROLL, Lewis (C.L. Dodgson), fantasist: 1832-98

CARTER, Angela, novelist: 1940-92

CASTIGLIONE, Baldassare, Italian, courtier and prose-writer: 1478-1529

CAVALCANTI, Guido, Italian, poet: *c*.1255-1300

CAXTON, William, printer and publisher: *c*.1422-91

CEPHALAS, Constantine, Byzantine Greek, anthologist: *fl. c*.AD900

CERVANTES SAAVEDRA, Miguel de, Spanish, novelist: 1547-1616

CÉSAIRE, Aimé, Martiniquais, politician and writer: *b*.1913

CHAPMAN, George, poet and playwright: *c*.1560-1634

CHAUCER, Geoffrey, poet: *c*.1340-1400

CHEKHOV, Anton, Russian, dramatist and short-story writer: 1860-1904

CHESTERFIELD, Philip Dormer Stanhope, Earl of, miscellaneous writer:
1694-1773

CHILD, Francis James, American, folklorist: 1825-96

CHOMSKY, Noam, American, linguistician: *b*.1928

CHRÉTIEN DE TROYES, French, poet: twelfth century

CICERO, Marcus Tullius, Roman, orator and statesman: 106-43BC

CIXOUS, Hélène, Algerian and French, literary theorist and novelist: *b*.1938

CLARKE, Arthur Charles, science-fiction writer: *b*.1917

CLEVELAND, John, poet: 1613-58

CLOUGH, Arthur Hugh, poet: 1819-61

COLERIDGE, Samuel Taylor, poet and critic: 1772-1834

COLLINS, William, poet: 1721-59

CONDELL, Henry, actor and editor: *d*.1627

CONGREVE, William, dramatist: 1670-1729

CONNOLLY, Cyril, novelist, autobiographer and critic: 1903-74

CONQUEST, Robert, poet and anthologist: *b*.1917

CONRAD, Joseph, Polish/British, novelist: 1857-1924

COPERNICUS, Nicolas, Polish, astronomer: 1473-1543

CORNEILLE, Pierre, French, dramatist: 1606-84

CORSO, Gregory, American, poet and novelist: *b*.1930

COWLEY, Abraham, poet: 1618-67

COWPER, William, poet: 1731-1800

CRABBE, George, poet: 1754-1832

CRANE, Hart, American, poet: 1899-1932

CRANE, Ronald Salmon, American, literary critic: 1886-1967

CRASHAW, Richard, poet: *c*.1612-49

CREELEY, Robert, American, poet and novelist: *b*.1926

CROCKETT, Samuel Rutherford, Scottish, novelist: 1860-1914

CULLEN, Countee, American, poet: 1903-46

CULLER, Jonathan Dwight, American, literary critic: *b*.1944

CUMMINGS, Edward Estlin, American, poet: 1894-1962

DANIEL, Arnaut, Provençal, poet: *fl. c*.1195
DANTE ALIGHIERI, Italian, poet: 1265-1321
DARWIN, Erasmus, scientist and poet: 1731-1802
DAVIES, William Henry, poet: 1871-1940
DAWE, Bruce, Australian, poet: *b*.1930
DAY, John, poet and dramatist: *c*.1574-1640
DEFOE, Daniel, novelist: 1660-1731
DE LA MARE, Walter, poet: 1873-1956
DEMOSTHENES, Greek, orator: 384-322BC
DENHAM, Sir John, poet: 1615-69
DE QUINCEY, Thomas, autobiographer and essayist: 1785-1859
DERRIDA, Jacques, French, linguistic philosopher: *b*.1930
DESCARTES, René, French, philosopher: 1596-1650
DE SICA, Vittorio, Italian, film director: 1902-74
DICKENS, Charles, novelist: 1812-70
DIDEROT, Denis, French, encyclopaedist: 1713-84
DISRAELI, Benjamin, Earl of Beaconsfield, novelist and politician: 1804-81
DOBELL, Sydney Thompson, poet: 1824-74
DOBSON, Henry Austin, poet: 1840-1921
DONLEAVY, James Patrick, Irish, novelist: *b*.1926
DONNE, John, poet: 1572-1631
DOSTOEVSKY, Fyodor Mikhaylovich, Russian, novelist: 1821-81
DOUGLAS, Gavin, Scottish, poet: *c*.1475-1522
DOUGLASS, Frederick, American, orator, journalist and autobiographer: 1817-95
DOWLAND, John, composer: 1563-1620
DOWSON, Ernest, poet: 1867-1900
DOYLE, Sir Arthur Conan, novelist and short-story writer: 1859-1930
DRAYTON, Michael, poet: 1563-1631
DREISER, Theodore, American, novelist: 1871-1945
DRUMMOND, William, of Hawthornden, Scottish, poet: 1585-1649
DRYDEN, John, poet, critic and playwright: 1631-1700
DUMAS (*père*), Alexandre, French, novelist and dramatist: 1802-70
DUNBAR, William, Scottish, poet: *c*.1460-*c*.1520
DUNCAN, Robert, American, poet: *b*.1919
DUNN, Douglas, poet: *b*.1942
DUNS SCOTUS, John, Scottish, scholastic philosopher: *c*.1275-1308
DURAS, Marguerite (Marguerite Donnadieu), French, novelist: *b*.1914

EAGLETON, Terry, critic: *b*.1943
EARLE, John, prose-writer: *c*.1601-65
EINSTEIN, Albert, German, physicist: 1879-1955
ELIOT, George (Mary Ann Evans), novelist: 1819-80
ELIOT, Thomas Stearns, American/British, poet and critic: 1888-1965
EMERSON, Ralph Waldo, American, philosopher and poet: 1803-82

EMPSON, Sir William, literary critic and poet: 1906–84
ENGELS, Friedrich, German, political theorist: 1820–95
ERASMUS, Desiderius, Dutch, humanist writer: 1466–1536
ESSLIN, Martin, scholar and literary critic: b.1918
ETHEREGE, Sir George, playwright: c.1635–91
EURIPIDES, Greek, tragic dramatist: c.484–c.406BC

FARQUHAR, George, playwright: c.1678–1707
FAULKNER, William, American, novelist: 1897–1962
FERLINGHETTI, Lawrence, American, poet and novelist: b.1919
FERRIER, Susan, Scottish, novelist: 1782–1854
FEYDEAU, Georges, French, dramatist: 1862–1921
FIELDING, Henry, novelist and dramatist: 1707–54
FIRTH, John Rupert, linguist: 1890–1960
FISH, Stanley, American, literary theorist: b.1938
FITZGERALD, Francis Scott, American, novelist: 1896–1940
FLAUBERT, Gustave, French, novelist: 1821–80
FLETCHER, John, dramatist: 1579–1625
FOLENGO, Teofilo, Italian, poet: 1491–1544
FORD, Ford Madox, novelist: 1873–1939
FORSTER, Edward Morgan, novelist: 1879–1970
FOUCAULT, Michel, French, literary and cultural theorist: 1926–84
FOWLES, John, novelist: b.1926
FRASER, George Sutherland, Scottish, poet and critic: 1915–80
FRAZER, Sir James George, Scottish, social anthropologist: 1854–1941
FREUD, Sigmund, Austrian, psychoanalyst: 1856–1939
FREYTAG, Gustav, German, literary critic: 1816–95
FRY, Christopher, dramatist: b.1907
FRYE, Northrop, Canadian, literary critic: 1912–91

GALILEO GALILEI, Italian, scientist: 1564–1642
GARCÍA MÁRQUEZ, Gabriel, Colombian, novelist: b.1928
GASCOYNE, David, poet and novelist: b.1916
GASKELL, Mrs Elizabeth, novelist: 1810–65
GAUTIER, Théophile, French, poet and novelist: 1811–72
GELLIUS, Aulus, Greek, miscellaneous writer: second century AD
GENET, Jean, French, prose-writer: 1910–86
GENETTE, Gérard, French, literary theorist: b.1930
GIBBON, Edward, historian and autobiographer: 1737–94
GIBBONS, Stella, novelist: 1902–89
GIDE, André, French, novelist and critic: 1869–1951
GILBERT, Sir William Schwenck, comic dramatist and poet: 1836–1911
GINSBERG, Allen, American, poet: b.1926
GISSING, George, novelist: 1857–1903

GODARD, Jean-Luc, French, film director: *b*.1930

GODWIN, William, political theorist and novelist: 1756–1836

GOETHE, Johann Wolfgang von, German, poet, novelist, dramatist and philosopher: 1749–1832

GOGARTY, Oliver St John, Irish, poet: 1878–1957

GOGH, Vincent van, Dutch, artist: 1853–90

GOLDING, Sir William, novelist: *b*.1911

GOLDSMITH, Oliver, Irish, poet, dramatist and essayist: 1730–74

GONCOURT, Edmond de, French, novelist: 1822–96

GONCOURT, Jules de, French, novelist: 1830–70

GÓNGORA Y ARGOTE, Don Luis de, Spanish, poet: 1561–1627

GOWER, John, poet: *c*.1330–1408

GRASS, Günter, German, novelist: *b*.1927

GRAVES, Robert, poet: 1895–1985

GRAY, Thomas, poet: 1716–71

GREENE, Robert, poet and miscellaneous writer: *c*.1560–92

GREGORY, Major Robert, Irish, airman and painter: 1881–1918

GREIMAS, Algirdas, Russian/French, semiotician: *b*.1917

GRIMM, Jakob, German, philologist and folklorist: 1785–1863

GRIMM, Wilhelm, German, philologist and folklorist: 1786–1859

GUINIZELLI, Guido, Italian, poet: *c*.1235–*c*.1276

GUNN, Thom, British/American, poet: *b*.1929

GUTENBERG, Johannes, German, printer: *c*.1398–1468

HALL, Joseph, satirist and prose-writer: 1574–1656

HALLAM, Arthur Henry, subject of Tennyson's *In Memoriam* (1850): 1811–33

HARDY, Thomas, poet and novelist: 1840–1928

HARVEY, William, scientist: 1578–1657

HAWTHORNE, Nathaniel, American, novelist: 1804–64

HAZLITT, William, critic and essayist: 1778–1830

HEANEY, Seamus, Northern Irish, poet: *b*.1939

HEGEL, Georg Wilhelm Friedrich, German, philosopher: 1770–1831

HEIDEGGER, Martin, German, phenomenological philosopher: 1889–1976

HELLER, Joseph, American, novelist: *b*.1923

HEMINGES *or* HEMING *or* HEMMINGE, John, actor and editor: 1556–1630

HEMINGWAY, Ernest, American, novelist: 1898–1961

HENRI, Adrian, poet: *b*.1932

HENRY, O. (William Sidney Porter), American, short-story writer and journalist: 1862–1910

HENRYSON, Robert, Scottish, poet: *fl.c*.1480, *d.c*.1506

HERBERT, George, poet: 1593–1633

HERRICK, Robert, poet: 1591–1674

HERVEY, John, Lord, courtier and memoir-writer: 1696–1743

HESIOD, Greek, poet: *c*. eighth century BC

HEYWOOD, John, dramatist: *c*.1497–*c*.1580
HILL, Geoffrey, poet: *b*.1932
HIPPOCRATES, Greek, physician: *c*.460–*c*.380BC
HOBBES, Thomas, philosopher: 1588–1679
HOBY, Sir Thomas, translator: 1530–66
HODGSON, Ralph, poet: 1871–1962
HOLBEIN, Hans, the younger, German, artist: 1497–1543
HOLINSHED, Raphael, historian: *d.c*.1585
HOMER, Greek, epic poet: probably eighth century BC
HOOD, Thomas, poet and humorist: 1799–1845
HOPKINS, Gerard Manley, poet: 1844–89
HORACE, Roman, poet: 65–8BC
HUGHES, Langston, American, poet, novelist and dramatist: 1902–67
HUGHES, Ted, poet: *b*.1930
HUGHES, Thomas, novelist: 1822–96
HULME, Thomas Ernest, philosopher and critic: 1883–1917
HUME, David, Scottish, philosopher: 1711–76
HUNT, Leigh, poet and essayist: 1784–1859
HUNT, William Holman, artist: 1827–1910
HURSTON, Zora Neale, American, novelist: 1903–60
HUSSERL, Edmund, phenomenological philosopher: 1859–1938
HUXLEY, Aldous, prose-writer: 1894–1963
HUYSMANS, Joris-Karl, French, novelist: 1848–1907

IBSEN, Henrik, Norwegian, dramatist: 1828–1906
IONESCO, Eugène, Rumanian/French, dramatist: *b*.1912
ISER, Wolfgang, German, literary theorist: *b*.1926

JAKOBSON, Roman, Russian, linguistician: 1896–1982
JAMES I, King of Scotland: 1394–1437
JAMES, Henry, American/British, novelist and critic: 1843–1916
JAMES, William, American, philosopher and psychologist: 1842–1910
JAMESON, Fredric, American, literary and cultural theorist: *b*.1934
JENNINGS, Elizabeth, poet: *b*.1926
JEROME, Saint, Eusebius Hieronymus, Dalmatian, biblical translator and
    monastic leader: *c*.AD347–419/20
JOHNSON, Bryan Stanley, novelist: 1933–73
JOHNSON, Linton Kwesi, poet: *b*.1952
JOHNSON, Lionel, poet: 1867–1902
JOHNSON, Dr Samuel, poet, lexicographer and critic: 1709–84
JONES, David, Anglo-Welsh, poet and artist: 1895–1974
JONES, Ernest, Welsh, psychoanalyst and biographer: 1879–1958
JONES, Inigo, architect and stage designer: 1573–1652
JONSON, Ben, dramatist and poet: 1572–1637

JOYCE, James, Irish, novelist: 1882–1941
JUNG, Carl Gustav, Swiss, psychiatrist: 1875–1961
JUVENAL, Roman, satiric poet: c.AD60–c.130

KAFKA, Franz, Austrian, novelist: 1883–1924
KANT, Immanuel, German, philosopher: 1724–1804
KEATS, John, poet: 1795–1821
KEBLE, John, clergyman and poet: 1792–1866
KENEALLY, Thomas, Australian, novelist: b.1935
KENNEDY, Walter, Scottish, poet: c.1460–c.1508
KEPLER, Johann, German, astronomer: 1571–1630
KEROUAC, Jack, American, novelist: 1922–69
KIERKEGAARD, Sören Aabye, Danish, philosopher: 1813–55
KINGSLEY, Charles, novelist and clergyman: 1819–75
KIPLING, Rudyard, poet and novelist: 1865–1936
KLINGER, Friedrich, German, dramatist: 1752–1831
KRISTEVA, Julia, French, linguist and semiotician: b.1941
KUNDERA, Milan, Czech, novelist: b.1929
KYD, Thomas, dramatist: 1558–94

LA BRUYÈRE, Jean de, French, satirist: 1645–96
LACAN, Jacques, French, psychoanalyst: 1901–81
LAMB, Charles, essayist: 1775–1834
LAMB, Lady Caroline, novelist: 1785–1828
LANDOR, Walter Savage, poet and prose-writer: 1775–1864
LANGBAUM, Robert, American, literary critic: b.1924
LANGLAND, William, poet: c.1331–c.1399·
LARKIN, Philip, poet: 1922–85
LA ROCHEFOUCAULD, François, French, moralist and essayist: 1613–80
LAWRENCE, David Herbert, novelist and poet: 1885–1930
LEAR, Edward, nonsense poet: 1812–88
LEAVIS, Frank Raymond, critic: 1895–1978
LEAVIS, Queenie Dorothy, critic: 1906–81
LE CARRÉ, John (David Cornwell), novelist: b.1931
LECONTE DE LISLE, Charles-Marie-René, French, poet: 1818–94
LEIBNIZ, Baron Gottfried Wilhelm von, German, philosopher: 1646–1716
LESAGE, Alain-René, French, novelist and dramatist: 1668–1747
LESSING, Doris, novelist: b.1919
LÉVI-STRAUSS, Claude, French, anthropologist: b.1908
LEWIS, Cecil Day, poet: 1904–72
LEWIS, Clive Staples, novelist and critic: 1898–1963
LEWIS, Matthew Gregory 'Monk', novelist: 1775–1818
LEWIS, Percy Wyndham, novelist and essayist: 1882–1957
LOCKE, Alain, American, editor and critic: 1886–1954

LOCKE, John, philosopher: 1632–1704
LOCKHART, John Gibson, Scottish, critic and biographer: 1794–1854
LODGE, David, literary critic and novelist: b.1935
LODGE, Thomas, poet and prose-writer: c.1558–1625
LONGFELLOW, Henry Wadsworth, American, poet: 1807–82
'LONGINUS', Greek, critic: probably first century AD
LORCA, Federico García, Spanish, poet and dramatist: 1893–1936
LORD, Albert Bates, American, classicist: b.1912
LORRIS, Guillaume de, French, poet: d.c.1235
LOVEJOY, Arthur Oncken, American, historian of ideas: 1873–1962
LOVELACE, Richard, poet: 1618–c.1658
LOWELL, Amy, American, poet: 1874–1925
LOWELL, Robert, American, poet: 1917–77
LOWRY, Malcolm, novelist: 1909–57
LUCRETIUS, Roman, philosophical poet: c.95–c.55BC
LUKACS, Georg, Hungarian, literary critic: 1885–1971
LUTHER, Martin, German, religious reformer: 1483–1546
LYDGATE, John, poet: c.1370–1449
LYLY, John, dramatist and prose-writer: c.1554–1606
LYOTARD, Jean François, French, philosopher: b.1924

MACAULAY, Thomas Babington, historian and poet: 1800–59
MACDIARMID, Hugh (Christopher Grieve), Scottish, poet: 1892–1978
MCGONAGALL, William, Scottish, poet: 1830–1902
MCGOUGH, Roger, poet: b.1937
MACHIAVELLI, Niccolò, Italian, political theorist: 1469–1527
MACKENZIE, Henry, Scottish, novelist: 1745–1831
MCLEISH, Archibald, American, poet and critic: 1892–1982
MCLUHAN, Herbert Marshall, Canadian, educator and critic: 1911–80
MACNEICE, Louis, Northern Irish, poet: 1907–63
MACPHERSON, James, Scottish, poet: 1736–96
MAILER, Norman, American, novelist: b.1923
MALLARMÉ, Stéphane, French, poet: 1842–98
MALORY, Sir Thomas, writer of romance: d.c.1471
MANN, Thomas, German, novelist: 1875–1955
MANSFIELD, Katherine (Kathleen Mansfield Beauchamp), New Zealander, short-story writer: 1888–1923
MARCEAU, Marcel, French, mime actor: b.1923
MARIE DE FRANCE, French, poet: late twelfth century
MARINETTI, Emilio Filippo, Italian, poet and publicist: 1876–1944
MARINI, Giovanni Battista, Italian, poet: 1569–1625
MARLOWE, Christopher, poet and dramatist: 1564–93
MARSH, Sir Edward, anthologist: 1872–1953
MARTIAL, Latin, epigrammatist: c.AD40–c.104

MARVELL, Andrew, poet: 1621–78
MARX, Karl, German, political theorist: 1818–83
MASCAGNI, Pietro, Italian, composer: 1863–1945
MASSINGER, Philip, dramatist: 1583–1640
MATURIN, Charles, Irish, novelist: 1782–1824
MAYAKOVSKY, Vladimir, Russian, poet: 1893–1930
MELVILLE, Herman, American, novelist: 1819–91
MENANDER, Greek, dramatist: c.343–c.291BC
MENIPPUS, Greek, philosopher: third century BC
MEREDITH, George, poet and novelist: 1828–1909
MERLEAU-PONTY, Maurice, French, phenomenological philosopher: 1908–61
MEUN, Jean de (Jean Chopinel), French, poet and translator: thirteenth century
MIDDLETON, Thomas, dramatist: c.1580–1627
MILL, John Stuart, philosopher and radical reformer: 1806–73
MILLAIS, Sir John Everett, artist: 1829–96
MILLER, Arthur, American, dramatist: b.1915
MILLER, Joseph Hillis, American, literary theorist: b.1928
MILLETT, Kate, American, feminist writer and autobiographer: b.1934
MILTON, John, poet: 1608–74
MOLIÈRE (Jean-Baptiste Poquelin), French, dramatist: 1622–73
MONTAGU, Lady Mary Wortley, miscellaneous writer: 1689–1762
MONTAIGNE, Michel Eyquem de, French, essayist: 1533–92
MOORE, George Edward, philosopher: 1873–1958
MOORE, Marianne, American, poet: 1887–1972
MOORE, Thomas, Irish, poet: 1779–1852
MORAVIA, Alberto (Alberto Pincherle), Italian, novelist: 1907–90
MORE, Sir Thomas, prose-writer: 1478–1535
MORÉAS, Jean (Iannis Pappadiamantopoulos), French, poet: 1856–1910
MORRIS, William, poet and designer: 1834–96
MOSCHUS, Greek, poet: second century BC
MOSLEY, Sir Oswald, Fascist politician: 1896–1980
MOZART, Wolfgang Amadeus, Austrian, composer: 1756–91
MUIR, Edwin, Scottish, poet: 1887–1959

NASH, Ogden, American, humorist and poet: 1902–71
NASHE, Thomas, pamphleteer, dramatist, poet and prose-writer: 1567–c.1601
NEWMAN, John Henry, Cardinal, Christian apologist: 1801–90
NEWTON, Sir Isaac, mathematician and philosopher: 1642–1727
NICHOLAS OF GUILDFORD, poet: fl.c.1250
NIETZSCHE, Friedrich, German, philosopher and poet: 1844–1900
NORTON, Thomas, dramatist: 1532–84
NOYES, Alfred, poet: 1880–1958

O'CASEY, Sean, Irish, dramatist and autobiographer: 1880–1964

OLSON, Charles, American, poet and literary theorist: 1910–70
OPIE, Iona, folklorist: *b*.1923
OPIE, Peter, folklorist: 1918–82
ORFF, Carl, German, composer: 1895–1982
ORTEGA Y GASSET, José, Spanish, critic and philosopher: 1883–1955
ORWELL, George (Eric Blair), novelist, journalist and political writer: 1903–50
OSBORNE, John, dramatist: *b*.1929
OVERBURY, Sir Thomas, prose-writer: 1581–1618
OVID, Roman, poet: 43BC–*c*.AD17
OWEN, Wilfred, poet: 1893–1918

PALGRAVE, Francis Turner, poet and anthologist: 1824–97
PARK, Mungo, Scottish, explorer: 1771–1806
PARMIGIANINO, Francesco, Italian, artist: 1503–40
PARNELL, Thomas, Irish, poet: 1679–1718
PARRY, Milman, American, classical scholar: 1902–35
PASCAL, Blaise, French, religious writer: 1623–62
PASTERNAK, Boris, Russian, poet and novelist: 1890–1960
PATER, Walter, essayist and critic: 1839–94
PATTEN, Brian, poet: *b*.1946
PAVESE, Cesare, Italian, novelist: 1908–50
PEELE, George, dramatist and poet: 1558–96
PEIRCE, Charles Sanders, American, philosopher: 1839–1914
PEPYS, Samuel, diarist: 1633–1703
PERCY, Thomas, Bishop, poet and antiquary: 1729–1811
PERRAULT, Charles, French, poet and fairy-tale writer: 1628–1703
PETRARCH, Francesco, Italian, poet: 1304–74
PETRONIUS ARBITER, Latin, satirist: probably first century AD
PHILIPS, John, poet: 1676–1709
PICASSO, Pablo, Spanish, painter: 1881–1973
PINDAR, Greek, poet: *c*.518–*c*.438BC
PINTER, Harold, dramatist: *b*.1930
PIRANDELLO, Luigi, Italian, dramatist and novelist: 1867–1936
PIRSIG, Robert, American, autobiographical novelist: *b*.1928
PISCATOR, Erwin, German, theatre director: 1893–1966
PLATH, Sylvia, American, poet: 1932–63
PLATO, Greek, philosopher: *c*.429–347BC
PLAUTUS, Roman, comic dramatist: *c*.254–184BC
PLOTINUS, Greek, philosopher: *c*.AD205–70
PLUTARCH, Greek, biographer: *c*.AD46–*c*.127
POE, Edgar Allan, American, poet, critic and short-story writer: 1809–49
POPE, Alexander, poet: 1688–1744
POUND, Ezra, American, poet: 1885–1972

PRIESTLEY, John Boynton, novelist, dramatist and miscellaneous writer: 1894–1984
PROCOPIUS, Greek, historian: c.AD499–c.565
PROPERTIUS, Sextus, Roman, poet: c.50–c.16BC
PROUST, Marcel, French, novelist: 1871–1922
PRUDENTIUS, Spanish, poet: AD348–c.410
PTOLEMY, Claudius Ptolemaeus, astronomer and geographer: second century AD
PUSEY, Edward Bouverie, theologian: 1800–82
PUSHKIN, Aleksandr Sergeevich, Russian, poet and story-writer: 1799–1837
PUTTENHAM, George, critic: c.1529–90

QUARLES, Francis, poet: 1592–1644
QUEVEDO Y VILLEGAS, Francisco, Spanish, poet: 1580–1645

RABELAIS, François, French, prose-writer: c.1494–c.1553
RACINE, Jean, French, dramatist: 1639–99
RADCLIFFE, Mrs Ann Ward, novelist: 1764–1823
RAINE, Craig, poet: b.1944
RALEIGH, Sir Walter, poet and historian: c.1554–1618
RANSOM, John Crowe, American, literary critic: 1888–1974
RASPE, Rudolph Erich, German, story-teller: 1737–94
READ, Sir Herbert, poet and critic: 1893–1968
REID, Christopher, poet: b.1949
REID, Thomas, Scottish, philosopher: 1710–96
RESNAIS, Alain, French, film-director: b.1922
RICHARDS, Ivor Armstrong, critic: 1893–1979
RICHARDSON, Dorothy, novelist: 1873–1957
RICHARDSON, Samuel, novelist: 1689–1761
RICOEUR, Paul, French, philosopher: b.1913
RIDING, Laura, American, poet: 1901–91
RIMBAUD, Arthur, French, poet: 1854–91
ROBBE-GRILLET, Alain, French, novelist: b.1922
ROCHESTER, John Wilmot, Earl of, poet: 1647–80
ROETHKE, Theodore, American, poet: 1908–63
ROGET, Peter Mark, physician and philologist: 1779–1869
RONSARD, Pierre de, French, poet: 1524–85
ROSSETTI, Christina, poet: 1830–94
ROSSETTI, Dante Gabriel, poet and painter: 1828–82
ROUSSEAU, Jean-Jacques, Swiss, novelist and philosopher: 1712–78
RUSHDIE, Salman, Indian/British, novelist: b.1947
RUSKIN, John, critic and art historian: 1819–1900
RYMER, Thomas, critic and historian: 1641–1713

SACKVILLE, Thomas, poet and dramatist: 1536–1608

SAINTSBURY, George, critic: 1845–1933

'SAKI' (Hector Munro), short-story writer: 1870–1916

SALINGER, Jerome David, American, novelist: b.1919

SAPPHO, Greek, poet: seventh century BC

SARRAUTE, Nathalie, French, novelist: b.1902

SARTRE, Jean-Paul, French, philosopher, novelist and dramatist: 1905–80

SAUSSURE, Ferdinand de, Swiss, linguistician: 1857–1913

SAVAGE, Richard, poet: c.1697–1743

SCARRON, Paul, French, dramatist: 1610–60

SCHILLER, Johann Christoph Friedrich von, German, dramatist, poet and literary theorist: 1759–1805

SCHLEGEL, August Wilhelm von, German, philosopher and critic: 1767–1845

SCHWITTERS, Kurt, German, artist and poet: 1887–1948

SCOTT, Sir Walter, Scottish, novelist and poet: 1771–1832

SEARLE, John Rogers, American, philosopher: b.1932

SELKIRK, Alexander, Scottish, sailor and buccaneer: 1676–1721

SENECA, Roman, philosopher and dramatist: c.4BC–AD65

SENGHOR, Léopold Sedar, Senegalese: b.1906

SEXTON, Anne, American, poet: 1928–74

SHADWELL, Thomas, dramatist: c.1642–92

SHAFTESBURY, Anthony Ashley Cooper, Earl of, philosopher: 1671–1713

SHAKESPEARE, William, dramatist and poet: 1564–1616

SHAW, George Bernard, Irish, dramatist: 1856–1950

SHELLEY, Mary Wollstonecraft, novelist: 1797–1851

SHELLEY, Percy Bysshe, poet: 1792–1822

SHERIDAN, Richard Brinsley, Irish, dramatist: 1751–1816

SHKLOVSKY, Viktor, Russian, critic and prose-writer: b.1893

SHOWALTER, Elaine, American, critic: b.1941

SIDNEY, Sir Philip, poet and prose-writer: 1554–86

SKELTON, John, poet: c.1464–1529

SMITH, Alexander, Scottish, poet: c.1829–67

SMOLLETT, Tobias, Scottish, novelist: 1721–71

SNOW, Charles Percy, novelist and scientist: 1905–80

SNYDER, Gary, American, poet: b.1930

SOCRATES, Greek, philosopher: c.469–399BC

SOLZHENITSYN, Aleksandr, Russian, novelist: b.1918

SONTAG, Susan, American, novelist and critic: b.1933

SOPHOCLES, Greek, tragic dramatist: c.496–406BC

SOUTHEY, Robert, poet: 1774–1843

SPENDER, Sir Stephen, poet: b.1909

SPENSER, Edmund, poet: c.1552–99

SPOONER, William Archibald, Reverend, academic: 1844–1930

STAËL, Anne-Louise-Germaine Necker, Madame de, French, novelist: 1766–1817

STEELE, Sir Richard, Irish, essayist and dramatist: 1672–1729

STENDHAL (Henri Beyle), French, novelist: 1783–1842
STERNE, Laurence, Irish, novelist: 1713–68
STEVENS, Wallace, American, poet: 1879–1955
STEVENSON, Robert Louis, Scottish, novelist and essayist: 1850–94
STOPPARD, Tom, dramatist: b.1937
STOWE, Harriet Beecher, American, novelist: 1811–96
STRACHEY, Lytton, essayist and biographer: 1880–1932
STRINDBERG, August, Swedish, dramatist: 1849–1912
STURLUSON, Snorri, Icelandic, poet: 1179–1241
SUCKLING, Sir John, poet: 1609–41
SUETONIUS (Gaius Suetonius Tranquillus), Roman, historian and biographer: c.AD70–c.160
SURREY, Henry Howard, Earl of, poet: c.1517–47
SWIFT, Jonathan, Irish, poet and satirical prose-writer: 1667–1745
SWINBURNE, Algernon Charles, poet: 1837–1909
SYMONS, Arthur, poet and critic: 1865–1945
SYNGE, John Millington, Irish, dramatist: 1871–1909

TACITUS, Gaius (?) Cornelius, Roman, historian: c.AD55–c.117
TASSO, Torquato, Italian, poet: 1544–95
TATE, Allen, American, poet and critic: 1899–1979
TAYLOR, Jeremy, prose-writer: 1613–67
TENNYSON, Alfred, Lord, poet: 1809–92
TERENCE, Roman, comic dramatist: c.195–159BC
THACKERAY, William Makepeace, novelist: 1811–63
THEOCRITUS, Greek, poet: c.310–c.250BC
THEOPHRASTUS, Greek, prose-writer: c.372–288BC
THOMAS, Brandon, dramatist: 1856–1914
THOMAS, Dylan, Welsh, poet: 1914–53
THOMAS, Edward, poet: 1878–1917
THOMSON, James, Scottish, poet: 1700–48
THOREAU, Henry David, American, philosopher and prose-writer: 1817–62
TIRSO DE MOLINA (Gabriel Téllez), Spanish, dramatist: 1584–1648
TODOROV, Tzvetan, Bulgarian, literary theorist: b.1939
TOLKIEN, John Ronald Reuel, philologist and novelist: 1892–1973
TOLSTOY, Count Lev Nikolayevich, Russian, novelist: 1828–1910
TOMLINSON, Charles, poet: b.1927
TOTTEL, Richard, publisher: d.1594
TOURNEUR, Cyril, dramatist: c.1575–1626
TREECE, Henry, poet: 1911–66
TROLLOPE, Anthony, novelist: 1815–82
TROLLOPE, Frances, novelist: 1780–1863
TROTSKY, Leon, Ukrainian, communist theorist and agitator: 1879–1940
TRUFFAUT, François, French, film director: 1932–84

TURGENEV, Ivan, Russian, novelist: 1818–83
TUSSER, Thomas, poet: c.1524–80
TWAIN, Mark (Samuel Clemens), American, novelist: 1835–1910
TYNDALE, William, biblical translator: d.1536
TZARA, Tristan, Rumanian/French, prose-writer and publicist: 1896–1963

VALÉRY, Paul, French, poet and literary theorist: 1871–1945
VANBRUGH, Sir John, dramatist: 1664–1726
VARRO, Roman, poet: 116–27BC
VAUGHAN, Henry, Welsh, poet: c.1621–95
VAUGHAN, Thomas, Welsh, mystic: c.1621–66
VEGA CARPIO, Lope Felix de, Spanish, dramatist and poet: 1562–1635
VERGA, Giovanni, Sicilian, novelist and short-story writer: 1840–1922
VERLAINE, Paul, French, poet: 1844–96
VERNE, Jules, French, novelist: 1828–1905
VIDAL, Pierre, Provençal, poet: fl.c.1200
VILLON, François, French, poet: 1431–c.1464
VIRGIL, Roman, poet: 70–19BC
VOLTAIRE (François-Marie Arouet), French, prose-writer and philosopher: 1694–1778

WAIN, John, poet, novelist and critic: b.1925
WALCOTT, Derek, West Indian, poet: b.1930
WALLER, Edmund, poet: 1606–87
WALPOLE, Horace, Earl of Orford, prose-writer: 1717–97
WALTON, Izaak, prose-writer: 1593–1683
WARREN, Robert Penn, American, novelist, poet and critic: 1905–89
WATSON, John, 'Ian McLaren', Scottish, novelist: 1850–1907
WATT, Ian, literary critic: b.1917
WAUGH, Evelyn, novelist: 1903–66
WEBSTER, John, dramatist: c.1580–c.1638
WEISS, Peter, German, dramatist: 1916–82
WELLEK, René, American, literary critic: b.1903
WELLS, Herbert George, novelist and prose-writer: 1866–1946
WESKER, Arnold, dramatist: b.1932
WHITMAN, Walt, American, poet: 1819–92
WIENE, Robert, German, film director: 1881–1938
WILDE, Oscar, Irish, dramatist, poet and essayist: 1854–1900
WILLIAMS, Tennessee, American, dramatist: 1911–83
WILLIAMS, William Carlos, American, poet: 1883–1963
WILSON, Colin, miscellaneous prose-writer: b.1931
WILSON, Thomas, politician and critic: c.1525–81
WIMSATT, William Kurtz Jnr., American, literary critic: 1907–75
WITHER, George, poet and pamphleteer: 1588–1667

WODEHOUSE, Sir Pelham Grenville, British/American, novelist and short-story writer: 1881–1975
WOLLSTONECRAFT, Mary, feminist writer: 1759–97
WOOLF, Leonard, prose-writer: 1880–1969
WOOLF, Virginia, novelist and critic: 1882–1941
WORDE, Wynkyn de, printer and stationer: *d.c.*1534
WORDSWORTH, William, poet: 1770–1850
WYATT, Sir Thomas, poet: 1503–42
WYCHERLEY, William, dramatist: 1640–1716
WYSS, David, Swiss, children's writer: 1743–1818

YEATS, William Butler, Irish, poet, dramatist and critic: 1865–1939
YOUNG, Edward, poet: 1683–1765

ZEPHANIAH, Benjamin, poet: *b.*1958
ZOLA, Émile, French, novelist: 1840–1902

Table of the Sovereigns since the Conquest

House	Name	Accession
Norman	William I	1066
	William II	1087
	Henry I	1100
	Stephen	1135
Plantagenet	Henry II	1154
	Richard I	1189
	John	1199
	Henry III	1216
	Edward I	1272
	Edward II	1307
	Edward III	1327
	Richard II	1377
Lancaster	Henry IV	1399
	Henry V	1413
	Henry VI	1422
York	Edward IV	1461
	Edward V	1483
	Richard III	1483
Tudor	Henry VII	1485
	Henry VIII	1509
	Edward VI	1547
	Mary	1553
	Elizabeth I	1558
Stuart	James I	1603
	Charles I	1625
	Commonwealth	1649
	Protectorate	1653
	Charles II	1660
	James II	1685
	William and Mary	1688
	Anne	1702
Hanover	George I	1714
	George II	1727
	George III	1760
	George IV	1820

House	Name	Accession
Hanover (*cont.*)	William IV	1830
	Victoria	1837
Saxe-Coburg	Edward VII	1901
Windsor	George V	1910
	Edward VIII	1936
	George VI	1936
	Elizabeth II	1952

APPENDIX THREE
Main periods of English literature

Old English (*or* Anglo-Saxon) Period *c*.450–*c*.1066

Middle English Period *c*.1066–*c*.1500
  (Anglo-Norman Period *c*.1100–*c*.1350)

The Renaissance *c*.1500–*c*.1660
  Elizabethan Age 1558–1603
  Jacobean Age 1603–1625
  Caroline Age 1625–1649
  Commonwealth Period 1649–1660

Neoclassical Period *c*.1660–*c*.1800
  The Restoration 1660–1700
  Augustan Age *c*.1700–*c*.1745
  Age of Sensibility *c*.1745–*c*.1800

Romantic Period *c*.1790–*c*.1830

Victorian Period 1832–1901

Edwardian Period 1901–1914

Modern Period *c*.1914–

The author of this Handbook

MARTIN GRAY was educated at the Universities of Perugia, Oxford and London. Since 1972 he has been lecturer in the Department of English Studies at the University of Stirling, where he is attached to the Centre for Commonwealth Studies and the Centre for Publishing Studies. His publications include *A Chronology of English Literature* (1989) and *The Penguin Book of the Bicycle* (with R.Watson).